新版
教室英語表現事典
英語で授業を行うために

染矢正一[著]

大修館書店

まえがき

　いろいろな分野で外国の人々との交流が頻繁に行われている今日，「聞いて話す」英語の力を伸ばすことが広く求められている。こうした時代の趨勢もあり，小学校から英語教育が導入された。会議を英語で行う企業も登場してきた。コミュニケーションを重視した英語をとりまく環境が大きく変化している証左である。

　英語を知識として知っていても，英語を聞き，話すこととは直結しない。英語を聞き，話すという習慣づけをしないと，なかなか話せるようになるのは難しい。英語が話せるためには，まず，英語を聞いて理解できなくてはならない。そのためには，できるだけ英語に音声で触れるという雰囲気づくりをする必要がある。

　ニュージーランドのある高等学校の日本語のクラスを参観する機会があった。このクラスは，半年間日本語を学んだ生徒が，さらに日本語の能力を高めるためのクラスであった。1年にも満たない日本語の学習にもかかわらず，生徒の会話力に驚嘆した。教材は日本語で書かれた8コマ漫画であったが，生徒はペアを組み，しっかりと声に出して反復練習をしていた。「外国語学習は音声から」ということを，あらためて感じた。

　多様化の中の国際化時代と言われて久しい。日本人が話す英語は，日本人的であってもいっこうにかまわない。むしろ，そのほうがよい。国が違えば人の顔が違うように，それぞれの国で学ぶ英語に特徴があって当然である。話す英語が英語の音韻組織から逸脱し，あまりに非文法的で意思の疎通ができない状態では困るが，そうでなければ，おおらかな気持ちでとにかく「英語で聞き，英語で話す」という習慣を早い時期からつけさせたいものである。

　こうした意図から，20年前に，英語の授業を英語で行うための一助として『教室英語表現事典』を上梓した。同書は，英語の教室で，始業から終業まで取り交わされるさまざま表現を分類整理した

ものである。しかし，20年の間に，語学教育環境は大きく変化した。教育内容は言うに及ばず，視聴覚機器などもめまぐるしく変化していった。例えば，一世を風靡したLL教室は，CALL教室にとって代わられた。パワーポイントを使う授業も，以前にはまったく見られなかった。

　時代の流れにそった『教室英語表現事典』の大幅な見直しが求められることになった。

　本書の改訂にあたっては，沖縄国際大学の津波聡先生，大修館書店編集部の辻村厚氏に一方ならぬお世話になった。大所高所から，また，微に入り細を穿ったコメントを随所にしていただいた。また，友人のFred Ferrasci氏には英文の校閲をしていただいた。3人の方々に心からお礼を申し上げたい。遺漏のないよう最善は尽くしたつもりだが，思わぬミスや誤りがあるかもしれない。それはひとえに私の浅学非才さによるものである。忌憚のないご意見やご教示を賜れば幸いである。

2013年7月

染矢正一

本書の使い方

①本として通読する
　英語の授業の流れに沿って編んでいるから，最初から順序だてて読むことができる。
②必要な箇所だけ拾い読みする
　平素の授業に必要な部分のみ拾い読みするのもよい。
③生徒に英語で質問させる
　「生徒」がよくする質問は，▶印で明示している。英語で質問させるときの参考になろう。
④語法上のポイントが学習できる
　ともすれば間違いやすいポイントや表現上の微妙な点について触れている。
⑤英作文の教材として利用できる
　日本文とその英文訳を併記しているので，任意の文を選んで英作文の教材としても使用できる。
⑥索引を利用する
　索引を利用して，担当科目に必要な英語表現を整理することも可能である。

目　次

まえがき　*i*
目次　*iv*

I　始業

1　着席　*3*
2　あいさつ　*6*
　A　始業のあいさつ　*6*
　B　年明け・休み明けのあいさつ　*9*
　C　新任教師のあいさつ　*10*
3　出欠　*11*
　A　出席の確認　*11*
　B　欠席　*14*
4　遅刻　*16*

II　授業の前提

1　授業の前提となる環境　*21*
　A　部屋の状態　*21*
　B　聞き取れるか　*26*
　C　黒板の字が見えるか　*30*
2　CALL 教室などの設備・機器　*32*
　A　入室　*32*
　B　CALL機器の操作　*32*
　C　退室　*41*
　D　機器のトラブル　*42*
3　規律　*46*
　A　クラスを静かにさせるとき　*46*
　B　生徒をしかる　*48*
　C　謝罪　*51*

目次　v

　　D　忘れ物　*54*
　　E　落書き　*55*
 4　例外的状況　*56*
　　A　身体状況・病気　*56*
　　B　途中での退室　*59*

III　授業活動

 1　授業開始　*63*
　　A　授業開始にあたって　*63*
　　B　既習部分の確認　*65*
 2　学習活動の指示　*67*
　　A　基本的指示　*67*
　　B　読ませる　*70*
　　C　書かせる　*84*
　　D　訳させる　*95*
　　E　教科書を使う　*104*
　　F　課題をさせる　*106*
　　G　聞かせる　*110*
　　H　書き取らせる　*114*
　　I　発音させる　*117*
　　J　手を上げさせる，発言させる　*119*
　　K　発表させる，意見を言わせる　*122*
　　L　下線を引かせる　*125*
　　M　ノートに写させる　*127*
　　N　ポイントの指示　*130*
　　O　視覚教材を使う　*135*
　　P　前のページに戻るとき　*137*
　　Q　次のページに進むとき　*138*
　　R　次の課・章などに移るとき　*139*
　　S　会話練習の指示　*140*
　　T　予習　*142*
　　U　復習　*150*
　　V　自習の指示　*151*
　　W　指名されて　*153*

X　間違いを指摘・訂正させる　*154*
 3　生徒とのやりとり　*157*
　　A　質問の有無　*157*
　　B　理解の確認　*162*
　　C　授業の進め方　*167*
　　D　生徒の返答に対して　*171*
　　E　生徒の学習への姿勢　*177*
　　F　間違い　*179*
　　G　生徒を励ます・慰める　*182*
　　H　生徒の感想・希望　*183*
 4　CALL 教室の授業　*184*
　　A　聞き取り・読みの練習　*184*
　　B　自分の声の録音　*187*
　　C　問題の指示　*188*
 5　パワーポイントを使う授業　*190*
　　A　スライドを見せる　*190*
　　B　スライドショーが終わって　*194*
 6　映画を使う授業　*196*
 7　教室で使ういろいろなもの　*202*
　　A　配布物・プリント　*202*
　　B　教科書　*207*
　　C　辞書　*211*
　　D　黒板・チョーク　*219*
 8　授業後・家庭学習の課題　*225*
　　A　宿題を出す　*225*
　　B　宿題の確認　*229*
　　C　宿題を受け取る　*231*
　　D　レポート　*234*
 9　授業でよく使う表現　*235*

Ⅳ　授業内容

 1　聞くこと　*253*
 2　発音　*257*
　　A　発音全般について　*257*

B　子音について　*264*
　　C　母音について　*269*
　　D　口の開き方　*272*
　　E　唇について　*275*
　　F　音節　*277*
　　G　発音記号　*280*
　　H　アクセント　*282*
　　I　イントネーション　*287*
3　読むこと　*290*
　　A　読み・音読　*290*
　　B　区切り　*294*
4　書くこと　*297*
　　A　書き方　*297*
　　B　つづり　*298*
　　C　句読点　*307*
5　作文　*311*
　　A　英作文　*311*
　　B　和文英訳　*322*
6　読解　*323*
　　A　語句の理解　*323*
　　B　文・文章の理解　*331*
　　C　和訳　*338*
　　D　文学作品　*339*
7　単語・語い　*345*
8　文法　*348*
　　A　主語　*348*
　　B　述語　*354*
　　C　目的語　*356*
　　D　補語　*359*
　　E　文型　*364*
　　F　名詞　*365*
　　G　代名詞　*370*
　　H　関係代名詞　*372*
　　I　動詞　*373*
　　J　助動詞　*378*

    K　形容詞　*380*
    L　副詞　*384*
    M　前置詞　*388*
    N　冠詞　*392*
    O　接続詞　*397*
    P　間投詞　*401*
    Q　語順　*402*
    R　疑問文　*406*
    S　付加疑問文　*407*
    T　態　*409*
    U　時制　*411*
    V　話法　*412*
    W　その他，文法に関して　*413*

V　英語の学習について

1　学習方法について　*417*
2　英語を学ぶ意義　*426*
3　英語や英語文化に関する知識　*430*

VI　テスト・試験

1　試験前後　*435*
  A　試験の予告　*435*
  B　試験の注意事項　*441*
  C　試験終了後　*453*
2　試験問題指示文　*455*
  A　基本的な指示文　*455*
  B　訳す　*456*
  C　正誤・異同を指摘する　*457*
  D　書く　*459*
  E　説明する　*460*
  F　書き換える　*460*
  G　つなぐ　*464*
  H　並べ換え・置き換え　*464*

I　埋める・空所補充　*465*
　　J　完成させる　*467*
　　K　選ぶ　*468*
　　L　○で囲む　*471*
　　M　下線を引く　*472*
　　N　×をつける　*473*
　　O　要約する・まとめる　*473*
　　P　句読点を打つ　*475*
　　Q　その他　*476*
　3　採点・成績　*476*
　　A　返却前　*476*
　　B　返却後　*478*
　　C　成績　*484*

VII　授業の周辺

　1　連絡・相談など　*489*
　　A　連絡・相談　*489*
　　B　生徒への気遣い　*495*
　2　教師についての質問　*496*
　　A　教師の経歴　*496*
　　B　教師の私的事柄についての質問　*500*
　　C　教師の身なり　*502*

VIII　終業

　1　終業間近　*505*
　2　連絡・指示など　*509*
　3　終業時の表現　*511*

IX　ネイティブスピーカーの英語表現実例

　1　ネイティブスピーカーの教師1　*515*
　　A　授業進行　*515*
　　B　生徒とのやりとり　*519*

　　　　C　トラブル・間違い　*521*
　　2　ネイティブスピーカーの教師2　*522*
　　　　A　授業進行　*522*
　　　　B　生徒とのやりとり　*523*
　　3　ネイティブスピーカーの教師3　*524*
　　　　A　授業進行　*524*
　　　　B　生徒とのやりとり　*524*
　　4　ネイティブスピーカーの教師4　*525*
　　　　A　授業進行　*525*
　　5　ネイティブスピーカーの教師5　*526*
　　　　A　授業進行　*526*
　　　　B　生徒とのやりとり　*527*
　　6　ネイティブスピーカーの教師6　*528*
　　　　A　授業進行　*528*
　　　　B　生徒とのやりとり　*529*

関連語い集　*530*
　　1　学問・学科名　*531*
　　2　文法関連語い　*539*
　　3　発音関連語い　*542*
　　4　英作文関連語い・表現　*546*
　　5　"読み"関連語い　*548*
　　6　意味・読解関連語い・表現　*549*

索引　*551*
参考文献　*564*

新版
教室英語表現事典

I 始業

1 着席

席についてください。
　Sit down.
　Be seated.
　　Be seated. の方が formal である。

番号の順番に座ってください。
　1. **Sit in the seat corresponding to your number.**
　2. **Sit according to your roll number.**
　3. **Sit in the booth with your number on it.**
　　1は席にも番号が書かれているような場合で指示がわかりやすい。2はどのように座るか，少しわかりづらい。3はCALL教室などに座る場合である。

班ごとに座ってください。
　1. **Sit in your group.**
　2. **Get into your group.**
　3. **Go to your group.**
　4. **Sit according to your groups.**
　　1～3はよく使われる。4はあまり自然な言い方ではない。グループ活動をする場合には，Let's work in groups now. などのように言う。

どこでもよいから座ってください。
   You can sit anyplace you wish.
   You can sit anyplace you want.
      want は wish に比べると，greater need を暗示させる。
      anyplace は any place のように，2 語に離して書くこともある。
      anywhere と同じ意味であるが，anyplace の方が口語的である。

みなさん座れますか。
   1. **Does everyone have a place to sit?**
   2. **Can everybody sit down?**
      2 は厳密には 3 つの意味に解釈できる。
         ① Please sit down.
         ② Are you physically able to sit down?
         ③ Does everyone have a place to sit?
      1 の文には 1 つの解釈しかない。2 の意味の違いは状況によって判断できる。

25 番の席は壊れていますから，空いている席に移ってください。
   1. **Seat 25 is broken. Move to another seat.**
   2. **Move to another seat since Seat 25 is broken.**
   3. **Move to another seat as Seat 25 is broken.**
      as は 2 つの事柄が同時に起こるときにしばしば使われる。
         She smiled as she sang.
      また，as は奇妙な心象を与えるときに使ったりする。
         Move to another seat as Seat 25 is in the process of being broken.
      as にはこうしたニュアンスがあるので，この場合 since を使った 2 の方が無難である。

▶ 机がガタガタするので，席を代わってもいいですか。
   My desk is wobbly. May I change seats?
   My desk is rickety. May I change seats?
   May I change seats, as my desk is wobbly?

May I change seats, as my desk is rickety?
　　wobbly は，一方が短く他方が長くてガタガタする家具などの形容でしばしば下記のように使われる言葉である。
　　　　This table's wobbling.
　　rickey は，unsafe, unsound の意味で a rickety ladder, rickety stairs などのように使う。「机がガタガタする」と言うときには，脚の長さが異なることによって生じる場合が多いので，wobbly という語の方がふさわしい。

35番を試してみてください。
Try No. 35.

▶どのように座ったらいいのですか。
How can we sit here?
　　この英語表現は状況によって，①どの席に座ったらよいか，②どのような方法で座ったらよいかという2つの解釈が成り立つ。

▶どこに座ったらいいのでしょうか。
Where should I sit?

▶男女別に座るのですか。
1. **Are the boys supposed to sit separately from the girls?**
2. **Are we supposed to sit by sex?**
3. **Are we supposed to sit according to sex?**
4. ***Are we supposed to sit in groups of boys and girls?**
　　1は適切な表現である。2, 3は，sex という語には，男女の性別の意味のほかに，別の意味もあるから，このような状況で生徒が使う表現としてはふさわしくない。4はあまり自然な表現ではない。

▶どこに座ってもいいのですか。
May we sit anyplace?
Can we sit anyplace?

May we sit anywhere?
Can we sit anywhere?

▶出席番号順に座るのですか。
Are we supposed to sit according to our roll number?
　　supposed のみの発音であれば [səpóuzd] であるが，次に続く前置詞 to の t が無声音であることから，同化作用により [səpóust] のように最後の子音の連結は無声音となる。

▶席を代わってもよいですか。
May I change seats?

▶山田さんと席を代わってもいいですか。
1. **May I change seats with Yamada-san?**
2. **May I trade seats with Yamada-san?**
　　1 は standard，2 は informal な表現である。

▶目が悪いので，前の方に座りたいのですが。
I have trouble with my eyes, so I'd like to sit in the front.

2　あいさつ

A　始業のあいさつ

▶起立，礼，着席。
Stand up, bow, sit down.
　　日本人の英語の発音が悪い例として，Sit down. がしばしば取り沙汰される。日本語ではサ行において，
　　サ [sa]　シ [ʃi]　ス [su]　セ [se]　ソ [so]
のように，高位置・前母音 [i] の前では，[s] が [ʃ] に変化してしまう。この日本語の音声変化をそのまま英語に適応すると，Sit

down. が，[ʃít dáun] と発音され，米英人の耳には，
　　　Shit down.（大便をしなさい）
と響いてしまう。生徒の発音が悪ければ，矯正が必要である。
　日本の学校では「起立」「礼」「着席」という号令をかけたりすることもあるが，英米ではこのような号令をかけることはない。英米の文化を学ばせるということからは，英語の時間内に限って「起立」「礼」「着席」の号令をかけずに授業を行うのも1つの方法であろう。

みなさん，おはよう。
Good morning, everyone.
Good morning, class.
　日本語では，「おはようございます」とだけ言うことが多いが，英語では Good morning, everyone. や Good morning, class. などのように，呼びかけの言葉をしばしば用いる。

▶高橋先生，おはようございます。
Good morning, Mr. Takahashi.
　日本語では，「先生」のように姓を付けずにしばしば敬称を呼称として用いるが，これをそのまま teacher という英語に変えて使うわけにはいかない。性別と結婚の状態に応じて
　　Mr. Suzuki（男の場合。既婚・未婚を問わない）
　　Miss Suzuki（未婚の女性の場合）
　　Mrs. Suzuki（既婚の女性の場合）
のように使い分けなくてはならない。
　性差別の解放を唱える女性解放論者の間から，男性の Mr. に相当する Ms（ミズ）を使う声が上がって久しい。商業文などではしばしば Ms が使われているものの，呼称として Ms を嫌うアメリカ人の女性も多い。

こんにちは，みなさん。
Good afternoon, boys and girls.
　afternoon は1語でつづることに注意。「みなさん」は every-

one, class のほか，このように boys and girls と言ってもよい。もちろん，男子校であれば boys, 女子高であれば girls となる。

▶ **高橋先生，こんにちは。**
Good afternoon, Mr. Takahashi.

元気ですか。
1. **Hello!**
2. **How are you?**
3. **How is everything?**
4. **How's everything going?**
5. **How are you doing?**
6. **I trust that everything is well.**
7. **How are you coming along?**
8. **How are you getting along?**
9. **How's life?**
10. **How's life been treating you?**
11. **How's it going?**
12. **How are things?**
13. **How are things with you?**
14. **It's good to see you.**
15. **Good to see you.**
16. **What's up?**

「元気ですか」に相当する英語表現は数多い。1 から 5 は standard, 6 は formal, 7 から 16 は informal な表現である。目上の人には 1 や 2 がよく使われる。上記に類似した表現に How are you feeling ...? があるが，この表現は，相手が病気であったり，疲れていたりするときによく使われる。

みなさん，元気ですか。
How are you, everyone?
How are all of you?

▶非常に元気です。先生はいかがですか。
I'm very fine, thank you. And you?

▶昨日は熱がありましたが，今日は元気です。ありがとうございます。
I had a fever yesterday, but I'm fine today, thank you.

やあ。
1. **Hi.**
2. **Hi, there.**
3. **Hello, there.**
4. **Howdy.**
5. **Hey.**
6. **G'day.**

　　2や3のthereは，There are two cameras on the table. などのように《存在》を表す副詞としてのthereの用法ではなくて，「満足」「激励」「慰め」などを表す間投詞（interjection）としての用法である。名前を付ける場合は，Hello, Suzuki-kun. としてもよい。

　　Hello there, Suzuki-kun. のように，thereと名前を同時に言う言い方はあまり自然ではない。

　　4はWestern Americaなどで使われる。5は非常にinformalな表現。6はオーストラリアで使われるinformalなあいさつ表現である。

B　年明け・休み明けのあいさつ

みなさん，あけましておめでとう。
1. **Happy New Year, everyone.**
2. **Happy New Year, class.**
3. **To all of you, a happy new year.**
4. **A happy new year, everyone.**

5. **A happy new year, class.**
  文語としては a happy new year もよく使うが，あいさつとしては不定冠詞の a を取って 1 や 2 のように言うことが多い。

休暇中は楽しかったですか。
  Did you have a nice time during the vacation?
  Did you enjoy yourself during the vacation?

楽しい休暇だったと思います。
  I hope you had a nice vacation.

きっとすばらしい冬休みだったと思います。
  I'm sure you had a wonderful winter vacation.

みんなの元気な顔を見て，安心しました。
  I'm relieved to find all of you fine.
  I'm happy to find all of you fine.
  I'm relieved to find all of you well.

みんな，色が黒くなったね。
  You all got a good suntan, didn't you?
  You all look brown.

C　新任教師のあいさつ

私は佐藤まりです。
  My name is Satoh Mari.
  I am Satoh Mari.
      表記的には Satoh でも Sato でもよい。

今学期，みなさんを教えることになります。
  I am going to teach you this term.

今年，みなさんに英会話1を教えることになります。
I'll be teaching you English conversation 1 this year.

《未来》のことは，be going to や will などを使うことが一般的であるが，be ～ing の進行形を使うこともできる。

今年は私がみなさんの担任です。
I'm in charge of your class this year.

私は教生です。
I'm a student teacher.

3　出欠

A　出席の確認

出席を取ります。
1. **Let me call the roll.**
2. **Let me call the register.**
3. **I'll call the roll.**
4. **I'll call the register.**

　　Let me ... の文型はよく使われる。1～4の表現には，日本語には存在しないlとrが出るので，正確に発音するのは意外と難しい。let のlは母音の前のlなので，聴覚的に明るい印象を与える。この種のlは「明るいl」と呼ばれる。一方，call のlは語尾に現れるlで，聴覚的に暗い印象を与えることから，「暗いl」と呼ばれる。

　　rは舌を反転させて発音するが，口腔内のどの部分にも接触しない。学生には，
　　　　fried rice（焼き飯）
　　　　fried lice（焼いたシラミ）
などを例として発音練習させると，興味を示すようである。

2 や 4 の register という語はイギリス英語で使われる。
(子音の発音の詳細については IV-2-B を参考のこと)

今日はだれが欠席していますか。
  Who is absent today?
  Who isn't here?

▶山内さんは欠席です。風邪を引いています。
  Yamauchi-san is absent today. She has a cold.

田中君はどうした？
  1. **What happened to Tanaka-kun?**
  2. **What's happened to Tanaka-kun?**
  3. **What has happened to Tanaka-kun?**

　　本当に英語的に授業を行うのであれば，姓ではなくて名前を直接呼び捨てにするのがよいが，出欠の確認をする場合には，このように「田中」などと姓で呼ぶのもおかしくない。
　　折り目正しい人であれば，3 のように言うかもしれない。

今日は博君はどうした？
  1. **What's the matter with Hiroshi-kun today?**
  2. **What's wrong with Hiroshi-kun today?**
  3. **What's up with Hiroshi-kun today?**

　1 が最も formal，2 が less formal，3 が最も informal な表現である。

▶昨晩，親戚の人が亡くなったと聞きました。
  I heard that one of his relatives died last night.

▶出席しています。
  Here.

　　日本語では，生徒は名前を呼ばれると「はい」と言い，「はい」に相当する Yes を使いがちである。名前を呼ばれて返事をする場

合は Yes ではなくて，Here という。

だれか今日博君を見ましたか？
Has anybody seen Hiroshi-kun today?

▶30 分ほど前，バスを待っているのを見ました。
I saw him waiting for the bus about thirty minutes ago.

博君がどこにいるか知っている人はいますか？
1. Does anybody know where Hiroshi-kun is?
2. Does anybody have any idea where Hiroshi-kun is?

　　2 は話し手には博がどこにいるかが全くわからないことを暗示する。

▶医者にいると先生に伝えてほしいと言っていました。昨晩，ひどく咳が出たようです。
1. He asked me to tell you that he is at the doctor's office. He coughed a lot last night.
2. He asked me to tell you that he is at the doctor's office. He had a lot of coughs last night.

　　2 は文法的ではあるが，1 の方が自然な響きがする。

前回は授業に出ていなかったようだけど，どこにいたのですか？
1. You weren't in class last time. Where were you?
2. You didn't come to the last class. Where were you?
3. You were absent from the last class. Where were you?
4. You failed to appear in the last class. Where were you?
5. You failed to appear at the last class. Where were you?

　　1，2，3 の間には意味上の差異はない。4 や 5 はかなり formal な響きのする言い方である。また，4 や 5 には，いつも欠席をするような学生に対して皮肉を込めて言うような意味合いもある。

B 欠席

山田さんは欠席ですか。
　Is Yamada-san absent?

山田さんが今日，欠席かどうか知っている人はいますか。
　Does anyone know if Yamada-san is absent today?

山田さんが今日，欠席かどうか知っている人はいませんか。
　Doesn't anyone know if Yamada-san is absent today?

佐藤君は欠席すると連絡がありました。
　I've heard that Sato-kun will be absent.

▶欠席の連絡をせずにすみませんでした。
　1. I'm sorry I didn't let you know I would be absent.
　2. I am sorry that I did not let you know I would be absent.
　　I'm は I am の，didn't は did not の省略形であるが，普通の会話ではほとんどの場合においてこのような省略形が使われる。I am や I did not のような形が使われる頻度は非常に少ない。2 のような言い回しは，unnatural, childish, non-native speaker な響きがする。2 が自然に響くのは，「自分」を強調したり，《否定》を強調する必要がある場合に限る。こうした省略形の使い方は，口語英語を学ぶ上でもっと力説されるべきである。

▶私は先週来ていました。欠席になっていますが何かの間違いではないでしょうか。
　I was here last week. According to this I was absent, but are you sure there's no mistake on the rollbook?

▶彼は欠席です。
　He is absent.

absent は present の反意語。「(当然いなければいけない状況でその場に) いない」というとき，absent を使う。

▶彼は風邪で欠席しています。
  1. **He is absent because of a cold.**
  2. **He is absent because he has a cold.**
  3. **He is absent because of the cold.**
  4. **He is absent owing to the cold.**
  5. **He is absent because he has the cold.**
  6. ***He is absent owing to cold.**
  7. ***He is absent because he has cold.**
   「風邪を引く」は catch a cold でも catch cold でもよいが，a を伴わない6や7のような表現には抵抗を示すネイティブスピーカーがいる。3，4，5は，「寒さのために欠席した」とも取れるので，1や2の方がよい。

▶博君がなぜ休んだのかわかりません。
  1. **I don't know why Hiroshi-kun is absent.**
  2. **I have no idea why Hiroshi-kun is absent.**
   2は1を強調した言い方である。

▶今日はまだ，彼に会っていません。
  I haven't seen him today.

▶私は今まで何回欠席しているでしょうか。
  How many absences do I have?

▶私は全部で何回欠席していますか。
  How many absences in all do I have?

▶私はまだ1回も休んでいません。
  I haven't been absent even once.

4　遅刻

博君，なぜ遅れましたか。
　Hiroshi-kun, why are you late?

▶夜ふかしをして，遅れました。
　I'm late because I stayed up (too) late last night.
　I came late because I stayed up late last night.
　　　I came late でも I'm late でもよいが，ネイティブスピーカーのなかには，I'm late の表現を好む人がいる。

▶夜ふかしをして，朝，起きられませんでした。
　I couldn't wake up because I stayed up too late last night.
　I couldn't get up because I stayed up too late last night.

▶自転車が途中でパンクしました。
　1. On the way here, my bicycle had a flat tire.
　2. My bicycle had a flat tire on the way here.
　3. On the way, my bicycle had a flat tire.
　4. My bicycle had a flat tire on the way.
　　　on the way here は副詞句であるから位置は比較的自由であるが，2よりも1の方を好むネイティブスピーカーが多いようである。1や2の方が，3や4よりも自然である。

▶ごめんなさい。寝過ごしてしまいました。
　I'm sorry I overslept.

博君，どこに行っていたのですか。
　Hiroshi-kun, where have you been?

▶ごめんなさい。体育館にいました。
  1. **I'm sorry I was in the gymnasium.**
  2. **I'm sorry, I was in the gymnasium.**
     1と2のいずれでもよいが，書く場合，2のように sorry のあとにコンマを付すことがある。この方が口語的な感じがする。

急いで座りなさい，博君。
  Hurry up and sit down, Hiroshi-kun.

▶遅刻してしまってすみません。
  1. **I'm sorry, I'm late.**
  2. **I'm sorry to be late.**
     1の方が2よりも casual な表現で，多く使われる。

博君，電車に乗り遅れたのですか。
  Hiroshi-kun, did you miss the train?

▶通学の途中で，自転車がパンクして遅れました。
  1. **I am late because my bicycle had a flat tire on my way to school.**
  2. **I am late because I had a flat tire on my way to school.**
  3. **I am late because I had a flat bicycle tire on my way to school.**
     日本語の「パンク」という言葉は puncture という英語に由来する。これは「パンクすること」とか「（刺してできたような）小さな穴」という名詞的な用法もあるし，「（タイヤなどを）パンクさせる」という動詞用法もある。しかし，日本語のように puncture を省略して punc のように用いることはできない。また，現在のアメリカ英語では，この言葉の代わりに to have a flat tire という表現をすることが多い。
     2には「自転車」という語はないが状況から判断できるし，3のように a flat bicycle tire のように言うと，ネイティブスピーカーにはあまり自然ではないようである。

博君，寝過ごしたのかね。
Hiroshi-kun, did you oversleep?

博君，授業がもう始まったから急ぎなさい。
 1. We've already started, so hurry up Hiroshi-kun.
 2. We've already started, so please hurry, Hiroshi-kun.

博君，遅れて来たら何と言いますか。
Hiroshi-kun, what do you say when you're late?

▶遅刻してごめんなさい。遅れないように注意します。
I'm sorry, I'm late. I'll be careful not to be late.

ちょうど時間に間に合ったな。授業を始められるように座りなさい。
You are just in time. Sit down so that we can start.

この次は遅刻しないようにしなさい。
 1. Try not to be late next time.
 2. Be careful not to be late next time.
 3. You had better not be late next time.
　　1は丁寧，2はやや強い，3はかなり強い表現である。

もう少し早く学校に来なさい。
Come to school a little earlier.

もう少し早く授業に来るようにしなさい。
Try to come to class a little earlier.

この次は定刻に来るようにしなさい。
Next time, try to be on time.
Try to be here on time next time.
　　be in time は「間に合って」，be on time は「定刻に」という意味で，まぎらわしい。

早寝早起きをすれば，遅刻がなくなります。
1. **Go to bed early and get up early, and then you won't be late.**
2. **If you go to bed early and get up early, you won't be late.**
    won't の方が will not よりも自然な表現である。
    1は《命令》で，2は《忠告》をしているというニュアンスの違いがある。

やむを得ず遅刻をするときには，電話で連絡してください。
1. **When you can't help being late, please call me.**
2. **When you can't help being late, please give me a call.**
    2は informal な表現である。

遅刻する正当な理由があったら，届け出てください。
   If you have a reason for being late, please report it.

▶**博君は医者に寄るので少し遅れて来るそうです。**
1. **Hiroshi-kun will be a bit late because he has to go to the doctor.**
2. **Hiroshi-kun will be a little bit late because he has to go to the doctor.**
3. **Hiroshi-kun will be a bit late because he goes to the doctor.**
    a bit でも a little bit でもよい。意味の違いはない。
    「かかりつけの医者」を意味する場合には the を付けるが，「任意の医者」を表す場合には a となる。
    3のように ... he goes to the doctor. と言うと，一度だけでなく，いつも医者に行くというニュアンスがある。

汽車が遅れて，私も遅れてしまいました。
   The train was delayed, so I am late.
   The train was delayed, so I was late.

大雨のためバスが途中で立ち往生して，遅れました。
1. **The bus got stuck because of the heavy rain, and I am late.**
2. **The bus got stuck because of the heavy rain, and I was late.**
3. **Heavy rain held up the bus I was on.**
4. **A heavy rain storm held up the bus I was on.**

　　3と4に注意。heavy rain と言うときには定冠詞は不要であるが，意味合いは少し変わるものの，次に storm などの名詞を置くときには不定冠詞の a が必要である。

II 授業の前提

1　授業の前提となる環境

A　部屋の状態

床が汚れているね。
　The floor is dirty, isn't it?

教室が汚いね。
　This classroom is messy.
　　　This class ... と言えば，the class members の意味になる。

床がほこりだらけだ。
　The floor is covered with dust.

黒板もきれいにしておきなさい。
　Clean the blackboard too.

今日の掃除当番はだれですか。
　Who is the cleaning monitor today?

掃除当番はゴミを捨てに行きなさい。
　Will the cleaning monitor take out the trash?

掃除当番は教室をもっときれいに掃除しなさい。
  The cleaning monitor should clean the classroom more neatly.

今日の掃除当番の人は，特に念入りに掃除をしなさい。明日は，授業参観日です。
  Today's cleaning monitors, clean the room more carefully than usual. Your parents are going to see your class.

部屋が暗すぎますか。
  Is the classroom too dark?

部屋が暗すぎませんか。
  Isn't the classroom too dark?

電気をつけてください。
  Please turn on the light.

部屋が暗いので，電気をつけてください。
  The room is dark, so could you turn on the light?
  Could you turn on the light, as the room is dark?
  Could you turn on the light, since the room is dark?

　　アメリカ英語では，事実を前提としたり，自明の理由がある場合に好んで since という接続詞を用いる。
　　because は，simply, partly, only などによってしばしば修飾されるが，since はこのような語で修飾されることはできない。
　　「電気をつける」と言うときの「電気」は light でよい。「蛍光灯」は fluorescent (light) である。LED は light-emitting diode の略である。

蛍光灯の調子がおかしいようだね。
  There seems to be something wrong with the fluorescent lights.

「蛍光灯」は，fluorescent lamp といってもよい。

まぶしいので，ブラインドを降ろしてください。
1. **It's glaring, so close the Venetian blind.**
2. **It's glaring, so close the Venetian blinds.**
3. **It's glaring, so let down the Venetian blinds.**

　　アメリカ英語では，ブラインドの意味で shade という単語を用いることもある。

　　ブラインドは blind のように単数でも，blinds のように複数でも表すことができる。one slat piece（1枚のブラインドの羽根板）が何枚も集まって1つのブラインドを構成しているとみなせば，blind となり，one slat piece のそれぞれが blind であるとすれば，ブラインド全体は blinds となる。

　　2の close と3の let down という動詞の違いを考えてみよう。close は，ブラインドを窓枠の下まで下げ，外の様子がうかがえる状態から，パタッと閉める場合に使う。let down は，ブラインドを窓枠の上にまとめてたぐり寄せた状態から，一気に窓枠の下までパッと下げる場合に使う。

まぶしいから，カーテンを閉めてください。
1. **Please close the curtains as there is a glare.**
2. ***Please close the curtains as it is glittering.**

　　太陽などのぎらぎらする光を形容するときには glare を使う。glitter は物が反射して断続的にぴかぴか光るようなときに使う。1は正しく，2は誤りである。

　　　cf. The sun glares down on the sand.
　　　　 The sun glared out of the blue sky.
　　　　 in the full glare of the sun
　　　　 Diamonds glitter in the dark.
　　　　 Cat's eyes glitter in the dark.
　　　　 All that glitters is not gold.

君たち寒いですか。
　Are you cold?

君たち寒くないか。
　Aren't you cold?

窓を閉めてもいいですか。
　May I close the window?

寒いので，窓を閉めなさい。
　It's cold, so close the window.

暖房を入れてほしいですか。
　Would you like me to turn on the heater?
　Would you like me to put on the heater?

君たち暑すぎますか。
　Are you too hot?

君たち，暑すぎませんか。
　Aren't you too hot?

窓を開けてもいいですか。
　May I open the window?

窓を少し開けよう。
　Let's open the windows a little.

暑いので，窓を開けなさい。
　It's hot, so open the window.

窓を開けてほしいですか。
　Would you like me to open the window?

雨が降り込むから，窓を閉めよう。
　The rain is coming in. Let's close the windows.

雨が降りだした。窓を閉めなさい。
　It has begun to rain. Close the windows.

部屋の空気を入れ換えよう。
　1. Let's air out the room.
　2. Let's change the air of the room.
　　　1 の air out は広く使われている表現である。2 の言い方は日本語に近いがあまり自然ではない。

▶窓を開けてもいいですか。
　May I open the window?

▶窓を少し開けましょうか。
　Shall I open the windows a little?

▶窓を閉めてもいいですか。
　May I close the window?

▶暑いので，上着を脱いでもいいですか。
　1. It's too hot. May I take my coat off?
　2. May I take my coat off, since it is too hot?
　3. Can I take my coat off, as it is too hot?
　　　日本語では「〜ので」となっているが，これを無理に1つの英文で訳すよりも，1のように2文で表現する方が自然である。助動詞の may と can は，あまり大きな意味の違いがなく使われることもあるが，クラスのような状況では may の方がふさわしいであろう。

▶寒いので，上着を着てもいいですか。
　It's cold. May I put my coat on?

May I put my coat on, since it is cold?
Can I put my coat on, as it is cold?

B　聞き取れるか

私の声が聞こえますか。
   Can you hear me all right?
   Can you hear me well?

みなさん，私の声が聞こえますか。
   Can you all hear me all right?
   Can you all hear me well?
   Can you all hear me?
   Can all of you hear me?
   Can you all hear what I'm saying?

▶はい，聞こえます。
   Yes, we can.

▶はい，よく聞こえます。
   Yes, we can. We can hear you well.

▶聞こえません。
   I can't hear you.
   We can't hear you.

▶もう少し大きな声でしゃべってください。
   Could you speak a little louder?
   Would you speak up a little?
   Could you speak up a little?

1 授業の前提となる環境　　27

後ろの人たちは，私の言うことが聞こえますか。
　Can people sitting at the back hear me?
　Can people sitting in the back hear me?
　Can people sitting at the back hear what I am saying?
　Can people sitting in the back hear what I am saying?

後ろの方は私の声がよく聞こえますか。
　Can you people sitting in the back hear me all right?
　Can you people sitting at the back hear me all right?
　Can you people in the back hear me?
　　　you という代名詞の次に guys などの普通名詞を付加できる。
　　you people ... という表現は，丁寧な意味を持つ。

▶**いいえ，聞こえません。**
　No, we can't.

私の声が聞こえにくい人は前の方につめてください。
　Those who cannot hear me well, please sit in the front.

CDの音が小さすぎますか。
　1. Is the sound of the CD too low?
　2. Is the sound of the CD loud enough?
　3. *Is the CD deck too low?
　　　3 は，「CDの位置が低すぎるのではないか」という解釈も成り立つので，1や2の方がよい。

後ろの人たちはCDが聞こえますか。
　Can the people in the back hear the CD?
　Can the people at the back hear the CD?
　Can you hear in the back?
　Can you hear at the back?

ボリュームを上げましょうか。
　Shall I turn up the volume?
　Do you want me to turn up the volume?

ボリュームの大きさはいいですか。
　Is the volume all right?

ボリュームが低すぎますか。
　Is the volume too low?

いいですか。
　Is it all right?

音がはっきりしていますか。
　Is the sound clear enough?

風邪を引いて声がよく出ません。
　I can't speak well because I have a cold.
　I can't speak well because of my cold.

▶声が小さくてちっとも聞こえません。
　1. I can't hear you at all because your voice is too soft.
　2. *I can't hear you at all because your voice is too small.
　　　声の大小をいうときには，loud と soft を用いる。big や small は使えない。
　　　生まれつき声が大きいとか小さいとかいう場合には，small や large で voice を形容することは可能である。

▶もっとはっきり話してください。
　Could you enunciate more clearly?

▶もう少しゆっくり話してください。
　Please speak a little slower.

▶聞こえないので，もう一度言ってください。
Could you say that once again? I can't hear you.
Could you say that again? I can't hear you.
Could you repeat once more? I can't hear you.
Could you please repeat what you just said? I can't hear you.
Could you repeat what you just said? I can't hear you.

▶後ろまで聞こえるように話してください。
Could you speak up so that people sitting in the back can hear?
Could you speak up so that people sitting at the back can hear?
　　アメリカ英語では前置詞 in がよく使われる。

▶マイクを使ってください。
Could you use the microphone?
Could you use the mike?

▶隣の教室がうるさくて，よく聞こえません。
The people next door are noisy. I can't hear you well.
I can't hear you well, as the people next door are noisy.
I can't hear you well, as the room next door is noisy.
　　*I can't hear you well, as the next door is noisy. のように訳すと，ドアがうるさいことになり，もとの文とは意味が違ってくる。「隣の教室」は，the people next door とか，the room next door のように訳したい。
　　as の代わりに since，because を使ってもよい。as と since は結果を，because は理由を強調したいときに使う傾向がある。

C 黒板の字が見えるか

黒板がよく見えますか。
　Can you see the blackboard well?

みなさん，黒板がよく見えますか。
　Can everybody see the board well?
　Can you all see the board well?

後ろの人は黒板が見えますか。
　Can you people sitting in [at] the back see the board?

後ろに座っている人は，黒板の字が見えますか。
　Can you people sitting in the back see the board?
　Can you people sitting at the back see the board?
　　「後ろに」と言うときの前置詞は，in でも at でもよい。

両横の人は，黒板が見えますか。
　Can people sitting on both sides see the board?
　　side という名詞は，前置詞 on との結び付きが強い。前文では sit in ～，sit at ～ と続いたが，この場合は side という名詞のからみで，sitting on both sides ... となる。

黒板の字が見えにくい人はいますか。
1. **Is anyone having trouble seeing the writing on the board?**
2. **Is there anyone who has trouble in seeing the letters on the board?**
3. **Is there anyone who has trouble seeing the letters on the board?**
　　1の方が2や3よりもよい。have trouble in seeing ... と言うと，視力の問題と取られやすい。

また，have trouble ... という形は，習慣的な問題を暗示させる。つまり，Is there anyone who has trouble seeing ...? と言うと，「いつも，ものが見えにくくて苦労してる人はいませんか」などの意味に解釈されやすい。

もとの日本語の意味を明確に英訳するには，is having という進行形を用いた１のようにするのがよい。

黒板の字が見えにくい人はいませんか。
1. **Isn't anyone having trouble seeing the board?**
2. **Isn't anyone having trouble seeing the writing on the board?**
3. **Isn't there anyone who has trouble in seeing the letters on the board?**
4. **Isn't there anyone who has trouble seeing the letters on the board?**

３や４のように言うと，「慢性的な視力の問題をかかえている人がいることを希望している」ような印象を与える。１や２のように表現するとよい。

黒板が見えにくい人は，空いている席に替わってもかまいません。
If you're having difficulty in seeing the board, you can move to an empty seat.

この場合も，you're having ... のように進行形にすること。you have ... というと，「慢性的な視力の問題」を暗示させることになる。

▶黒板の字が見えにくいのですが。
I can hardly see what is written on the board.

▶黒板がまぶしくて，字が読めません。
I can't read the board because of the glare.
I can't read the letters because of the glare on the board.

glare には，加算名詞と不加算名詞の両方の用法がある。「まぶ

しい光」という意味では通常 the を付けて，the glare とすることが多い。

2　CALL教室などの設備・機器

A　入室

ブースが具合の悪い人はいますか。
　1. Is there anyone having trouble at his booth?
　2. Is anyone having trouble at his booth?
　　　1の there を省略して2のように言ってもよい。

CALL教室には飲食物を持ち込まないでください。
　Don't bring in any food and drink in the CALL room.
　Don't bring in any food and drink in the CALL lab.
　　　以前は語学の授業はLL教室で行われることが多かったが，現在ではCALL教室で行われることが多い。LLは language laboratory の略，CALLは computer-aided language learning の略である。computer-assisted language learning の略と考えてもよい。

CALL教室では，食べたり飲んだりすることはできません。
　You are not allowed to eat or drink in the CALL room.
　You are not allowed to eat or drink in the CALL lab.

B　CALL機器の操作

CALLで授業を受けたことのない人はいますか。
　1. Is there anybody who has never had a class in the CALL?
　2. Is there anybody who has not had a CALL class?

3. **Is there anybody who has not had any CALL classes?**
  4. **Is there anybody who has not had any class in a CALL?**
  5. **Is there anybody who has not has any class in the CALL?**
　　1，2，3の方が4よりも自然である。

まず，CALLの機械の使い方について説明しましょう。
First of all, let me tell you how to use the CALL machines.
First of all, let me explain how to use the CALL machines.

メインスイッチを入れてください。
Turn on the main switch.
Put on the main switch.

スイッチの位置がわかりますか。
Do you know where the switch is?

スイッチが入るとランプが点灯します。
  1. **The light will come on when you put the switch on.**
  2. **The light will come on when you turn the switch on.**
  3. ***The light will be on when you put the switch on.**
  4. ***The light will be on when you turn the switch on.**
　　come on には，「(灯火などが) ともる，つく」という意味がある。putの代わりに turn を使ってもよい。
　　3や4のように be on ～を使うと，「スイッチをつける前からライトがすでについている」ことを暗示させるのでおかしい。

まず，IDを入れてください。
  1. **First, enter your ID.**
  2. **First, put in your ID.**
　　1の方がより自然な言い方である。

次に，自分のパスワードを入れてください。
  1. **Next, enter your password.**

2. **Next, put in your password.**
3. **Put your password in.**
 1，2，3の順で自然な言い方である。

それからログインをしてください。
 Then, please log in.

パスワードを入れてログインします。
 You enter your password to log in.
  ログインが名詞で使われるときは，loginのように1語で書く。

しばらくすると，パソコンが立ち上がります。
 After a while, your computer will be ready.

今後はこのようにしてパソコンを立ち上がらせてください。
 From now on, please boot up your computer in this way.

パソコンが立ち上がらない人はいますか。
 1. **Is there anyone who is (still) having trouble starting with their computer?**
 2. **Is there anyone who failed to start their computer?**
  1の方が2よりも自然で，親切な表現である。

再起動してみてください。
 Please restart your computer.

表示画面をスクロールしてください。
 Scroll the viewing area.
 Scroll down the page.

ポインターが画面の右端に来るまでマウスを動かしなさい。
 Move your mouse until the cursor comes to the right edge of the screen.

マウスボタンを押したままでドラッグしてください。
  Press and hold the mouse button, and drag (the icon).

CDを入れてください。
  Put the CD in.

録音する準備をしてください。
  Get ready to record.

録音のボタンを押しなさい。
  Push the record button.

録音のボタンを押すと，赤いランプが点灯します。
  When you push the record button, the red lamp will come on.
  When you push the recording button, the red lamp will come on.

プログラム3から音声を流します。
  You can hear the sound on Program 3.
  I'll put the sound on Program 3.
    「音声を流す」を直訳的に，*to make the sound run と言うのはおかしい。

ヘッドセットを使ってみましょう。
  Let's use the headset.

ヘッドセットがコンセントに入っていますか。
  Is the headset plugged in?

ヘッドセットがコンセントに入っていることを確かめなさい。
  Make sure your headset is plugged in.

今，私の声が聞こえますか。
　Can you hear me now?

ヘッドセットは大丈夫ですか。
　Is your headset working?

今，自分で録音することができます。
　You can record on your own now.

コールボタンがどこにあるかわかりますか。
　Do you know where the call button is?

もし何か問題があったら，コールボタンを押してください。
　Press your call button if you have any problems.
　Push down your call button if you have any problems.

マイクを上に押し上げるとスイッチが切れます。
　1. If you put your mike upward, it will be switched off.
　2. If you raise your mike, it will be switched off.
　3. If you point your mike upward, it will be switched off.
　　　上下に移動できるマイクの場合である。1と2は，3とは異なる意味を持つ。前者は「マイク全体の位置を上げる」意味であり，3は「マイクの基部は固定したままで，録音する面のみを上方に向ける」意味である。

マイクをあまり口に近づけないように。
　Don't put your mike too close to your mouth.

本番の録音前に，機械が正常に動いているかどうかチェックしてみましょう。
　Before we begin with the actual recording, let's check the machines to see if they are working properly.
　Before we begin the actual recording, let's check the ma-

chines to see if they were working properly.
Before we begin with the actual recording, let's make a test run.
Before we begin the actual recoding, let's make a test run.

それでは録音します。準備はいいですか。
　Well, let's record now. Are you ready?

録音できなかった人は手を上げてください。
　Those who couldn't record, raise your hand.

録音に失敗した人はいませんか。
　1. Is there anyone who has failed to record?
　2. Isn't there anybody who has failed to record?
　3. *Is there anyone who has failed in recording?
　4. *Isn't there anyone who has failed in recording?
　　1, 2の両方が可能であるが, 1の方がよい。2のように言うと, だれかが失敗するのを期待するニュアンスがあるからである。
　　anyone と anybody とは同じ意味と解してよい。
　　3, 4では fail in ～ing という形が使われている。この形は個人的な失敗などを暗示させるので, 一斉録音の失敗などについて言うときにはふさわしくない。

しばらく録音してみましょう。
　Let's record for a while.

ここで止めてみます。
　Let me stop here.

CDがきれいに録音できているかどうか調べてごらんなさい。
　1. Why don't you check your CD to see if everything recorded well?
　2. Why don't you check your CD to see if everything is re-

corded well?
3. **Why don't you check your CDs to see if everything recorded well?**

　文法的には1のように recorded という能動態でも，2のように受動態でもよいが，1の言い方が標準的である。

　3のように CDs という複数形を使うと，CD が何枚か録音されたことになる。

今度は各自で録音してみなさい。
This time, record on your own.

後藤君，マイクに向かって大きな声で話してください。
Goto-kun, speak loudly into the microphone.
Goto-kun, speak aloud into the microphone.

　aloud という副詞は「(人に聞こえるように) 声を出して」という意味であり，speak aloud, read aloud (音読する)，think aloud (独り言を言う) のような熟語的表現として使うことがある。ネイティブスピーカーの中には，speak aloud という表現が，speak は「声を出して話す」のであるから，aloud とは重複しておかしいと抵抗を示す人もいる。

教室のモニタースピーカーから音声を流します。
1. **I'm going to put it through the classroom monitor speaker.**
2. **You will hear it through the speaker.**

　正式には教室のモニタースピーカーであるが，状況から判断できるので，2のように省略してもよい。

今度はヘッドセットから音を流しましょう。
This time, let me run the program through the headset.

君と山田君をつなぎます。
I'll connect you with Yamada-kun.

ボリュームを調節しなさい。
  Adjust the volume.

ボリュームの上げ下げのしかたはわかりますか。
  1. **Do you know how to turn the volume up and down?**
  2. **Do you know how to turn the volume up or down?**
  3. *** Do you know how to turn up or down the volume?**
     turn up, turn down を一緒にした言い方が turn up and down であるが, 3 のように言うことはできない。1 や 2 のように, turn の次に目的語を置いて, そのあとに up and down あるいは turn or down を入れること。

質問のある人は, コールボタンを押してください。
  If you have questions, press the call button.
  Those who have some questions, press the call button.

▶機械の操作のしかたを教えてください。
  Please tell me how to use the machine.

▶CDを忘れました。
  I forgot to bring the CD.
  I forgot to bring my CD.
  I forgot to bring a CD.

▶予備のCDを貸してください。
  May I borrow the spare CD?
  May I borrow a spare CD?
     特定の唯一のCDであればthe, 不特定のCDであればaを使う。後者の場合には, 予備のCDが2枚以上あることを暗示させる。

▶どのプログラムを使うのですか。
  Which program are you going to use?

▶CDを家に忘れました。
I left my CD at home.

▶CDを持ってくるのを忘れました。
I forgot to bring my CD.

▶CDを忘れてしまいました。1枚貸していただけませんか。
I forgot my CD. Could I borrow one?

▶予備のCDを貸していただけませんか。
May I borrow an extra CD?
Could I borrow an extra CD?
Do you have an extra CD I could borrow?

▶先生のCDを貸してください。ダビングをしたいと思いますので。
1. Could I borrow your CD, as I'd like to copy it?
2. Could I borrow your CD, as I want to make a copy of it?

　　1の方が丁寧で，学生の立場としてはふさわしい。
　　厳密には make a copy は，copy the thing or the material, as well as the recorded contents という解釈も成り立つので，copy という語の方がよい。
　　「ダビング」は日本語ではコピーの意味で使われるが，英語で dub は
　　　I dubbed this CD to make it more interesting.
　　　Let's dub some music on the CD.
のように，「編集」の意味で用いる。用法の差異に注意。

▶CDは何枚必要でしょうか。
How many CDs do we need?

▶DVDは，どこのメーカーのものが一番いいですか。
1. What brand of DVD is best?
2. As for the DVD, which make is the best?

1, 2のいずれも可能であるが, 1の方が自然である。なお,「一番よい」という日本語の訳として, 1のようにbestという形で使うこともできるし, 2のように定冠詞のtheを入れてthe bestとしてもよい。

C 退室

スイッチを切ってください。
1. **Turn the switch off.**
2. **Put the switch off.**
3. **Move the switch to the off position.**

　　2のput offは「(電灯・ラジオなどをスイッチを作動させて)消す」という意味であるが, イギリス英語的用法。
　　1や2の方が3よりも簡潔でよい。

CALLの機械はすべてチリを嫌います。消しゴムのくずはきれいに取って, ゴミ箱に捨ててください。
　All the machines in the CALL room are sensitive to dust. Collect any eraser dust and put it in the trash can.

教室を出る前に, ヘッドセットを机の中に入れてください。
　Put your headset in your desk before you leave.

教室を出る前に, ヘッドセットをかけてください。
　Hang up your headset before you leave.

この次は60分CDを1枚持ってきなさい。
　Bring a sixty-minute CD next time.

いすをちゃんと机の下に入れてください。
　Put your chair under your table neatly.

これで終わります。
  1. **That's it for today.**
  2. **That's about it.**

  1の方がよい。2の場合には，本当に授業で終えるべきところを終わったのかどうか，ややあいまいさが残った感じがするからである。

それでは時間がきたので，パソコンを閉じてください。
  1. **Well, time is up. Please shut down your computer.**
  2. **Well, the time is up. Please shut down your computer.**

  1の方が2よりも普通に使われる。

パソコンをログアウトしてください。
  Please log out.

  「パソコンを使用したあとはログアクトするように」という掲示は，Log out when done. などのように言えばよい。

D　機器のトラブル

何か問題がありますか。
  1. **Does anyone have a problem?**
  2. **Is anyone having a problem?**
  3. **Is there a problem?**
  4. **Is there any trouble?**

  4はあまり自然な言い方ではない。

すべて正常ですか。
  Is everything all right?

機械の調子の悪い人は，空いている席に移ってください。
  If you have trouble with your machine, move to an empty booth.

機械の調子の悪い人は，どこでもいいですから，ほかの席に移ってください。
If you have any trouble with your machine, move to whichever seat is available.

どうも調子が悪いようだ。
There seems to be something wrong with this.

プロジェクターが故障しています。
The projector is out of order.

これは大丈夫です。
This is all right.
This is OK.

リモコンが動かない。
The remote control does not work.

▶よく聞こえません。
I can't hear you well.

▶音が出ません。
The sound doesn't come on.

▶音が聞こえません。
I can't hear the sound.

▶音声が全く聞こえません。
I can't hear any sound.
I can't hear anything.

▶CDの声が非常に小さいのです。
1. The voice on the CD is very soft.

2. **The voice on the CD is very low.**
3. **The voice on the CD is not loud enough.**
4. **The voice on the CD is inaudible.**
5. ***The voice of the CD is inaudible.**

　「CDの声」というときの前置詞は on を使う。of はふさわしくない。The Voice of America とか the voice of the majority というときには of が可能である。この場合には America や the majority がそれ自体で voice を持っていると見なされるからである。

▶ボリュームを上げてください。
Could you turn up the volume?

▶スイッチが入りません。
1. **I can't turn on the switch.**
2. **I can't turn on the machine.**
3. **The machine won't turn on.**
4. **The switch is stuck.**
5. **I can't put on the switch.**
6. **I can't get the switch on.**
7. **The switch doesn't work.**

　2と3では switch という言葉ではなく machine が使われているが，1や4と文意は変わらない。

　put の場合には「努力」は別に伴わないが，get の場合には「努力」を伴う。

▶スイッチが切れません。
I can't turn off the switch.

▶スイッチがおかしいようです。
There seems to be something wrong with the switch.

▶スイッチはどこにあるのでしょうか。
Where is the switch?

▶録音できません。
I can't record.
I can't get anything on my tape.

▶CDが急に回らなくなりました。
All of a sudden, the CD got stuck.

▶CDが動きません。
The CD won't move.

▶機械の調子が悪いので，席を代わってもいいですか。
1. **May I change seats since something is wrong with this machine?**
2. **Can I change seats since something is wrong with this machine?**
3. **May I change seats since there is something wrong with the machine?**
4. **Can I change seats since there is something wrong with the machine?**

　　1，2 では接続詞 since のあとの主語は something となっている。3，4 では since に導かれる節が there is something ... で始まっている。1，2 の方が 3，4 よりも自然な言い方である。

　　また，1，2 では this machine，3，4 では the machine という形が使われている。日本語の訳は「この機械」とはなっていないが，英訳としては this machine とした方が明確である。

　　may，can のいずれも可能であるが，may の方がより丁寧な表現である。

▶（CALL機器などで）**雑音がひどいようです。**
1. **There is a lot of static.**
2. **There is a lot of noise.**

　　noise は「部屋の外からの騒音」という意味合いもあるので，1 の方がよい。また，noise には不可算名詞としての用法も，可

算名詞としての用法もある。しかし，上記の日本語を*There are lots of noises. と訳すと，ネイティブスピーカーにあまり自然には響かない。

3 規律

A クラスを静かにさせるとき

静かにしなさい。
   Be quiet.
   Button your lips.
   Silence.
   Pipe down.
   Put a lid on it.
   Can the talking.

　　shut up は日本語の「黙れ！」に相当する，強い響きをもつ粗暴な感じのする言葉である。本当にクラスが騒々しいときには，効き目のある言葉である。学生になじみの深い言葉でもあるし，言葉の持つ響きの効果もあるのであろう。
　　「静かにしなさい」という英語の言い方は数多い。Put a lid on it. の it は，your speaking を意味する。
　　Can the talking. の can は stop の意味である。この can は Can the shit.（Stop trying to fool me.）などのように，命令文で俗語的によく使われる。

みなさん，静かにしてください。
   Everybody, please be quiet.

話をやめてください。
   Stop talking now.

私語をしないように。
　Don't whisper to your friends.
　Don't talk with your friends.

私語はほかの人の迷惑になります。
　If you chatter, you'll bother other people.
　Your talking disturbs other people.

聞いてください。
　Please listen.

ちょっと聞いてください。
　May I have your attention?

騒がしい。
　You guys are too noisy.
　You're being too noisy!

シー！
Shhh!
　　英語でも人を静かにさせるときに Shhh! という表現を用いることができる。Shhh! の h の数は別に決まってはいない。強く言うのであれば h の数を増やせばよい。
　　日本語で赤ん坊にオシッコをさせるとき，同様に「シー」と言うことがあるが，英語ではこの場合には Shhh! とは言わない。

静かになるまで始められません。
　1. We can't start until everyone quiets down.
　2. We can't start until everyone is quiet.
　3. I can't start until everyone quiets down.
　4. I can't start until everyone is quiet.
　　　until と till は同じ意味であるが，前者の場合には l が 1 つ，後者の場合には l が 2 つであることに注意。つづりがまぎらわしい。

イギリス英語では quiet down の代わりに quieten という動詞を使うことができる。
　　　主語は we でも I でもよい。また，be 動詞の is の代わりに becomes を用いてもよい。ネイティブスピーカーは，それぞれ 2 よりも 1，4 よりも 3 を好む人がいる。

授業が始められるように，自分の席に戻ってください。
　Return to your seats so that we can start.
　　　"Return to your seats and fasten your seat belts." は，しばしば飛行機の中で耳にする表現である。return という動詞は前置詞の to と結び付くことが多い。

皆が静かになるのを待っているんです。
　I'm waiting for you to quiet down.
　I'm waiting for you to be quiet.

私語をするなら英語でしなさい。(ジョーク)
　If you want to whisper, do it in English.
　If you want to whisper, do that in English.

B　生徒をしかる

田中さん，私語をやめなさい。
　Tanaka-san, stop chattering.
　Tanaka-san, don't talk with your friends.
　Tanaka-san, don't whisper to your friends.

山下君，後ろの人と話さないように。
　Yamashita-kun, don't talk with the person behind you.
　Yamashita-kun, no talking with the person behind you.

よそ見をしてはいけません。
　Don't look the other way.
　Keep your eyes forward.

よそ見をしないでこちらを向きなさい。
　1. Keep your eyes on me.
　2. Don't look over there. Look at me.
　3. Don't look the other way. Look at me.
　4. Don't look around. Look at me.
　5. Pay attention.
　6. *Don't stare around. Look at me.
　　　2は,「反対側を見るな」という意味になる。
　　　stare は, look long and directly with the eyes wide open という意味であるから, この言葉に6のように around を付けて言うのはおかしい。

居眠りをしないように。
　Try not take a nap.
　Try not to doze off.

山下君, 居眠りをしているとわからなくなるぞ。
　Yamashita-kun, you can't keep up if you continue dozing off.
　Yamashita-kun, you'll be lost if you continue dozing off.

毎日早く寝るようにしなさい。そうすれば英語の時間に眠くならないだろう。
　Try to go to bed early, and you won't be sleepy during the English class.
　Going to bed early will keep you from getting sleepy during English class.

岡田君が眠っているので，起こしなさい。
   Okada-kun is asleep. Wake him up.

山下君，いすを後ろに傾けないようにしなさい。
   Yamashita-kun, don't lean back on your chair.

山下君，いすをガタガタさせないようにしなさい。
   1. Yamashita-kun, stop banging your chair on the floor.
   2. Yamashita-kun, stop rocking in your chair.
      rock one's chair は，rock an empty chair つまり，「だれも座っていないいすをぐらつかせる」という意味であるが，rock in one's chair と言えば rock one's chair while one's sitting in it つまり，「座っているいすをぐらつかせる」という意味になる。

教科書を忘れて来たら授業ができないじゃないか。
   1. How can you study if you didn't bring your textbook?
   2. You can't study anything unless you bring your textbook.
   3. You forgot to bring your textbook. You can't study anything.
      1や2の方が3よりもよい。3はやや stilted な感じがある。

これからは教科書を忘れないようにしなさい。
   Never forget to bring your textbook.
   Always remember to bring your textbook.

これからはちゃんと予習をしておきなさい。
   From now on, be sure to study in advance.

私の言うことをしっかりと聞いておきなさい。
   Listen to what I say very carefully.

3 規律 *51*

同じことを繰り返さないから，私の言うことをよく聞きなさい。
  1. **Listen carefully to what I am going to say because I am not going to say the same thing again.**
  2. **Listen carefully to what I am going to say because I am not going to say the same thing twice.**
  3. **Listen carefully to what I am going to say because I am not going to repeat it.**
  4. **Listen to what I am going to say carefully because I am not going to say the same thing again.**

　　副詞の位置はほかの品詞に比べて自由であるが，carefully の位置は１〜３の方が４よりもよい。４のように言うと，「(教師が)注意深く言うこと」を聞きなさいという意味にも取れるからである。

C　謝罪

ごめんなさい。先週は風邪で休んでいました。
  I'm sorry I was absent last week because of a cold.
  I'm sorry I was absent last week because I had a cold.
  I'm sorry I was absent last week because I had a bad cold.
  I'm sorry I was absent last week because I was sick in bed with a cold.

　　いずれでもよい。I'm sorry のあとにコンマを付してもよい。

ごめんなさい。まだ，先週のテストを採点していません。
  I'm sorry I haven't graded your test papers yet.

ごめんなさい。まだ，先週のテストを採点し終わっていません。
  I'm sorry I haven't finished grading your test papers yet.

ごめんなさい。ラッシュにかかって遅れました。
  1. **I'm sorry I was late because the (rush-hour) traffic was**

heavy.
2. I'm sorry I was late because I ran into a traffic jam.
3. I'm sorry I was late because I got stuck in a traffic jam.
4. I'm sorry I was late because I encountered a traffic jam.
5. *I'm sorry I was late because I had to fight against the traffic jam.

　1 は standard な表現，2 と 3 は informal，4 は formal な表現である。5 は不自然である。上記の例文ではいずれも I was late ... になっているが，I'm late ... と言ってもよい。

ごめんなさい。バスがストで遅れました。
I'm sorry I was late because of the bus strike.

▶すみません。静かにします。
I'm sorry. I'll be quiet.

▶これからは忘れないようにします。
I'll be careful not to forget.

▶すみません。つい，眠ってしまいました。
I'm sorry. I fell asleep.
I'm sorry. I ended up falling asleep.

▶これからは気をつけます。
I'll be careful from now on.

▶もう二度と同じことはしません。
I won't let it happen again.

▶二度と同じことをしないと約束します。
I promise not to do the same thing again.

▶大変うかつなことをしました。
It was very careless of me.
How foolish I was!
How foolishly I acted!
How stupid I was!
　　これらの文は，さまざまな状況で使うことが可能である。

▶友達ではなくて，私が一人で全部それをしました。
1. I did it all by myself. No one helped me.
2. I did it all by myself. I didn't have any help from any of my friends.
3. I did it all by myself. I didn't have any help from my friends.
4. I did it all by myself. No one else was involved.
5. I did it all by myself. My friend was not involved.
6. I did it all by myself. My friend didn't help me.
7. I did it all by myself. My friend did not help.
　　5〜7のように my friend と言うと，友人が1人しかいないという意味になる。
　　友人が何人もいれば，1〜4のように言えばよい。4はやや formal な言い方である。

▶私に責任があります。
I'm responsible for that.

▶私が責任者でした。
1. I was in charge.
2. I was in charge of it.
　　of it は付さない方が自然である。しかし，it が event を指す場合には，2の表現でもよい。I'm responsible for that. でもよい。

▶私が不注意でした。
I was careless.

D 忘れ物

ああ，しまった。教科書を持ってくるのを忘れてしまった。
　Oh, I forgot to bring my textbook with me.
　Oh, I forgot to bring the textbook with me.

あ，しまった！　CDプレーヤーを職員室から持ってくるのを忘れた。
　1. **Oh, no! I forgot to bring a CD player from the teacher's room.**
　2. **Whoops! I forgot to bring a CD player from the teacher's room.**
　　　1の方が自然である。

職員室にチョーク箱を忘れてしまった。
　I left the chalk box in the teachers' room.

チョークを持ってくるべきだった。
　I should have brought some chalk.

答案用紙を家に忘れてしまった。
　I left the test papers at home.

森山君，鉛筆をちょっと貸してくれないか。
　Moriyama-kun, can you lend me a pencil for a while?

どれくらいの人が辞書を忘れてきましたか。
　How many people forgot to bring a dictionary?

こんなに多くの人が辞書を忘れてきたんですか。
　This many people forgot to bring a dictionary?

▶宿題を持ってくるのを忘れました。
I forgot to bring my homework assignment with me.

▶テキストを忘れました。
I forgot my textbook.

▶筆記用具を忘れました。
I forgot to bring something to write with.

▶英語の試験が今日あるということを全く忘れていました。
I had forgotten all about our having the English test today.

▶消しゴムを貸していただけませんか。忘れてしまいました。
 1. May I borrow an eraser? I left mine at home.
 2. Could I borrow an eraser? I left mine at home.
 3. May I borrow an eraser? I forgot mine.
 4. Could I borrow an eraser? I forgot mine.

　　mine を it で置き換えることはできない。it を使うと，貸してもらう消しゴムと忘れた消しゴムとが同一のものになってしまうからである。
　　どこに忘れたか場所が明確であるときは，leave という動詞を使う。忘れた場所が定かでない場合には forget を使う。学校で消しゴムを忘れる場合は家庭に置き忘れることが多いので，1 や 2 の文の方が，3 や 4 よりもより自然な文である。

▶これからは忘れないようにします。
I'll be careful not to forget.

E　落書き

机に落書きをしないように。
　Don't scribble on the desk.

机やいすは皆のものだから，落書きはしないように。
Don't scribble on the desks and chairs, as they belong to everybody.

　　この場合の as は自然に聞こえる。話し手が教師であり，as を使うことによって大人的な口調を印象づけることができる。
　　since や because でもよい。

4　例外的状況

A　身体状況・病気

日ごろ元気なのに，今日はどうしたの。
You've been fine up to now, but what's the matter today?
You've been fine, but what's the matter today?

　　What's the matter? に類似した表現に What's the matter with you? がある。これは Why aren't you doing the right thing? の意味である。

君は顔色が悪いようだが。大丈夫ですか。
You look pale. Are you all right?

　　Look と同様に，主格補語をとる動詞に，seem, taste, grow, feel, appear, remain, sound, keep, become, be, get などがある。

松下君，風邪気味ではないのか。
Matsushita-kun, aren't you catching a cold?
Matsushita-kun, aren't you getting a cold?

▶斉藤先生，ありがとうございます。少し熱っぽいですが，大丈夫だと思います。
1. Thank you, Mr. Saito. I'm a little feverish, but I think I'm

OK.
2. **Thank you, Mr. Saito. I have a fever, but I think I'm OK.**
　　1 は feverish という形容詞，2 は fever という名詞を使った表現。いずれでもよい。

顔が少し赤いけど，熱があるの？
1. **You look a little flushed. Do you have a fever?**
2. **You look flushed. Do you have a fever?**
3. **Your face looks red. Do you have a fever?**
4. **You look a little pink. Do you have a fever?**
5. ***You look a little red. Do you have a fever?**
6. ***You look reddish. Do you have a fever?**
7. ***You look a little flushed. Don't you have a fever?**
8. ***You look flushed. Don't you have a fever?**
9. ***Your face looks red. Don't you have a fever?**
10. ***You look a little pink. Don't you have a fever?**

　　flush は，「(興奮・怒り・運動・熱などで)〈顔などが〉紅潮している」ときに使う言葉である。1，2 は自然な表現である。
　　red は 3 のように，Your face looks red. と言うことはできるが，5 のように You を主語にして使うことはできない。red の代わりに pink という言葉を使って 4 のように言うことは可能である。
　　red から派生した reddish も *You look reddish. のように使うことはできない。
　　「顔が少し赤いけど，熱があるんじゃないか」という日本語は変ではないが，これを直訳して英語を否定疑問にするとおかしくなる。7 〜 10 のように言えば，英語的感覚からすると，「熱があるに違いない。そうだろう」という気持ちを強く押し出したことになり，相手が病気であることを期待するような印象を与えるからである。否定の日本文を英文に訳すときには注意を要する。

▶**急におなかが痛くなりました。**
　My stomach just started to hurt.
　My stomach just started hurting.

My stomach suddenly started to hurt.

▶田中先生，山口君が苦しがっています。
  1. **Mr. Tanaka, Yamaguchi-kun is suffering.**
  2. **Mr. Tanaka, Yamaguchi-kun doesn't feel well.**
     1は，ongoing serious pain, mental or physical の場合である。それほど由々しい状態でなければ2のように言うべきである。

▶田中先生，山口君の様子が何か変です。
  There's something wrong with Yamaguchi-kun.

▶田中先生，山口君の顔色が悪いようです。
  1. **Mr. Tanaka, Yamaguchi-kun looks pale.**
  2. **Mr. Tanaka, Yamaguchi-kun is pale.**
  3. **Mr. Tanaka, Yamaguchi-kun has a pale face.**
     自然な英語の順番は 1 > 2 > 3 である。

斎藤君，制服が汚れているよ。
Saito-kun, your uniform has a stain on it.
    日本の中学校や高等学校では制服を着ることが多いが，アメリカではほとんど私服である。

斎藤君，その包帯はどうしたの。
  1. **Saito-kun, what happened to the bandage?**
  2. **Saito-kun, why are you wearing a bandage?**
  3. **Saito-kun, what is that bandage for?**
     実際にだれかが包帯をしているのを見たあとは，3のように言うよりも1や2のように言った方が親切な気持ちを表すことになる。

B 途中での退室

これからちょっと用事があるから，自習をしておいてください。
1. I'll let you study by yourselves. I have some business to do now.
2. I'll let you study by yourself. I have some business to do now.

　　1のように by yourselves と言えば，複数の生徒を対象に授業をしている場合である。2のように言えば，1人を対象に授業をしている場合となる。

30分ほど自習をしておいてください。また，戻ってきますから。
Please study by yourselves for about thirty minutes. I am coming back here.
Please study by yourself for about thirty minutes, as I am coming back here.

ちょっと用事を思い出したから職員室まで行ってきます。10分したら戻ってきます。
1. Oh, I have something I have to do in the staff room. I'll be back in ten minutes.
2. Let me go to the staff room. I just remembered I have some work to do. I will be back in ten minutes.
3. Oh, I have some work to do in the staff room. I'll be back in ten minutes.
4. Let me go to the staff room. I just remembered I have some business to do. I will be back in ten minutes.
5. Oh, I have some business to do in the staff room. I'll be back in ten minutes.

　　I have some business to do. は「トイレに行く」の euphemism（婉曲表現）でもあるので，ほかの表現を使うことが望ましい。some business to do を some work to do と言えば，「ト

イレに行く」という含みはなくなる。このような理由から，1，2，3の方が4や5よりもよい。

山下さん，家からすぐ帰ってくるようにという電話がありました。
1. **Yamashita-san, there was a phone call saying you should go home right away.**
2. **Yamashita-san, there was a phone call saying you should go home soon.**

　1のright awayは「即刻」という意味であるが，2のsoonは，wishy-washy, uncertainなニュアンスがある。日本語の英訳としては1の方がよい。

▶トイレに行ってもいいですか。
1. **May I be excused?**
2. **May I go to the restroom?**

　「トイレに行く」という表現は，日本文化でも欧米文化でも直截的な言い方はできるだけ避ける傾向にある。Excuse me. I'll be right back.（失礼します。すぐ戻ってきます。）とだけ言ってトイレに行くことを表す場合もある。

　1は2よりも普通に使われる表現。

▶気分が悪いので，ちょっと保健室に行ってきてよいですか。
1. **I am not feeling well. May I go to see the nurse?**
2. **I am not feeling well. May I go to the nurse's office?**
3. **May I go to the nurse's room because I am not feeling well?**
4. **May I go to the nurse's office because I am not feeling well?**
5. ***May I go to the health room because I am not feeling well?**

　日本語の「保健室」を直訳して，health roomと言うことはできない。英語ではthe nurse's roomとかthe nurse's officeと言う。

▶頭が痛いので，保健室に行ってきてもよいですか。
  May I go to the nurse's room, as I have a headache?
  May I go to the nurse's office because I have a headache?

▶気分がよくありません。斉藤先生，家に帰ってもいいですか。
  I'm not feeling well. Mr. Saito, can I go home?

松下君，気分が悪かったら帰ってもいいですよ。
  1. Matsushita-kun, you can go home if you are not feeling well.
  2. *Matsushita-kun, you can go home if you are not feeling all right.
      日本語で考えると2もよさそうであるが，意味的に2では弱すぎるし，通常，all right は否定形では使わない。

▶おなかが痛いので，家に帰ってもいいですか。
  I have a stomachache. May I go home?

▶熱がありますので，失礼してもいいですか。
  1. I have a slight fever. May I be excused?
  2. I have a slight fever. May I leave the room?
  3. I have a little fever. May I be excused?
  4. I feel like I have a slight fever. May I be excused?
  5. I feel like I have a slight fever. Please be excused.
      3のように have a little fever という言い方はあまり自然ではない。
      「熱がある」といっても，もし体温計で実際に熱を測っていないのであれば，4，5のように言うのが自然である。

▶頭がひどく痛いので，医務室に行ってもいいですか。
  May I go to the school doctor now, as I have a terrible headache?

▶辞書をロッカーの中から取ってきていいですか。
  1. **May I go get my dictionary from my locker?**
  2. **Can I go get my dictionary from my locker?**
  3. **May I go get my dictionary from the locker?**
  4. **Can I go get my dictionary from the locker?**
　　それぞれの学生に1つずつロッカーがある場合には1や2のように my locker となり，すべての生徒用にただ1つのロッカーがある場合には3や4のように the locker となる。実際には前者のケースが多いであろう。

▶家に連絡しなければならないことがありますので，電話してきてもいいですか。
  May I go and make a telephone call, as I have to call my family?

▶前の授業でノートを忘れましたので，取りに行ってもかまいませんか。
  1. **May I go and get my notebook, as I left it in my last class?**
  2. **May I go and get my notebook, as I left it where I had my last class.**
  3. **May I go and get my notebook, as I left it in the last classroom?**
　　1が最も自然な表現である。

III 授業活動

1 授業開始

A 授業開始にあたって

では始めます。
 Well, let's start.
 Well, let's begin.
 Well, let's get started.
 Well, let's get on with our lesson.

今から授業を始めます。
 1. **I'll start class now.**
 2. **I'll start the lesson, now.**
 3. *__I'll start the class now.__

  class は「(クラスの) 授業」の意味で用いるときには抽象名詞,「クラスや授業時間の数」の意味で用いるときには普通名詞の扱いをする。
   I have to go to [attend] class today.
   (今日は授業に出なくてはならない。)
   I have five classes today.
   (今日は5つの授業がある。)
  また now の前のコンマはあってもなくてもよい。

それでは始めましょう。
　Let's get started.
　Let's start.
　Let's begin.
　Let's get on with our lesson.
　It's time to start now.

それでは張り切っていきましょう。
　Let's get on the ball.
　Let's get the ball rolling.
　　　get on the ball は「一生懸命に働く，勉強する」という意味の俗語的なアメリカ英語である。
　　　イギリス英語では get the ball rolling という言い方をする。

みなさん，いいですか。/ みなさん，準備ができましたか。
　1. Are you ready?
　2. Are you ready to start?
　3. Is everyone ready to start now?
　　　1 が最もよく使われる表現である。

▶はい，できました。
　Yes, I am.

準備ができたと思います。
　I hope you are all ready to start class.

英語の授業で何をしたいですか。
　What would you like to do in English class?

▶今日はどんなことをするのですか。
　What are we supposed to do today?

B　既習部分の確認

先週は何を勉強しましたか。
　　What did we study last week?

先週はどこまでやりましたか。
　　Where were we last week?
　　Where did we leave off last week?
　　How far did we get?
　　　　学生に応答練習をさせるために，絶えずこの質問をクラスの始めにするのもよい。
　　　　イギリス英語では How far did we get up to? という表現も可能である。

このあいだは，10ページの3行目まで行きました。
　　1. **We left off at line 3 on page 10.**
　　2. **We stopped at line 3 on page 10.**
　　3. **We finished up to line 3 on page 10.**
　　　　3よりも1や2の方を好むネイティブスピーカーが多い。

先週は，5課を終わりましたね。
　　We finished Lesson 5, didn't we?
　　We went through Lesson 5, didn't we?
　　We were through with Lesson 5, weren't we?

今日はどこからかわかりますか。
　　Do you know where we are today?

これは前回の授業でもう説明しましたね。
　　I had explained this in my previous lesson, hadn't I?
　　I explained this in my previous lesson, didn't I?
　　I explained this in a previous lesson, didn't I?

▶鈴木先生，52ページは先週終わりました。今日は53ページからです。
Mr. Suzuki, we finished page 52 last week. We'll begin with page 53 today.

▶佐藤先生，25ページはまだやっていません。
1. Mrs. Satoh, we haven't done page 25 yet.
2. Mrs. Satoh, we haven't covered page 25 yet.

　　2は「まだ，25ページは全くやっていない」という意味にも解釈できるし，「すでに25ページに入ったが，まだ，仕上げてはいない」という意味にも解釈できる。Mrs. Satoh, we are not through with page 25 yet. といえば，「すでに25ページに入ったが，まだ仕上げてはいない」という意味になる。

▶小川先生，そこは先週済みました。
1. Miss Ogawa, I think we finished that last week.
2. Miss Ogawa, I'm sorry, but we finished that last week.
3. Miss Ogawa, we finished that last week.
4. Miss Ogawa, we covered that last week.
5. *Miss Ogawa, we covered there last week.

　　1～4はどれでもよいが，1や2のように，I think あるいは I'm sorry を入れると穏やかな表現となる。3と4は直截的な表現である。

　　there は location や place を指す場合に使う。日本語に引かれて that を there にしてはいけない。5は不自然な表現である。

▶その問題はすでに済みました。今日はDをする予定です。
We have already finished the exercise. We are going to do D today.
We have already finished the exercises. We are going to do D today.

　　問題を1つ済ませたのであれば the exercise，いくつもやったのであれば the exercises のように複数形にする。

日本語の「問題」という訳にとらわれると，ついつい problem という語を使ってしまいがちであるが，problem を使うのは誤りである。

2　学習活動の指示

A　基本的指示

立ちなさい。
　Stand up.

座りなさい。
　Sit down.

　「座る」という表現に Have a seat. があるが，これは特定の場所ではなく，「(どこでもよいから) 座る」という状況で用いる言葉である。
　Sit down. は，「(特定の場所に) 座る」という意味なので，クラスの中で決まった席に生徒を座らせる場合にはこちらを使うのが望ましい。

答えなさい。
　Answer it.

読みなさい。
　Read it.

発音しなさい。
　Pronounce it.

書きなさい。
　Write it.

聞きなさい。
　　Listen to it.
　　Listen.

黒板をご覧なさい。
　　Look at the board.

よく黒板を見なさい。
　　Look at the board carefully.
　　Look at the board closely.

黒板の文章を見てみましょう。
　　Let's look at the sentences on the board.

私のあとからくり返しなさい。
　　Please repeat after me.

黒板に行きなさい。
　　Go to the board.

黒板まで出てきなさい。
　　Come up to the board.

黒板に書きなさい。
　　Write it on the board.

ノートに書きなさい。
　　Write it in your notebooks.

空欄の部分を埋めてみましょう。
　　Let's fill in the blanks.

ノートを出しなさい。
　Take out your notebooks.
　Take your notebooks out.
　Take your notebook out.
　Get out your notebooks.
　Get your notebook out.
　　　notebooks, notebook のいずれでもよい。

ゆっくり考えたまえ。
　Why don't you take time and think?

では次の問題に答えてください。
　Well, answer the next question.
　Well, do the next exercise.
　Well, solve the next problem.
　　　question は，数学以外の history, reading, grammar, essay などいろいろな事柄について使うことができる。
　　　problem は，数学の時間などで使われる。

自分の力でやりなさい。
　Work on your own.
　Work by yourself.
　Do your own work, please.
　Look at your own paper.

個人個人でやってごらんなさい。
　Try to work individually.

みなさん，ほかの人に頼らずにやりなさい。
　Everybody work independently.

隣の人の邪魔をしないように。
　Don't disturb your neighbor.

遠慮なく質問してください。
　Please don't hesitate to ask me questions.

では次の問題に進みましょう。
　Well, let me go on to the next exercise.
　Well, let me go on to the next question.

席がえをしよう。
　Let's change seats.

B　読ませる

まず，私が読んでみます。
　First of all, I'll read it to you.
　I'll read it to you first.

先に私が読んでみましょう。
　Let me read first.
　I'll read first.

私のあとについて読んでください。
　Please read after me.

私のあとについて，大きな声で読みなさい。
　Please read aloud after me.

私のあとについて，新出単語を読んでください。
　Say the new words after me.
　Repeat the new words after me.
　*Read the new words after me.
　　日本語では「読んで」だが，read という語に直訳すると，おかしい。say や repeat という語を使うべきである。

状況から学生はどの新出単語かわかるので，定冠詞の the を付ける必要がある。

私のあとについて，15 課を読んでください。
　Please read Lesson 15 after me.

私のあとについて，15 課のダイアローグを読んでください。
　Please read the dialog in Lesson 15 after me.

私のあとについて，15 課の例文を読んでください。
　I'd like you to read the sample sentences in Lesson 15 after me.

CD のあとについて読んでみましょう。
　Let's read after the CD.

それでは，本を開き，CD のあとについて読む練習をしてごらんなさい。
　Well, practice reading after the CD with a book open.

　　状況から誤解なく判断できる場合もあるが，この文で with a book open という語句を省略するとまぎらわしい文が生まれる。
　　　Well, practice reading after the CD.
　　この文では，"Is the CD projecting words?" という疑問が生じる。repeat after the CD（CD のあとについて読む［言う］）はよく使われる文であるが，read after the CD は普通の言い方ではない。with a book open があれば「本を開いて，CD を聞きながら読む」という意味が明確に伝わる。

テキストを自分で読みなさい。
　Read the text to yourselves.

だれか新しい課が読めますか。
　1. **Can anyone read the new lesson?**

2. **Can anybody read the new lesson?**

1のanyoneと2のanybodyとは意味も用法も同じであるが，anybodyの方がより口語的な表現である。授業ではanyoneの方がよく使われるようである。

だれか一人で読めますか。
  Can anybody read it by themselves?
  Can anyone read it by himself/herself?
  Can any of you read it by yourself?
  Can any of you read it by yourselves?
  ***Can any of you read it by himself/herself?**

anybodyは元来単数の扱いであるが，口語ではその代名詞を複数形で受けるのがふつうである。

Anybody → they，their，them，themselves

anyoneをany oneのように文脈によって2語につづることもある。oneにストレスがある場合やoneが「物」を表す場合である。

Any one of them can do such a thing.
（彼らのうちだれでもそんなことはできますよ。）
Any one of them will do.
（どれでもかまいませんよ。）

森君，読み始めてください。
  You start reading, Mori-kun.

次郎君，読み始めてください。
  Jiro-kun, start reading.

太郎君から読みなさい。
  Taro-kun will begin.

森君，続けてください。
  You go on, Mori-kun.

森君，続けて読んでください。
  Mori-kun, go on reading.

もう1文読みなさい。
  Read one more sentence.

次の文も読んでください。
  Read the next sentence, too.

貴志君，もう1つ文を読んでください。
  Takashi-kun, please read one more sentence.

みんなで読んでみましょう。
  Let's read in chorus.
  Let's read all together.
    chorus の発音は [kɔ́ːrəs] であることに注意。

順番に読みましょう。
  Let's take turns reading.

前から順番に，1段落ずつ読みなさい。
  Starting from the front seat, read the passage paragraph by paragraph.
  Starting from the front of the row, read the passage paragraph by paragraph.

前から順番に，1文ずつ読みなさい。
  Starting from the front seat, read the passage sentence by sentence.
  Starting from the front of the row, read the passage sentence by sentence.

1段落ごとに読みなさい。
　Read one paragraph each.

次のところを読み始めてください。
　Start reading the next section.

次郎君，太郎君が終わったところを続けて読みなさい。
　Jiro-kun, go on from where Taro-kun left off.

今のところをもう一度読んでください。
　1. Please read the same thing again.
　2. Please read it again.
　3. Please read the same passage once again.
　4. *Please read the same place once more.
　　　1と2が最も普通な言い方である。3はformalすぎる。once again の once は省略可。
　　　4の言い方は日本文には近いが，不自然である。

文の意味を考えながら，もう一度本文を読んでください。
　Read the text once more, thinking about the meaning of the sentences.
　Read the text one more time keeping in mind the meaning of the sentences.
　Read the text one more time keeping the meaning of the sentences in mind.
　Read the text one more time bearing in mind the meaning of the sentences.

さあ，意味がはっきりしたので，もう一度読んでみましょう。
　Well, now that the meaning is clear, let's read it once more.
　Well, as the meaning is clear now, let's read it once more.
　　　now that ... の方が as ... よりも話し言葉としては自然である。as は pedantic, dry, formal といったニュアンスがある。

2 学習活動の指示　75

それでは佐藤さん，最初から読んでください。
Well, Sato-san, please read from the beginning.
OK, Sato-san, please read from the beginning.
　　「最初から〜」というときは，定冠詞の the がやはり必要である。また，OK は，上記のように well と同様な意味合いで使うこともできる。

次のところを少し読んでください。
1. **Read a little bit of the next section.**
2. **Read the next section for a little bit.**
3. **Read the next section for a little while.**
4. **Read the next section a little bit.**
　　a little bit の位置によって文の意味が異なってくる。1 は amount of reading の意味であるが，2 は 3 と同様，duration of reading を表す。4 のように言うと，読む量が少しなのか，読む時間が少しなのか不明瞭である。時間に言及するのであれば，2 や 3 のように前置詞の for を入れるとよい。

森君，最初の5行だけ読みなさい。
Mori-kun, read the first five lines.

山内君，3つ目の文を読んでください。
Yamauchi-kun, read the third sentence.

8行目から読み始めなさい。
Start reading from line 8.

14 行目の終わりまで読みなさい。
Read as far as to the end of the 14th line.
Read down to the end of the 14th line.

39 ページの第2の段落を読んでください。
Read the second paragraph on page 39.

39ページの第2の段落から読んでください。
Read from the second paragraph on page 39.

第2の段落ではなくて，第3の段落です。
Not the second paragraph, but the third paragraph.

25ページの上から3つ目の文まで読みなさい。
Read to the third sentence from the top of page 25.

79ページの5行目から80ページの3行目まで読みなさい。
Read from line 5 on page 79 to line 3 on page 80.
　　「上から下まで」と対句的に言う場合には，lineやpageに定冠詞のtheは使わない。

8ページの一番上の文の終わりまで読みなさい。
Read to the end of the top sentence on page 8.

2分間時間を与えますから，その間に5課を読んでください。
I'll give you two minutes to read Lesson 5.
You have two minutes to read Lesson 5, starting now.

山内君，下線の部分に注意して，3つ目の文を読んでください。
Yamauchi-kun, read the third sentence, paying attention to the underlined parts.

斉藤君，89ページの新出単語を読んでください。
Saito-kun, please read the new words on page 89.

はい。そこまで。
OK, Good.

そこでやめなさい。
Stop there.

そこまででいいですよ。
1. Okay. That's fine.
2. Okay. That's enough.
3. Okay. That will do.
　　　教師によっては，Thank you. とだけ言う人もいよう。1が一番よい。2と3は読み方によっては「もういい。それ以上聞きたくない」という意味にも取れるので注意が必要である。

次の人，どうぞ。
Next, please.
Next person, please.
Next one, please.

だれかほかの人，お願いします。
Someone else, please.

次郎君，文の途中で止めてはいけません。
Jiro-kun, don't stop in the middle of the sentence.

もっとゆっくり読んでください。
Please read more slowly.

テキストを大きな声で読みなさい。
Read the text aloud.

みなさん，大きな声ではっきりと読んでください。
Everybody, read loudly and clearly.

山内君，3つ目の文を大きな声で読んでください。
Yamauchi-kun, read the third sentence aloud.

みなさん，口を大きく開けて読みましょう。
1. Everybody, open your mouth wide and read.

2. *Everybody, open your mouth widely and read.

日本語を考えると widely という副詞を使いたくなるが, widely は誤り。1のように wide という形を使わなくてはいけない。widely という副詞は「(違いが) 大きく」とか「広範に」という意味で使われる。

wide には形容詞としての用法もあるし副詞としての用法もある。「(口などを) 大きく開いて」というような状況では wide という副詞を使わなくてはならない。日本語としては「口を大きく開けて読む」という言い方は自然であるが, 英語を母語とする人々の中には, Open your mouth wide and read. という文は不自然だと指摘する人もいる。口を大きく開けると, 唇を使って作る [p], や [f] などの発音ができなくなるからだというのがその理由である。

貴志君, 大きな声でもう一度読んでください。
Takashi-kun, please read aloud once more.
Takashi-kun, please read aloud one more time.

貴志君, 大きな声でもう1つ読んでください。
Takashi-kun, please read aloud one more sentence.

もう少し大きな声を出してください。
Please speak a little louder.

もう少し大きな声で読みましょう。
Please read a little louder.

声が小さすぎます。大きな声で読んでください。
Your voice is just too low. Read in a louder voice.
Your voice is just too low. Read louder.

聞こえません。もう一度大きな声で読みなさい。
I can't hear you. Read it aloud once more.

大きな声で，2回読んでください。
Read it aloud twice.

8ページを大きな声で一度読んでください。
1. Read page 8 once aloud.
2. Read page 8 once out loud.
3. Read page 8 once in a loud voice.
4. *Read page 8 once with a big voice.
　　日本語には3が近いが，英語としては1や2の方が自然である。out loud は「大きな声で」「はっきりと」という意味の熟語的表現。
　　He has a big voice. と言えば，「彼は生まれながらにして大きな声をしている」という意味になるので，4はおかしい。

自分でこの文章を2度，大きな声で読みなさい。
1. Please read these sentences aloud twice to yourself.
2. Please read aloud these sentences twice individually.
　　1のように，individually よりも yourself の方を好むネイティブスピーカーが多い。2の言い方では意味がわかりにくい。
　　また read these sentences aloud の方が，read aloud these sentences よりも自然である。

各自で3回大きな声を出して読んでください。
1. Read aloud three times to yourselves.
2. *Read aloud three times for yourselves.
　　for oneself は「（他人に頼らず）自分の力で」という意味である。この場合，2はおかしい。

めいめいで3回大きな声を出して読みなさい。
Each of you, read aloud three times to yourself.
Read aloud three times to yourselves.
　　you には「あなた」と「あなた方」という単数と複数の意味があるから，学生に対して言うときには yourself, yourselves の

いずれの形を使ってもよい。

各自で会話を大きな声で読む練習をしてごらんなさい。
Practice reading the dialogue aloud by yourself.
Practice reading the dialogue aloud to yourselves.
Practice reading the dialogue aloud to yourself.
> dialogue は dialog でもよい。

抑揚に注意しながら教科書を読んでください。
Read the textbook, paying attention to intonation.
Pay attention to intonation as you read the text.
> textbook, text のいずれでもよい。ついでながら，教科書の教授用書は，teacher's book とか teachers' book などのように言う。

個々の単語の発音よりも，むしろ全体の文の調子に気をつけて5ページを読んでごらんなさい。
Read page 5, paying attention to the rhythm of the whole sentence, rather than the pronunciation of individual sounds.
Read page 5, paying attention to the entire rhythm pattern, rather than the pronunciation of the individual sounds.

8ページの会話文を読んでみましょう。森君，John のところを読んでください。
Let's read the dialog on page 8. Mori-kun, you take John's role.

あなたがたのうち1人は John となって，もう1人は Betty となって会話を読んでごらんなさい。
Read the dialog with one of you as John and the other as Betty.

隣の人と役割を決めて，読みの練習をしなさい。
　Practice reading your assigned role with your partner.

もう一度会話を読んでみましょう。しかし，今度は役割を代えてごらんなさい。
　Let's read the dialog again. But this time, switch roles.

黒板の文をみんな読みましょう。
　Let's all read the sentences from the board.

黒板の文を，みんなで一斉に読みましょう。
　Let's read the sentences on the board in chorus.
　Let's read the sentences on the board all together.

黒板に書いた文を，私のあとについて読んでください。
　Please read the sentences on the board after me.

黒板の文を，2回ずつ読みましょう。
　Let's read the sentences on the board twice.

黒板の文を，1行飛ばしに読みましょう。
　1. Let's read every other sentence on the board.
　2. Let's read every two sentences on the board.
　　　1の方がよりわかりやすい文である。

▶先生，字が小さすぎて読めません。
　1. Your writing is too small to read.
　2. We can't read your writing. It's too small.
　3. We can't read what you wrote since your writing is too small.
　4. We can't read what you wrote because your writing is too small.
　5. *We can't read as your writing is too small.

日本語を中心に考えると5もよさそうであるが，不自然な言い方である。1〜4は正しいが，1，2の方が3，4よりも簡潔でよい。

▶もっと大きい字を書いてください。
Could you write a little larger?

▶そこは訳せますが，うまく読めません。
  1. **I can translate that, but I cannot read it well.**
  2. ***I can translate there, but I cannot read it well.**
    日本語は「そこは」で，これを there に訳すとあまり自然ではない。1の方がよい表現である。

8課を黙って一度読みなさい。
  Read lesson 8 once, silently.
    「黙読する」は，read to yourselves と表現してもよい。

5ページを黙読しなさい。
  Please read page 5 to yourselves.

今CDで聞いたところを黙読しなさい。
  Read what you heard on the CD silently.

第3課を一度黙読してください。
  Read Lesson 3 silently once.

12ページの5行目から，13ページの8行目まで黙読しなさい。
  1. **Read silently from line 5 on page 12 to line 8 on page 13.**
  2. **Read from line 5 on page 12 to line 8 on page 13 silently.**
    1の方が2よりもよい。

この章を黙読して，内容を理解してみましょう。
  1. **Let's read this chapter silently and try to understand it.**
  2. ***Let's read this chapter silently and understand it.**

2のように and の後に try to を入れないと，突然命令した感じを与えたり，文尾で twist した感じを与えてしまう。文頭と呼応させるためには try to を入れたい。

▶どこを読んだらいいのですか。
1. **What part should I read?**
2. **Where should I read?**

　　日本語に近いのは2であるが，where を使うよりも what part を使う方がより英語的である。

▶どこまで読んだらいいのですか。
1. **How far should I read?**
2. **Up to where should I read?**
3. **Up to what sentence should I read?**
4. ***Until where should I read?**

　　1と2がよい。3は明確であるが，あまり自然な英文ではない。4の Until where という表現はおかしい。

▶どこからどこまで読んだらいいのですか。
Where should I start and how far should I read to?
From where to where should I read?

▶読むだけでいいんですか。
Can I just read it?
Can I simply read it?

▶今，どこを読んでいるのですか。
Where are you reading now?

▶先生の読むのが速すぎて，ついていけません。
I can't follow you because you read too fast.
I can't keep up with you because you read too fast.
I can't catch up with you because you read too fast.

I can't catch up with you because you're reading too fast.
　　厳密には，keep up は follow の意で，catch up は reach the place の意である。

▶ もう少しゆっくり読んでいただけませんか。
Could you read a little slower?
Could you read more slowly?

▶ よく読めません。
I can't read well.

▶ 48 ページの上から3行目，前から2つ目の単語の読み方がわかりません。
I don't know how to read the second word on the third line from the top on page 48.

▶ 私はだれと組めばいいのでしょうか。
Who should I pair with?

C　書かせる

名前を大文字で書きなさい。
　Write your name in big letters.

それを小文字で書きなさい。
　Write it in small letters.

ブロック体で書きなさい。
　Write it in block letters.
　　字体をいうときは，前置詞は in を使う。

名前をブロック体の大文字で書きなさい。

1. **Write your name in block capitals.**
2. **Write your name in block caps.**

  2 の caps は colloquial な言い方である。

筆記体ではなく，ブロック体で書いてください。

1. **Print. Don't write.**
2. **Print. Don't use script.**
3. **Print. Don't write in cursive.**

  「ブロック体で書いてください」は 1，2，3 のいずれでもよい。2 や 3 はやや専門的な感じがする。自然な形としては 1 ＞ 2 ＞ 3 の順である。

きれいに書きなさい。

Write neatly.

もっときれいに書きなさい。

Write more neatly.

もう一度きれいに書きなさい。

Rewrite it neatly.

十分時間をかけて書きなさい。

1. **Take your time writing.**
2. **Take your time in writing.**
3. **Take your time while writing.**

  1 が最も自然な表現である。

書くときはあわてないようにしなさい。

Take your time writing.
Don't hurry while writing.

小さい字で書かないようにしましょう。
　Let's not write small.

行間をたっぷり空けて書きなさい。
　1. Leave a lot of space between lines when you write.
　2. Write, leaving a lot of space between the lines.
　　　２の方が日本語に近い感じがするが，１の方がより英語的な表現である。

忘れないように，これをノートに書き留めておきなさい。
　Jot this down in your notebooks so that you won't forget it.

これは大変重要だから，ノートに書いておきなさい。
　Take this down since it is very important.
　　　「ノートに書き留める」という言い方は，take down, write down, put down, copy down, get down などのようにいろいろと可能である。

これはノートのどこかに必ず書き留めておきなさい。
　Be sure you make a note of this somewhere in your notebook.
　Make sure you make a note of this somewhere in your notebooks.

これはノートに書く必要はありません。
　You don't have to write this down in your notebooks.

テキストの空白部分にこれを書いておきなさい。
　Write this down in the margin of your textbooks.

５ページの上の空白部分にそれを書いておきなさい。
　Write it down in the upper margin of page 5.

2 学習活動の指示　87

ノートを1ページ使ってそれを書きなさい。
Write it using the whole page of your notebook.

ペンで書きなさい。
1. Write it in ink.
2. Write in ink.
3. Use a pen when you write it.

　　代名詞のitは2のように省略してもよい。
　　「ペンで」とか「鉛筆で」という場合には，前置詞はinを使うことに注意。

鉛筆で書いてはいけません。
Don't write it in pencil.
Don't write in pencil.

濃い鉛筆を使いなさい。
Use a dark pencil.

書くときには，濃い鉛筆を使いなさい。
Use a dark pencil when you write it.

答案用紙にはHB以上の鉛筆を使いなさい。
1. Use a pencil darker than HB on the answer sheet.
2. Use a darker pencil than HB on the answer sheet.

　　日本語的発想からすると2のようにa darker pencilとしたくなるが，1のようにa pencil darker than ... と続けた方がよい。

家で書いてきなさい。
Write it at home.

質問の文章をノートにきれいに書きなさい。
Write the question sentences out neatly in your notebooks.

　　「ノートに書く」というとき，前置詞はonではなく，inを使

うことに注意。

なお,「ノート」の英語は notebook である。この意味で note とは言わない。

教科書 22 ページの答えをノートに書きなさい。
1. **Write the answers to the questions on page 22 in your notebooks.**
2. **Write the answers to the exercises on page 22 in your notebooks.**
3. ***Write the answers on page 22 in your notebooks.**

1 と 2 は standard な表現である。3 は the answers on page 22 の意味が曖昧である。

問題を黒板に書きますから,その答えをノートに書きなさい。
I'm going to write the questions on the board, so write the answers in your notebooks.

句読点に注意して答えを書きなさい。
Write your answer, paying attention to punctuation.

新出単語を5回ずつノートに書きなさい。
1. **Write the new words five times each in your notebooks.**
2. **Write the new words out five times in your notebooks.**

1 の方が 2 よりも自然である。

板書する文の中に新しい語句があったらノートに書きなさい。
1. **If there are any new words in the sentences I am going to write on the board, write them in your notebooks.**
2. **If there are any new words in the sentences that I write on the board, write them in your notebooks.**

1 と 2 のいずれでもよい。しかし,ニュアンスが異なる。1 は「これから書こうとする」場合であり,2 は「毎日書く」という習慣を表す。

この表現を使って，英文を2つ書いてみなさい。
　Write two English sentences using this expression.

感想をノートに書きなさい。
　Write your impressions in your notebooks.

ノートに書く時間はあとであげます。
　1. I'll give you some time later to write in your notebooks.
　2. I'll give you some time later so that you can write in your notebooks.
　　　1 は standard な表現。2 もよい。

▶佐藤先生，鉛筆で書くんですか。それともペンで書くんですか。
　Mr. Sato, should we write in pencil or in ink?

▶書くものを持っていないんですが。
　I don't have anything to write with.

▶いつまでに，書き終えたらいいんですか。
　1. What time should we finish writing?
　2. What time should we be finished writing?
　3. By when should we finish writing?
　　　日本語の「いつまでに」に相当する英語は by when であるが，この形をあまり好まないネイティブスピーカーがいる。1 や 2 の方が 3 より自然である。

それを黒板に書きなさい。
　Write that on the board.

前に出て黒板にその文を書きなさい。
　Come and write that sentence on the board.
　Come up and write that sentence on the board.

正しい答えを黒板に書きます。
　I'll write the correct answers on the board.

答えをきちんと黒板に書きなさい。
　1. **Write the answer on the board.**
　2. **Write out the answer on the board.**
　　　2 の write out は，「(あますところなく) 完全に文を書き取る」ときの表現である。

この問題がわかる人は，黒板に来て答えを書きなさい。
　1. **If you can do this question, come and write the answer on the board.**
　2. **If you can do this question, come here and write the answer on the board.**
　3. **If you can do this question, come up and write the answer on the board.**
　4. ***If you can answer this question, come and write the answer on the board.**
　　　一般的には question が目的語の場合には動詞 answer を使い，problem が目的語の場合には solve を使う。(ただし，数学の場合には answer the problem という表現が可能である。)
　　　このようなルールからすると 4 もよさそうであるが，If you can answer ... という言い方には抵抗がある。If you can answer ... で文が始まれば，I'll be happy. とか You'll understand the lesson. などのように《未来》と関係のある文が来るのが自然である。1～3 のように If you can do ... と言えば，「すでに答えを解いてしまっている」ことを前提にした問いかけになるから，後続の come and write the answer on the board. という《現在》を表す文とも呼応する。1～3 のように言いたい。

ここにチョークがあるから，A の答えを黒板に書きなさい。
　Here is a piece of chalk. Write the answer to A on the board.

山中君，ノートに書いてあることを黒板に書いてください。
　Yamanaka-kun, please write what you have in your notebook on the board.
　　黒板に書く場合には write を，黒板の文字をノートに書く場合には copy を使う。

この問題のわかる人は，黒板に出て答えを書きなさい。
　If you can do this question, come and write the answer on the board.
　If you can answer this question, come and write the answer on the board.
　If you can answer this question, come here and write the answer on the board.
　If you can answer this question, come up and write the answer on the board.
　If you can solve the problem, come here and write the answer on the board.
　If you can solve this problem, come up and write the answer on the board.
　　1 の do this question はよく使われる表現である。
　　question が目的語の場合，動詞には answer を使い，problem が目的語の場合，動詞には solve を使う。ただし，数学の場合には answer the problem という表現が可能である。

今から名前を呼ぶ人は，板書しなさい。
　Those who are called, come here and write on the board.
　Those who are called, come and write on the board.
　Those who are called, come up and write on the board.

まだ黒板に出てない人はだれですか。
　Who hasn't been to the blackboard yet?
　Who hasn't been up to the board yet?

授業の前に（３）の問題の解答を黒板に書いておきなさい。
Write the answer to (3) on the board before class.

それをここに書きなさい。
Write it here.

それをあそこに書きなさい。
Write it there.

それはあの言葉の横に書きなさい。
Write it next to that word.

その文の右横にそれを書きなさい。
Write it to the right of that sentence.

その文の左側にそれを書きなさい。
Write it to the left of that sentence.

３の文の上にそれを書きなさい。
Write it above sentence 3.

４と５の文の間にそれを書き入れなさい。
Write it in between sentence 4 and sentence 5.

政雄君の文の横に文を書きなさい。
Write your sentence next to Masao-kun's.

政雄君の文の右に文を書きなさい。
Write your sentence to the right of Masao-kun's.

政雄君の文の下に答えを書きなさい。
Write the answer under Masao-kun's sentence.

山内君,(黒板の)一番上から書いてください。
　Yamauchi-kun, write from the top.

もっと行間を空けて書きなさい。
　Write with more space between lines.

まっすぐ書くようにしなさい。
　Try to write straight.
　Try to keep your writing straight.

もっと大きな字を書きなさい。
　Write on the board in larger letters.
　Write in larger letters on the board.
　　「黒板に書く」場合には,write in のように前置詞の in が必要である。

後ろの人が見えるように,大きな字で書きなさい。
　Write in larger letters so that people in the back can see.
　Write in larger letters so that people at the back can see.

字が小さいと皆が見えません。
　If you write small, people can't see your writing.
　If you write small, nobody can see your writing.

字が小さいと皆が読めません。
　If you write small, people can't read your writing.
　If you write small, nobody can read your writing.

できるだけ文字はきれいに書きなさい。
　1. Write as neatly as you can.
　2. Write neatly as much as you can.
　　　1の方が2より自然な表現である。

黒板の下は見えにくいので，空けておいてください。
　Leave the bottom of the board blank, as it is hard to see.

君たち，あとの人が書けるように，もっとつめて書いてください。
　You people, write closer together so that the others can write.
　You people, write closer together so that the other people can write.
　You people, write closer together so that the others have room to write.
　You people, write closer together so that the other people have room to write.

みんなが見えるように片側に寄りなさい。
　Move to one side so that we can all see.

クラスの人があなたの書いたことが見えるように脇に寄りなさい。
　Step aside so that the class can see what you've written.

▶どこに書いたらいいんですか。
　Where are we supposed to write?

▶私の書いたものが読めますか。
　Can you read my handwriting?
　Can you read my writing?

▶書くのが下手ですみません。
　1. I'm sorry I have terrible writing.
　2. I am sorry I am an awful writer.
　3. I'm sorry I'm a terrible writer.
　　　1は「書く文字が下手」という意味であるが，2や3の場合には「作文が下手」という意味になる。

▶私はあまり速く書けないのです。
I can't write fast.

▶どこからどこまで書いたらいいのでしょうか。
1. **Where shall we start and finish writing?**
2. **Where shall we begin and where shall we end?**
3. **Where shall we begin and end?**
4. **What do you want us to write?**
5. **From where to where shall we write?**

　　1，2，3 はある特定の場所を書き写すときの質問である。
　　4 は何を書いたらいいのかを尋ねる言い方でもある。
　　「どこからどこまで」を直訳すると from where to where となるが，これはあまり自然な英語表現ではない。

▶私の答えは正しいのでしょうか。
1. **Is this right?**
2. **Am I right?**

　　1 は，生徒が板書し，書いた答えを指さしながら，教師にそれが正しいかどうか尋ねる場合などに使われる。
　　2 は，
　　　Do you agree with me?
　　　Do you agree with my statement?
　　　Do you agree with what I said?
　　などと同じ意味に解釈される。

D　訳させる

この連語を訳しなさい。
　Translate this compound word.
　Translate this phrase.

この文を和訳しなさい。
　　Translate this sentence into Japanese.
　　Put this sentence into Japanese.

最初の４つの文を日本語に訳しなさい。
　　Translate the first four sentences into Japanese.

今の文をもう一度訳してください。
　　Please translate the same sentence once more.

この文章を読んで，日本語に訳しなさい。
　　Read these sentences and translate them into Japanese.

一度読んでから訳してごらんなさい。
　　Read once and translate.

はい。読みはそこまで。次は訳しなさい。
 1. Good. So much for reading. I'd like you to translate now.
 2. Good. So much for reading. I'd like you to do some translating now.
 3. *Good. So much for reading. I'd like you to translate this time around.

　　　this time around は，同じことを別の方法で行うようなときに用いる表現である。例えば，
　　　　You listened with your books open. This time around, let's listen with your books closed.
　　などの場合である。

おおよその訳でいいですよ。
　　A rough translation is OK.

　　　OK はアメリカで好んで使われる表現である。イギリスでは all right をよく用いる。
　　　OK は，O.K., Okay, okay, Okey, Okeh などのように，い

ろいろなつづりが可能であるが，Okey, Okeh はあまり使われない。

まず，直訳してごらんなさい。
1. **First, try translating it literally.**
2. **First, try to translate it literally.**
3. **First, try literal translation.**
   3 はやや stilted な感じの表現である。

直訳でもかまいませんよ。
The literal translation will be all right.
The literal translation is all right.

この場合「直訳」は，ある特定の文章の直訳のことであるから，定冠詞の the が必要である。

will be all right も is all right も正しいが，will be all right の方がより好まれる。

literal は「直訳的な」という意味であるが，literary は「文学的な」という意味。両者はまぎらわしい。

意訳が難しければ，直訳でもかまいません。
If you have difficulty in translating freely, the literal translation will be all right.

直訳でいいから，9行目の文を日本語に訳しなさい。
A literal translation is OK. Translate the sentence on the 9th line into Japanese.
A word-for-word translation is OK. Translate the sentence on the 9th line into Japanese.

山田君，直訳でいいから最初の段落を訳しなさい。
Yamada-kun, translate the first paragraph. A literal translation will be OK.
Yamada-kun, translate the first paragraph. You can do it lit-

erally.

まず，直訳し，それから意訳を考えてごらんなさい。
　First, try to translate literally. Then, translate freely.

意訳でも直訳でもかまいません。
　Either literal translation or free translation will be OK.
　Either literal translation or free translation is OK.
　Both literal and free translation are OK.

一語一語訳してはいけません。
　Don't translate word for word.

できるだけ直訳は避けなさい。
　Try to avoid literal translation.

山田君，直訳は避けなさい。
　Yamada-kun, avoid literal translation.
　Yamada-kun, don't translate literally.
　Yamada-kun, don't translate word for word.

直訳ではなくて，自然な日本語に訳しなさい。
　Do not translate literally, but put it into natural Japanese.

できるだけ自然な日本語に訳しなさい。
　Translate into as natural Japanese as you can.

山田君，意訳しなさい。
　Yamada-kun, translate freely.
　Yamada-kun, free translation will do.
　Yamada-kun, free translation will be OK.

2 学習活動の指示　99

この文を訳せる人は手を上げなさい。
Those who can translate this sentence, raise your hands.

ここが訳せる人はいませんか。
1. **Can anyone translate this?**
2. **Can anybody translate this?**
3. ***Can anyone translate here?**
4. ***Can anybody translate here?**
　　「ここ」という日本語を英訳するとhereであるが，3，4は不自然である。1や2の方がよい。

出席番号順に，Lesson 8 を訳していきなさい。
1. **Translate Lesson 8 according to your roll number.**
2. **Translate Lesson 8 by your roll numbers.**
　　2はあまり自然な言い方ではない。

出席番号順に，Lesson 8 を1文ずつ訳していきなさい。
Translate Lesson 8 one sentence at a time according to your roll number.

この列から訳しなさい。
Will the students in this row start translating.
　　「この列から訳しなさい」というとき，Translate from this row. という英語が考えられるが，状況から判断できるものやや意味が不明瞭である。

9ページの 25 行目から，10 ページの 3 行目まで訳しなさい。
Translate from line 25 on page 9 through line 3 on page 10.
Translate from line 25 on page 9 to line 3 on page 10.

だれか，15 ページの 8 行目から 13 行目まで和訳してください。
Some, translate from line 8 through line 13 on page 15 into Japanese.

Some, translate from line 8 to line 13 on page 15 into Japanese.

15ページの8行目から13行目まで和訳しなさい。
1. Translate the passage from line 8 to line 13 on page 15 into Japanese.
2. Translate from line 8 to line 13 on page 15 into Japanese.
   1の方が2よりも明確である。

13ページの2番目のパラグラフを読んで訳しなさい。
Read the second paragraph on page 13 and translate it.

はい，そこまででいいです。
OK, that's enough.
OK, that's fine.
OK, that will do.
OK, that's far enough.

この文を英訳しなさい。
Translate this sentence into English.
Put this sentence into English.

日本語を英語に訳しなさい。
Translate from Japanese into English.
Put the Japanese into English.

日本文を英語に訳しなさい。
Put the Japanese sentences into English.

これから言う日本語を英語に訳しなさい。
Translate what I am going to say in Japanese into English.
Put what I am going to say in Japanese into English.

日本文の意味をよく考えて英訳しなさい。

1. Translate the Japanese sentence into English, keeping the meaning of the sentence in mind.
2. Think about the meaning of the Japanese sentence and (then) translate it into English.
3. *Translate the Japanese sentence into English, thinking the meaning of the sentence well.

   1, 2 は standard な表現であるが, 3 は不自然な表現である。

時制に気をつけて和文英訳してください。

1. Bear in mind the tense when translating the following sentence into Japanese.
2. Bear in mind tenses when translating the following sentence into Japanese.
3. *Translate the Japanese sentence into English, bearing in mind the tense.

   1 と 2 は standard な表現であるが, 3 は不自然な表現である。
   1 は時制とかかわる部分が 1 か所の場合, 2 は 2 つ以上の時制がかかわる場合である。

▶どこを訳すのですか。
Where do I have to translate?
Where am I supposed to translate?

▶どこを訳したらいいんですか。
1. Which passage should I translate?
2. Which sentence should I translate?
3. What is the passage I should translate?
4. What is the sentence I should translate?
5. What should I translate?
6. *Where shall I translate?

   日本語の原文を考えると, 6 のように言いたくなるが, この表現はあまり自然ではない。

1や2の表現が最も自然である。

▶どこまで訳したらいいのですか。
How much should I translate?
Until where should I translate?
To what point should I translate?

▶何行訳したらいいんですか。
How many lines should I translate?

▶最初に読むんですか。
Am I supposed to read first?
Should I read first?
Do I have to read first?

▶訳せません。
1. I can't translate that.
2. *I can't translate.
　2は正しくない。translateは他動詞であるから目的語が必要である。

▶この文はどう訳すのですか。
How would you translate this sentence?

▶ここの訳し方がよくわかりません。
1. I cannot understand how to translate this.
2. I don't understand how to translate this.
3. *I cannot understand how to translate here.
4. *I don't understand how to translate here.
　「ここの〜」という英語はhereを使いたくなるが，3と4は英文として自然ではない。1や2のようにthisを使うこと。

▶直訳でもかまいませんか。
　Can I translate literally?
　Is it all OK to translate literally?
　Is it all right for me translate literally?
　Is it all right if I translate literally?
　Do you mind if I translate literally?

▶直訳は避けた方がいいんですか。
　Is it better to avoid literal translation?

▶意訳してもよいですか。
　May I give a free translation?
　May I translate freely?
　May I give a loose translation?
　May I translate loosely?

▶この文は直訳すると…となりますが，意訳するとどうなりますか。
　The literal translation of this sentence is ..., but what would be a free Japanese translation?

▶文の修飾関係がわかりません。
　I don't understand what modifies what in the sentence.

▶単語の意味はわかりますが，文の意味がわかりません。
　1. I understand the meaning of the words, but I can't understand the meaning of this sentence.
　2. I understand the meaning of the words, but I cannot understand the meaning of this sentence.
　3. I understand the meaning of the words, but I can't understand the sentence meaning.
　　1のようにcan'tと言ってもいいし，2のようにcannotと言ってもよい。cannotの方が強い表現となる。

▶ 54 ページの３行目から訳していただけませんか。
　Could you translate from the third line on page 54?
　Can you translate from the third line on page 54?

E　教科書を使う

教科書を出してください。
　Take out your textbooks.
　Take your textbooks out.
　Get out your textbooks.
　Get your textbooks out.

教科書の 18 ページを開けてください。
　1. Please open your textbook to page 18.
　2. *Please open your textbook at page 18.
　　　１のように open 〜 to ... のように言う。

72 ページを見てください。
　Look at page 72.

65 ページの９行目の文を見てください。
　Look at the 9th line on page 65.
　Look at line 9 on page 65.

教科書の 25 ページの上から６行目を見てください。
　Please look at line 6 from the top on page 25.
　Please look at the sixth line from the top on page 25.
　Please look at page 25, line 6 from the top.
　　　いずれでもよい。いずれも standard な言い方である。

教科書の 32 ページの下から４行目を見てください。
　1. Please look at the fourth line from the bottom on page

32.
2. **Please look at page 32, the fourth line from the bottom.**
3. *****Please look at line 4 from the bottom on page 32.**

　1と2はともによい。ふつう行数はそれぞれのページの上から数字を入れているので，3のline 4というのは自然な言い方ではない。

38ページの上から7行目の文から始めます。
We are going to start on the 7th line from the top of page 38.

　「上から〜」と言うときは，from the topと言う。反対に，「下から〜」と言うときは，from the bottomと言う。

まず，6ページの左上隅の写真を見なさい。
First, look at the picture at the upper left-hand corner of page 6.
First, look at the picture in the upper left-hand corner of page 6.

　the picture at the upper ... でもよいし，the picture in the upper ... でもよい。

　「6ページ」と言うとき，前置詞はonを用いてon page 6のように言う。ところがcornerという名詞は，

　　the corner of a table（テーブルのかど）
　　look out the corner of one's eyes（横目を使って盗み見る）
　　all the corners of the earth（世界のすみずみ）

などのように，前置詞ofを従える。

　上記の例文では，いわば前置詞のonとofとが衝突した形になっている。この場合にはofがonに優先することになる。したがって，

　　*First, look at the picture on the upper left corner on page 6.

は不自然な英語となる。

28ページの図1を見てください。
Look at Diagram 1 on page 28.

「図1」などというときは，Diagram 1 のように言い，定冠詞の the を付けないことに注意すること。

教科書の89ページを開いてください。
Open your textbooks to page 89.

Open your textbooks at page 89. のように，前置詞の at を使うのはイギリス英語。アメリカ英語では to を使う。

読んで訳しなさい。
Read and translate.

隣の人と役割を決めて，読みの練習をしなさい。
Practice reading your assigned role with your partner.

私のあとについて，教科書を読みなさい。
Read the textbook after me.

教科書を伏せてください。
Please turn your textbook over.

F 課題をさせる

教科書61ページの練習問題2をやってください。
Please do Exercise 2 on page 61.

プリントの2番と5番の問題だけしてごらんなさい。
Do only No. 2 and No. 5 on your handout.
Do only No. 2 and No. 5 in your handout.

プリントの表に書けなくなった人は，裏も使ってください。

Those who have used up the front, you can write on the back.

Those who have used up the front, use the back as well.

If you have used up all the space on the front, you can write on the back.

▶表に書けなくなったので，裏に書いてもよいですか。

May I write on the back, as I've run out of space on the front?

May I write on the back, as I don't have any more room on the front?

Can I write on the back, as I've run out of space on the front?

　　Is it all right to write on the back? には「表に書けなくなったので」という日本語の訳は現れていないが，よく使われる英語表現である。

今配ったプリントを，20分で終えてください。

1. Finish the handout you've just received within twenty minutes.
2. Finish the handout you've just received in twenty minutes.

　　1の within twenty minutes は，not more than twenty minutes という意味であり，「20分以内」が強調された形である。

　　2の in twenty minutes は，場合によっては twenty-one minutes ということが有り得ることを暗示させる。

プリントを終えることができなかった人は，家で終えてきてください。

Those who haven't finished the handout, please finish it at home.

答えのチェックが終わったら，プリントは回収します。
  When you finish checking the answers, please give your handout back to me.
  When you finish checking the answers, let me have your handout.
  When you finish checking the answers, let me collect your papers.
  When you finish checking the answers, hand in your papers to me.

この問題の答えは2つ以上ありますので，よく考えてみなさい。
  1. There is more than one answer to this question, so think about it some more.
  2. There is more than one answer to this question, so give it more thought.
  3. *There is more than one answer to this question, so think more deeply.

　more than 〜は，誤解を生じやすい表現である。「2つ以上」という日本語は，英語では more than one となる。「1つより多い」という言い方をする。
　英語では，ある考えを動詞を主体に使う場合と，名詞を主体に使う場合とがある。1のように名詞的表現を好むネイティブスピーカーが多いようである。
　「よく考える」は think more deeply という日本語が当てはまりそうだが，ここではふさわしくない。

考える時間を10分与えます。
  1. I'll give you ten minutes to think.
  2. I'll give you ten minutes so that you can think.
　　1の方が2よりも自然な言い方である。

▶今からこの問題を解くのですか。
  Are we supposed to do these exercises?

2 学習活動の指示　109

▶今からこの問題をするんですか。
 1. **Are we supposed to work on this problem now?**
 2. **Are we supposed to work on these problems now?**
 3. **Are we supposed to solve this problem now?**
 4. **Are we supposed to solve these problems now?**
　　1, 2 の work on の方が 3, 4 の solve よりもよい。work on には,「最善を尽くして仕事に取り組み, 納得のいく答えが出るまで頑張る」という意味合いがあるからである。

▶今からするんですか。
Are we supposed to do this now?

▶全部するんですか。
Are we supposed to do everything?

▶どれをすればよいのですか。
Which one are we supposed to do?

▶何分ですればよいのですか。
 1. How many minutes do we have for this?
 2. How many minutes do I have to do this?
 3. *Within how many minutes should we do this?
　　日本人的な考え方からすると 3 がぴったりであるが, 英語表現としては冗長で奇異な感じがする。

▶あと何分ありますか。
How many more minutes do we have?

▶友達と一緒にやってもよいのですか。
May we do this with our friends?
Can we do this with our friends?
May we work on this with our friends?

110　Ⅲ　授業活動

▶5番の問題の意味がわかりません。
　I don't understand the fifth question.
　I cannot understand the fifth question.
　I don't understand question (No.) 5
　I cannot understand question (No.) 5.

G　聞かせる

よく聞いて，英語の音に慣れてください。
　1. Listen to spoken English often, and you'll get used to English sounds.
　2. Listen to spoken English well, and get used to English sounds.
　　　1の方が自然な言い方である。

英語を聞いたあと，すぐ真似をしてみてください。
　1. After you listen to English, try to imitate what you have just heard.
　2. After you listen to English, try to imitate soon.
　　　1は自然であるが，2はあまり自然な言い方ではない。

しゃべり方が速すぎますか。
　Am I talking too fast?

▶いいえ。そのままでかまいません。
　No. That's OK.

もっと速くしゃべってもかまいませんか。
　May I talk faster?
　Is it all right if I talk faster?
　*Can I talk faster?
　　　Can I ...? はふさわしくない。Am I (physically or mentally)

capable of ...? の意味に解釈されるからである。

▶はい。よく理解できました。
Now, I understand (very well).
　　括弧内の語はしばしば省略される。口語的な表現として，I get it や I got it. はよく使われる。

聞き取りが苦手な人はいますか。
  1. **Is there anyone who has trouble listening?**
  2. **Is there anyone who is not good at listening?**
　　1 は自然であるが，2 はあまり自然な言い方ではない。

教科書を見ないようにして，CDをよく聞いてください。
  1. **Listen to the CD carefully without looking at your textbook.**
  2. **Listen to the CD carefully without trying to look at your textbook.**
　　1 は普通に使われる表現であるが，2 も正しい。

教科書を閉じなさい。CDを聞いてみましょう。
  1. **Close your textbook. Let's listen to the CD.**
  2. **Shall we close your textbooks and listen to the CD?**
　　1 は命令調であるが，2 の方は生徒にややおもねった表現である。

CDを聞いて，まず，内容を理解するようにしてください。
　First, try to understand what is being said by listening to the CD.
　Listen to the CD and try to understand what is being said.

ちょっと戻ってみましょう。
　Let me go back a little bit.

ここで止めてみます。
　Let me stop here.

ここでしばらく止めて，いくつか質問をしてみます。
　Let me stop here for a while and ask you some questions.

▶もう少しゆっくり話してください。
　Could you speak a little slower?
　Please speak more slowly.

▶スピードについていけません。
　1. It's too fast for me.
　2. It's going too fast for me to keep up.
　3. You're going too fast for me to keep up.
　4. *I can't catch up with the speed.
　　　4 は meaningless である。1 が最もよい。

▶英語が全く聞き取れません。
　1. I cannot understand English at all.
　2. I cannot catch English at all.
　　　1 の方が 2 よりもよい。

▶今のところをもう一度聞かせてください。
　Could you let us hear that part once more time?
　Could you let us hear the passage once more?

▶ちょうどそこで止めてください。
　Please stop right there.

▶先週学んだところをもう一度聞かせてもらえませんか。
　Would it be possible for us to listen to what we covered last week?

▶何度聞いてもわかりません。
No matter how many times I listen to the passage, I can't understand it.
No matter how many times I listen to this part, I can't understand it.

▶全く理解できません。
I can't understand it at all.
I can't understand at all.
　　シェークスピアからきた表現であるが,「全くわからない」という言い方に It's all Greek to me. というのがある。

▶よくわかりませんので, もっと易しい英語で言ってください。
I can't understand you very well, so could you explain it in simpler English?
I can't understand you very well, so could you explain it in easier English?

▶今のところはよく理解できなかったので, 日本語で説明してください。
1. As I couldn't understand what you said, could you say it in Japanese?
2. As I couldn't understand what you said, could you explain in Japanese?
　　1の方が2よりも自然な英語表現である。

▶質問を英語で言えませんので, 日本語を使ってもいいですか。
I'm afraid I can't state my question in English. May I use Japanese?
I'm afraid I can't state the question in English. May I use Japanese?

H　書き取らせる

さあ，次は書き取りをしましょう。
　Well, let's do dictation next.
　Well, let's do some dictation next.

さあ，次は書き取りの練習です。
　Well, let's have a dictation exercise next.
　Well, let's do a dictation exercise next.

今から言う文を書きなさい。
　Write the sentences I am going to say to you.
　Write the sentences I am going to dictate to you.

今から英文を言いますから，書き取ってください。
　Please write the English sentences down as I give them to you.
　Please write the English sentences down as I say them to you.
　Please write the English sentences down as I read them to you.
　　「英文を言う」と言うとき，動詞は give, say, read のいずれでもよい。

黒板で説明する代わりに，口で言うからノートに書いてください。
　1. I am not going to use the board, so write what I tell you in your notebook.
　2. Write in your notebooks what I am going to tell you since I will not use the board.
　　1の方が語順や語の選択において2よりも自然である。

2 学習活動の指示　115

ゆっくり言いますから，ノートに写しなさい。
1. As I slowly tell the story, please write it down in your notebook.
2. I'm going to tell you the story slowly. Please write it down in your notebook.
3. I'm going to say it slowly. Please write it down in your notebook.
4. *I'm going to tell you slowly. Please write it down in your notebook.

　　4 の，... tell you slowly. のように言うのは不自然である。1 や 2 のように目的語の the story などを付さなくてはならない。
　　3 のように say を使えば，... say it slowly. で標準的な言い方となる。

今度はもっとゆっくり話します。用意はいいですか。
I'll speak a little bit slower this time. Are you ready?

3つの英語の文をゆっくり読みますので，書き取ってください。
1. I am going to read three English sentences slowly. Please take them down.
2. Since I am going to read three English sentences slowly, please take them down.

　　日本語の「～ので」を無理に訳さない方がいいというネイティブスピーカーも多い。1 の方が無難である。

普通の速さで3回読みますから，文章を書き取ってみましょう。
I am going to read three times at normal speed. Write the sentences down.

まず，日本語を書き取って，その次に英語に直してください。
First, write the Japanese sentences down, and then translate them into English.
First of all, write the Japanese sentences down, and then

translate them into English.
First, write down the Japanese sentence, and then put it into English.

first of all を使うと,「そのあとすべきことがたくさんある」ことを暗示する。first の場合は,そう強くは暗示させない。

状況から判断して,書き取る日本語はどれであるか理解できる。したがって,Japanese sentences ではなく,the Japanese sentences としたい。

▶書き取るのが苦手です。
I am not good at writing sentences down.
I am not good at writing things down.

▶もっとゆっくり言ってください。速く書けません。
Could you speak a little slower. I can't write so fast.
Could you speak a little more slowly. I can't write so fast.

▶速くノートに書き取れませんので,ゆっくり言ってください。
1. I can't take notes quickly. Could you speak a little slower?
2. I can't take notes fast. Could you speak more slowly?
3. I can't write fast enough. Could you slow down a little?

1〜3 はいずれも standard な表現である。

▶速くノートに写せませんので,ゆっくり言ってください。
1. I can't copy fast. Please speak more slowly.
2. I can't copy fast in my notebook. Please speak more slowly.
3. I'm not a fast copier. Please speak more slowly.

状況から「ノートに写す」ことは理解できるので,2 のように ... in my notebook をいう語句をわざわざ入れる必要はない。wordy かつ unnecessary である。

3 のように名詞を使って表現してもよい。

I 発音させる

発音の練習をしましょう。
　Let's practice pronunciation.

今度は発音練習をしましょう。
　1. Now, we'll do pronunciation exercises.
　2. Now, let's do pronunciation exercises.
　3. This time, let's do pronunciation exercises.
　　　1や2の方が3より自然な表現である。

大きな声を出して発音練習をしましょう。
　1. Let's do our pronunciation exercises with good, strong voices.
　2. Let's do our pronunciation exercises in a loud voice.
　　　ネイティブスピーカーによっては，in a loud voice という言い方に抵抗を示す人もいる。loud には「(声・音などが) 大きい」という意味のほかに，「不快で，うるさい」という negative な意味もあるからである。1のように言えばだれに対しても positive な印象を与える。

パートナーとしばらく発音練習をしてみてください。
　Why don't you practice pronunciation with your partner?
　How about practicing pronunciation with your partner?
　　　practice はアメリカ英語のつづりであり，イギリス英語では practise のようにつづる。

新出単語の発音練習をしましょう。
　Let's practice pronouncing the new words.

下線を施している部分に注意して，発音練習をしましょう。
　Let's practice pronunciation, paying special attention to the

underlined parts.
　文中のコンマはあってもなくてもよい。

1つずつ，単語の発音練習をしてみましょう。
Let's pronounce each word.

まず，単語の発音練習をしましょう。
1. **First of all, let's practice pronouncing words.**
2. **First of all, let's practice pronouncing the words.**

　一般的な発音練習を意味するときには1のように the を付けず，特定の単語の発音練習を意味するときには2のように the を付ける。

私のあとについて，新出単語の発音練習をしましょう。
1. **Repeat the new words after me.**
2. **Repeat after me, and let's practice pronouncing the new words.**

　1の方が2よりも自然な表現である。

もう一度聞いて，私のあとについて言ってごらんなさい。
Listen again, and say it after me.

私の言うのを聞いて，くり返しなさい。
Listen to me, and repeat after me.

個々の単語の発音が正確にできますか。
Can you accurately pronounce individual words?

その単語は，どのように発音するのですか。
How do you pronounce the word?
How is the word pronounced?

この単語を発音しなさい。
　Pronounce this word.

この単語の発音のしかたがわかりますか。
　Do you know how to pronounce this word?

r-e-f-r-i-g-e-r-a-t-o-r から成っている単語はどのように発音しますか。
　How do you pronounce the word consisting of [ɑːr], [iː], [ef], [ɑːr], [ai], [dʒiː], [iː], [ɑːr], [ei], [tiː], [ou], [ɑːr]?

bird と 3 回言ってください。
　Say *bird* three times.

私のあとをつけて，3 回 [bə́ːrd] と言ってください。
　Say [bə́ːrd] three times after me.

▶この単語が読めません。
　I can't read this word.

J　手を上げさせる，発言させる

わかった人は手を上げてください。
　Those who understand, please raise your hand.
　Those who understand, raise your hand.
　Those who have understood, raise your hand.
　Those who got it, raise your hand.
　Those who get it, raise your hands.

　　　関係代名詞節の中は，現在形・過去形・現在完了形のいずれも可能である。

　　　raise your hands のように hand を複数形にすると，狭義には「両手を上げなさい」という解釈もなりたつ。

「わかった人は〜」というとき，日本語で考えると The people who ... でよさそうであるが, Those who ... の形の方が自然である。

書き上げた人は，手を上げてください。
  1. **Those who have finished writing, raise your hands.**
  2. **Everyone who has finished writing, raise your hands.**
     1の方が2よりも自然である。

まだよくわからない人は手を上げてください。
  Those who do not understand the point, raise your hands.
  Those who have not understood the point, raise your hands.
  Those who didn't get the point, raise your hands.
     the point の the は，this と言い換えてもよい。また，the point を what I said と言い換えることもできる。

まだよくわからない人は手を上げなさい。
  Those who still don't understand, raise your hands.

手を真っすぐ上げてください。
  Raise your hands straight up.
  Raise your hands high.
    「真っすぐ」は straight だけではなく，up をそえて straight up のように言わなくてはいけない。
    straight up の代わりに high と言ってもよい。

手の上がり方が少ないようですね。
  1. **There don't seem to be many hands up.**
  2. **There don't seem to be many hands.**
     1の方が2よりもよい。

恥ずかしがらずに手を上げてください。
  1. **Don't be shy about raising your hand.**

2. **Don't be afraid to raise your hand.**
3. **Don't hesitate to raise your hands.**
　　１が最もよい表現である。３は非常に formal で，(生徒にあまり考えず) 早く手を上げるよううながしているニュアンスがある。

２番目の段落の意味がわかる人は手を上げなさい。
If you understand the second paragraph, raise your hand.
Those of you who understand the second paragraph, raise your hand.

黒板に書いた文が理解できた人は手を上げてください。
Those who have understood what is written on the blackboard, please raise your hand.

この単語をどのように発音するかわかる人は手を上げてください。
1. **If you know how to pronounce this word, please raise your hand.**
2. **If you can pronounce this word, please raise your hand.**

　　１はもとの日本語に近いが，２のように簡便に言ってもよい。

この列から順番に，練習問題３の答えを言ってください。
Starting from this row, give me your answers to Exercise 3 in order.

間違ってもよいから，答えを言ってみてください。
1. **Don't worry about making mistakes. Give me your answers.**
2. **Don't worry about mistakes. Give me your answers.**
3. **Don't worry about messing up. Give me your answers.**

　　１〜３はいずれもよい。１と２は standard，３は informal な表現である。

この文の意味がわかる人は言ってみてください。
　　If you understand this sentence, please tell me.

K　発表させる，意見を言わせる

この章の内容を，簡単に説明してください。
　　Please explain the contents briefly.

発表する人は，平常点に加えます。
　　Those who speak up in class will get credit.
　　Those who speak up in class will get points toward their final grade.
　　Those who speak up in class will get points towards their grade.
　　　　toward はアメリカで，towards はイギリスで使われる傾向がある。

山田さん，調べてきたことを発表してください。
　　Yamada-san, please tell us what you have studied.

山田さんに，調べてきたことについて発表してもらいます。
　　I'd like Yamada-san to tell us about that she studied.

２番目の段落の大意を言いなさい。
　　Sum up the second paragraph.

君の誕生日を英語で言ってみなさい。
　1. Say when your birthday is, in English.
　2. Tell us when your birthday is, in English.
　3. Tell us your birthday in English.
　4. Tell me when your birthday is in English.
　5. Tell us your birthday. Try to do it in English.

6. **Say your birthday, in English.**
7. **Say your birthday in English.**

　　Say ... という言い方は時折ジョークの材料となることがある。例えば，教師と生徒の間で次のような会話が考えられる。

　　　教師：Say your birthday in English.
　　　生徒：Your birthday in English.

　　酒を注ぐとき，Say when (you have enough). (ころあいを言ってくれ) と言うと，相手が When. と切り返すジョークはよく知られている。

　　7の表現はこうしたジョークの可能性を秘めた表現であるから，6のように，birthday の後にややポーズを置けばよい。

　　6や7よりも，1〜5の方が明確に意味が伝わりやすい。

森さんの言ったことについて，どう思いますか。
What do you think about what Mori-san said?
What do you think of what Mori-san said?

森さんの言ったことについて，何かコメントはありますか。
Do you have any comments on what Mori-san said?

森さんの言ったことについて，賛成しますか。
1. **Do you agree with what Mori-san said?**
2. **Do you agree to what Mori-san said?**

　　2は「森さんが提案したことをする」という意味である。

鈴木君は…だと言っていますが，それについてどう思いますか。
Mr. Suzuki says that ..., but what do you think about it?
Mr. Suzuki says that ..., but what do you think?

　　... think about it. の about it は省略可能である。

今，田中君の言ったことについて，反対意見はありますか。
1. **Is there anyone who disagrees with what Tanaka-kun just said?**

2. **Is there anyone who disagrees with what Tanaka-kun said just now?**
3. **Is there anyone who has difficulty accepting about what Tanaka-kun just said?**
4. **Is there anyone who is against what Tanaka-kun just said?**
5. **Is there anyone who is against what Tanaka-kun said just now?**

　to be against what someone said という言い方は非常に強い響きを持った表現であるから，極力避けた方がよい。選挙の場合には，

　　I'm for the proposal.
　　I'm against the proposal.

という言い方が可能である。自分の立場を明確に示す必要があるからである。

　ほかの人が発言したことについて同様に考えているかどうかを単に尋ねるような状況では，disagree with という表現をした方が無難である。

　disagree with を使う代わりに3のように言ってもよい。

今，田中君の言ったことについて，反対意見はありませんか。

1. **Isn't there anyone who disagrees with what Tanaka-kun just said?**
2. **Isn't there anyone who disagrees with what Tanaka-kun said just now?**
3. **Who does not agree with Tanaka-kun?**
4. **Who does not agree to what Tanaka-kun said just now?**

　1に比べて2は「今言った」という時間を重視している感じがある。

　"Isn't there ...?" と聞くときには，だれかが反対意見を出すのを期待している感じがあるので，状況を判断して Is there ...? と Isn't there ...? を使い分ける必要がある。

　「《人》に同意する」というときには agree with 〜を使い，「《人

の言った内容など》に同意する」というときには agree to ～の形を使う。

　3と4は1や2とは異なる意味を持っている。3は Who doesn't think the same about this? ということであり，4は Who doesn't agree to do what he suggested? ということである。

▶こんな言い方でアメリカ人に通じますか。
1. **Do you think this expression can be understood by Americans?**
2. **Do you think this expression will be understood by Americans?**
3. **Will this expression be understood by Americans?**
4. **Can this expression be understood by Americans?**

　1や2のように，Do you think ...? という語句を文頭に加えた方が丁寧である。「皆…できるか」とか「だれも…できないか」ということを人に尋ねるときには，しばしば尋ねられた人を helpless, angry, annoyed といった気持ちにさせるので注意が必要である。

L　下線を引かせる

今から言う英語表現に，下線を施しなさい。
1. **Please underline the words that I say.**
2. **Please underline the words as I say them.**
3. **Please draw a line under the words that I say.**
4. **Please underscore the words as I say them.**

　「下線を引く」の項目で辞書を引くと，4の underscore という語句が出てくることがある。しかし，この語が奇異に聞こえる人もいる。formal, technical な響きがするというのも彼らの印象である。

文の中の形容詞に下線を引いてごらんなさい。
　Underline the adjectives in the sentence.

次の文の主語と動詞に下線を引きなさい。
　Underline the subject and the verb of the following sentence.

重要な表現に下線を引きましょう。
　Let's underline some important expressions.

本のタイトル名には下線を引くべきです。
　We are supposed to underline the title of a book.

この文で，文法的に誤っている語に下線を引きなさい。
　Underline the words that are grammatically wrong in this sentence.
　In this sentence, underline the word or words that are grammatically wrong.

この文で，つづりが間違っている語に下線を引きなさい。
　1. Underline the misspelled words in this sentence.
　2. Underline the wrongly spelled words in this sentence.
　　　1の方がよい。2はやや不自然な表現。

この文で，誤っている箇所に下線を引きなさい。
　Underline the part of the sentence that is wrong.

▶下線を引いてある部分はどういう意味ですか。
　1. What does the underlined part mean?
　2. What does the underlined passage mean?
　3. What does the underlined section mean?
　4. What is the meaning of the underlined part?
　　　下線部が長ければ2のように passage を使うとよい。

4 の言い方は堅苦しい感じがする。

▶どこに下線を引いたらよいのかわかりません。
1. **I don't know where to underline.**
2. **I don't know where to draw underlines.**

　1と2はいずれでもよいが，1の方を好むアメリカ人がいる。2は wordy, unnatural な感じがするという。

▶本のタイトル以外，どんな場合に下線を引くのですか。
1. **In what cases do you underline, except for the title of a book?**
2. **Except for book titles, are there other cases in which we underline?**
3. **In what cases do you underline, excepting the title of a book?**
4. ***In what cases do you underline except the title of a book?**
5. **Besides the titles of books, what other groups of words are underlined?**

　ふつう，文全体を修飾する場合は except for ～を使い，語を修飾する場合には except ～を使う。前者は文頭に置くこともできるし，文尾に置くこともできる。文尾に置く場合には，1のように except の前にコンマを置く。

M　ノートに写させる

これをノートに写しなさい。
　Copy this down in your notebooks.

これをノートにそのまま写しなさい。
　Copy this straight into your notebooks.

今やったところをノートに写しなさい。
　Copy what we've just done in your notebook.

ノートに黒板の文を写しなさい。
　Please copy the sentence on the board in your notebooks.

できるだけ速くノートに写しなさい。
　1. Copy it in your notebook as soon as you can.
　2. Copy it in your notebook as soon as possible.
　　　1の方が自然な言い方である。2はstiltedな感じがする。

新出単語をノートに写しなさい。
　Copy the new words in your notebook.

新出語句をノートに写しなさい。
　Copy the new words and expressions in your notebook.
　Copy the new words and phrases in your notebook.

板書した単語をノートに写しなさい。
　Write the words on the board in your notebook.

黒板の文をノートに書きなさい。
　Write the sentences that are on the board in your notebooks.
　Write the sentences on the board in your notebooks.

教科書の56ページの基本文型をノートに写しなさい。
　Write the basic sentences on page 56 in your notebook.

黒板の文章をノートに写し終わったら，教科書の28ページを黙読しなさい。
　1. When you finish copying the sentences from the board into your notebook, read page 28 of your textbook silent-

ly.
2. **When you finish copying the sentences on the board, read page 28 of your textbook silently.**

  2のように ... copying the sentences on the board と言うと，「文章を黒板に写すのか」，「黒板の文章を写すのか」，意味が不明瞭である。

スペリングに注意しなさい。
 Watch your spelling.
 Pay attention to your spelling.

ノートが速く取れるようにしなさい。
 1. **Try to take notes quickly.**
 2. ***Try to take note quickly.**

  take notes のように，note に -s を付けた形で熟語的に用いる。*take note は誤りである。

ノートが速く取れることは大切です。
 Taking notes quickly is important.

▶ノートを取るのですか。
 Should we take notes?
 Are we supposed to take notes?

▶どこをノートに写したらいいのですか。
 What should we copy in our notebooks?
 What should be copied in our notebook?

▶どの部分をノートに写すのですか。
 1. **What part should we copy in our notebooks?**
 2. ***Where should we copy in our notebooks?**

  1のように言わなくては，もとの日本文の意味に取りにくい。
  2のように言うと，what part of the notebook か what part of

the passage on the board か定かでない。

▶どこからどこまでノートに写すのですか。
From where to where should we copy in our notebook?

▶どこからどこまで書き取るのですか。
1. **What are we supposed to transcribe?**
2. ***From where to where are we supposed to transcribe?**

　　transcribe には，①〜を書き写す，②〈音声など〉を発音記号で書き表す，という意味がある。英語のクラスでよく「ディクテーション」という言葉を使うが，これは「口述」の意味である。
　「どこからどこまで」という日本語を英訳すると，from where to where となるが，この言い方に強い抵抗を示すネイティブスピーカーが多い。文法的には問題ないが from 〜 to ... と疑問詞を組み合わせることに抵抗があるようだ。「どこからどこまで」の訳としてはこの場合，1のように what を使うのが無難である。

▶何行めから何行めまで書き取るのですか。
From what line to what line are we supposed to transcribe?
From which line to which line are we supposed to transcribe?

▶それは何という単語ですか。
What is that word?

▶2番目の字は何ですか。
What is the second letter?

N　ポイントの指示

これは非常に大切です。
　This is very important.

2 学習活動の指示　　*131*

これは非常に大切です。是非，理解してください。
　This is very important. Please make sure you understand.

これは基本です。しっかり覚えておくように。
　1. **This is fundamental. Try to understand it.**
　2. *__This is a basis. Try to understand it.__
　　　2 は自然な言い方ではない。

ここは大切ですから，よく理解しないといけません。わかりましたか。
　1. **This is important, so you need to understand it. OK?**
　2. **This is important, so you have to understand it. OK?**
　3. **This is important, so you have to understand. OK?**
　　　2，3 の have to よりも 1 の need to の方がよい。have to は pushy で counter-productive な感じがする。
　　　3 では ... understand it の it が省略されているが，it はあった方が文意が明確になる。

ここは重要なセクションだから，しっかり復習しておきなさい。
　This is an important section, so review it carefully.

ここは非常に大切だから，よく復習しておきなさい。
　Since this is very important, go over it thoroughly.

これは大変重要だから，二重丸をしておきなさい。
　1. **Double-circle this because it is very important.**
　2. *__Make a double circle because this is very important.__
　　　make は make an appointment, make a reservation などのように，「～する」という意味で使うことがある。しかし，2 のように言うことはできない。

この文は大切だから，頭に印を付けておきなさい。
　Place a check-mark in front of this sentence because it is

very important.
　英語の文化圏では，しばしばチェックマーク（✓）を使う。二重丸（◎）や米印（※）などはあまり使わない。

この単語は重要だから，〇で囲んでおきなさい。
Put a circle around this word because it is important.

この文は大切だから，赤線を引いておきなさい。
Draw a red line under this sentence because it is important.

重要なポイントを繰り返します。
1. **Let me repeat the important points.**
2. **Let me repeat the important parts.**
3. **Let me repeat the important places.**

　重要な場所は一度説明した部分であるから，話し手も聞き手も共通の認識がある。したがって，定冠詞の the を使って the important parts や the important points などのように言う。
　3のように places という語を使う場合には，教科書などについて top of page 18 とか，bottom of page 35 という場合である。1や2の方が3よりも一般的な表現である。

ここは暗記しておきなさい。
Memorize this.

　「ここ」という意味の英語に here があるが，これを名詞的に使って *Memorize here. とは言えない。

これは基本的な文です。
This is a basic sentence.

こんなところはテストに出そうです。
Phrases like this may appear on the test.
Things like this may appear on the test.

「こんなところ」という日本語に引かれて place を使うのは，この場合ふさわしくない。「こんな〜」という日本語を英訳する場合には，like 〜 や such as 〜 という表現が便利である。

ここは大切ですから，必ずテストに出します。
1. This is important. It will surely be on the test.
2. This is important. The test will surely cover it.
3. This is important. It is surely to be covered on the test.
4. This is important. It is surely to be covered in the test.

　1〜4 はどれでもよいが，1 は最も自然な表現である。4 はイギリス英語。

難しい点をいくつか見てみましょう。
Let's look at some of the difficult points.
Let's have a look at some of the difficult points.

難しい点をいくつか復習してみましょう。
Let's go over some of the difficult points.
Let's review some of the difficult points.

ここは難しいから，間違ってもがっかりしないように。
1. Don't be discouraged even if you make a mistake here since this is difficult.
2. Don't be discouraged even if you make a mistake here because this is a little tricky.
3. Don't be disappointed even if you make a mistake because it is difficult here.
4. Don't be discouraged even if you are mistaken here because this is difficult.

　1, 2 は standard であるが，3 と 4 はやや不自然である。

　3 では，... it is difficult here. という言い方が不自然さを与えている。

　4 では，you are mistaken ... の使いかたが不自然さを与えてい

る。you are mistaken は，you have made a mistake ということよりも，you have the wrong idea ということを意味するからである。You are mistaken は，
> You're mistaken when you say that Chinese and Japanese are alike.

のように使う。

諸君が思うほど難しくはありませんよ。
1. **It is not as difficult as you might think.**
2. **It is not so difficult as you might think.**

前の as は 2 のように so にしてもよいが，as の方を好むネイティブスピーカーが多い。

この課には 2, 3 難しいポイントがあるかもしれません。
There may be a few difficult points in this lesson.

そんなに難しくはありませんよ。あきらめないように。
Don't give up. It is not so difficult.

▶どこが重要なのですか。
1. **What are the important points?**
2. ***Where are the important points?**

日本語では「どこが」となっているが，これを直訳的に Where are ... で英訳すると不自然な感じがする。「重要な箇所はどこか」と場所を聞く言い方でも，英語表現としては 1 のように言いたい。

▶ポイントはこういうことですか。
Is this the point?

▶どこが特に大切ですか。
What points are especially important?

▶この章の主なポイントは何ですか。
  1. **What is the main point of this chapter?**
  2. **What points does this chapter make?**
     「この章のポイントは何ですか」という日本文は、おおよそ「この章の主なポイントは何ですか」という文と同義だと見なされよう。しかし、前者を英語に訳し、
       What is the point of this chapter?
     とすると、1や2とは意味が異なってくる。この文は、
       What good is this chapter?
       Why did they bother to write this chapter?
     と解釈されるので注意が必要である。

▶どの点に注意したらいいのでしょうか。
  What points should we pay attention to?

▶もう一度大切なポイントを説明してくださいませんか。
  Could you explain the important points once again?

O　視覚教材を使う

それではビデオを見せましょう。
  Let me show you the video now.

それではこのビデオを見てください。
  Please look at this video clip now.
     video は音声に対しての画像を言い、video clip は画像の1カットを言う。

これを見てください。
  Look at this one.
     スライドを見せているとき、「次を見てください」という日本語は不自然ではない。しかし、この日本文を英訳して、

*Look at the next one.

と言うと，自然な英語としては受け取れない。next と言うときには，まだ，前のスライドを見ているわけであるから，next slide を見ることはできない。したがって，Look at the next one. は illogical な文になってしまう。

次に移ります。
I'll go on to the next one.
Let me go on to the next one.

こっちを見てください。
Look at it this way.
　　　*Look at here. のようには言わない。Look at it here. であればよい。また，Look here! という表現は可能であるが，スライドを見せながら説明するような場合には唐突な感じがするので適切ではない。

右側の写真を見なさい。
1. **Look at the picture on the right.**
2. **Look at the right-hand picture.**
3. **Look at the right picture.**
　　　3は正しいが，1，2の方がよい。3は「正しい写真」という意味にも解釈できる。

画面の図を見てください。説明します。
Please look at the chart on the screen. I'll explain it.

画面の3図を見てください。同じ図がハンドアウトにもあります。
1. **Please look at Figure 3. You'll find it on your handout, too.**
2. **Please take a look at Figure 3. It's on your handout, too.**
3. **Please take a look at Figure 3. The same figure is on your handout, too.**

1，2は自然だが，3はあまり自然な表現ではない。

左から3番目のイラストを見なさい。
　Look at the third illustration from the left.

真ん中の地図を見なさい。
　Look at the map in the center.

一番上の表を見てください。
　Please look at the table at the top.

一番下のグラフを見てください。
　Please look at the graph at the bottom.

P　前のページに戻るとき

93ページに戻ります。
　We are going back to page 93.

31ページを復習してみましょう。
　Let's review page 31.

先週やった46ページを開いてください。
  1. Please turn to page 46, which we covered last week.
  2. Please look at page 46 which we covered last week.
  3. Please open your book to page 46, which we covered last week.
  4. *Please open to page 46 we covered last week.
　　　日本語で考えると4はよさそうであるが，openの目的語として bookが必要である。

138　Ⅲ　授業活動

85ページの「まとめ」を見てください。**重要なポイントを思い出しましょう。**
　Look at the Summary on page 85, and let's remember the important points.
　Look at the Summary on pape 85, and let's go over the important points.
　Look at the Summary on page 85, and let's review the important points.

Q　次のページに進むとき

さあ，46ページに進みましょう。
　Now, let's turn to page 46.
　Now, let's move on to page 46.

質問がなければ，次のページに進みます。
　Unless you have questions, I'll move on to the next page.
　Unless you have questions, let me go on to the next page.

質問はありませんか。なければ，次のページに進みます。
　Do you have any questions? If you don't, I'll move on to the next page.
　If you don't have any questions, I'll go on to the next page.

この課は大切ですから，内容がまだよく理解できない人は，次のページに進む前に質問してください。
　This lesson is important. If you don't understand the content well, please ask me questions before we move on to the next page.
　This lesson is important. If there's something you don't understand, please ask me questions before we move on to the next page.

3ページ飛ばします。
   1. **We will skip three pages.**
   2. **I will skip three pages.**
      １の方が自然な表現である。

3課は自分でやっておいてください。では5ページ飛ばします。
   Please do Lesson 3 by yourselves. Well, let me skip five pages then.
   Please do Lesson 3 by yourselves. Well, I'm skipping five pages.
   Please do Lesson 3 by yourselves. Well, I'll pass the next five pages.

3課は自分でやっておいてください。8ページにいきます。
   Please do Lesson 3 by yourselves. Turn to page 8.

▶後藤先生，2ページ飛ばしました。
   Mr. Gotoh, you skipped two pages.

R　次の課・章などに移るとき

では，次の章に移ります。
   Well, let me go on to the next chapter.
   Well, let's move on to the next chapter.

次の課にいく前に，何か質問はありますか。
   Before we move on to the next section, do you have any questions?

次の課にいく前に，何か質問はありませんか。
   Before we move on to the next section, don't you have any questions?

このように否定形で聞くと，肯定の形よりも押し付けがましい感じになる。

質問がなければ次の課にいきます。
　Unless you have questions, let me go on to the next section.
　Unless you have questions, I'll go on to the next section.

質問はありませんか。もしなければ，次の課にいきましょう。
　Don't you have any questions? If you don't, let's move on to the next section.

S　会話練習の指示

ロールプレイをしましょう。
　Let's do a role-play exercise.

隣の人と，ロールプレーをしてごらんなさい。
　Role-play with your partner.

役割を決めて読み合わせをする動作を role-play というが，この語は動詞としても使うことができる。

隣の人とペアを組みなさい。
　Make a pair with your neighbor.
　Pair up with your neighbor.

隣の人がいなかったら，移動してもよいですよ。
　If you don't have a neighbor, you can move around.

立ち歩いてもよいですよ。
　You can walk around.

2 学習活動の指示　　141

相手を探すために，立ち歩いてもよいですよ。
　　You can walk around to find your partner.

4人のグループを作りなさい。
　　Make a group of four.
　　Split up into groups of four.

5人のグループを8つ作りなさい。
　　Make eight groups of five people.
　　Split up into eight groups of five people.

相手と向かい合ってください。
　　1. Face your partner.
　　2. Sit face-to-face with your partner.
　　3. *Face to face with your partner.
　　　　1と2はよいが，3は文法的誤りである。face to face は副詞である。

会話練習をしなさい。
　　Work together to do the conversation exercise.
　　Work together and do the conversation exercise.

1回読み終えたら，役割を交代しなさい。
　　1. When you finish once, change roles.
　　2. When you finish once, change your roles.
　　　　1の方が2よりも自然である。change roles は決まった言い方である。

会話練習を5分間行ってください。
　　Practice the dialog exercise for five minutes.

T 予習

予習を必ずやってきなさい。
　Be sure to prepare for class.

予習をやってきましたか。
　Have you prepared for the lesson?
　Have you prepared for class?
　　　「授業」を意味する class という語を使うときには，定冠詞の the は不要である。
　　　イギリス英語では，class という語の代わりに，しばしば lesson が使われる。

予習はちゃんとしてきましたか。
　Did you study for this class?
　Did you study the lesson before class?

何時間予習をしましたか。
　How many hours did you study for this class?
　How many hours did you study before class?
　How many hours did you put into studying for this class?

少なくとも2時間は予習をしなさい。
　Spend at least two hours studying this lesson.
　Spend at least two hours on this lesson.
　Study the lesson for at least two hours.
　Spend a minimum of two hours studying this lesson.
　Spend a minimum of two hours on this lesson.
　Study the lesson for a minimum of two hours.

2～3時間は予習をしなさい。
　Study the lesson for two or three hours before class.

2 学習活動の指示　*143*

8課をよく予習しておきなさい。
　Study Lesson 8 well, before class.
　Study Lesson 8 carefully before class.
　Familiarize yourself with Lesson 8 before class.
　Make sure you fully understand Lesson 8 before class.

8課の予習を必ずしておきなさい。
　Make sure you study Lesson 8 before class.

これからはちゃんと予習をしておきなさい。
　From now on, be sure to study in advance.

94ページまで予習をしておきなさい。
　1. Prepare through page 94.
　2. Prepare up to and including page 94.
　3. Prepare as far as page 94.
　4. Prepare up to page 94.
　　「94ページまで」と言うとき，ふつう94ページも含まれるので，1と2のように言うとよい。3，4は94ページが予習分野に含まれるかどうかあいまいである。94ページを含まない場合は，Prepare as far as page 94. Don't do 94. などと言うとよい。

教科書の98ページをよく調べておきなさい。
　1. Please study page 98 in your textbook.
　2. Please study page 98 of your textbook.
　　1の方が2よりもよい。

予習をした方がいいですよ。
　I advise you to study beforehand.
　You had better study beforehand.

もし僕が君だったら予習をするよ。
　If I were you, I would study beforehand.

予習をしてわからないところを質問しなさい。
Study the lesson before class and ask me questions.

日本語では「わからないところを質問する」という表現はさほど不自然ではないが，英語に直訳して

To ask the things which you don't understand.

と言うと，不自然である。「わからないから質問する」のは当然であると考えるからである。

まず，復習をした上で予習をしなさい。
1. **First review what we've done and then study the next lesson before class.**
2. ***First review and study the lesson before class.**

もとの日本語を直訳すると，2のような文も形の上では考えられるが，論理的にはおかしくなる。目的語が the lesson であるから，同一の lesson を復習し，予習するということになるからである。

復習よりも予習に時間をもっとさきなさい。
Spend more time on preparation than on review.
Spend more time for preparation than for review.

予習と復習とどちらに時間をさいていますか。
1. **Which do you spend more time on, reviewing or preparation?**
2. **Which do you spend more time on, reviewing or preparing for the next class?**
3. **Which do you spend more time on, reviewing or studying the lesson before class?**

1，2，3の順序でよい。

予習したところで，どこが難しかったですか。
1. **Which of the sections you studied before class did you find most difficult?**

2. Which of the points you studied before class did you find most difficult?
3. Which of the passages you studied before class did you find most difficult?
4. *Which did you find difficult among the places you studied before class?

   4 はもとの日本語の意味に近いが，英語として不明瞭である。1，2，3 のように表現したい。

わからない単語は，辞書を引いておくように。

If there are any words you don't know, please look them up in the dictionary.

予習をして，質問に答えられるようにしておきなさい。

1. Study the lesson in advance, and be ready for questions.
2. Study the lesson in advance, and be ready to answer questions.
3. Prepare for your lessons and be ready for questions.
4. *Prepare your lessons and be ready to answer questions.

   be ready for 〜という形も可能であるし，be ready to 〜という不定詞の形も可能である。

   prepare for one's lesson は「授業のための準備をする」という意味があるが，prepare one's lessons は「自分で直接まとめたり作ったりする」という意味である。文脈から 3 のように前置詞の for が必要である。

学校に来る前に，新しい単語の意味は辞書で調べておきなさい。

1. Before you come to school, look up the new words in your dictionary.
2. Before you come to school, look the new words up in your dictionary.
3. *Before you come to school, look new words up in your dictionary.

新出単語については，教師も生徒もテキストのどの部分であるかお互いに了解しているので，定冠詞の the が必要である。
　1と2はいずれでもよい。

学校に来る前に，新しい単語の意味は必ず辞書で調べておきなさい。
Before you come to school, be sure to look the new words up in your dictionary.
Before you come to school, make sure to look the new words up in your dictionary.
Before you come to school, be certain to look the new words up in your dictionary.
Before you come to school, remember to look the new words up in your dictionary.

次の授業から新しい課に入るので，新出単語の意味を必ず調べておきなさい。
Since we are going to do a new lesson next time, be sure to look up the new words in the dictionary.
　　「新出単語」という場合，「新しい課」に出る単語のことをいうから，定冠詞の the が必要である。

▶予習のしかたがわかりません。
I don't know how to prepare my lessons.

▶予習はどのようにしたらよいのでしょうか。
How can I study for my lessons?
How can I get ready for my lessons?
How can I prepare my lessons?
How can I prepare my lessons before coming to school?
How should we study the lesson before class?
How should we study before class?

2 学習活動の指示　147

▶予習は何時間くらいしたらいいのでしょうか。
　How many hours should we study before class?
　How many hours should we study the lesson before class?

▶予習はどれくらいしたらいいのでしょうか。
　How long should we study before class?
　How long should we study the lesson before class?

▶授業についていくには，どのような予習をしたらいいですか。
　How should I prepare in order to keep up?
　How should I prepare in order to keep up with you?
　How should I study in advance so that I can keep up with you?

▶どこまで調べてくればいいのですか。
　1. How far should we go?
　2. To where should we go?
　3. How much should we check?
　　　1や2の方が3よりもよい。3では意味が不明瞭である。

▶次回はどこからどこまで予習したらよいですか。
　1. What pages should I study for next time?
　2. Which sections should I study for next time?
　3. *From where to where should I prepare next time?
　　　3は最も日本文に近いが，英語としては不自然である。1や2の方がよい。

▶来週までに，どのような準備をすればいいのでしょうか。
　What should we prepare by next week?
　What should we prepare for next week?
　What should we do by next week?
　What should we do for next week?

▶辞書に載っていない単語はどのようにして意味を調べたらいいのですか。
How can we check the meaning of a word that is not in the dictionary?

▶辞書に載っていない単語の意味を調べることができません。
We can't check the meaning of a word that is not in the dictionary.

▶予習と復習はどちらが大切でしょうか。
Which is more important, preparing or reviewing?

▶英語では，予習と復習はどちらが大切ですか。
In English, which is more important, reviewing or studying the lesson before class?
In English, which is more important, reviewing or studying for the next class?

▶授業についていくには，予習をすべきでしょうか，それとも復習をすべきでしょうか。
In order to catch up on class, which should I do, preparation or review?

▶ここは予習したけどよくわかりません。
I studied this, but I don't understand it very well.
I studied this, but I don't understand it so well.
　　「非常に」「大変」という意味を持つ言葉に very や so がある。ここでは否定文なので「あまり（〜でない）」という意味で使われているが，very の方がより好まれる。また，so は女性が好んで使う傾向もある。

▶予習をしましたが，内容がよくわかりませんでした。
I studied the lesson, but I couldn't understand the content

well.
I studied the lesson, but I couldn't understand it well.
I studied the lesson, but I couldn't make heads or tails of the lesson.

▶予習してきませんでした。
I didn't study the lesson before class.

▶復習はしましたが，予習はしませんでした。
I reviewed the lesson, but I didn't study the next lesson before class.
I reviewed the lesson, but I didn't study for today's class.

▶ごめんなさい。予習をするのを忘れました。
I'm sorry, but I forgot to study the lesson before class.
I'm sorry, but I forgot to study for class.

▶宿題が多すぎて，予習をする時間がありませんでした。
There was too much homework, so I didn't have time to study the lesson before class.
There was so much homework that I didn't have time to study the lesson before class.

▶単語の意味を調べてくるのを忘れました。
1. I forgot to check the meanings of the words.
2. I neglected to check the meaning of the words.
3. I failed to check the meaning of the words.
　　　2と3はformalで，やや stilted な感じがする。

150 Ⅲ 授業活動

U 復習

今日学んだことを必ず復習しておきなさい。
 Be sure to review what you have learned today.

今日学んだことは，今日のうちに復習しておきなさい。
 1. Review what you have learned today when you get home.
 2. Review what you have learned today before you go to bed.
 3. Review what you have learned today within today.
    1 は standard，2 はやや informal，3 はやや stilted な表現である。

8課を必ず復習しておきなさい。
 Be sure to review Lesson 8.

50点未満以下だった人は今日の午後，私と一緒にもう一度復習しましょう。
 1. If you scored under 50 points, let me help you study the lesson again this afternoon.
 2. Those who have scored under 50 points, let's study together in the afternoon.
    もとの日本語にとらわれると，2 のように study together という言い方をしたくなるが，study together というと，教師が生徒と一緒に勉強し，生徒から学ぶことも有り得ることを示唆する。

復習は非常に大切です。
 Reviewing is very important.

予習，復習はいつもするように心がけてください。
 Please bear in mind that you should review and prepare

lessons.
Please bear in mind that you have to review and prepare lessons.

　　いずれも standard な表現である。

復習すると，授業内容が理解できます。
By reviewing you can understand what you have learned in class.

家で予習し，学校で集中し，家で復習することを勧めます。
I recommend that you prepare at home, concentrate your attention at school, and review at home.

復習をすればするほど，頭に入ります。
The more you review, the more you can understand.

V　自習の指示

早く終わったので，自習しなさい。
We finished a little earlier than usual. Please study on your own.
We finished a little early. Please study by yourselves.

3限目は自習にします。
You'll have study hall third period.
You'll have study hall during third period.
You'll study on your own during third period.

　　study hall には「自習室」「自習時間」の意味がある。third period は前置詞なしに副詞句として使われている。「3限目に」は in the third period でもよさそうであるが，あまり自然な英語ではない。

静かに自習をしなさい。
　Please study quietly on your own.

自習時間は何をしてもかまいません。
　You can do anything you want during study hall.
　You can do whatever you want during study hall.

自習時間には何をしたいですか。
　What would you like to do during study hall?

自習時間は立ち歩いてはいけません。
　1. Don't walk around during study hall.
　2. Don't play around during study hall.
　3. Don't horse around during study hall.
　4. Don't fool around during study hall.
　5. You are not allowed to walk around during study hour.
　6. You are not to walk around during study hour.
　　6 の be to ... の形には《命令》の用法がある。

自習時間にはプリントの問題をします。
　You should do the exercises on your handout during study hour.
　　「プリント」は print ではなく, handout という語を使う。なお,「プリントの問題」の英訳は exercises on your handout のように言い, handout exercises のような言い方は不自然である。

図書館で自習を行ってください。
　1. Study on your own in the library.
　2. Study on your own at the library.
　　「図書館で」という場合の前置詞は in でも at でもよいが, in the library は the school library を, at the library は the city library を暗示させる。この場合は1の方がよい。

課題が終わったら，委員長が全員のノートを集めなさい。
When you finish the assignment, the class secretary should collect all the students' notebooks.
When you finish the assignment, the class secretary will collect all the students' notebooks.

▶自習が終わったら，ノートを提出しなくてはいけませんか。
1. After study hour, are we supposed to turn in our notebook?
2. After study hour, do I have to turn in my notebook?
3. After study hour, are we supposed to turn in our notebooks?
4. After study hour, do I have to turn in our notebook?

　　1, 2, 4のようにnotebookという単数形を用いても，3のようにnotebooksという複数形を用いてもよい。主語はweでもIでもよい。

W　指名されて

▶（突然指名されてあわてて）何ページを読んだらいいのでしょうか。
What page should I read?
Which page should I read?

▶今どこをやっているのですか。
Where are we now?

　　"内職"をしていて，急に当てられた生徒が口にする言葉。疑問詞で始まる文は，常に下降調のイントネーションとは限らない。上昇調にすると，「やさしさ」「丁寧さ」などが加わる。

▶質問の意味がわかりません。
I don't understand the question.

▶ごめんなさい。何をしてよいのかわかりません。
I'm sorry I don't know what to do.

▶わかりません。
I don't understand.

▶この訳はできません。
1. I can't translate this.
2. I cannot translate this.
　　1は普通の表現である。upset, frustrated な状態であれば not を強調した2の表現を使う。

▶どこまで訳したらいいんでしょうか。
How much shall I translate?

▶上から3行目の2番目の単語の発音ができません。
I don't know how to pronounce the second word in the third line from the top.
I don't know how to pronounce the second word on the third line from the top.

▶予習をしていません。
I haven't prepared for class.

X　間違いを指摘・訂正させる

黒板の文には、何か間違いがありますか。
　Are there any mistakes in the sentences on the board?

黒板の文はどこが間違っていますか。
　What's wrong with the sentences on the board?
　What's the problem with the sentences on the board?

2 学習活動の指示   155

どうすれば黒板の文が正しくなると思いますか。
　1. **How can we correct the sentence on the board?**
　2. **What do you think we should do to correct the sentence on the board?**
　3. **What do you think should be done in order to make the sentence on the board correct?**
　　　1＞2＞3の順でよい。3は冗長すぎる。特に，in order to make ～ correct という言い回しがそうである。

２番目の文は正しいでしょうか。
　Is Sentence 2 correct?

この文の文法上の誤りを正しなさい。
　Correct the grammatical mistakes in this sentence.

間違っている言葉を消しなさい。
　1. **Erase the incorrect word.**
　2. **Erase the wrong word.**
　3. **Rub out the incorrect word.**
　4. **Rub out the wrong word.**
　　　1～4はいずれでもよいが，1と3は standard，2と4はやや informal な表現である。
　　　rub out はイギリス英語。アメリカ英語では rub out は murder の意味で使われる。

この文のなかで，間違っている言葉を括弧でくくりなさい。
　Put parentheses around the word in this sentence.

２の文には間違いが２つあります。どこが間違いですか。
　1. **There're two errors in Sentence 2. Where do you think they are?**
　2. **Sentence 2 has two errors. Where are they?**
　3. **Can you find the two errors in Sentence 2?**

3は1文であるが，もとの日本文と文意は同じである。

2の文には間違いが2つあります。それを探しなさい。
1. **There're two errors in Sentence 2. Find them.**
2. **Sentence 2 has two errors. Tell me where they are.**
3. **Sentence 2 has two errors. Can you locate them?**
4. ***There're two errors in Sentence 2. Point them out.**
5. ***Sentence 2 has two errors. Point them out.**

4や5のように point out という語句を使うと不自然になる。point out は，

He pointed out that his students should study harder.

などのように使うのはよい。

5の文は間違っています。正しい文に直しなさい。
1. **Sentence 5 is wrong. Correct it.**
2. **Sentence 5 is erroneous. Correct it.**
3. **Sentence 5 is not correct. Correct it.**
4. **Sentence 5 is wrong. Change it into a correct sentence.**

4は wordy な表現である。1〜3のように言った方がよい。

この文を正しくするにはどうしたらよいと思いますか。
1. **How can we correct this sentence?**
2. **How can this sentence be corrected?**
3. **What do you think should be done to make this sentence correct?**

1と2は standard，3は formal な表現である。日本語の英訳としては3が近いが，1と2の方が簡潔である。

この文は正しいでしょうか，間違いでしょうか。
1. **Is this sentence right or wrong?**
2. **Is this sentence correct or incorrect?**
3. **Is this sentence right or is there something wrong?**
4. ***Is this sentence right or incorrect?**

5. *Is this sentence correct or wrong?

　　1〜3は standard であるが，4と5は不自然である。right の反意語は wrong，correct の反意語は incorrect である。

この文は正しくありません。その理由がわかりますか。
　　This sentence is not correct. Do you know why?
　　There's something wrong with this sentence. Do you understand why?

3　生徒とのやりとり

A　質問の有無

何か質問はありませんか。
　　Do you have any questions?
　　Are there any questions?
　　Any questions?

　　普通は，簡単に Any questions? と教師が生徒に問いかけることが多い。any questions と複数の -s を付けても，any question のように -s を付けなくてもよい。

この点について何か質問はありませんか。
　　Are there any questions about this?
　　Are there any questions on this point?

95 ページまで，何か質問はありませんか。
　　Don't you have any questions up to page 95?

この前のクラスで 25 ページまで終わりましたが，質問はありませんか。
　　We finished everything up to page 25, but do you have any

questions so far?

わからないところがあれば質問してください。
　If there is anything you don't understand, ask me.
　If you have anything you don't understand, ask me.
　If there is something you don't understand, ask me.
　If you have something you don't understand, ask me.

質問がある人は，手を上げてください。
　If you have any questions, raise your hands.

質問があったら，何でも遠慮なく聞いてください。
　If you have any questions, please do not hesitate to ask me.
　If you have any questions, please be sure to ask me.
　　いずれでもよい。

いつでも質問をしてください。
　Ask me questions any time you want to.

いつでもわからないときには質問してください。
　Please ask me questions whenever you can't understand.

質問のある人は，紙に書いてもかまいません。
　If you have any questions, you can write them on your paper.
　If you have any questions, you can write them on the paper.
　If you have any questions, you can write them on a piece of paper.
　　your paper か the paper か a piece of paper かは，どういう種類の紙であるかによる。自分の紙である場合には your paper, 特定の紙であれば the paper, 不特定の紙であれば a piece of paper となる。

質問のある人は，放課後職員室に来なさい。
1. **If you have questions, please come to the staff room after school.**
2. **Students who have questions, please come to the staff room after school.**

　　関係代名詞を使えば2のように言えるけれども，1の言い方の方が自然である。

ほかに何か尋ねたいことはありますか。
Is there anything else you would like to ask about?

ほかに何か尋ねたいことはありませんか。
Isn't there anything else you would like to ask about?

　　別の質問を期待しているときの表現である。

質問がなければ，私からいくつか聞いてみますよ。
If you don't have any questions, let me ask *you* some questions.
If you don't have any questions. I'll ask *you* some questions.

　　イタリックの you は強調して言わなくてはいけない。

質問をする人には平常点をあげます。
Students who ask questions will get extra credit.
Students who ask questions will get extra points.

予習をしなくては質問も生まれません。
If you don't prepare lessons, you won't have any questions.
Unless you prepare lessons, no questions will come up.
Unless you prepare for class, no questions will come up.

それはいい質問です。すぐあなたの質問にもどります。
That's a good question. Let me get back to you.

> あることの説明の途中や，質問に答える前に何かについて触れたいときの表現である。

それはいい質問です。調べてみます。
That's a good question. Let me look into it.

それは難しい質問です。一晩考えさせてください。
That's a tough question. Let me sleep on it.

> 自分がなかなか答えられないような質問を受けた場合に，英語では That's a good question. という言い方をすることが多い。sleep とは「一晩考える」という意。前置詞は on を使う。

ごめんなさい。質問に答えられません。調べておきます。
I'm sorry. I'm not able to answer your question. Let me think about it.
I'm sorry. I'm not able to answer your question. Let me think on it.
I'm sorry. I'm not able to answer your question. Let me look into it.
I'm sorry. I'm not able to answer your question. Let me study about it.

▶**質問があります。**
I have a question.

▶**質問がいくつかあります。**
I have some questions.

▶**質問をしてもいいですか。**
May I ask some questions?
May I ask you a question?

▶先週習ったことについて，質問をしてもかまいませんか。
May I ask you a question on what we learned last week?

▶まだ that の使い方がよくわからないのですが。
I still can't understand how to use *that*.

▶これはつまらない質問かもしれませんが。
This may be a silly question, but ...

▶今から何をすればいいのでしょうか。
What should we do now?

▶質問の意味がわかりません。
I don't understand the question.
I don't get the question.

▶なぜそこはそのようになるのですか。
1. Why should it be that way?
2. Why should that be as it is?
　　　1の方が，2よりも自然な表現である。

▶なぜそこは間違っているのですか。
Why is that wrong?
What's wrong with this?

▶この答えはどうしていけないのでしょうか。
Why is this answer wrong?

▶この問題はどのようにして考えればいいのですか。
How should I tackle this problem?
How should I go about solving this problem?

▶この課ではどんなところが大切ですか。
  What things are important in this lesson?
  What should I pay special attention to in this lesson?

▶この問題の答えを教えてください。
  Could you tell us the right answer to this question?

▶問題集には解答が付いていますか。
  1. Do you have the answers for the exercise book?
  2. Do you have the answers for the work book?
  3. *Do you have the answers to the exercise book?
  4. *Do you have the answers to the work book?
     answer という語と前置詞の使い方には次のような関係がある。
       answers to questions
       answers for the book
     したがって，1，2の使い方が正しい。

B 理解の確認

わかりましたか。
  1. Did I express my ideas clearly?
  2. Did I express myself clearly?
  3. Were you able to understand me?
  4. Did I make my ideas clear?
  5. Did I make myself clear?
     5を使うときには注意を要する。強い響きを持つ言い方で，両親が子供をしかったあとなどにしばしば使う。

すべて理解できますか。
  Do you understand everything?
  Did you understand everything?
  Is everything clear?

3 生徒とのやりとり　　*163*

私の言うことがわかりましたか。
　Do you understand?
　Did you understand?
　Did I make myself clear?
　Did you make out what I said?
　Do you get what I'm saying?
　Do you understand what I'm saying?
　Did you get what I said?
　Did you understand what I said?
　Did I express my ideas clearly?
　Did I express myself clearly?
　Were you able to understand me?
　Did I make my ideas clear?
　　　現在形と過去形の両方が可能なものが多い。

わからないことが何かありますか。
　Is there anything you don't understand?

はっきりしない点が何かありますか。
　1. Is there any part you are not sure of?
　2. Are there any parts you are not sure of?
　3. Are there any points you are not sure of?
　　　parts を 3 のように points にしてもよいが，parts を好むネイティブスピーカーが多い。

知らない単語や表現が何かありますか。
　1. Are there any words or expressions you are not familiar with?
　2. Are there any words or expressions you do not know?
　3. Are there any new words or expressions?
　4. *Are there any strange words or expressions?
　　　英会話の道案内の場面などで，道順を尋ねられた人が不案内なとき，"I'm a stranger here." と言ったりする。この場合は「よく

知らない」という意味合いで stranger を使うことができるが,「知らない単語や表現」というとき strange という語を 4 のように使うと, unnatural の意と解されてしまう。4 の言い方は誤解されるのでふさわしくない。

すべての新出単語の意味が理解できますか。
Do you understand the meaning of all the new words?

だれか,この問題がわかる人がいますか。
Is there anyone who can solve this exercise?

だれかこの問題がわかる人はいませんか。
Can anybody answer this question?
Can anybody understand this question?
Can anybody solve this problem?
Can anybody understand this problem?
Can anyone solve this problem?
Can anybody solve this problem?

　　anyone を anybody としてもよいが, anyone の方を好むネイティブスピーカーが多いようである。
　　to answer this problem は数学の問題などについていう。

今の説明でわからなかった人はいませんか。
1. **Is there anyone who did not understand what I just said?**
2. **Isn't there anyone who did not understand what I just said?**

　　これは自然な日本文であるが,英語を直訳すると日本語にはないニュアンスが生じてくる。英語で Isn't there ...? と聞くと,「ないこと」を期待している話者の気持ちを表すことになってしまう。教師は自分の説明をできるだけ学生に理解してほしいわけであるから, Isn't there ...? と問いかけるのはふさわしくない。1 のようにしたい。

どこがわかりませんか。
　What can't you understand?

3番の問題を間違えた人はいますか。
　Is there anyone who missed No. 3?
　Is there anyone who made a mistake in No. 3?
　Is there anyone who made a mistake on No. 3?
　Which of you missed No. 3?
　Who has made a mistake in No. 3?

3番の問題を間違えた人は手を上げなさい。
　Those who made a mistake in No. 3, raise your hand.

5つ以上間違えた人は手を上げなさい。
　Raise your hand if you made more than five mistakes?
　Those who made more than five mistakes, raise your hand.

5つ以上間違えた人は追試験を行います。
　If you made more than five mistakes, I'll give you a make-up test.
　I'll give a make-up test to those who made more than five mistakes.
　I'll give a make-up test to those who made mistakes more than five.

最初は難しく感じるかもしれませんが，次第にわかるようになります。
　You may have difficulty at first, but you'll soon be able to understand.

それについて説明しましょうか。
　Do you want me to explain about it?
　Shall I explain about it?

Would you like anything explained?

それについてもっと詳しく知りたいですか。
　　Would you like to know more about it?

例をあげて説明しましょう。
　　Let me explain this to you with some examples.

先程言ったことを，繰り返しましょう。
　　Let me repeat what I said a minute ago.

▶もう一度言ってください。
　　Could you repeat that once more?
　　Could you repeat that once again?

▶ちょっと待ってください。
　　Just a second, please.
　　Just a minute, please.
　　Just a moment, please.

▶そこがわかりません。
　　I don't understand that.
　　I don't get that.

▶日本語でそれを説明してください。
　　Could you explain that in Japanese?

▶自分ではこの章がわかったつもりでいるんですが。
　　I think I understand this chapter.

▶5ページの問題が，まだよく理解できません。
　　I still can't understand the question on page 5.
　　I still can't understand the exercise on page 5.

I still can't understand the problem on page 5.

　　数学などのテスト問題は，problem でよい。

▶これは前の時間やったのですが，まだ，よくわかりません。
1. **Even though we did this last time, I still don't understand it.**
2. **Even though we did this last time, I still don't understand it very well.**
3. *****Even though we did this last time, I still didn't understand it well.**

　　3 の ... still didn't ... という言い方はおかしい。また，well という語を単独に使うのもおかしい。very well のように使わなければならない。

▶講義の内容があまりよくわかりません。
I can't understand the lecture very well.

▶私は内容を問う問題が苦手です。
I am not good at kinds of questions asking about the content(s).

C　授業の進め方

授業の進み方はちょうどいいですか。
1. **Am I teaching at the right pace for you?**
2. **Am I going at the right pace for you?**
3. **Is the pace just about right?**
4. **Is the speed of instruction just about right?**

　　4 は直訳に近く，あまり自然な表現ではない。

授業の進め方をどう思いますか。速すぎますか，それとも遅すぎますか。
　What do you think of the pace of my teaching? Too fast or too slow?
　What do you think of the pace of my lessons? Too fast or too slow?
　What do you think of the speed of my teaching? Too fast or too slow?

ちょっと速すぎますか。
　Am I going too fast?

私の説明が速すぎたら，そのように言ってください。
　If I go too fast, just tell me (so).

ちょっと遅すぎますか。
　Am I going too slow?

授業の進め方で何か提案はありませんか。
　1. Do you have any suggestions regarding my pace?
　2. As to the pace of instruction, do you have any suggestions?
　3. As to the speed of instruction, do you have any suggestions?
　　　1が最もよい。2や3は formal な言い方である。

もう少しゆっくり説明しましょうか。
　Shall I explain more slowly?

ここは大切だからちょっとゆっくり説明しましょう。
　Since this is important, let me explain a little more slowly.
　Since this is important, let me explain a little slower.

3 生徒とのやりとり　　*169*

今度はもっとゆっくり話します。用意はいいですか。
　　I'll speak a little bit slower this time. Are you ready?

▶はい，お願いします。
　　Yes, please.

▶先生，速すぎます。
　　You are going too fast.

▶授業が速すぎてついていけません。
　　I cannot keep up with you.

▶授業のペースが速すぎます。もう少しゆっくり進めてください。
　　You are going too fast. Could you slow down a little bit?

▶もう少しゆったりとしたペースで授業をしてください。
　　Could you slow down a little?
　　Could you go at a slower pace?
　　Could you go at a slower tempo?
　　Could you conduct your class at a slower pace?
　　Could you conduct your class at a slower tempo?
　　　　tempo の発音は，[témpou] のように o が二重母音であることに注意。tempo はしばしば音楽用語として使われる。

ここは最も大切なポイントですから，もう一度説明しましょう。
　　Since this is the most important point, let me go over it once more.
　　Since this is the most important point, let me explain once more.
　　　　go over は「〈説明など〉を繰り返す」という意味でよく使われる。

同じことを言っているんじゃないだろうか。

1. **I'm afraid I'm repeating myself.**
2. **I am afraid I am saying the same thing again.**

  1の方が自然な言い方である。

遠慮なく質問してください。

 Feel free to ask me questions.
 Please don't hesitate to ask me questions.

質問があればいつでもいいですよ。

 If you have any questions, you may ask at any time.
 If you have questions, you may ask at any time.

  日本では授業中に質問するのをためらって，授業が終わって質問をする光景がよく見かけられるが，アメリカなどでは授業中にさかんに質問がなされる。

わからないときには，いつでもそう言ってください。

1. **Whenever you don't understand, please let me know.**
2. **Please let me know whenever you don't understand.**
3. ***Whenever you don't understand, please say "No".**

  日本文の意味は，「（話の内容が）理解できないときは（遠慮なく）わからないといってほしい」という意味であるから，1や2の英訳がよい。3は，わからないときには，その都度「ノー！」という声を call out しなさいという意味に解釈される。

わからないことがあればわかるまで説明します。

 If you have anything you don't understand, I will explain until you can understand.

▶難しいので，もう一度説明してください。

 Could you explain it once again as it is difficult?

▶重要なところをもう一度繰り返していただけませんか。
　Could you repeat the main point again?
　Could you repeat the important part again?
　Could you repeat the important thing again?

▶学期の初めは授業がよくわかったのですが，だんだんわからなくなってきました。
　1. **I understood everything at the beginning of the term, but I'm having more and more difficulty these days.**
　2. **I understood the lessons all right at the beginning of the term, but gradually I came to have difficulty with them.**
　　　1の方が2よりも自然な表現である。

▶授業についていけなくて現在悩んでいます。
　I am worried because I can't keep up with the lessons.

D　生徒の返答に対して

よくできました。
　Good.
　You did a good job.
　Right.
　That's right.
　You're right.
　Fine.
　Yes.
　　　yes は日本語式発音では [íes] となりがちである。y の発音は母音ではなくて半母音であるから，[jés] のように発音しなくてはならない。
　　Correct.
　　That's correct.
　　That's it.

Uh-huh.
　　　Um-hum.
　　　M-hum.
　　　You've got it.
　　　You've got the idea.
　　　You are right on the money.
　　　You hit the nail on the head.
などのような面白い表現もある。

大変よくできました。
　Congratulations!
　Very good.
　Very fine.
　That's very good.
　Excellent!
　Magnificent!
　Marvelous!
　Terrific!
　Wow!
　Fantastic!
　You did a very good job.
　Well done.

　　Congratulations! は，努力をして何かを成就した相手に対しての褒め言葉である。日本語の「おめでとう」におおよそ相当するが，結婚式で花嫁には言ってはならないとされていた。「男を探し続けてやっと結婚できましたね」という意味に解釈されるからであるが，最近ではそうでもないようである。

その通りです。
　That's it!
　Exactly.
　Perfect.
　You said it.

I quite agree with you.
That's exactly the point.
That's perfectly correct.
What you said was perfectly correct.
What you said was perfectly all right.
That's just what I was looking for.
You didn't make a single mistake.
You are quite right.
You took the words right out of my mouth.
You took the words out of my mouth.

それはなかなかいい説明です。
 That's a very interesting explanation.

大体いいですよ。
 Almost right.
 You've almost got it.
 You're almost there.
 You're on the right track.

なるほど，そんな考え方もありますね。
 I see. That is possible, too.
 Indeed, that makes sense, too.
 That makes sense, too.
 Uh-huh, it is OK, too.
 Um-hum, that's a good idea, too.
 Well, that's OK, too.

それは場合によります。
 It depends.

それは全く状況次第です。
 It all depends.

そんな可能性もあります。
It's possible.
It could be.
It could be possible.
It might be.
I suppose so.
It might be possible.
Perhaps.
Maybe.
Probably.
Probably so.
It is likely.

> 可能性が高い場合には，次のような表現が使える。
> It is most likely.
> It is highly likely.

それの方がいいですね。
That's better.
That's much better.
That's far better.
That's far better than before.
That's more like it.
That's a bit more like it.
That's a lot better.
You've improved a little.
You've improved a lot.
You've made a lot of progress.
You've made great progress.
Yours is much better than mine.

その答えでいいのですが，どうしてそのようになるのですか。
1. That's right, but why is that so?
2. Your answer is OK, but why is that?

1 の方がよい。

答えはそれでいいけれども，もう少し詳しく説明してください。
1. **That's right, but can you explain in a little more detail?**
2. **That's right, but can you give a little more detailed explanation?**
3. **Your answer is correct, but can you elaborate on that?**

　　1 と 2 はごく普通に使われる表現である。
　　3 の elaborate は学会などで耳にする非常に formal な響きのする言葉である。

もう一度言ってください。
Please say it again.
Please repeat it once more.

もう一度やってごらんなさい。
Try it once again.
Try it once more.
Try again.
Try it again.
Try it one more time.
Have another try.
Have a try.

間違いです。
1. **I'm afraid that's not quite right.**
2. **I don't think you are quite right.**
3. **I am afraid I have to disagree with you on that.**
4. **Good try, but not quite right.**
5. **Not quite.**
6. **Not exactly.**
7. **Not really.**
8. **Unfortunately not.**

9. **It's wrong.**
10. **This is wrong.**
11. **That is wrong.**

　　9, 10, 11 は強い響きをもっているので, 少し穏やかに言うには 1 〜 8 の表現の方がよい。

気にしないように。
Don't worry.
Don't worry about it.

間違いを気にしないように。
Don't worry about making mistakes.

　　「間違いを気にせず言いなさい」という意味と, 間違った生徒を元気づける意味の両方が可。

間違いを気にする必要はありません。完全な人間なんていないから。
You don't have to worry about making mistakes. Nobody is perfect.
You don't have to worry about making mistakes. Everyone makes mistakes.
You don't have to worry about making mistakes. Everybody makes mistakes.

　　everyone を everybody としてもよいが, 呼びかけでは everybody の方が普通である。

急がなくてもかまいません。
We have plenty of time.
There's no hurry.
There's no need to hurry.

落ち着きなさい。
Calm down.

わかりました。それでは説明します。
　　I see. Then, let me explain it to you.
　　I see. Then, I'll explain it to you.

はい。よろしい。着席しなさい。
　　OK. Good. Sit down.

▶少し考えさせてください。
　　Please let me think for a while.
　　Please give me some time to think.

▶説明が十分できないので，日本語で説明してもいいですか。
　　I am afraid I can't explain this well, so may I use Japanese?
　　I am afraid I can't explain this well, so may I explain it in Japanese?
　　I am afraid I can't explain this well, so may I use Japanese to explain it?

E　生徒の学習への姿勢

一生懸命に練習しなさい。
　　Practice hard.
　　Study hard.

大きな声を出しなさい。
　　Speak up.

元気がよくて大変よろしい。
　1. I'm glad that you are very fine.
　2. I'm happy that you are very fine.
　3. *You're very fine. That's nice.
　　　　3はあまり自然な表現ではない。

そのように努力を続けたら，きっと英語がうまくなります。

1. If you keep on trying like this, you will surely be a good English speaker.
2. If you keep making efforts like that, you will sure be a good English speaker.

   1の方が自然な表現である。2はstiltedな感じがする。

どんどん英語がうまくなっていますよ。

1. Your English is getting much better.
2. Your English is getting better and better.

   いずれでもよいが，1の方がよい。

思い出したように勉強しても駄目だ。いつもコンスタントに勉強しなさい。

1. It's no use studying on and off. You have to study constantly.
2. It's no use studying only some of the time. You have to study constantly.
3. You need to study a little each day, not a lot at one time.
4. You need to develop regular study habits.
5. It's no use studying by fits and starts. You have to study constantly.

   1〜4はstandardな表現，5はinformalな表現である。

努力の成果が現れていますよ。

1. Your effort is paying off.
2. Your effort is getting a result.

   1の方が2よりもよい。

コツコツ努力することが大切です。

1. It is important to keep on trying.
2. It is important to make efforts little by little.
3. It is important to plug away.

2 と 3 はあまり自然な表現ではない。plug away は「コツコツ努力する」という意味で使われることがあるが，3 の使い方は自然ではない。He is plugging away at his math. のように言うと自然である。

最近は集中して勉強しているようですね。
1. **These days you are studying hard.**
2. **These days you are studying intensively.**

   1 の方が自然な言い方である。2 はやや stilted な感じがする。

F　間違い

8ページの A はミスプリントです。
A on page 8 is a misprint.

ごめんなさい。間違いました。
I'm sorry. I've made a mistake.
I'm sorry. I made a mistake.
I'm sorry. I made an error.

   mistake と error は上記のように類義語として使うことがあるが，英語学では mistake は「知っていながらうっかりしていて犯す誤り」，error は「知らずに犯す誤り」という意味で区別する。

ごめんなさい。私が先週言ったことは間違いでした。
I'm sorry. What I said last week was misleading.
I'm sorry. What I said last week was wrong.
I'm sorry. I was mistaken about what I said last week.

私が先週言ったことは間違いでしたので，訂正します。
What I said last week was wrong. Let me correct it.
Let me correct the mistake I made last week.

間違ったら訂正してください。
　If I make a mistake, please correct me.
　If I have made a mistake, please correct me.
　If I am mistaken, please correct me.
　If I'm wrong, please correct me.
　　板書するときなどに生徒に言う表現。

間違いをしない人などいません。
　1. **Nobody is perfect.**
　2. **No one is perfect.**
　3. **We all make mistakes.**
　4. **Everyone makes mistakes.**
　5. **There's no one who doesn't make any mistakes.**
　　no one [no-one] は意味的には nobody と同じであるが，呼びかけとして使う場合は，nobody を用いるのが普通である。
　　3，4 は肯定表現であるが，文意は 1，2 と同一である。
　　5 はもとの日本語の意味に近いが英語としては awkward である。1〜4 のように言った方が自然である。

英語の先生でも間違えることはあるんですよ。
　1. **Even English teachers sometimes make mistakes.**
　2. **Even English teachers make mistakes sometimes.**
　　副詞の sometimes の位置は，1 の方が 2 よりも自然である。

英語はたくさん間違いをしながら次第に上手になっていきます。
　You can improve your English through making lots of mistakes.

間違いを恐れる必要はありません。
　You don't have to worry about mistakes.

間違いを恐れないようにしなさい。
　Try not to worry about making mistakes.

間違いをしても大したことではありません。
It doesn't matter if you make mistakes.
　　間違いを恐れず発言することをうながす場合も，間違った生徒を慰める場合にも言う。

間違いを恐れてはいけません。
Don't worry about making mistakes.

間違いを恐れないで英語を話してごらんなさい。
1. **Speak English without worrying about mistakes.**
2. **Speak English without worrying about making mistakes.**
　　2は正しい英語表現であるが，1の方が簡潔である。

答えが合っているのに×をされた人はいませんか。
Whose answer has not been graded properly?
Is there anyone who had an answer misgraded?
　　採点の間違いについては p. 479 〜参照。

▶レポートに英語の間違いがあったら直していただけませんか。
1. **If there are English mistakes in my report, could you correct them?**
2. **If there are mistakes in my English in my report, could you correct them?**
　　2は，前置詞の in が2度現れるので，不自然な感じがする。1のように言いたい。

▶つづりが間違いではないでしょうか。
Is the spelling all right?
Is there a mistake in the spelling?

▶小川先生，スペリングが間違っています。
Mr. Ogawa, is this spelling OK?

直訳的に This spelling is not correct. とすると，生徒同士ではよいとしても，生徒から先生に対しては少し直截的過ぎる。疑問文の形にすると，柔らかいニュアンスになる。

G　生徒を励ます・慰める

君たち，やればできるじゃないか。
　You see, you can do it!
　You made it!
　You've made it!
　You have made it!
　You've done it!
　You can do it!

　　You've made it. の方が You have made it. よりも自然な表現である。会話の中では，You have made it. のように，個々の単語を等しく発音することは少ない。

努力する者が最後には勝ちます。
  1. Effort will be rewarded.
  2. Those who try hard will succeed in the end.
  3. Those who try hard will win in the end.
  4. Those who try hard will come out ahead.
  5. Those who make efforts will win in the end.

　　1～4 は自然な言い方である。5 はやや stilted な感じがある。

私は努力する者にいい評価を与えます。
  1. I will reward those who make an effort.
  2. I'll give good grades to those who try.
  3. I'll be generous to those who try.

89ページの長文の意味のわからなかった人はしかたがありません。まだ，習ってない構文が入っていましたから。
1. Don't worry if you didn't understand the long passage on page 89. There are some sentence patterns that haven't been taught yet.
2. Those who haven't understood the long story on page 89, don't worry about it. There are some sentence patterns that haven't been taught yet.

　　1の方が2よりもよい。2はwordyである。

中間テストで悪かった人は，期末テストで頑張ればいいのです。
1. If you didn't do well on the midterm test, you can make up for it on the final exam.
2. Don't worry if you didn't do well on the midterm tests. You can make up for it on the final exams.
3. Those who didn't do a good job in the midterm exams. Don't worry about it. You can make up for it in the final exams.

　　1や2の方が3よりもよい。3はwordy, stiltdな感じがする。

いままで発表していない人にチャンスを与えましょう。
Let me give a chance to those who have not spoken yet.
I will give priority to those who have not spoken yet.

　　そのほか，生徒の間違いを慰める表現はp. 180を参照のこと。

H　生徒の感想・希望

▶英語は思ったより面白いです。
English is more interesting than I had thought.

▶英語がだんだん面白くなってきました。
English has become more and more interesting.

▶英語が好きになりました。
1. **I've come to like English.**
2. **I came to like English.**

　　1 は「以前は英語が好きでなかったが，好きになった。現在でも英語は好きだ」という意味である。

　　2 は，過去において「英語が好きになる」経験があったことを述べた文で，現在も英語が好きであるかどうかは明らかにしていない。1 の方がよい。

▶それについてもっと話をしてください。
Could you tell us more about it?

▶山本先生，英語の歌のリスニングをしましょう。
Mr. Yamamoto, let's do some listening exercises with English songs.
Mr. Yamamoto, shall we do some listening exercises with English songs?

4　CALL 教室の授業

A　聞き取り・読みの練習

聞き取りの問題をやってみましょう。
Let's do the dictation-cloze exercises for a while.

　　音声を聞きながら空欄を埋めていく種類の聞き取り練習を dictation-cloze exercises という。大まかなことから問う方式を top-down approach，細部から問うものを bottom-up approach と言ったりする。

今度はもっとゆっくり話します。用意はいいですか。
I'll speak a little bit slower this time. Are you ready?

後ろの人たちは，私の言うことが聞こえますか。
　Can people sitting at the back hear what I am saying?
　Can people sitting in the back hear what I am saying?
　Can people sitting at the back hear me?
　Can people sitting in the back hear me?

CDの内容が聞き取れましたか。
　Did you understand what the CD said?
　Did you understand what was on the CD?

どこがわかりませんか。
　What can't you understand?

録音を終わった人は，ユニット8を2度聞いてみてください。
 1. If you are through with the recording, listen to Unit 8 two times, first.
 2. If you are through with the recording, listen to Unit 8 twice, first.
 3. If you are through with the recording, listen to Unit 8 two times before you do anything else.
 4. *If you are through with the recording, first listen to Unit 8 two times.
 5. *If you are finished with the recording, first listen to Unit 8 twice.

　「～が終わる」という日本語に相当する英語表現としては，be through with も be finished with も可能である。しかし，定冠詞の用法上の違いがある。be through with ～の場合には，必ず次に the を必要とするが，be finished with ～の場合には the が必要でない場合もあり得る。つまり，be through with ～は《特定》なものに使い，be finished with ～の場合には《特定》《不特定》のいずれの場合にも使うことができる。

それでは，しばらくCDのあとについて読む練習をしてごらんなさい。
Well, practice reading after the CD for a while.

CDを聞いたあと，しばらく読みの練習をしなさい。
Practice reading after listening to the CD for a while.

5分間与えますから，しっかり読みの練習をしてください。
1. I'll give you 5 minutes. Practice reading, trying hard to do it well.
2. *Let me give you 5 minutes. Practice reading hard.

　　Let me ... の形はしばしば I'll ... で表現できることが多いが，この場合には1のようにI'll ... を使った方が自然である。
　　「しっかり読みの練習をしてください」を直訳して*Practice reading hard とするのは awkward である。少し語句を補って1のように言うべきである。

こちらでモニターできるように，口の前にマイクを当てて読みの練習をしばらく行ってください。
Put your microphone closer to your mouth and practice reading so that I can monitor you.

CDの速さに負けないように，速く読んでみなさい。
Try to read rapidly in order to keep up with the CD.
Try to read fast so as not to fall behind the CD.

大きな声でCDのあとにくり返してごらんなさい。
Repeat aloud after the CD.
Repeat after the CD in a loud voice.

B 自分の声の録音

今度は自分の声を録音してごらんなさい。
　This time, why don't you record your own voice?

マイクを口の前にもってきます。
　1. Put the microphone in front of your mouth.
　2. Put the microphone in front of your lips.

　　日本語で microphone のことをマイクと言うが，英語の俗語的表現でも mike という語を使うことがある。[k] 音が mike のように ke というつづりになることに注意。
　　日本語では「口の前」となっているが，あえて「口」にとらわれる必要はない。英語では 2 のように lips という語を使うこともできる。

マイクに向かって話しなさい。
　Speak into the microphone.

　　前置詞の into の代わりに，through を使うこともできる。

録音された自分の声をどう思いますか。
　What do you think of your recorded voice?

自分で納得のいくまで練習をしてください。
　Practice until you are satisfied.

明確に発音するようにしなさい。
　Try to enunciate clearly.

英語を速く話す必要はありません。それよりも，正確に話すことの方が大切です。
　You don't have to speak English fast. It is more important to be able to speak correctly.

You don't have to speak English fast. It is more important to be able to speak accurately.

個々の単語の発音よりは、全体の調子に気をつけなさい。
Pay attention to intonation rather than to the pronunciation of individual sounds.
Pay attention to intonation rather than the pronunciation of individual sounds.
  than の次の to は省略できる。

切るところ，上がるところ，下がるところに特に注意して，もう一度自分の声を録音してごらんなさい。
Pay special attention to pauses, rising intonation and falling intonation. Record your own voice once more.

C 問題の指示

ストーリーについて，いまからいくつか質問をします。
Let me give you some questions on the story.

問題は回答器で答えてください。正しいものには1，誤っているものには2のボタンを押しなさい。
Answer the questions using the analyzer. If the statement is correct, press button 1 and if it is wrong press button 2.

今から英語で問題を出しますから，英語で答えてください。
Now, we're going to do an exercise in English, so answer me in English.
Now, I am going to give you some exercises in English, so answer me in English.

英語で説明するのが難しすぎるなら，日本語でもかまいません。
　　If it is too difficult to explain in English, Japanese will be all right.
　　If it is too difficult to explain in English, it will be all right to use Japanese.
　　If it is too difficult to explain in English, it is all right to use Japanese.
　　If it is too difficult to explain in English, you can do it in Japanese.

もう一度質問を繰り返します。
　1. I'll repeat the question.
　2. Let me repeat the question again.
　3. Let me ask the question again.
　4. Let me say the question again.
　5. Let me state the question again.
　　　1では again という言葉が使われていないが，2，3，4，5では使われている。どちらでもよい。ただし，again を使うと，すでに質問を1回，あるいはそれ以上繰り返していることを暗示させる。

質問は一度しかしませんから，よく注意して聞いてください。
　1. As I am going to give each question only once, please listen very carefully.
　2. As I am going to give you the question only once, please listen very carefully.
　　　1の each question は2つ以上の質問がある場合，2の the question は質問が1つだけの場合である。

質問の意味がわかりましたか。
　　Did you understand the question?
　　Did you get the question?

5　パワーポイントを使う授業

A　スライドを見せる

ブラインドを閉めてください。
　Please close the blinds.

ライトをつけてください。
　Please turn the lights on.

これはロンドンで写したものです。
　This was taken in London.

絵を換えます。
　1. **Let me go on to the next slide.**
　2. **Let me go on to the next picture.**
　3. **Let me change the slide.**
　4. **Let me change the picture.**
　　　1〜4のいずれでもよいが，1と2の方がよい。

少し前に戻してみましょう。
　Let me back up a little.
　Let me go back a little.

おおっと，1枚飛ばしました。
　Whoops! I skipped one slide.
　　　Whoops! は，ちょっとした失敗をしたときなどに発する驚きの表現である。Oops! と同義である。

この写真は漁師の波止場の前で撮られたものです。
　This picture was taken in front of Fisherman's Wharf.

5 パワーポイントを使う授業　*191*

この写真は少しボケています。
　This picture is a little blurred.

この表からはっきりとわかるように，…
　As this table clearly shows, ...

▶先生，スライドが反対になっています。
　The slide is reversed.
　The slide is backward.
　The slide is in backward.
　The slide is the wrong way round.

▶もう少しゆっくり見せてください。
　1. Could you show the slides a little slower?
　2. Could you slow down a little?
　3. Could you show us the slides a little slower?
　4. Could you show the slides to us a little slower?
　　　2はスライドのときだけでなく，いろいろな状況で使うことができる。授業のペースが速すぎるときなどによく使われる。
　　　3と4ではusとto usという語句がそれぞれ使われているが，showがmain verbであるから，ともに省いた方がよい。

このグラフから，どんなことがわかりますか。
　1. What does this graph show?
　2. What do you notice by looking at the graph?
　3. What do you notice when you look at the graph?
　4. What can you learn from looking at this graph?
　5. What can you learn from this graph?
　　　1〜4はstandard，5はやや informal な表現である。

このグラフは年ごとにどのように人口が変化していったかを表しています。
　1. This graph shows how the population has changed from

year to year.
2. **This graph shows how the population has changed over the years.**
3. **This graph shows how the population has changed year after year.**

　1 は standard，2 はやや informal な表現である。3 は year after year には continue to happen every year という意味があるから，この場合ふさわしくない。year after year は，
　　He works hard *year after year*.
　　The weather is getting warmer *year after year*.
のように使う。

縦軸は英検の受験者数を，横軸は受験年を表しています。
The vertical axis shows the number of the *Eiken* (English Step Test) takers and the horizontal axis shows the year in which they had the test.

　had the test の代わりに，took the test と言ってもよい。

これは 10 年前の受験生の数を表しています。
This shows the number of the test-takers who took the test ten years ago.

このグラフは，はっきりと TOEIC の受験者が増加していることを示しています。
This graph clearly shows the number of TOEIC test-takers has increased.

数字が次第に上昇しています。
The number is gradually rising.

数字が最近突然上昇しました。
The number has suddenly risen recently

数字は一度下降し，そのあと，再び上昇しました。
1. The number dropped but has risen again.
2. The number has dropped and after that it has risen again.

　　　1の方が2よりも自然な言い方である。

数字は驚くほど上昇しました。
1. The number has increased remarkably.
2. The number has remarkably increased.

　　　1の方が2よりも自然な言い方である。

10年前の数字を比べると3倍ののびです。
The number has almost tripled since 2005.

数字は小数点以下を切り捨てています。
1. The numbers omit the figures after the decimal point.
2. The numbers omit the figures after the decimal fractions.

　　　1は明確であるが，2はわかりづらい。

この図は昨年，あなたたちに対して行ったアンケート調査の結果を示したものです。
1. This chart shows the results of the questionnaire that you filled out last year.
2. This chart shows the results of the questionnaire that was administered to you last year.

　　　1の方が自然な表現である。2はformalでstiltedなニュアンスがある。

ほぼ全員がアンケートに答えています。
Almost everybody answered the questionnaire.
Nearly everyone filled in the questionnaire.

　　　いずれもstandardな表現である。

3分の1の生徒が「英語が好きだ」と答えています。
1. **One-third of the students answered, "Yes, I like English."**
2. **One-third of the students said that they like English.**

　　1のように直接話法で言っても，2のように間接話法で言ってもよい。

50パーセントの人が，大学に進学したいと回答しています。
　Fifty percent of the students want to go to college.

B　スライドショーが終わって

スライドは以上です。
　That's all the slides.
　That's all of the slides.

これだけです。
　That's all I have.

面白かったですか。
1. **Did you have a good time?**
2. **Did you enjoy the slides?**
3. **Did you enjoy yourself?**
4. **Did you enjoy yourselves?**

　　アメリカ英語では enjoy yourself, enjoy yourselves の形は undertone of sarcasm あるいは talk down といったニュアンスがあるので，1，2のように表現することが望ましい。

　　enjoy という動詞を使うときには，目的語を忘れないようにしないといけない。*I enjoyed.（私は楽しかった）のように言うと誤りとなる。I enjoyed myself. とか，I enjoyed playing the piano. などのように，目的語を入れること。

5 パワーポイントを使う授業　*195*

この続きは，またいつか見せてあげましょう。
　I'll show you the rest some other time.
　Let me show you the rest some other time.

今日はこれで終わります。
　So much for today.

だれか電気をつけてください。
　1. Someone, please turn on the lights.
　2. Someone, please turn the lights on.
　　　1，2はどちらでもよいが，1の方がよく使われる。

カーテンを開いてください。
　Please open the curtains.

ブラインドを開いてください。
　Please open the blinds.
　　　II章のp. 23参照

プロジェクターを片付けてください。
　Please put the projector away.

▶大変面白かったです。
　I had a really good time.
　I enjoyed myself very much.
　　　自分自身のことについて言及する場合には，enjoy myselfという形は何ら抵抗はない。

▶またいつかスライドを見せてください。
　Please show us slides again, sometime.

▶来週も見せてください。
　Could you show us some more next week?

196　Ⅲ　授業活動

▶なかなかきれいなスライドですね。
　The slides are very beautiful, aren't they?

▶もっとスライドが見られたらなあ。
　I wish we could see more slides.

▶ああ，首が痛くなった。
　My neck got stiff.

6　映画を使う授業

今日の授業は映画鑑賞です。
　1. We'll see a movie in class today.
　2. I'll let you watch a movie in class today.
　　　2のように言うと，教師の態度がやや尊大に感じられる。

これから映画を見せましょう。
　1. I'm going to show you a movie now.
　2. I'll show you a movie, now.
　3. Starting right now, I'll show you a movie.
　4. We'll watch a movie now.
　5. Now, let's watch a movie.
　6. Let's see a movie now.
　7. Let's watch a movie now.
　8. *From now, I'll show you a movie.
　9. *Let's now see a movie.
　10. *Let's now watch a movie.
　　　1から7までは正しい。8のfrom nowは，「これから」という日本語にぴったりの英語表現であるが，英語ではfrom nowだけを独立させて文頭におくのは不自然である。しかし，文末で次のように使うのはよい。

a. If you don't eat more, you'll be hungry thirty minutes from now.
  b. I wonder what I'll be doing two years from now.

 a や b の場合には,それぞれ thirty minutes, two years という修飾語句を伴って,「30 分後」「2 年後」という《未来の時》を表している。

映画は我々にいろいろなことを教えてくれます。
  Movies can tell us many things.
  We can get many things from movies.

これから見る映画は,世界の名作の 1 つです。
  The movie you are going to watch is one of the world's great movie masterpieces.
  The movie you are going to watch is one of the great masterpieces of the movie world.
  The movie you are going to watch is a great movie masterpiece.
  The movie you are going to watch is one of the movie masterpieces of the world.

これはトム・クルーズの主演する映画です。
  This is a movie starring Tom Cruise.

『カサブランカ』という映画を見た人はいますか。
  Has anyone ever watched the movie entitled *Casablanca*?
  Has anyone over watched the movie called *Casablanca*?
  Has anyone ever watched the movie, *Casablanca*?

この映画は 1942 年にアメリカで作られましたが,今でもなおわたしたちの心に深い感動を与えます。
  1. This movie was made in America in 1942, but it still has great power to impress us deeply.

2. **This movie was made in America in 1942, but it still has great power to move us deeply.**
3. **This movie was made in America in 1942, but it still has the power to impress us deeply.**
4. **This movie was made in America in 1942, but it can still make a deep impression on us.**
5. **This movie was made in America in 1942, but it can move us to tears.**
6. **This movie was made in America in 1942, but it still has power to move us to tears.**
7. ***This movie was made in America in 1942, but it still moves us deeply.**
8. ***This movie was made in America in 1942, but it still moves us to tears.**

　7, 8 は日本語の訳としてはふさわしく思われるが, 英語を母語とする人々にとっては抵抗のある文である。同一の映画でも, その映画によって受ける印象は人それぞれに異なる。ほかの人が素晴らしいという映画も自分にとってはつまらないこともあろうし, 逆の場合もありうる。個人主義を尊ぶ英米人は, 7や8のような文に対して, 強い反感を抱くことが多い。it still moves ... と断定的な表現を避けて, it can still move ... のように言えば, 容認可能な表現となる。

字幕は出ません。
There will be no subtitles.

字幕は見ないようにしなさい。
1. **Try not to look at the subtitles.**
2. **Avoid reading the subtitles.**
3. **Avoid looking at the subtitles.**
4. **Avoid subtitles.**

　時によってせりふの言葉が字幕に現れないことがある。これは一度に画面に表す字数には制限があるからである。ふつう, 画面

の下には2行，それぞれの行には10〜13文字くらい入る。
　4の文は正しいが，1，2，3の文に比べて意味が明確でない。

字幕はできるだけ見ないようにしなさい。
　Try to look at the subtitles as little as possible.
　Try not to look at the subtitles any more than you have to.

字幕はありますが，できるだけ見ないようにしてください。
　There will be subtitles, but try not to look at them.

　　　「見る」はこの場合 look at を使う。see は使えない。「(意識的に)見る」が look at で，「(自然に，見ようとしなくても) 見える」が see である。

字幕に頼らないようにしなさい。
　Try not to depend on the subtitles.

洋画を理解するのは大変難しいから，わからなくてもがっかりしないように。
　It is difficult to understand English movies, so don't be disappointed even though you have trouble understanding them.

今から見る映画の中で，主な登場人物の役割に注意しなさい。
1. **Pay attention to the roles of the main characters in the movie we are going to watch now.**
2. **Pay attention to the roles of the main characters in the movie we are going to begin watching now.**
3. ***Pay attention to the roles of the main characters in the movie we are going to watch from now.**

　　1, 2 の now の使い方は正しいが，3 の from now の使い方は誤りである。
　　2 の begin は start という語に置き換えてもよい。

映画を見ながら，人々のジェスチャーに注意してみましょう。
As you watch the movie, pay attention to people's gestures.

映面を見ながら，聞き取れた語句を書き取ってください。
As you watch the movie, write down the expressions you understand.

映画を見ながら聞き取れた英語の表現があったら，何でもいいからノートに書き取ってごらんなさい。
Write down whatever expressions you have understood in your notebook while watching the movie.

洋画を見るとき，英語表現をいちいち日本語に置き換えないようにしましょう。
When you watch English movies, try not to translate into Japanese word for word.

映画を見終わったら，感想文を書いてください。
When you are through with the movie, I'd like you to write your impression of it.

映画を見終わったら，簡単な感想文を英語で書いてください。
When you finish watching the movie, write a simple description of your impressions.

映画が終わったらいくつか質問をしてみます。
When you finish watching the movie, I'll ask you some questions about it.
When you finish watching the movie, I'll ask you some questions on it.

映画は何パーセントわかりましたか。
What percent of the movie did you understand?

percent は可算名詞の扱いをし，What percent ...? や How many percent ...? の形で使うことが多い。

今見た映画は何パーセントくらいわかりましたか。
What percent of the movie you just watched did you understand?

この続きは来週見せます。
Let me show you the rest of the movie next week.

来週映画を見たい人は手を上げなさい。
Those who want to watch a movie next week, raise your hands.

前回は映画を見ましたが，どこまで見たか覚えている人は教えてください。
We watched a movie last time, but please tell me where we left off, if there's someone who remembers (it).
文の最後の代名詞 it は省略することができる。

▶映画を見せてください。
Please show us some movies.

▶映画をときどき見せていただけませんか。
Could you let us watch movies once in a while?

▶その映画はいつ封切られましたか。
When was that movie released?

▶私は，その俳優が主演する別の映画を見たことがあります。
I have seen another movie starring the same actor.

▶来週，続きを見せてください。
Please show us the sequel next week.

▶映画が全く理解できません。
I don't understand the movie at all.

7　教室で使ういろいろなもの

A　配布物・プリント

今からプリントを配ります。
I'm going to give you a handout.

今からプリントを2枚配ります。
I'm going to give you two handouts.
　　複数枚の紙をホッチキスでとめたものが2セットある場合はtwo sets of papers と言う。

この列からプリントを2枚配ります。
1. I'm going to give two handouts starting with this row.
2. I'm going to give two handouts beginning with this row.
3. I'm going to give two pages starting with this row.
4. I'm going to give two pages beginning with this row.
5. *I'm going to give two handouts from this row.
　　「この列から」を英語に直訳すると from this row と言いたくなるが，starting with this row，あるいは beginning with this row などのように言わなくてはいけない。

配布するものが多いので，ちょっと手伝ってください。
1. There're a lot of handouts, so could you help me out?
2. There're a lot of handouts, so could you help me?

7 教室で使ういろいろなもの　　*203*

3. There're a lot of handouts, so can you help me out?
　　理論的には can も could も可能であるが，この場合，1 や 2 のように could を使う方がより自然である。
　　help out は「困って助けを必要とする」場合などに使う。

プリントが2枚あるかどうか確かめてください。
Please check to see if you have two handouts.
Please check to see that you have two pages.
Make sure you have two handouts.
Make sure you have two pages.

プリントは足りましたか。
Are there enough handouts?
Did you have enough handouts?

プリントは全部で5枚あるはずです。
There should be five handouts in all.
There should be five handouts in total.
There should be five handouts all together.
All in all, there should be five handouts.
　　all in all は，文頭で使われることが多い。

プリント3枚をホッチキスでとめた資料が30部あります。
1. **There are thirty sets of three sheets stapled together.**
2. **There are thirty, three sets of papers stapled.**
　　1 の方が明確な表現である。

プリントが余ったら，私に返してください。
If you have some handouts left, please return them to me.
If there are extra handouts, please return them to me.

プリントが足りなかった人はいませんか。
1. **Is there anyone who doesn't have a handout?**

2. **Is there anyone who hasn't got a handout?**
3. ***Is there anyone who has not had a handout?**
　　3は不自然である。一度はプリントを持っていて，なくしてしまったという意味合いになる。

広田君，今日欠席している山田君にもプリントを渡しておいてください。

Hirota-kun, could you give these handouts to Yamada-kun, who is absent today.

Hirota-kun, could you make sure Yamada-kun, who is absent today, get these handouts?

見えにくいプリントがあったら取り換えます。

1. **If you have a handout that is hard to read, let me exchange it for a better one.**
2. ***If you have a handout that you can hardly see, let me exchange it with a better one.**

　　日本語の「見えにくいプリント」を直訳して2のように … a handout that you can hardly see … と訳すと，「印刷されている文字が見えにくい」ということではなく，「プリントそのものを見ることが困難」という意味に解される。

ミスプリントがいくつかあります。

There're some misprints.

There're some typographical errors.

There're some typos.

　　「プリントが足りません。」などというとき print とはいえないが（正しくは handout），misprint はれっきとした英語。misprint の替わりに，a typo あるいは a typographical error などと言ってもよい。ついでながら，typo は typographical error の省略形であるので，*a typo error ということはできない。

プリントに日付を書くのを忘れないようにしなさい。
　Please don't forget to write the date on your handout.
　Make sure you write the date on your handout.

プリントの問題を全部する必要はありません。
　1. You don't have to answer every question on the handout.
　2. You don't have to answer every question in the handout.
　3. *You don't have to answer every question of the handout.
　　　1のように on the handout とすると，「プリントは1枚しかない」という意味に解される。2のように in the handout とすると，「プリントは2枚以上ある」ということが暗示される。

来週は，今配ったプリントに関するテストを行います。
　Next week, you're going to have a test based on the handout you've just got.

来週のこの時間は自習ですが，プリントを用意します。
　You'll have study hall this hour next week, but let me prepare handouts.
　You'll have to study on your own this hour next week, but I'm going to prepare handouts.
　You'll have study hall this period next week, but let me prepare handouts.
　You'll have to study on your own this hour next week, but I'm going to prepare handouts.
　You'll have to study by yourselves this hour next week, but I'm going to prepare handouts.

クラスで配るプリントはいつもきれいに整理しておきなさい。
　Please put the handouts given in class in order.

▶同じものが２枚あります。
　I have two sheets of the same paper.
　Two of my sheets are the same.

▶No. 1のプリントが足りません。
　I need a No. 1 handout.
　I need a copy of the No. 1 handout.

▶プリントが１枚足りません。
　We need one more handout.

▶プリントが１枚余りました。
　There is an extra handout.

▶５枚余りました。
　I have five extra ones.

▶プリントの文字がよく見えませんので，交換していただけませんか。
　1. I can hardly read this handout. Can you give me another one?
　2. I can hardly read the handout. Can you give me another one?
　　　１のように this handout と言っても，２のように the handout と言ってもよい。

▶全部で何枚ありますか。
　How many sheets of paper are we supposed to have?

▶これは白紙です。
　This is a blank sheet of paper.
　This is blank.
　This is a blank.

▶3枚目のプリントは破れています。
The third handout is torn.

▶3枚目の紙は汚れています。
The third paper is smeared.

▶これは汚れていますので，新しいのと取り換えていただけませんか。
May I exchange this for a new one as, it is smeared?
Could I exchange this for a new one, as it is smeared?

▶これはミスプリントではないでしょうか。
I'm afraid this is a misprint.

▶締め切りはいつですか。
When is this due?
When is the due date?

▶辞書を見てもよいですか。
1. Is it all right to use our dictionaries?
2. May we use our dictionaries?
3. May I use my dictionary?
4. Can we use our dictionaries?
　　3のように，we を I に換えて言ってもよい。4は少し informal な感じがする。

B　教科書

新しい課の新出単語の意味は少なくとも調べておきなさい。
1. At least check the meaning of the new words for the new lesson.
2. At least check the meaning of the new words in the new

lesson.
3. **At least check the meaning of the new words of the new lesson.**

　1のように for を使うと,「新しい課のために」という意味になる。

　「新しい課の」という意味では in the new lesson, of the new lesson のいずれでもよいが, in を好む人の方が多いようである。

教科書を忘れてきた人はいませんか。
　Is there anyone who forgot to bring the textbook?
　Who forgot to bring their textbook?
　Has anyone forgotten to bring his textbook?

教科書を忘れてきた人は，隣の人に見せてもらいなさい。
1. **Those who forgot to bring the textbook, ask your neighbor to let you look on.**
2. ***Those who forgot to bring the textbook, have your neighbor look his textbook.**

　1の look on という表現は,「人と一緒に本を見る」という意味である。

　　Would you like to look on with me?
　　（私と一緒に本を見ませんか。）
　2の表現は garbled な感じがする。1のように言いたい。

これからは教科書を忘れないようにしなさい。
　Please try not forget to bring your textbook.
　Please don't forget to bring your textbook.
　Make sure you don't forget to bring your textbook.

だれか教科書を学校に忘れていましたよ。
1. **Someone left his textbook at school.**
2. **Someone left his textbook behind at school.**
3. ***Someone forgot his textbook at school.**

忘れた場所が明確な場合には，forget ではなく，leave を使わなくてはいけない。したがって，3 は誤りである。

教科書をできるだけ見ないようにして会話練習をしましょう。
　　Try not to look at your textbook and practice conversation.
　　Try not to look at your textbook when you practice conversation.
　　Try not to look at your textbook as you practice conversation.

▶**教科書を忘れたので，隣の人に見せてもらっていいですか。**
　1. I forgot to bring my textbook. May I ask my neighbor to let me look at his book?
　2. I forgot to bring my textbook. May I ask my neighbor to show his book to me?
　3. I forgot to bring my textbook. Can I ask my neighbor to let me look at his book?
　4. I forgot to bring my textbook. Can I ask my neighbor to show his book to me?

　　　厳密には
　　　　look at = long enough to read
　　　　show = can be done in 1/2 second
　　の意味であるから，1 や 3 の方が 2 や 4 の使い方よりもよい。

▶**これからは教科書を忘れないようにします。**
　I will be careful not to forget my textbook.

▶**数学の教科書を間違えて持ってきました。**
　I brought my math textbook by mistake.

▶**教科書はどのように予習したらいいんですか。**
　How should we study our textbook before class?
　How should we study our textbook beforehand?

▶何回このダイアローグを読むのですか。
How many times are we supposed to read this dialog?

▶教科書はどのように復習したらいいんでしょうか。
How should we review our textbook?
How should we go over our textbook?

▶教科書の上手な使い方を説明してください。
Could you tell us a better way of using our textbook?
Could you tell us how to use our textbook effectively?
Could you tell us how to use our textbook well?

▶実力考査には，教科書の問題も出ますか。
Does the proficiency test cover anything in our textbook?
Does the proficiency test cover our textbook?

▶教科書を徹底的に勉強すれば，大学入試は大丈夫ですか。
1. Will we be all right in the entrance exams if we study our textbook thoroughly?
2. Will we be all right on the entrance exams if we study our textbook thoroughly?
3. Will we be all right on the entrance exams if we thoroughly study our textbook?

　　in the entrance exams でも on the entrance exams でもよい。
　　副詞の位置は比較的自由であるが，1 や 2 の thoroughly の位置の方が，3 の thoroughly の位置よりも自然である。

▶どこから読めばいいんでしょうか。
1. Where should I start reading?
2. From where should I read?

　　「どこから」という日本語を英訳すると 2 のように From where ...? と言いたくなるが，1 のように Where ...? のように聞くのが自然である。

▶どんなところが大切ですか。
What things are important?
What should I pay special attention to?

▶今日の大事なポイントは何ですか。
What are the most important points today?

▶なぜそこはそのようになるのですか。
1. **Why should it be that way?**
2. **Why should that be as it is?**
    1の方が，2よりも自然な表現である。

▶少し考えさせてください。
Please let me think for a while.
Please give me some time to think.

▶一晩考えさせてください。
Please let me sleep on that.
    sleep は「眠り」という意味の名詞としても，「眠る」という意味の動詞としても使うが，sleep on で「(問題などを) 一晩考える」「(決定を) 翌日にもちこす」という意味にも用いる。

▶今から何をすればいいのでしょうか。
What should we do now?

C　辞書

単語のつづりは辞書を引いて確かめなさい。
　Check the spelling by using your dictionary.

新しい単語に出くわしたら，辞書で調べなさい。
　When you come across a new word, look it up in the dic-

tionary.
When you come across a new word, consult the dictionary.

その単語を辞書を引いて確かめなさい。
Look up the word in the dictionary.
Look the word up in the dictionary.

その言葉は辞書に載っていますか。
Can you find the word in your dictionary?

辞書の使い方を説明しましょう。
Let me explain how to use a dictionary.
Let me tell you how to use a dictionary.

まだ，辞書の使い方がわからない人はいますか。
Is there anyone who does not know how to use the dictionary yet?
Is there anyone who does not know how to use a dictionary yet?

いつも英語の授業には辞書を持ってくるようにしなさい。
Try to bring your dictionary with you whenever you have an English class.
Try to bring your dictionary with you whenever you have English class.

辞書を持っていない人は手を上げてごらんなさい。
1. Raise your hand if you don't have a dictionary.
2. Raise your hand if you didn't bring a dictionary.
3. Raise your hand if you didn't bring your dictionary.
4. If you don't have dictionary, raise your hand.
5. Those who do not have a dictionary, raise your hand.

　　５の表現はネイティブスピーカーによっても使われるが，１〜

4 の方が使用頻度が高い。

辞書はいつも引かなくてはいけません。
1. **You must always use a dictionary.**
2. **You must always use dictionaries.**
　　生徒は，英語の辞書は 1 冊しか持っていないことが多いので，1 の方がふさわしい。

辞書は引けば引くほど慣れてきます。
The more you use your dictionary, the more you will get used to it.

一度引いた単語や文章にアンダーラインを引くと記憶に残りやすいでしょう。
1. **If you underline the words or sentences that you look up, they will stay in your mind.**
2. **If you underline the words or sentences that you once looked up, they will stay in mind.**
3. ***If you underline the words or sentences that you once looked up, they will stick to your mind.**
　　1 が最も自然な言い方である。3 のように，stick to ... mind という表現は少し奇異である。

ぼろぼろになるまで，辞書を使いなさい。
Use your dictionary until it gets worn to tatters.

辞書は大切にすればいつまでも使えます。
If you take good care of your dictionary, you can use it for a long time.

君たちはどんな辞書を使っていますか。
1. **What kind of dictionary have you been using?**
2. **What kinds of dictionaries have you been using?**

1，2のいずれでもよい。1は1種類の辞書を，2は複数の辞書を念頭に入れた表現である。
　　最近では電子辞書を使う人が多くなった。電子辞書は electronic dictionary, computerized dictionary, electronic lexicon, IC dictionary などの言い方がある。以下，辞書に関係した表現で，必要に応じて「辞書」を「電子辞書」に置き換えて言うとよい。

辞書には多くの種類があります。
There are many kinds of dictionaries.

目的に合った辞書を使うことが大切です。
It is important to use a dictionary that fits your purpose.

できるだけ英英辞書を使うようにしましょう。
Let's try to use an English-English dictionary as much as we can.
Let's try to use an English-English dictionary as much as possible.

辞書ほど頼りになるものはありません。
Nothing is more dependable than a dictionary.
　　これは教師が大げさに言った表現である。辞書にも誤りはある。特に和英辞書を使うときには注意を要する。和英辞書にはあたかも1つの日本語にぴったり相当する英語があるかのように書かれているが，register に注意しないと木に竹を接いだような英文が生まれやすい。

辞書が常に正しいとは限りません。
1. **Dictionaries are not always accurate.**
2. **Dictionaries are not always right.**
3. ***Dictionaries are not always true.**
　　辞書が「正確である」と述べるときには，accurate の方が right や true よりもよい。

辞書に書かれた発音記号が読めますか。
　Can you read the phonetic symbols written in the dictionary?

小さな辞書は弱形の発音を載せていません。
　Small dictionaries do not take up the pronunciation of weak forms.

俗語は普通の辞書には載っていないことが多いから，大きな辞書で調べなさい。
　Ordinary dictionaries do not usually take up slang expressions, so look them up in large dictionaries.

この単語は普通の辞書には載っていないでしょう。
　Ordinary dictionaries may not have this word.
　Ordinary dictionaries may not take up this word.

単語のつづりを言いますから，辞書で意味を確かめてください。
1. I'm going to give you the spelling. Please check the meaning in your dictionary.
2. As I give you the spelling, please check the meaning in your dictionary.
3. I'm going to give you the spelling, so please check the meaning in your dictionary.
4. *As I will give you the spellings, please check the meaning in your dictionary.

　　例文では word となっているが，もし2語以上あればもちろん words と言わなくてはいけない。

　　日本語の「から」をあえて as を使って英訳すると不自然な英文になる。1の方が2や3よりも自然な英語である。

　　4では as に導かれる節の中で助動詞の will を使っているが，これは正しい用法ではない。

　　1と2とはやや異なる意味を持つ。つまり，2は次の単語のつ

づりを言う前に，意味を調べる必要があるということを暗示するが，1にはそのようなニュアンスはない。

彼は「生き字引」です。
He is a walking dictionary.

▶辞書の使い方を説明してください。
Could you explain how to use a dictionary?
Could you tell me how to use a dictionary?

▶辞書の上手な使い方を教えてください。
1. Please tell me how to use a dictionary effectively.
2. Please tell me how to use a dictionary efficiently.
3. Please tell me how to use a dictionary well.
   effectively が efficiently や well よりも自然である。

▶この電子辞書の引き方を教えてください。
Please tell us how to use this electronic dictionary.

▶この単語は，私の辞書には載っていません。
1. My dictionary does not have this word.
2. This word is not in my dictionary.
3. *My dictionary does not carry this word.
   3の carry は新聞などで見かけるが，この場合には自然に響かない。

▶昨日習った単語の言葉は，私の辞書に載っていませんでした。
The word we learned yesterday is not listed in my dictionary.
   listed の代わりに carried を使うこともできるが，全く省いて
      The word we learned yesterday is not in my dictionary.
   のように表現してもよい。

▶辞書には，この単語のたくさんの意味が載っていますが，この場合，どの意味が一番いいのでしょうか。
The dictionary shows many meanings for this word. Which one fits in this case?
There are many meanings of this word in the dictionary, but which one fits in this case?
There are many meanings of this word in the dictionary, but which one is the best in this case?
This word has many meanings in the dictionary, but which one is the best in this case?

▶テキストが難しすぎて，いつも辞書ばかり引いています。
The textbook is too difficult, so I always have to use my dictionary.

▶いくら辞書を引いても単語を覚えられません。
No matter how often I use my dictionary, I'm not able to learn words.
No matter how often I use my dictionary, I'm not able to acquire words.

▶辞書は毎日学校に持ってこなければいけませんか。
Do we have to bring our dictionaries to school every day?

▶辞書を持ってくるのを忘れました。
I forgot to bring a dictionary with me.

▶友人から辞書を借りてもよいですか。
May I borrow a dictionary from one of my friends?

▶英語の辞書にはどんな種類があるのですか。
What kinds of English dictionaries do you have?

▶書店には数多くの辞書があるので，どれを買っていいのかわかりません。
1. I don't know which dictionary I should get, as there are so many in the book stores.
2. I don't know which dictionary I should get, since there are so many in the book stores.
 ネイティブスピーカーの中には，1の方を2よりも好む人が多いようである。

▶和英の辞書を買いたいのですが，どれがいいでしょうか。
1. I'd like to buy a Japanese-English dictionary, but which one do you recommend?
2. I'd like to buy a Japanese-English dictionary, but what would you recommend?
 1の方が2よりもよい。「どれが」という日本語は what という英語を連想するかもしれないが，which という語の方が，より具体的である。

▶和英辞書では，どこの出版社が一番いいですか。
Which is the best publisher of Japanese-English dictionaries?

▶英英辞書では，どこの出版社が一番いいですか。
Which publisher puts out the best English-English dictionaries?

▶今度の試験では辞書を使ってもいいのですか。
Can we use our dictionary on the next test?

D 黒板・チョーク

黒板で説明しよう。
　　Let me explain it on the board.
　　I'll explain it on the board.

これは大切だから，板書しましょう。
　　This is important. I will write it on the board.

新出単語を黒板に書いてみます。
　　Let me write the new words on the blackboard.
　　I'll write the new words on the blackboard.
　　　blackboard の発音は，black の部分を強く発音する。black も board も同じ強さで発音すると「黒い板」の意味になる。その場合は2語に分ける。

特に重要な文に下線を引きました。
　　I underlined the especially important sentences.

黒板の文について，何か質問はありませんか。
　　Don't you have any questions on the sentence on the board?

黒板の3番目の文について，1つ質問をします。
　　Let me ask you a question on the third sentence on the board.

黒板の文について，何かコメントはありませんか。
　　Do you have any comments on the sentence on the board?

これは消さないようにしてください。
　　1. Please don't erase this.

2. **Please try not to erase this.**
     日本語には 2 の方がぴったり当てはまるが，1 の方が自然な英語である。

黒板を消してもいいですか。
  May I erase the board?

▶まだ消さないでください。
  Please don't erase the board yet.

▶左側は消してもかまいません。
  You can erase the left side of the board.

まだ書いている人は，書き終わったら全部消しておいてください。
  Those who are still copying, please erase everything on the board after copying.
  Those who are still copying, please erase everything on the board after you finish.

これはピリオドではなくて，黒板の傷です。
  1. **This is not a period but a scratch on the board.**
  2. ***This is not a period but a scratch in the board.**
     2 では前置詞 in が使われているが，in では黒板の表面ではなくて黒板の内部に傷がある印象を与える。1 の on の場合には黒板の表面に傷があることになる。

だれが黒板を消すことになっていますか。
  Who is supposed to erase the board?

衛藤君，黒板をきれいにしてください。
  Etoh-kun, please clean the board.

授業の前に黒板をよく消しておきなさい。
Erase the board completely before class.
Clean the board before class.

黒板の粉をきれいにしておきなさい。
Clean the chalk tray.
Clean out the chalk tray.

「チョークの受け皿をきれいにしておきなさい。」という英訳である。これを，
*Clean the chalk dust.
のように言うと，「chalk dust をきれいにする」意味になってしまう。

上記の文の代わりに，
Remove the chalk dust.
と言ってもよい。

黒板の粉をちゃんと取っておきなさい。
Take the chalk dust out.

黒板ふきが汚いね。
1. **This eraser is dirty.**
2. **The eraser is dirty.**

もし教師が黒板ふきを持っているのであれば，1 の方が 2 よりもよい。

黒板ふきはどこにあるのだろう。
1. **I wonder where the eraser is.**
2. **Where's the eraser?**
3. **Where's the blackboard eraser?**
4. ***Where's the board eraser?**

「黒板ふき」は blackboard eraser と言うが，冗長な言葉なので，通常は eraser とだけ言う。board eraser とは言わないので 4 は誤りである。

222　Ⅲ　授業活動

ここにチョークがあります。
Here's a piece of chalk.

チョークがなくなった。
I've run out of chalk.

赤いチョークを使いなさい。
Use a piece of red chalk.

赤いチョークがないね。
1. **There's no red chalk.**
2. **There is no red chalk.**

　　1は2の短縮形であるが，There's ... という形の方が自然な言い方である。

カラーのチョークがほしい。
I want some colored chalk.

カラーのチョークがあればなあ。
I wish I had some colored chalk.

　　アメリカ英語は color，イギリス英語は colour。

白いチョークが3本ほしい。
1. **I'd like to have three pieces of white chalk.**
2. **I need three pieces of white chalk.**
3. ***I need three white chalk.**

　　1と2は正しい。1の方が2よりもやや丁寧な表現である。chalk は不可算名詞であるから，3のように three white chalk のように言うことはできない。

だれかチョークを取ってきてくれませんか。
1. **Would anyone like to get some chalk for me?**
2. ***Could anybody like to get some chalk for me?**

would も could も同じように使える場合があるが，Could 〜 like ...? という言い方は誤りである。for me は省略できる。

だれかチョークを職員室から持ってきてくれませんか。
1. Would someone go and get some chalk from the staff room for me?
2. Would anyone go and get some chalk from the staff room for me?
　　疑問文では any ... を使うというルールがあるが，《肯定の応答》を予期する場合には some ... を使うのが普通である。1の方がよい。

だれかチョークがどこにあるか知っていますか。
Does anyone know where the chalk is kept?
Does anyone know where the chalk is?

隣の部屋にチョークがないかどうか見てきてくれないか。
Go and see if there's any chalk next door.

▶たった今おっしゃったことを黒板に書いてください。
Could you write what you said just now on the board?

▶黒板に書いて，詳しく説明してください。
Could you write it on the board and explain it in greater detail?
Could you write it on the board and explain it to us in more detail?
Could you write it on the board and explain it in more detail?

▶黒板に書かれた3番目の文を，文法的に説明してください。
1. Could you explain the grammar of the third sentence written on the board?
2. Could you explain the third sentence written on the

board from a grammatical point of view?
 3. Could you explain the third sentence written on the board grammatically?
 4. *Could you grammatically explain the third sentence written on the board?

　　1は2を平易に述べた言い方である。
　　3は,「文法的に説明する」のか,「文法的に黒板に書かれた文」を説明するのかわかりづらい。2のように言えば誤解が少ない。
　　4は「文法的な間違いをせずに黒板に書かれた3番目の文章を説明してください」という意味に解されるからふさわしくない。

▶最初の行の2番目の単語は何ですか。
What is the second word on the first line?

▶野中先生, beautiful のつづりが間違っています。
 1. Mr. Nonaka, *beautiful* is misspelled.
 2. Mr. Nonaka, I am afraid the spelling of *beautiful* is not correct.
 3. Mr. Nonaka, I am afraid your spelling of *beautiful* is not correct.

　　2と3は正しい文であるが,やや冗長な感じがする。1の方がよい。

▶このへんに書いてもいいですか。
 1. May I write here?
 2. May I write around here?

　　「この辺に」という日本語に相当する英語表現に around here という言い方があるが, 2のように around here を使うと, this part of the room というニュアンスが強くなる。1の方がよい。

▶口頭で説明しにくいので,黒板に答えを書いてもいいですか。
 1. Since it is difficult to explain, may I do it on the board?
 2. Since it is difficult to explain orally, may I go up to the

board and write the answer?
3. **Since it is difficult to explain orally, can I go up to the board and write the answer?**

　　「口頭で」という日本語を無理に orally という英語に訳さなくてもよい。
　　2 や 3 の方がもとの日本文に近いが，1 の方が自然な表現である。may と can はいずれでもよい。

▶黒板が見えません。横に動いていただけませんか。
I can't see the board. Could you move over a little bit?

　　move over のかわりに，move aside, step aside と言ってもよい。

8　授業後・家庭学習の課題

A　宿題を出す

これは宿題にします。
　This will be an assignment.
　This will be a homework assignment.
　This will be homework.

このページを宿題にします。
　This page is your homework.

この課を今週の宿題にします。
　This lesson is your homework for this week.

今日は宿題はありません。
1. **I am not going to give you any assignment tonight.**
2. **I am not going to give you any assignment today.**

3. **There's no assignment tonight.**
　　日本語では「今日は宿題はない」というように,「今日」という言葉を使うのが普通であるが, 英語的表現としては today よりも tonight の方が自然である。ただし, tonight は, 締め切りが翌日の場合である。

来週までに宿題をやってきてください。
Finish the assignment by next week.

このプリントを明日までにやって, 授業のときに提出しなさい。
Complete this handout and turn it in tomorrow in class.
Finish this handout and turn it in tomorrow in class.

練習問題の残りを家でやってきなさい。
Complete the rest of the exercise at home.
　　the rest of the exercise を簡単に this exercise と言い換えてもよい。

練習問題（5）は, 家でやっておきなさい。
Complete Exercise (5) at home.

今日の宿題は3課の新出単語を調べてくることです。
1. **Your homework for today is to check the meaning of the new words in Lesson 3.**
2. **Your homework for today is to check the meaning of the new words for Lesson 3.**
　　... the new words in Lesson 3 でも the new words for Lesson 3 でもよい。

明日は教科書の35ページの小テストをするので, 今晩はよく勉強しておくように。
You're going to have a quiz on page 35 of the text, so study hard tonight.

練習問題の残りを家でやり終えて，この次の時間に提出しなさい。
1. Finish the rest of the exercise at home, and turn it in next time.
2. Finish the rest of the exercise at home, and turn it in at the next class.
3. Finish the rest of the exercise at home, and turn it in at our next class.

　　1の next time という言い方が最も自然である。

来週の水曜日までに，15 課を準備しておきなさい。
Prepare Lesson 15 for next Wednesday.

宿題に，29 ページの練習問題の（4）をしてきなさい。
For your homework, do Exercise (4) on page 29.

この随筆の内容を 100 字以内の英語でまとめて，来週の月曜日に提出してください。
Summarize this essay in 100 English words, and turn it in next Monday.

教室を出るときに，宿題の用紙を取りなさい。
Pick up a copy of the homework as you leave.

今度の中間テストは，宿題と大いに関係があります。
This coming midterm exam will have a lot to do with the homework.
This coming midterm exam will be based mainly on the homework.

8ページと9ページの問題をやっておきなさい。近いうちにそこに関連した試験をします。
1. Do the exercises on pages 8 and 9. There will be a test on them in the near future.

2. **Do the exercises on page 8 and page 9. There will be a test on them sometime soon.**

　2のように page 8 and page 9 と言うよりも，1のように pages 8 and 9 と言う方がよい。

5課の新出単語を勉強しておきなさい。この次の時間にテストをします。
Learn the new words in Lesson 5. I will give you a quiz next time.

Learn the new words for Lesson 5. I will give you a quiz next time.

今日授業で学んだことをよく復習しておきなさい。来月のいつか，それについてテストをします。
Review what you have learned in class today. I will test you on it sometime next month.

Review what you have learned in class today. I will give you a test on it sometime next month.

Go over what you have learned in class today. I will test you on it sometime next month.

Go over what you have learned in class today. There will be a test on it sometime next month.

Go over what you have learned in class today. You can expect a test on it sometime next month.

Go over what you have learned in class today. You can expect to be tested on it sometime next month.

15ページと19ページがテストに出るので，よく勉強しておきなさい。
Pages 15 and 19 will both be on the test, so pay special attention to them.

Pages 15 and 19 will both be appearing on the test, so pay special attention to them.

Pages 15 and 19 will both appear on the test, so pay special attention to them.

be 動詞の次に appearing を入れてもよいし，will appear ～としてもよい。

▶宿題はいつまでに出したらいいのですか。
When is the assignment due?
What is the due date for the assignment?
When should we turn in the assignment?
When do we have to turn in the assignment?

▶宿題は何に書いたらいいんですか。
What shall we write the assignment on?
What should we write the assignment on?

▶宿題はレポート用紙に書くんですか。
Are we supposed to write the assignment on report paper?

▶この宿題はテストに出ますか。
1. **Will this assignment be put on the test?**
2. **Will this assignment be included in the test?**

   1の方が自然な表現である。

B 宿題の確認

宿題はやってきましたか。
Did you do your homework?
Have you done your homework?
Have you finished your homework?
Have you completed your homework?

宿題を忘れないように。
1. **Don't forget your homework.**
2. **Remember your homework.**

   1の方が2よりもよい。

宿題をするのを忘れないように。
1. **Don't forget to do your homework.**
2. **Remember to do your homework.**

   1は「宿題を必ずするように！」という気持ちを強く伝えるが、2は気持ちの表し方が弱いというニュアンスの違いがある。

必ず宿題を持ってくるように。

   Make sure you bring your homework with you.
   Be sure to bring your homework with you.

宿題は必ず期限を守ってください。
1. **Be sure to turn in your homework on time.**
2. **Be sure to turn your homework in on time.**
3. **Be sure to turn in the homework assignment by the due date.**
4. **Be sure to turn in the homework assignment by the date it is due.**

   1や2の方が、3や4よりもよく使われる表現である。

宿題は今週の金曜日が期限です。

   The assignment is due this Friday.

宿題をきちっとしないと、単位がありませんよ。

   If you don't do your homework regularly, you will not get any units for this course.

宿題でわからなかった問題がありますか。

   Do you have any questions on the homework assignment?

宿題をまだ終えてない人は手を上げなさい。
　Those who have not finished the homework, raise your hand.
　Is there anyone who hasn't finished the homework? Raise your hand if you haven't.

▶宿題の量が多すぎます。
　1. This assignment is too long.
　2. This assignment asks for too much.
　3. The assignment is too much.
　　　3は日本語に近いが，あまり自然な言い方ではない。1や2のように言いたい。

C　宿題を受け取る

宿題は難しかったですか。
　Was the homework assignment difficult?
　Was the homework assignment hard?
　Was the homework assignment tough?

宿題を提出してください。
　Turn in the homework assignment.
　Hand in the homework assignment.
　Turn in your homework assignment.
　Hand in your homework assignment.

授業が終わったら宿題を提出しなさい。
　Hand in your homework assignment when the class is over.
　Hand in your homework assignment when you leave today.

宿題を提出するのを遅れないように。
  1. **Don't turn in your homework late.**
  2. **Don't be late in turning in your homework.**
     2よりも1の方が自然な表現である。

宿題を前に順に送って提出しなさい。
  Hand in your reports by passing them forward.
  Hand in your papers by passing them to the person in front of you.
     イギリス英語では，forwardという語を「前に」という意味の副詞として使う場合には，forwardsのようにsを付けて使うことが多い。

それぞれの列の最後の人がエッセイを集めてください。
  Could the last person in each row collect the essays, please?
  Would the last person in each row collect the essays, please?
     couldとwouldの丁寧さの度合いはネイティブスピーカーによって意見が異なる。同じ程度と考えてよい。

▶**宿題を忘れた人はどうしたらいいですか。**
  What should those who forgot to do their homework do?

▶**宿題をしていましたが，家に忘れてきました。**
  1. **I did my homework, but I left it at home.**
  2. **I had done the homework, but I left it at home.**
     この2つの文章はいずれでもよいが，I did my homework ... の形がより自然な表現である。

▶**宿題の提出は来週でもかまいませんか。**
  1. **May I turn in my homework next week?**
  2. **Can I turn in my homework next week?**

3. **May I turn my homework in next week?**
4. **Can I turn my homework in next week?**
5. **May I turn in the homework next week?**
6. **Can I turn in the homework next week?**

　1, 3, 5 の may は標準的な表現。2, 4, 6 の can はくだけた感じのする表現である。また, can を使うと lazy, whiny な響きがする。

　文法的には my homework でも the homework でもよいが, my homework という形を好むネイティブスピーカーの方が多いようである。

　動詞＋前置詞で句動詞を作る場合, turn in my homework でもよいし, turn my homework in でもよい。ただし, 代名詞を目的語にとる場合には, turn it in は正しいが, *turn in it は誤りとなる。

▶すみません。宿題を忘れました。
I'm sorry. I forgot to do my assignment.
I'm sorry. I forgot to do my homework.
I'm sorry. I forgot about my homework.

▶すみません。宿題を持ってくるのを忘れました。
I'm sorry. I forgot to bring my homework.

▶宿題をしましたが家に忘れました。ごめんなさい。
I did my homework, but I left it at home. I'm sorry.

▶宿題を家に忘れましたので，明日持ってきてもいいですか。
I left my homework at home. May I bring it tomorrow?
I left my homework at home. Can I bring it tomorrow?

D　レポート

5課についてレポートを書きなさい。
　Write a report on Lesson 5.

レポートは今月の15日までに提出してください。
　Turn in your report by the 15th of this month.

レポートに，名前を書くのを忘れないようにしなさい。
　Don't forget to write your name on your report.

レポートを後ろから順番に集めてください。
　Collect the reports in order starting from the back of the class.
　Collect the reports in order starting from the back of the room.
　Collect the reports in order starting from the back row.
　Collect the reports in order starting with the back of the class.
　Collect the reports in order starting with the back row.
　　start from の方が start with よりもよく使われる。
　　the back of the class の方が the back row よりも自然な表現である。
　　日本人は report という語をしばしば使用する。厳密には report や essay, composition には次のような違いがある。
　　A report is an account of something that has happened or a summary of one's research. An essay is a statement of one's opinion on an issue. A composition is a story written by the student.

▶提出期限を延ばしてください。
　Could you postpone the due date?

Could you postpone the date due?
Could you put off the deadline?
Could you put the deadline off?

▶提出期限にレポートが間に合いません。期限を延ばしてください。
I can't turn in the report by the due date. Could you put it off?
I can't turn in the report by the due date. Could I have a little longer?
I can't turn in the report by the due date. Could we have a little longer?
I can't turn in the report by the due date. Could I have a little more time?
I can't turn in the report by the due date. Could we have a little more time?

▶提出期限にレポートが間に合いません。もっと時間をください。
I can't turn in the report by the due date. Could you give me some more time?

9　授業でよく使う表現

◇話を切り出すとき

授業を始めるにあたっての表現は，p. 63 の授業開始を参考のこと。

◇授業の予定を述べるとき
今日は7課をやります。
Today, we will do Lesson 7.

今日は7課から始めます。
We will begin with Lesson 7 today.

◇順序だって話すとき
First ... Second ... Third ... Finally ...
Firstly ... Secondly ... Thirdly ... Finally ...
To begin with,
To start with,
In the first place,
In the beginning,
In the second place,
Second of all,

上記の表現は，いずれも formal speaking や writing で用いられる。

◇「…と言われている」と言うとき
It has been said (that) ...
It has been claimed (that) ...
It has been asserted (that) ...
It has been argued (that) ...
It has been advocated (that) ...

上記の表現は，いずれも formal speaking や writing で用いられる。

◇「〜には…と書かれている」と言うとき
The Bible says (that) ...
Today's newspaper says (that) ...

Informal な表現である。

◇「したがって…」と言うとき
1. **Then,**
2. **Because of 〜**
3. **This [That] is why ...**

4. **Therefore,**
5. **Thus,**
6. **(And) Hence,**
7. **As a result,**
8. **As a consequence,**
9. **For that reason,**
10. **For this reason,**
11. **Accordingly,**
12. **Consequently,**
13. **In consequence,**
14. **So,**
15. **And so,**

　　1 〜 3 は standard，3 〜 13 は formal，14 〜 15 は informal な表現である。

　　12 の方が 13 よりは頻繁に使われる。

　　Thus の前に，しばしばコロンやセミコロン，あるいは and を置く。

◇「〜によると」と言うとき
1. **By 〜**
2. **According to 〜**
3. **In accordance with 〜**
4. **In line with 〜**

　　1 と 2 は standard，3 と 4 は formal な表現である。

◇「伝説によると」と言うとき
Legend has it that ...

　　formal な表現である。

◇「〜するために」と言うとき
... to ...
... in order to 〜
... in order that ...

... so that ...
   ... so as to 〜
   　　いずれも standard な表現である。

◇「〜について話す」と言うとき
   1. **speak about 〜**
   2. **discuss 〜**
   3. **go into 〜**
   4. **elaborate on 〜**
   5. **talk about 〜**
   6. **tell us about 〜**
   7. **tell me about 〜**
   8. **talk of 〜**
   9. **speak of 〜**

   　　1〜3 は standard な表現である。2 と 3 は，少し詳しく話すような場合に使う。4 は formal な表現で，詳しく話す場合に使う。5〜7 は informal な表現である。8 と 9 は，こうした状況では，ほかの表現ほど用いられない。

◇「〜から判断すると」と言うとき
   1. **Judging from 〜**
   2. **Judging by 〜**
   3. **Looking at 〜**
   4. **Going by 〜**

   　　1 と 2 は standard，3 と 4 は informal な表現である。

◇「〜にもかかわらず」と言うとき
   1. **Although ...**
   2. **Even though ...**
   3. **Even if ...**
   4. **Admitting (that) ...**
   5. **Granted (that) ...**
   6. **In spite of 〜**

7. **Albeit ...**
8. **Despite** ～
9. **Though ...**

　1～5 は standard, 6 はやや formal, 7 は formal, 8 はやや informal, 9 は informal なニュアンスがある。

　though は even though と同様な意味で使われるが, 口語的な表現である。しかし, even though と言うが, even although とは言えない。

◇「～については」と言うとき
1. **Regarding** ～
2. **Concerning** ～
3. **As for** ～
4. **As to** ～
5. **As far as ... is concerned,**
6. **Relating to** ～
7. **In terms of** ～
8. **In regard to** ～
9. **In regards to** ～
10. **From the viewpoint of** ～
11. **In reference to** ～
12. **In connection with** ～
13. **With respect to** ～
14. **With regard to** ～
15. **With reference to** ～
16. **About** ～
17. **On,**
18. **Respecting** ～

　「～については, 関しては」という表現は数多い。1～7 は standard, 8～15 は formal, 16～17 は informal な表現である。18 は頻繁には使われていない。

◇詳しく述べるとき
1. **In detail,**
2. **To be more specific,**
3. **More particularly,**
4. **Elaborately**
5. **Minutely**
6. **At great length**

　　1～3 は standard な表現である。4～6 は文頭では使われない。
　　　He explained it elaborately.
　　　He examined the problem minutely.
　　　He went into it at great length.

◇例をあげて言うとき
1. **For example,**
2. **For instance,**
3. **To take ... as an example,**
4. **As an example,**
5. **... such as A, (B and C)**
6. **By way of illustration,**
7. **To illustrate my point,**

　　1～5 は standard，6 は formal，7 は informal な表現である。

◇特徴について述べるとき
have the characteristics of ～
be characterized by ～
have the features of ～

　　いずれも standard な表現としてよく使われる。

◇ものの大きさを比較するとき
AはBの5倍である。
　A is 5 times as big as B.

AはBの２倍である。
  A is twice as big as B.

AはBの５分の１である。
  A is one fifth of B.

AはBの５分の３である。
  A is three fifths of B.

AはBの半分である。
  A is one half of B.

AはBの 30 パーセントである。
  A is thirty percent of B.

AとBとの割合は２対３である。
  1. The ratio of A to B is two to three.
  2. The ratio between A and B is two to three.
    １はよく使われる表現であるが，２はあまり使われる表現ではない。

◇「きりがない」と言うとき
数え上げればきりがない
  1. The list is endless.
  2. Too many to mention
  3. Too numerous to mention
  4. And so on and so forth
    １〜３は standard，４は informal な表現である。

◇同じことを繰り返して言うとき
  1. To recapitulate 〜
  2. Again,
  3. To repeat myself,

1 は standard，2 と 3 は informal な表現である。

◇換言するとき
1. **In other words,**
2. **To put it another way,**
3. **That is,**
4. **i.e.**
5. **That is to say,**

　1 ～ 3 は standard，4 は formal，5 はやや informal な表現である。

　i.e. は id est というラテン語の省略形で，[áií:] と発音したり，[ðætíz] と発音したりする。i.e. も id est も改まった感じのする表現である。頻度から言うと，id est と書き表すことはあまりない。

◇わかりやすく証明するとき
To illustrate ～

◇二つの異なる意見を述べるとき
1. **However,**
2. **On the other hand,**
3. **On the contrary,**
4. **Conversely,**
5. **But then,**
6. **Then again,**
7. **But,**

　1 ～ 3 は standard，4 は formal，5 ～ 6 はやや informal，7 は informal な表現である。

◇付け加えて言うとき
1. **On top of that,**
2. **In addition,**
3. **Additionally,**
4. **Besides,**

5. **Also,**
6. **As well,**
7. **Moreover,**
8. **What is more,**
9. **Furthermore,**
10. **Further,**
11. **Likewise,**
12. **I may add (that) ...**

　　1 〜 11 はいずれも standard，12 は informal な表現である。9 の方が 10 よりもよく使われる。

◇確信して言うとき

1. **Certainly,**
2. **It is certain (that) ...**
3. **It is quite natural (that) ...**
4. **There is no doubt (that) ...**
5. **There is no question (that) ...**
6. **There is no denying that ...**
7. **It is quite clear (that) ...**
8. **I'm absolutely sure that ...**
9. **I am convinced (that) ...**
10. **I have a deep conviction (that) ...**
11. **I am 100 percent sure (that) ...**
12. **Nobody denies the fact (that) ...**
13. **It is crystal clear (that) ...**
14. **I am sure (that) ...**
15. **I am positive that ...**
16. **I bet (that) ...**

　　1 〜 11 は standard，12 は formal，13 はやや informl，14 〜 16 は informal な表現である。

　　16 は，bet が「〈お金など〉を賭ける」という意味が原義であることから，強くそう思うと言うときに使う。

◇同意するとき

1. **Of course,**
2. **I agree with** 〜
3. **I agree to** 〜
4. **Agree with the idea (that) ...**
5. **I agree to the idea (that) ...**
6. **I approve** 〜
7. **I consent to** 〜
8. **I assent to** 〜
9. **I am in line with** 〜
10. **Actually,**
11. **In fact,**
12. **In effect,**
13. **Indeed,**
14. **In reality,**
15. **I am confident of ...**
16. **I am positive of ...**
17. **I am sure about ...**
18. **I am sure of ...**
19. **I am in agreement with** 〜
20. **I am in accord with** 〜
21. **I go along with** 〜
22. **I am for** 〜
23. **Truly,**
24. **Really,**
25. **In truth,**

　1〜17 は standard, 18 はやや formal, 19 は formal, 20〜24 は informal な表現である。25 はあまり頻繁には使われない。6 は許可を与えるような状況で使われる。7 は依頼を受け入れるときなどに使われる。6 の方が 7 よりもよく使われる。11〜13 は in reality の意味である。17 と 18 では、of の方が formal な感じで、about に比べて確実性が高い。

◇反対意見を述べるとき
基本的には「同意する」表現を否定すればよいが，そのほか次のような言い方も可能である。

disagree with ～
be opposed to ～
be against ～

上記の表現は，いずれも standard な表現である。言い方を和らげるには，相手の主張にまずは理解を示し，but など使って意見を述べるとよい。

◇仮定して言うとき
Figuratively,
Figuratively speaking,

いずれも standard な表現である。Generally (speaking), Frankly (speaking) などの場合と同様に，speaking はあっても省略してもよい。

◇自分の考えを言うとき
1. **I think (that) ...**
2. **I believe (that) ...**
3. **I assume (that) ...**
4. **I suppose (that) ...**
5. **I presume (that) ...**
6. **In my opinion,**
7. **In my view,**
8. **In my observation,**
9. **It is my belief (that) ...**
10. **My belief is (that) ...**
11. **My thought is (that) ...**
12. **I feel (that) ...**
13. **I figure (that) ...**

1 ～ 7 は standard, 8 ～ 11 は formal, 12 はやや informal, 13 は informal な表現である。9 は 10 よりもよく使われる。11

はほかの表現よりも頻度は低いようである。

◇自分の言うことをまとめるとき
私が言いたいことは，
1. **What I want to say is ...**
2. **What I am trying to say is (that) ...**
3. **What I mean is (that) ...**
4. **What I am driving at is (that) ...**
5. **What I am referring to is (that) ...**
6. **I want to say (that) ...**
7. **I just want to say (that) ...**
8. **I am saying (that) ...**

1～4 は standard，5 は formal，6 と 7 はやや informal，8 は informal な表現である。

◇感想を述べるとき
筆舌に尽くしがたい。
   It's beyond description.
      standard な表現である。

それは想定内でした。
   It was within the scope of my assumption.
      formal な表現である。

それは想像以上でした。
   It was beyond (my) imagination.
      standard な表現である。my はあっても省略してもよい。

◇生徒に必ず何かをしてほしいとき
1. **You have to ...**
2. **You must ...**
3. **Be sure to ...**
4. **You should ...**

5. Make sure ...
6. You ought to ...
7. You had better ...
8. You need to ...
9. Bear in mind (that) ...
10. Keep in mind (that) ...

　　1〜10はいずれもstandardな表現である。ニュアンスの違いは，1〜3は4〜7よりも強い言い方であり，5〜7は，4のshouldと同じ意味である。9と10は，「いつも心に留めておくように」という意味である。1から10は，意味合いの強いものから弱いものの順になっている。

◇本題に戻るとき
話を元に戻しますと…
　　Coming back to the point,
　　Returning to the main point,
　　Getting back to the original topic,
　　Getting back to what I was talking about,
　　Getting back to what I was saying,
　　　いずれもstandardな表現である。

話を少し元に戻しましょう。
　　Let me back up a little bit.
　　　Standardな表現である。

ちょっと脱線しましたが，
　1. **I was sidetracked for a minute, but ...**
　2. **I went off the track for a minute, but ...**
　3. **What I said was beside the point, but ...**
　4. **To get back to what I was talking about, ...**
　5. ***I went off the rails, but ...**
　　1〜4はいずれもstandardな表現である。1と2を比べると，1の方が2よりもよい。

3の文には,「脱線」に相当する言葉はないが, be beside the point は内容的に「脱線する」に当たる。

go off the track とは言っても, 5 のように *go off the rails とは言わない。

本題に入りましょう。
Let's go on to the main subject.
Let's go on to the main topic.
Let's get down to business.

いずれも standard な表現である。

さて,授業を続けましょう。
Well, let's continue with our lesson.

冗談はさておき,
1. Joking aside,
2. Aside from joking,
3. All kidding aside,

1 と 2 は standard な表現であるが, 1 の方が 2 よりもよく使われる。3 は informal な表現である。

今のは冗談です。
1. I was just joking.
2. I was just kidding (you).
3. I was just teasing (you).
4. I was just pulling your leg.
5. I said that just for fun.
6. I said it just for fun.

1 は standard, 2 〜 6 は informal な表現である。

私が言ったことは冗談事ではありません。
1. I was quite serious when I said ...
2. What I said is no joking matter.

3. **I wasn't kidding when I said ...**
　　1, 2 は standard, 3 はやや informal な表現である。

まじめに言うと,
　Seriously,
　In all seriousness,
　　いずれも standard な表現である。

◇忘れる，思い出す
振り返ってみると
　In retrospect,

…と言い忘れるところでした。
　I almost forgot to say that ...

このことを言い忘れたら，私に思い出させてください。
　If I forget to say this, please remind me to say it.
　If I forget to say this, please remind me during class.
　　いずれも standard な表現である。

ちょうど…を思い出した。
　I just remembered (that) ...

それで思い出した。
　1. **That reminds me.**
　2. **It sounds familiar.**
　3. **It rings a bell.**
　4. **It rang a bell.**
　　1, 2 は standard, 3, 4 はやや informal な表現である。
　　3 の ring a bell は口語的表現である。4 のように rang という過去形を使うよりは，3 のように ring という現在形を使う方が自然である。
　　1 は突然何かをしなければならないことを思い出したとき，2

〜4はぼんやりと記憶にあったことをはっきり思い出したときに言う。

ああ，思い出した。アヘン戦争は 1840 年に勃発しました。
　Oh, I just remembered. The Opium War broke out in 1840.
　Oh, I just recalled that the Opium War broke out in 1840.

▶ **enshrine という語の意味をどうしても思い出せません。**
　1. **I can't remember the meaning of the word enshrine.**
　2. **I can't recall the meaning of the word enshrine.**
　3. **I can't recollect the meaning of the word enshrine.**
　　　1，2 は standard，3 は formal な表現である。

◇要約するとき
端的に言うと，
　1. **In short,**
　2. **Briefly,**
　3. **Frankly,**
　4. **Frankly speaking,**
　5. **To be frank,**
　6. **To be frank with you,**
　7. **In all frankness,**
　8. **Honestly,**
　9. **To be honest with you,**
　　　1〜9 はいずれも standard な表現であるが，ニュアンスの違いがある。つまり，1と2は「要点をまとめる」ときに使うが，3〜9は，「あまり好ましくないことについて言おうとする」ときに使う。

要約すると，
　1. **In a word,**
　2. **In one word,**
　3. **In one sentence,**

4. **In short,**
5. **To summarize,**
6. **To sum up,**
7. **In brief,**
8. **In summation,**
9. **In summary,**
10. **To make a long story short,**

　　1〜7 は standard, 8 は formal, 9, 10 はやや informal である。

大雑把に言えば,
Generally speaking,
In general,

　　両方とも standard な表現である。

簡単に言えば,
To be brief,
In short,
In a word,
In a few words,
To put it briefly,

　　いずれも standard な表現である。

作者が言いたいことは,
What the author wants to say is that ...

作者がここで言っていることは,
1. **What the author is saying here is ...**
2. **What the author argues here is that ...**
3. **What the author claims here is that ...**

　　1〜3 はいずれも standard な表現であるが, 1 が最も普通に使われる表現である。

作者は…と言っているようです。
   The author seems to say that ...
   It seems that the author is saying ...
   I think the author is trying to say ...
   いずれも standard な表現である。

◇重要な点を述べるとき
最も重要なことは
   The most important thing is (that) ...

特に重要なことは
   1. **What is particularly important is (that) ...**
   2. **Of particular importance is (that) ...**
   3. **What is of prime importance is (that) ...**
   　　1 は standard，2 と 3 はやや informal な表現である。

◇授業の終わりが近づいたとき
   これに関連した表現は，p. 502 を参考のこと。

◇最後に述べるとき
   Finally,
   Lastly,
   To close,
   In conclusion,
   To conclude
   　　いずれも standard な表現である。

◇授業の終わり
   これに関連した表現は p. 508 を参考のこと。

Ⅳ 授業内容

1 聞くこと

話す前に，まず，聞くことが大事です。
Before you speak, it is important to listen.

聞いた内容が理解できれば，英語が話せるようになります。
You'll be able to speak English if you can understand what you hear.

英語が話せるようになるには，英語が聞き取れないといけません。
In order to be a good speaker of English, you have to be able to understand spoken English.

英語をよく聞いていると，だんだん英語の音に慣れてきます。
1. You'll get used to English sounds as you practice listening to English.
2. As you listen to English well, you'll get used to English sounds.

    1はよいが2はあまり自然な言い方ではない。

話されている英語が聞けるためには，英語の語句をよく理解しておく必要があります。
1. In order for you to able to understand spoken English, it is necessary to understand English words and expres-

sions well.
2. In order for you to able to understand spoken English, it is necessary to understand English words well.
3. In order for you to able to understand spoken English, it is necessary to develop a good vocabulary.

1 はよい。2 はあまり自然ではない。3 はいくぶん意味が異なるが，自然な言い方である。

▶ネイティブスピーカーの言うことが全くわかりません。
1. I can't understand what the native speakers say at all.
2. I can't understand what native speakers say at all.

特定のネイティブスピーカーでない場合には，2 のように言う。

▶英語は少し話せますが，アメリカ人同士が話しているのは理解できません。
1. I can speak English a little, but I can't understand what Americans talk about to each other.
2. I can speak English a little, but I can't understand when Americans talk to each other.
3. I can speak English a little, but I can't understand what Americans say to each other.

1 のように what を使えば talk about のように about が必要で，2 のように what の代わりに when を使えば about は不要である。3 のように say を使えば to を伴う。

▶英語の聞き取りは苦手です。
I am not good at listening to English.

▶聞き取りの力をつけるにはどうしたらよいでしょうか。
How can I improve my listening ability?

▶聞き取りがうまくなる何か特別の方法はありますか。
Is there any special way to improve listening ability?

Is there any special way we can improve our listening ability?
Is there any special way we can improve listening ability?

▶簡単なことは英語で言えますが、聞き取りがほとんど駄目です。
I can say simple things in English, but my listening is very poor.
I can express simple things in English, but I'm not good at listening.
I can express simple things in English, but I'm poor at listening.

▶どんな点に注意して英語の聞き取りをすればよいのでしょうか。
What point should we pay attention to when listening to English?

▶機能語はなぜ聞き取りにくいのでしょうか。
Why is it difficult for us to hear function words?
Why is it difficult for us to catch function words?

▶機能語にはいくら聞いてもわかりにくいものがあります。
1. Some function words are hard for me to catch, no matter how carefully I listen.
2. Some function words are hard for me to catch, no matter how hard I try.
3. Some function words are hard for me to catch, no matter how hard I try to catch them.
4. *I cannot understand some function words no matter how hard I try to catch them.

  上記の場合、catch とは、
    be able to hear the sounds of the function words distinguish their sounds from the sounds of the other words around them

の意味であるから，1のように listen という語を使うか，3のように catch を繰り返すか，あるいは2のように省略する方がよい。4のように understand を使うのはおかしい。

▶読解力と聴解力には何が関係がありますか。
Are reading ability and listening ability related in any way?
Are reading ability and listening ability related?
Is there a relationship between reading ability and listening ability?
Is there any relationship between reading ability and listening ability?

▶ [l] と [r] の区別ができません。
I cannot tell the difference between [l] and [r].
I cannot distinguish between [l] and [r].
I can't make a distinction between [l] and [r].
I never can distinguish between [l] and [r].
I never can distinguish [l] and [r].
I never can distinguish [l] from [r].
I have a hard time distinguishing [l] from [r].
I have great trouble distinguishing [l] from [r].
I have great trouble distinguishing [l] and [r].

母語が日本語であれば，かなり英語が堪能になっても [l] と [r] を聞き取るのは困難な課題であるようだ。ちょうど，ネイティブスピーカーが，日本語の単母音と長母音とをいつまでたっても区別できにくい現象と似ている。

▶ヒアリングの問題は試験に出るのですか。
Will listening exercises be on the test?

2 発音

A 発音全般について

発音が悪くては通じません。
　You can't make yourself understood if your pronunciation is bad.

発音が悪いと，通じないことがあります。
　1. If your pronunciation is not good, you may not be able to make yourself understood.
　2. If your pronunciation is not good, you will sometimes not be able to make yourself understood.
　　　1の方が2よりもよい。

発音に注意しましょう。
　Be careful of your pronunciation.

英語は，正しい発音をマスターすることが大切です。
　In English it is important to master correct pronunciation.

発音は練習していれば次第に上手になります。
　1. You can keep improving your pronunciation as long as you keep practicing.
　2. You can improve your pronunciation as long as you keep practicing.
　　　1と2とは意味が異なる。1と2はそれぞれ
　　　1. Your pronunciation will continue to improve as long as you continue practicing.
　　　2. Provided you keep on practicing pronunciation, you can improve it.

大きな声で読めば読むほど発音はうまくなります。
1. **The more you read out loud, the more your pronunciation will improve.**
2. **The more you read out loud, the more your pronunciation will become improved.**
   1の方が2よりも自然な表現である。

舌がどのように歯に触れるか注意しなさい。
Notice how my tongue touches my teeth.

音の出し方を説明しましょう。
Let me explain how to make the sounds.
I'll explain how to make the sounds.

2番目の音は lion の [l] の音です。
The second sound is [l] as in lion.

あなたは sink と言いましたが、正しい発音を聞いてみましょう。
You said *sink*, but let's listen to the correct pronunciation.

その言葉はまだ正しく発音されていません。
The word is not pronounced correctly yet.

lice と rice という言葉を一緒にしないように。
1. **Try not to confuse the words lice and rice.**
2. **Try not to mix up the words lice and rice.**
   1の方がより自然な英語表現である。
   [l] と [r] の区別は、日本人でも話すときに注意して発音すればネイティブスピーカーに間違えて取られることは少ない。[l] は必ず舌先を上の歯茎に触れるようにし、[r] は舌をのどの奥の方に向けて折り曲げるようにして発音すること。[r] の発音をすると

きには，舌先が口のどの部分にも触れていないようにする。また，[r] を発音するときには，両方の唇をすぼめるようにすることが大切である。

6行目の2番目の語は，[páil] と発音されます。
The second word on line 6 is pronounced [páil].

発音が素晴らしいですよ。
1. **Your pronunciation is very good.**
2. **Your pronunciation is great.**
3. ***Your pronunciation is wonderful.**
    pronunciation のほめ言葉として wonderful を使うのはおかしい。Your speech was wonderful. ならよい。

発音が素晴らしくよくなりましたよ。
1. **Your pronunciation has improved a great deal.**
2. **Your pronunciation has improved a lot.**
3. **Your pronunciation has really improved.**
4. **Your pronunciation has improved very much.**
    1〜3の方が4よりもよい。very much という言い方はこの場合あまり自然ではない。

発音はまあまあですね。
Your pronunciation is so-so.
Your pronunciation is all right.

発音が次第によくなっていますよ。
Your pronunciation is getting better gradually.
Your pronunciation is getting better little by little.

発音に間違いがありました。
There was a mistake in your pronunciation.
Your pronunciation was off a little.

個々の単語の発音は，文の中では変わってきます。
The pronunciation of each word is subject to change in a sentence.

機能語は弱く，内容語は強く発音することになります。
You are supposed to pronounce the function words weakly, but the content words strongly.
You are supposed to pronounce function words weakly, but content words strongly.

　　特定の機能語や内容語に言及しているのであれば，定冠詞の the を使うことになり，特定なものではなくて一般的な機能語や内容語ということであれば定冠詞の the は使わない。

英語を話すときには，リズムをつけることが大切です。
When you speak English, it is important to have rhythm.

sick と kick とは韻を踏んでいます。
Sick rhymes with *kick*.

cat と韻を踏む語は何ですか。
1. **What is the word that rhymes with *cat*?**
2. **What is a word that rhymes with *cat*?**
3. **What word rhymes with *cat*?**

　　話の内容から，cat と韻を踏む語が1つしかないというような状況では1のように the word とする。cat と韻を踏む語がいくつか考えられ，そのうちの1つを挙げればよい状況では2のように a word とする。cat と韻を踏む語が複数考えられる場合には3のように言う。

つづりと発音の関係について説明しましょう。
Let me explain the relationship between spelling and pronunciation.

▶これはどのように発音したらいいのでしょうか。
Could you tell me how to pronounce this?
　　学生が本の中の単語を指さして言うときなどの表現。

▶その言葉の発音はどのようにすればいいのでしょうか。
How should I pronounce the word?

▶この単語の発音のしかたがわかりません。
I don't know how to pronounce this word.
How do you pronounce this word?
How should I pronounce this word?

▶この単語の発音のしかたを教えてください。
Please tell me how to pronounce this word.
Could you tell me how to pronounce this word?

▶橘先生，その言葉をもう一度発音していただけませんか。
Mr. Tachibana, will you pronounce the word once again?
Mr. Tachibana, could you pronounce the word once again?

▶ Extraordinarily はどのように発音したらよいのでしょうか。
1. How should I pronounce the word *extraordinarily*?
2. How do I pronounce the word *extraordinarily*?
　　1 の should の方が 2 の do よりも自然である。

▶新出単語の発音をもう一度お願いします。
1. Could you pronounce the new words again?
2. Could you pronounce the new words once more?
3. Could you pronounce the new words one more time?
4. Could you pronounce the new words once again?
　　4 のように，once again という言い方はあまりしない。

▶新出単語の発音がよくわからないので，もう一度発音してください。
I don't know how to pronounce the new words, so could you pronounce them again?
I don't know how to pronounce the new words, so could you pronounce them one more time?
I don't know how to pronounce the new words, so could you say them again?

▶その単語をゆっくり発音してください。
Could you pronounce the word slowly?
Could you pronounce that word slowly?

▶この言葉は，[ráiz] と発音するのですか。
Is this word pronounced [ráiz]?

▶単語の発音は，文の中では変化するのですか。
1. Does the pronunciation of a word change within a sentence?
2. Does a word's pronunciation change within a sentence?
3. *Is the pronunciation of a word changed in a sentence?
 1が2よりもよい。3は意味が明確ではない。

▶ and の発音は，文の中ではどのように変化しますか。
How does the pronunciation of the word *and* change within a sentence?

▶発音が苦手です。
I am not good at pronunciation.

▶英語の単語の発音がどうも苦手です。
I'm not good at pronouncing English words.

▶発音はどうしたらうまくなるのでしょうか。
  1. How can I improve my pronunciation?
  2. How can we improve our pronunciation?
  3. How can we better our pronunciation?
      better にも動詞用法があるので3も文法的には可能であるが，1や2の表現の方がより普通な言い方である。

▶自分で発音を上達させるには，どうしたらいいでしょうか。
What should I do to improve my pronunciation?

▶発音の悪いところを直してください。
Could you correct my pronunciation?

▶発音がうまくなるためには，どうすればいいのでしょうか。
How can I study to improve my pronunciation?

▶イギリス英語とアメリカ英語の発音の違いは何ですか。
  1. What are some pronunciation differences between British English and American English?
  2. What is the difference in pronunciation between British English and American English?
  3. What is the difference between British English and American English in pronunciation?
      3のように in pronunciation を American English に付けて言うと，
      What is the difference between *British English* and *American English in pronunciation*
      のように取られる可能性もあるから，1や2のように言いたい。
      母音の後の r を響かせて発音するのはアメリカ英語，r の発音をしないのはイギリス英語の大きな特徴である。

264 Ⅳ 授業内容

B 子音について

空気の流れが肺から上がってくるとき，舌や唇などの発音器官によって妨げられるときがあります。そうして作られる言語音は子音と呼ばれます。
　When a stream of air comes up from the lungs, it is sometimes obstructed by speech organs such as the tongue and the lips. The speech sound made in such a manner is called a consonant.

f は上の歯で下の唇を軽くかんで発音します。
　When you make an *f* sound, you press your upper teeth lightly against your lower lip.

　　f は [ef] と発音するので，冠詞を付す場合には a ではなく an となる。不定冠詞の a, an の選択は，あくまで次の語の語頭音が母音であるか否かによる。

[f] の音を作り，声帯を振動させれば [v] となります。
　If you make the [f] sound and vibrate your vocal cords, you can make the [v] sound.

　　[f] のように [ ] に囲まれて示される場合は，実際に発音される音を意味するから，エフと読むことはできない。上の歯で下唇を軽くかんで「フ」と言わなくてはならない。

[f] の音と，[h] の音を混同しないように注意しましょう。
　Be careful not to confuse the [f] and [h] sounds.

▶ [f] と [h] の違いが聞き取れません。
　I can't hear the difference between [f] and [h].
　I can't distinguish [f] from [h] by listening.

[θ] の音は，舌先を軽くかんで発音します。
　When you make a [θ] sound, you press your teeth lightly against your tongue tip.

[θ] の子音は，舌の先を上歯と下歯の間に入れて作ります。
　The [θ] consonant is made by putting the tip of the tongue between the upper and lower teeth.

[ð] は，[θ] の有声音です。
　[ð] is the voiced form of [θ].
　[ð] is the voiced version of [θ].
　[ð] is the voiced counterpart of [θ].

[l] の音は，舌先を上の歯茎に付けて作ります。
　The [l] sound is made by placing the tip of the tongue against the upper gum ridge.

[l] の音を作るときには，舌先を上の歯茎に付けなさい。
　When you make the [l] sound, place the tip of the tongue on the upper gum ridge.

[l] は舌先を上の歯茎に付けて発音します。
　[l] is pronounced by putting the tip of the tongue on the upper gum ridge.

語頭の [l] は明るいl（エル）とよばれ，語尾の [l] は暗いl（エル）とよばれます。
　The word-initial l is called a light [l], and the word-final l is called a dark [l].

[r] は，舌を後ろにグッと丸めて発音しますが，舌は口のどの部分にも触れません。
　[r] is pronounced by curling the tongue backward, but the

tongue does not touch any part of the mouth.

日本語の「ラ」は，舌先を上歯の裏に付けて作ります。
  The Japanese ラ is made by placing the tip of the tongue against the upper teeth.

[l] と [r] は，日本人にとって一番発音が難しい子音です。
  [l] and [r] are the most difficult consonants for Japanese people to pronounce.

日本語にも英語にも破裂音はありますが，英語の破裂音は強く息を出して作ります。
  Both Japanese and English have plosive sounds, but those in English require more vigorous aspiration.

　　「破裂音」は plosive というほかに，stop（閉止音）ともいう。肺から上がってきた空気の流れである呼気の流れを，唇・歯・喉彦（のどびこ）などの調音器官で一時的に止めて，さらに破裂させる音であるから，《破裂》を重視すれば「破裂音」，《閉止》を重視すれば閉止音となる。

舌先を上歯で軽くかんで [θ] や [ð] を作ります。
  1. You make [θ] and [ð] by pressing your tongue lightly against your upper teeth.
  2. You make [θ] and [ð] by biting your tongue tip with your upper teeth lightly.

　　もとの日本文とは異なるが，1 の方が 2 よりも自然な英語表現である。

▶v（ブイ）の発音をする時の唇の形がわかりません。
  I don't know the shape of the lips for pronouncing the [v].
  I don't know the shape of the lips needed for pronouncing the [v].

▶ th はどんなとき「ス」と発音し，どんなとき「ズ」と発音するのでしょうか。
  1. **When do we pronounce th as [θ] and when do we do it as [ð]?**
  2. **When do we pronounce th as [θ] and when do we pronounce it as [ð]?**
     英語では，同じ言葉の反復をさけてある語句を省略することがあるが，この場合，
         *When do we pronounce the th as [θ] or [ð]?
     のように言うのは自然な表現ではない。少し長くはなるが，1か2のように言いたい。

▶ 英語の子音，たとえば [θ] や [ð] などの発音のしかたを教えてください。
  1. **Could you explain how to pronounce English consonants like [θ] and [ð]?**
  2. **Could you tell me how to pronounce English consonants like [θ] and [ð]?**
     1の方が2よりもよい。

▶ l（エル）の発音のしかたを教えてください。
  Could you tell me how to pronounce [l]?

▶ [l] の発音をするとき，舌先はどこに置いたらいいのでしょうか。
  When you pronounce [l], where do you put the tip of the tongue?

▶ l（エル）を発音するとき，舌はどうなりますか。
  When you pronounce [l], what happens to the tongue?

▶ [r] の発音のしかたがわかりません。
  I don't know how to make the [r] sound.

▶ r（アール）を発音するとき，舌をどうしたらいいのですか。
When pronouncing [r], what should I do with my tongue?

▶ [r] を発音するときには，舌をどのようにしたらいいのですか。
When pronouncing [r], what do you do with your tongue?

▶ [r] の発音は舌をどのようにしたらいいのでしょうか。
1. What do I do with my tongue when I pronounce an [r] sound?
2. How should I place my tongue when I pronounce an [r] sound?
3. How should I place my tongue when I pronounce [r]?

　　1や2の an [r] sound の代わりに，the [r] sound, this [r] sound という言い方も可能である。
　　日本語にとらわれると，
　　*How can I do with my tongue when I pronounce [r] sound?
のように言いたくなるが，How can I do with ...? とは言えない。

▶ [t] を発音するとき，舌はどこに置いたらいいのでしょうか。
Where do you put your tongue when you pronounce the [t] sound?

　　[t] は日本語にも英語にもある発音であるが，厳密には発音のしかたが異なる。日本語では舌先を上の歯に付けて発音するが，英語では上の歯茎に付けて発音する。微妙な差であるが，後者の場合には破裂音の特徴が著しい。

▶ス（th）を発音するとき，必ず舌先を上歯でかまなくてはいけないのですか。
1. When you pronounce *th*, do we always have to press our tongue tip against the bottom of our upper teeth?
2. When you pronounce *th*, do we always have to bite our tongue tip with our upper teeth?

　　1の方が2よりもよい。

▶舌をかまなければならない英語の子音は，いくつくらいありますか。
1. **How many consonants are made by putting the tongue against the teeth?**
2. **How many consonants are made by biting the tongue?**
   2のように biting を使うと，ネイティブスピーカーは，"sounds painful" というような印象を受けやすい。

C　母音について

母音は空気の流れを調音器官によって妨げられることなく，口から押し出して作ります。
　Vowels are made by pushing a stream of air out of the mouth without being obstructed by speech organs.

母音は舌の高さ，舌の位置，口の開き方の度合いによって細分化されます。
　Vowels can be sub-classified according to tongue height, tongue position and degree of mouth opening.

[u], [o], [ɔ] などの母音を，円唇母音といいます。
　Vowels such as [u], [o], and [ɔ] are called rounded vowels.

[u] を作るときには，後舌面が軟口蓋に近くに置かれて，唇は緊張しています。
　When making [u], the back of the tongue is placed close to the soft palate and the lips are tense.

[ʊ] は [u] に似た方法で作りますが，両唇と舌は [u] を作るときほど緊張はしません。
　[ʊ] is made in a way similar to [u], but both the lips and the tongue do not become tense as in the production of [u].

[i] の母音を作るとき，上歯と下歯はほとんど触れています。
  1. When making the [i] vowel, the upper and lower teeth are almost touching each other.
  2. When making the [i] vowel, the upper teeth and the lower teeth are almost touching each other.
    1 の方がより自然な言い方である。

[ɪ] は [i] に似ていますが，口は [ɪ] を作るときの方が [i] を作るときよりも開いています。
  [ɪ] is similar to [i], but the mouth is more open when making [ɪ] than in [i].

母音のシュワ [ə] は，中立母音とも呼ばれ，英語では大きな役割を果たします。
  The schwa vowel [ə], also called a neutral vowel, plays a big role in English.

[ə] の母音を作るときの舌の位置は，ほかの母音に比べて中立で，口の開き方もほかの母音に比べて中立的な位置にあります。
  1. The position of the tongue when making the vowel [ə] is neutral compared with other vowels, and mouth is open(ed) to a medial position in comparison with other vowels.
  2. The position of the tongue when making the vowel [ə] is neutral compared with other vowels, and the opening of the mouth is also in the medial position in comparison with other vowels.
    1 は自然であるが，2 はあまり自然な言い方ではない。

英語では，強勢を受けない母音は [ə] に変わる傾向があります。
  1. There is a tendency for unstressed vowels to be pronounced as [ə] in English.
  2. There is a tendency that in English, unstressed vowels

become changed into [ə].
　1 は自然であるが，2 はあまり自然な言い方ではない。

up や duck のような言葉では，[ʌ] の母音が [ə] の代わりに使われます。
In words like *up* and *duck*, the vowel [ʌ] is used instead of [ə].

[ə] の強勢をを受けた形は，ときどき [ʌ] として示されます。
The accented form of [ə] is sometimes shown as [ʌ].

[æ] を作るには，口は [ɛ] を作るときよりもさらに開いています。
In order to make [æ], the mouth is more open than when making [ɛ].

[æ] を作るときには，口や唇のような調音器官は緊張し，唇は広がっています。
When making [æ], the articulatory organs such as the mouth and the lips are tense, and the lips are spread.

[æ] という発音記号は，[a] と [e] の両方が結合していることを暗示させます。
The phonetic symbol [æ] implies that both the [a] and [e] are conjoined.

口を大きく開けて，[ɑː] と言ってごらんなさい。
1. Say [ɑː] with your mouth open wide.
2. Say [ɑː] with your mouth wide open.
　1 の方がよい。2 のように wide open と言うと，gross な感じがする。いろいろなことが連想されるからである。

英語の [ɑ] は日本語の「ア」よりも，もっと口を開けます。
1. You have to open your mouth wider for the English [ɑ]

than the Japanese ア.
2. **You have to open your mouth wider when making the English [ɑ] than the Japanese ア.**

　2の … when making … のように言うと，unbalanced で garbled な感じがする。1のように言いたい。

[ɑː] と言いながら唇をすぼめなさい。そうすると [ɔ] を作ることができます。
Pucker up your mouth saying [ɑː], and you can make [ɔ].
Pucker up your lips saying [ɑː], and you can make [ɔ].

▶母音の [ə] は，どれくらい口を開けて発音するのでしょうか。
How much should I open my mouth to pronounce the vowel [ə]?

▶英語にはあって日本語にはない母音には，どんなものがありますか。
What are the vowels that exist in English but not in Japanese?

D　口の開き方

口を閉じなさい。
Close your mouth.

口を少し閉じなさい。
Close your mouth a little bit.

口をもう少し閉じなさい。
Close your mouth a little bit more.

口を完全に閉じなさい。
　Close your mouth completely.

口を開きなさい。
　Open your mouth.

口を少し開きなさい。
　Open your mouth a little bit.

口をもう少し開きなさい。
　Open your mouth a little bit more.

口を大きく開けなさい。
　Open your mouth very wide.
　　「大きく」を widely としたくなるが，wide という形容詞の形を使うこと。

口を大きく開けないと，正しい英語の母音を作ることはできません。
　1. Unless you open your mouth wide, you will not be able to make the correct English vowel sound.
　2. *Unless you open your mouth wide, you will not be able to make a correct English vowel.
　　英語にはおよそ 11 の母音がある。この中には [i] や [ə] などのようにあまり口を開けないで作るものもあるので，2 のように make a correct English ... と言うと誤ってしまう。1 のように定冠詞の the を使って make the correct English ... のように言わなくてはならない。

自分の口の開き方を鏡を見て確かめなさい。
　1. Check to see how far to open your mouth by looking in the mirror.
　2. Check to see how much to open your mouth by looking in the mirror.

3. *Check to see how to open your mouth by looking in the mirror.
　　1か2のように言わなくてはならない。3のように言うと、「単なる口の開き方」の意味になり、「どのような格好で口を開くか」という意味ではなくなってしまう。口をどうやって開くかだけであれば、だれでも赤ん坊のときから知っている。

口を正しく開けているかどうか鏡を見なさい。
　Look in the mirror to see if you're opening your mouth the right amount.

私の口をよく見なさい。
　Watch my mouth carefully.

どのように私の口が開いているかごらんなさい。
　See how my mouth is open.
　　あまり自然な表現ではない。次のように具体的に言った方がよい。

どれくらい私の口が開いているかごらんなさい。
　1. See how far my mouth is open.
　2. See how wide my mouth is open.
　3. See how much my mouth is open.
　　1や2の方が3より自然である。

▶**どれくらい口を開けたらよいのですか。**
　How much should I open my mouth?

▶**どのように口を開けたらよいのですか。**
　1. What is the right amount to open our mouth?
　2. What is the right way to open our mouth?
　3. *How should we open our mouths?
　4. *How should we open our mouth?

3 と 4 は awkward である。1 や 2 のように言いたい。

▶口の開き方がわかりません。
  I don't know how far to open my mouth.
  I don't know the right amount to open my mouth for the ... sound.

▶もう少し口を大きく開けるのでしょうか。
  Should I open my mouth wider?

▶もう少し口を閉じるのでしょうか。
  Should I close my mouth a little more?

E 唇について

英語では唇の使い方が大切です。
  In English, the use of the lips is important.

私の唇をよく見なさい。そうすれば音の出し方がわかります。
  Watch my lips closely, and you'll understand how to make the sound.

[f] の音を作るには、上の歯で下唇を軽くかみ、息を出します。
  1. In order to make [f], you bite your lower lip lightly with your upper teeth and push your breath out with pressure.
  2. In order to make [f], you bite your lower lip lightly with your upper teeth and push your breath out under pressure.

　　1 の方が 2 よりもよい。2 のように under pressure と言うと、under stress あるいは in a nervous state の意味にも解されるからである。

[u] や [o] や [ɔ] の母音を発音するときには，唇をすぼめるようにします。
When pronouncing [u], [o], and [ɔ], try to pucker up your lips.

[r] の発音をするときにも，唇をすぼめるようにします。
When you pronounce the [r], try to pucker up your lips too.

[ʃ] という子音を発音するときには，少し唇をすぼめなさい。
When you pronounce the [ʃ] consonant, pucker up your lips a little bit.

▶英語のどんな音を作るとき，唇を丸めるのですか。
For what English sounds should we round our lips?

▶[r] の発音のとき，唇はどうしたらいいのですか。
When pronouncing [r], what should we do with our lips?

▶[f] の子音を作るには，下の唇が上の歯にどのように触れるべきでしょうか。
How should our lower lip touch our upper teeth when we make the consonant [f]?

　日本語では [f] の子音の作り方を説明するとき，しばしば「上の歯で下唇を軽くかむ」と言うが，これを bite という単語を使って訳すと「かむ」という意味合いが強すぎてしまう。touch という語の方が自然である。

▶[f] の音を作るには，上の前歯で下唇を軽くかめばいいのですね。
  1. Our lower lip is supposed to touch our upper front teeth when we make [f], isn't it?
  2. We are supposed to bite our lower lip with our upper front teeth in order to make [f], aren't we?

　1の方が2よりも自然である。

F 音節

この語は3つの音節からなります。
　This word consists of three syllables.

strength は1つの音節です。
　1. *Strength* has one syllable.
　2. *Strength* is a one-syllable word.
　3. *Strength is one syllable.
　　　3は誤りである。

この語を音節に分けなさい。
　Divide this word into syllables.

英語には数多くの音節の種類があります。
　There are many kinds of syllables in English.

日本語の音節構造は比較的簡単です。
　The structure of Japanese syllables is comparatively simple.

英語の音節構造は，日本語の音節構造より複雑です。
　1. The structure of English syllables is more complicated than that of their Japanese counterparts.
　2. The structure of English syllables is more complicated than that of Japanese ones.
　　　1の方が2よりも自然である。

音節とは，1つの母音あるいは1つ以上の子音から成る，単語の構成要素となっている最も小さな音の固まりを言います。
　A syllable is, the smallest possible sound cluster containing a vowel or one or more consonants acting as a con-

stituent of a word.
A syllable is, the smallest cluster of sounds containing a vowel or one or more consonants acting as a constituent of a word.

単語の音節の切れ目は辞書に明示してあります。
Dictionaries tell us how to divide a word into syllables.

ネイティブスピーカーは，無意識のうちに単語を音節に分けることができます。
1. Native speakers are able to divide a word into syllables automatically.
2. Native speakers can divide a word into syllables without having to think about it.
3. Native speakers can divide a word into syllables without consciously thinking about the process.
4. Native speakers can unconsciously divide a word into syllables.

「無意識のうちに」という意味の英語として unconsciously がしばしば使われるが，この単語は unintentionally の意味で，どちらかというと否定的な文脈の中で使われる。

I knocked over my glass of water unconsciously, while I was thinking.

He was biting his nails unconsciously.

このような理由で，3と4はあまり自然な言い方ではない。1と2の方がよい。

▶音節とは何ですか。
What is a syllable?

▶音節がよく理解できません。
I cannot understand syllables well.

音節の分け方
①接頭辞や接尾辞は音節を構成する。
   impersonality → im-per-son-al-i-ty
   displacement → dis-place-ment
②合成語はそれぞれの構成単位で音節を構成する。
   greenhouse → green-house
   blindfold → blind-fold
③母音 [iː], [uː], [ɔ], [ei], [ai], [au], [oi], [ou] は音節の最後に現れることがある。
④強勢を受けない短母音 [i], [e], [æ], [ə], [ɑ], [u] は後に子音を従えて音節を作ることがある。
⑤同一の子音が続いて現れるときは、はじめの子音は最初の音節、2番目の子音は次の音節を構成する。
⑥強勢のない [ə] や [i] は、音節の最後に現れることがある。

▶この単語はどの音節を強く読むのですか。
  1. **Which syllable are we supposed to accent in this word?**
  2. **What syllable are we supposed to read strongly in this word?**
     1の方が2よりもよい。

▶どの音節が強勢を受けるのですか。
  Which syllable is stressed?
  Which syllable is accented?
  Which syllable gets accented?
  Which syllable gets the stress?

▶ "language" には、いくつ音節がありますか。
  How many syllables are there in *language*?

280 Ⅳ 授業内容

▶音節に分けるには何かルールがあるのですか。
1. **Are there any rules for dividing words into syllables?**
2. **Are there any rules as to how to divide a word into syllables?**

　　1の方が2よりもよい。

G　発音記号

発音記号が読めますか。
　Can you read phonetic symbols?
　　　phonetic symbols を phonetic signs にしてもよいが, phonetic symbols の方がより広く使われている。

発音記号が書けますか。
1. **Are you able to write phonetic symbols?**
2. **Can you write phonetic symbols?**

　　1の方が2よりもよい。

発音記号には, LSAとIPAの2種類があります。
　There are two kinds of phonetic symbols : LSA and IPA.
　　　LSAとは Linguistic Society of America（アメリカ言語学会）の略, IPAは International Phonetic Association（国際音声学協会）の略である。発音記号にはいろいろな種類があるが, この2つの組織が用いる発音記号が世界的によく知られている。日本では昔はIPAの発音記号だけが用いられていたが, 現在ではLSAの発音記号も使われている。

いくつか単語を言いますから, 発音記号で書いてみなさい。
　I am going to give you some words, so please write them in phonetic symbols.
　I am going to give you some words, so please write them in phonetic signs.

発音記号に習熟すると，知らない単語でも，その単語の発音記号を見て発音することができます。
After you've learned to read phonetic symbols, you'll be able to figure out the pronunciation of words you are not familiar with by looking at the (phonetic) symbols.
When you have mastered the phonetic symbols, you can pronounce words you are not familiar with by looking at the (phonetic) symbols.

master は，すべての発音記号を暗記する必要があることを暗示させる言葉である。実際には，(辞書に) 示された発音記号を手掛かりにして，figure out するわけであるから，master の域に達していなくてもよい。

phonetic symbols という語がそれぞれの文で2度使われているが，2度目に現れるときには，phonetic を省略した方がすっきりする。

発音記号を見ながら，私のあとについて単語を読んでごらんなさい。
Read the words after me while looking at the phonetic symbols.

学生に発音記号を見せながら発音させる練習は，発音記号に習熟させる上で，大変効果のある方法である。

▶**発音記号が読めません。**
I can't read phonetic symbols.

▶**発音記号がよくわかりません。**
I don't understand phonetic symbols well.

▶**この発音記号の読み方がわかりません。**
I don't know how to read this phonetic symbol.

▶**この発音記号はどう読んだらいいのですか。**
1. How is this phonetic symbol read?

2. **How do you read this phonetic symbol?**
3. **How can I read this phonetic symbol?**
   1と2の方が3よりも自然な言い方である。

▶どうしたら発音記号が読めるようになりますか。
  What should I do in order to be able to read phonetic symbols?

▶発音記号をもう少し詳しく説明していただけませんか。
  Could you explain phonetic symbols in more detail?

▶英語には全部でいくつ発音記号がありますか。
  How many phonetic symbols are there for English?

▶6ページの3行目の2番目の単語を発音記号で書いてみてください。
  Please write the second word on line 3, page 6, in phonetic symbols.

H アクセント

アクセントにはストレスアクセントとピッチアクセントの2種類があります。
  There are two kinds of accents : stress accent and pitch accent.

ふつう「アクセント」と我々が呼んでいるのは，ストレスアクセントのことです。
  What we usually call "accent" is in fact stress accent.

ストレスはアクセントと同じ意味で使われます。
  1. *Stress* **has practically the same meaning as** *accent*.

2. *Stress* and *accent* have practically the same meaning.
3. *Stress* is used as the same meaning of *accent*.
　　3 はやや不自然である。

ストレスは声の大きさと関係があります。
Stress is connected with the loudness of the voice.
Stress has to do with the loudness of the voice.

英語はストレスの言語と呼ばれたりします。
English is sometimes called a stress language.
　　language は可算名詞であるから，stress language の前には不定冠詞の a が必要である。

英語では，必ず1つの音節をほかの音節よりも強く発音しなくてはいけません。
In English you have to pronounce one syllable stronger than the others.
　　いくつかあるもののうち，1つを取り出して残り全部に言及する場合には the others と言わなくてはならない。
　　2つあるもののうち1つを取り出して，もう一方のことを言う場合には the other と言う。
　　たくさんのものの中から1つを取り出して，残りの中からある不特定のものを取り出す場合には another と言う。

アクセントの位置に注意しなさい。
1. **Be careful where you put your accent.**
2. **Be careful where you put the accent.**
3. **Watch where you place your accent.**
4. **Be careful of the position of the accent.**
　　1 と 2 は自然な表現である。
　　3 の文では watch out としないように注意すること。

どちらの音節を強く読んだらいいと思いますか。
　　Which syllable do you think should be stressed?

この単語のアクセントはどこにありますか。
　　Where is the accent in this word?
　　Where is this word accented?
　　Where does the accent fall in this word?
　　Where is the stress in this word?

この単語はどの音節に第1アクセントがありますか。
　　1. Where is the main accent in this word?
　　2. Where is the primary accent in this word?
　　3. Where is the grave accent in this word?
　　4. Where is the first accent in this word?
　　5. Where is the primary accent of this word?
　　　　2 の the primary accent という言い方は専門的なニュアンスが強い。1 の the main accent の方が一般的である。

次の単語にアクセント符号を付けてごらんなさい。
　　Place accent marks on the following words.

46ページ，上から3行目の前から5番目の単語はどこにアクセントがありますか。
　　Where is the accent in the fifth word from the beginning of the third line from the top of page 46?

その単語は，第3音節にアクセントがあります。
　　The word is accented on the third syllable.

この単語には第3音節にアクセントがあります。
　　1. The accent is on the third syllable in this word.
　　2. The accent is over the third syllable in this word.
　　　　1 の方が好んで使われる。

第1アクセントは第3音節にあります。
The main accent falls on the third syllable.
The main accent is on the third syllable.
The third syllable has the main accent.
The primary accent falls on the third syllable.

第2アクセント，第3アクセントはそれぞれ secondary accent, tertiary accent と言う。厳密に言うと，音節の数だけアクセントの数はあると言われているが，辞書には第3アクセント以下はふつう書かれていない。

アクセントのある音節にアクセント符号を付けなさい。
1. Put an accent mark on the accented syllable.
2. Put an accent mark on the syllable where the accent is.
3. Put an accent mark on the syllable that gets stressed.
4. Put an accent mark on the syllable that gets accented.

1 が最もよい。

ストレスを第2の音節に置いて，[ədǽpt] と発音しなさい。
Pronounce [ədǽpt] with the second syllable stressed.
Place the stress on the second syllable and pronounce [ədǽpt].
Stress the second syllable and say [ədǽpt].

ストレスを第2の音節に置いて [ədǽpt] と発音します。
[ədǽpt] is pronounced with the stress on the second syllable.

▶**アクセントとは何ですか。**
What is an accent?

▶**第2アクセントとは何ですか。**
1. What do you mean by "secondary accent"?
2. What is the "secondary accent"?

1の方が2よりも具体的でわかりやすい。

▶ピッチアクセントとはどんな意味ですか。
What do you mean by pitch accent?

▶ストレスアクセントとピッチアクセントとの違いは何ですか。
What is the difference between stress accent and pitch accent?

▶イントネーションとストレスとは，どのように違うのでしょうか。
What is the difference between intonation and stress?

▶この単語の第1アクセントはどこにあるのですか。
Where is this word's main accent?
Where is the primary accent in this word?

▶この単語の第2アクセントはどこにありますか。
 1. Where is the secondary accent in this word?
 2. Where is the secondary accent of this word?
　　1の方がより自然な英文である。

▶ Extraordinarily の第1アクセントはどこにあるのでしょうか。
 1. Where is the main accent in *extraordinarily*?
 2. Where is the primary accent in *extraordinarily*?

▶私のアクセントは正しいのでしょうか。
Is my accent correct?
Is my accent right?

▶英語のアクセントのルールについて説明してください。
Could you tell me about the rules for English accents?
Could you tell me about the rules for accenting in English?

この文では主語の you を強く発音します。なぜだかわかりますか。
　You pronounce the subject *you* strongly in this sentence. Do you know why?

アクセントの位置に気をつけて，次の文章を読んでみましょう。
　Let's read the following sentences, paying attention to the position of the accents.

どの単語を最も強く読んだらいいと思いますか。
　1. **What word do you think you should emphasized?**
　2. **What word do you think should be stressed?**
　3. **Which word do you think should be stressed?**
　4. ***What word do you think should be read emphasized?**
　　　1〜3は standard な表現であるが，4はやや不自然な表現である。

機能語でも，文脈で大切な働きをする場合には強く読みます。
　Even function words are stressed when they play an important role in the context.
　Even function words are stressed when they have an important role in the meaning.

I　イントネーション

イントネーションとは，話すときの声の上げ下げの調子を言います。
　Intonation is the way your voice goes up and down when you speak.
　Intonation is the way your voice goes up and down when speaking.
　　　いずれも standard な表現である。

全体のイントネーションに注意してごらんなさい。
Be careful of the intonation contour.
　　contour は「輪郭」という意味。女性の体の線などについてもこの contour という語を使うことができる。

抑揚に注意しながら教科書を読んでください。
1. **Pay attention to intonation as you read the text.**
2. **Read the textbook, paying attention to intonation.**
　　1 と 2 はいずれでもよいが，1 の方が standard な表現である。

疑問詞で始まる文は，一般に語尾を下げて読みます。
Sentences beginning with a question word generally have falling intonation.

Yes-No で始まる疑問文は，語尾を上げます。
Yes-no questions have rising intonation.
　　イントネーションの上下をいう場合は，定冠詞や不定冠詞を付さない。

端的に，日本語は抑揚の言語，英語はリズムの言語です。
Simply put, Japanese is an intonation language and English is a rhythm language.

同じ文でも，イントネーションによって意味が変わることがあります。
1. **The meaning of a sentence is often affected by intonation.**
2. **The meaning of a sentence differs according to intonation.**
3. **Even in the same sentence, the meaning becomes different according to intonation.**
　　1 ～ 3 はいずれもよいが，1 が最も standard な表現である。2 は 1 ほど明確ではない。3 は日本語に近いがやや不自然な表現で

ある。

平叙文でも文尾を上げると疑問文に変わることがあります。
1. Raising the intonation at the end of a declarative sentence can sometimes change it into a question.
2. Raising the intonation at the end of a declarative sentence can sometimes make it into a question.
3. *By raising the end of a declarative sentence, you can sometimes change it into a question.
   1 は standard, 2 はやや informal, 3 は不明確な表現である。

文尾を上げると, 丁寧さを表すことがあります。
You can sometimes show politeness by raising the intonation at the end of a sentence.

文の終わりで声を下げなさい。
Let your voice fall at the end of the sentence.

文の終わりで声を上げなさい。
Raise your voice at the end of the sentence.
Let your voice rise at the end of the sentence.
   raise と rise に注意。自動詞の rise を使うときには let ... rise とする。

▶イントネーションにはどんなルールがありますか。
What are the rules for intonation?
What rules do you have for intonation?

▶どんなとき肯定文でも抑揚を上げるのですか。
When would you have rising intonation with affirmative sentences?
In what cases do you have rising intonation for affirmative sentences?

▶選択疑問文では，いつも or の前で抑揚を上げ，or の後で下げて読むのですか。
For an alternative question, do you always have to raise the intonation before *or* and lower the intonation after *or*?
With an alternative question, do you always have to raise the intonation before *or* and lower the intonation after *or*?

▶この文は，文末を上げるのですか。
Do you have rising intonation at the end of this sentence?
    intonation は通常，不可算名詞の扱いをする。

3 読むこと

A 読み・音読

英語を読むことは大変大切です。
Reading English is very important.

大きな声で読まないと，英語はうまくなりません。
Unless you read aloud, you will not be able to be a good speaker of English.

速く読む必要はありません。
You don't have to read fast.

正確に読む練習をしましょう。
Let's practice reading accurately.

速く読むことよりも，正確に読むことの方が大切です。
Reading accurately is more important than reading fast.

It is more important to read accurately than to read fast.
To read accurately is more important than to read fast.

文章の意味を考えながら読むことが大切です。
It is important to think about the meaning while you read.
It is important to think of the meaning as you read.
It is important to think of the meaning while you are reading.

意味を考えながら本文を読まなくてはいけません。
1. You have to think about the meaning while you read the text.
2. You have to read the text while keeping the meaning in mind.
　　1の方が2よりよい。

英語の文章を繰り返し読んでいると，書かれていることの意味が理解できるようになるでしょう。
If you read English sentences over and over, you will be able to grasp the meaning of things written in English.

何度も何度も読んでいるうちに，英語の勘が養われます。
You will get a feel for English by reading it over and over.
You will get a feeling for English by reading it over and over.
As you read again and again, you will be able to get a sense of English.
As you read over and over, you will be able to get a sense of English.
　　「英語の勘」というとき，a feel for English あるいは a feeling for English の方が，a sense of English よりもぴったりした表現である。

英文を何回でも慣れるまで読んでください。そうすればだんだんすらすら読めるようになります。
1. Read English sentences over and over until they become part of you. Then you will be able to read them with ease.
2. Read English sentences over and over until you get used to them. Then you will be able to read them with ease.
3. Read English sentences many times until you get used to them. Then you will be able to read them with ease.

　　1や2の方が3よりも自然な表現である。

家で何回読んできましたか。
How many times did you read it at home?

もう新出単語はすらすらと読めますか。
1. Can you read the new words smoothly now?
2. *Can you read the new words fluently now?

　　状況から判断して「特定の箇所の新出単語」であるから，the new words のように定冠詞の the が必要である。この場合，日本語の「すらすら」に相当する英語として2のように fluently を使うのはおかしい。fluently は flowingly ということである。つまり，言葉づかいがすらすらとよどみないことなどを形容する言葉であるから，新出単語を読むときに使うのはふさわしくない。新出単語は break を置きながら丹念に読んでいく作業だからである。fluently でなく1のように smoothly を使いたい。

ここが読める人は手を上げなさい。
1. Raise your hand if you can read this.
2. Those who can read this raise your hand.
3. Those who can read here raise your hand.

　　1, 2, 3の文章は，1 > 2 > 3の順で自然である。日本語では「ここが」となっているが，英語では here というよりも this と表現した方がよい。here を使った3の表現に対しては，誤りと感じ

るネイティブスピーカーすらいる。

命令文で Raise your hand ... の方が,Those who ... と言うよりも,より口語的で,より普通に見受けられる表現である。

この文の読み方について,何か質問はありませんか。
1. **Do you have any questions on how to read this sentence?**
2. **Don't you have any questions on how to read this sentence?**

「～ありませんか」という日本文はごく普通に使われるが,これを直訳して Don't you ...? と英語で言うと普通の言い方ではない。「質問があって当然」という強い気持ちを表すことになるので,英語としては1のように言うべきである。

▶私はあまり速く読むことができません。
I can't read so fast.

▶私はすらすら英語を読むことはできません。
I can't read English smoothly.

▶英語を読むときには,どのような点に注意して読んだらよいのでしょうか。
When reading English, what points should we pay attention to?

▶速く読める方法を教えてください。
1. **Could you tell me how to read faster?**
2. **Could you tell me how to read fast?**
3. ***Could you tell me the way of reading fast?**

1の方が2よりもよい。2の read fast という言い方は,「意味を理解せずに,ずさんにただ素早く読む」というニュアンスがある。

read faster という場合は,「意味の理解を損なうことなく,現在よりも読むスピードをアップする」というニュアンスがある。

▶アメリカの大学生は1分間にどれくらいの語を読むことができますか。
How many words a minute can American college students read?

▶スピードリーディングはどのように訓練するのですか。
How can you practice speed reading?
How can you train yourself to read faster?
How can we train ourselves to read faster?

▶形容詞が名詞を修飾する場合には，どちらを強く読むのですか。
When an adjective modifies a noun, which one should we stress?
When an adjective modifies a noun, which one is supposed to be stressed?
When an adjective modifies a noun, should the adjective or the noun be stressed?
When an adjective modifies a noun, should we stress the adjective or the noun?

B 区切り

正しいところにポーズを置く練習をしましょう。
Let's practice pausing in the proper places.
Let's practice putting pauses in the proper places.

そこで切って読んではいけません。
1. There shouldn't be a pause there.
2. You shouldn't pause there.
3. You cannot have a pause there.
　　1＞2＞3の順で自然である。

この文ではどこにポーズを置くのでしょうか。
Where should we pause in this sentence?

この文を1か所切って読むとしたら，どこでしょうか。
1. If we want a pause in this sentence, where should it be?
2. If we want to have a pause in this sentence, where should we put it?
3. If we want to read this sentence with a pause, where should we put the pause?
4. *If you place a pause in this sentence, where is it?
5. *If we are to read this sentence with a pause, where should we have it?
　　4と5は不自然な表現である。1〜3のように言いたい。

休止の位置に注意して読みの練習をしましょう。
Let's practice reading, paying attention to the position of pauses.
Let's practice reading, paying attention to pauses.
Let's pay attention to the position of pauses while we practice reading.
Let's pay attention to pauses while we practice reading.
　　the position of は省略してもよい。
　　practice とつづればアメリカ英語，practise とつづればイギリス英語である。

ポーズの前でどんな抑揚になるか説明してください。
Could you explain what kind of intonation is used before a pause?
Could you explain what kind of intonation is used before pausing?

▶どこを切って読んだらいいのですか。
1. Where should I pause?
2. Where should the pauses be?
3. Where should I put pauses?
　　1，2の方が3よりもよい。

▶接続詞 that の前で切って読むのですか，それとも後で切って読むのですか。
Are we supposed to pause in front of the conjunction *that* or after it?
Are we supposed to have a pause in front of the conjunction *that* or after it?

▶文を区切るときのルールについて説明してください。
Please explain the rules for how to place pauses in a sentence.
Please explain the rules for placing pauses in a sentence.
Please explain the rules for pauses within sentences.
Please explain the rules on how to place pauses in sentences.

▶どんなときにポーズを置くのですか。
When do you pause?
In what cases do you pause?
In what cases do you put pauses?
In what cases do you have pauses?
In what cases do you need pauses?

▶ポーズと句読点の関係を説明してください。
Could you explain the relationship between pauses and punctuation?

４　書くこと　　297

4　書くこと

A　書き方

速く英語が書けることも大切です。
　It is also important to be able to write English fast.

問題の答をノートに書き終わったら見せなさい。
　When you finish writing the answers to the questions, please let me see them.

この答は動詞の使い方がおかしいです。
　The way the verb is used in this answer is odd.
　The usage of the verb in this answer is odd.
　The way the verb is used in this answer is strange.
　The usage of the verb in this answer is strange.
　The way the verb is used in this answer is funny.
　The usage of the verb in this answer is funny.
　　odd は strange よりも「突飛さ」を強調した表現である。

これは必ず書き留めておきなさい。
　Make sure you jot this down.

こんなにごちゃごちゃ書いているとわからないよ。
　Your paper is messy. I can't read what you wrote.
　　「わからない」という日本語は，I don't know という表現も考えられるが，この場合は目的語が what you wrote であるから I don't know を使うのはおかしい。

▶書くのは苦手です。
　I am not good at writing.

▶速く書けるようになるにはどうしたらいいのでしょうか。
1. What should we do to write fast?
2. What should we do if we want to be able to write fast?
3. What should we do to be able to write fast?
　　1の言い方が簡潔で最もよい。

▶書き方の上で，アメリカ英語とイギリス英語とでは何か違いがありますか。
Are there any differences in writing between American English and British English?

B　つづり

つづりと発音は英語ではいつも一致するとは限りません。
　In English, spelling and pronunciation do not always match.

アメリカ英語とイギリス英語とでは時々つづりが異なります。
1. Sometimes there are differences in spelling between American English and British English.
2. *Once in a while, there is a difference in spelling between American English and British English.
　　once in a while は「時々」という日本語に相当するが，人が行う事柄や，（自然に，あるいは偶然に）起こる事柄を描写するときに使われる言葉である。例えば，
　　　Once in a while, he takes a bath.
　　　Once in a while, it snows in Kobe.
　などのように使う。つづりの違いについて述べる上記のような状況では once in a while を使うことはできない。
　　2 の ... there is a difference ... も複数形の ... there are differences ... と直す必要がある。

英語にはたくさんの外国語が入っていますので，つづりが難しいことがあります。
1. English spelling can be difficult because English contains many words of foreign origin.
2. English spelling can be difficult because English contains many words from foreign sources.
3. English spelling can be difficult because so many words having foreign origin have come into English.
4. English spelling can be difficult because so many words have come into English from other languages.
5. *English spelling is sometimes difficult because English contains many foreign words.

　　5 はおかしい。is difficult を can be difficult に変えたい。
　　もとの日本語を直訳して ... English contains many foreign words. という言い方もおかしい。語源的には外国語であっても借用されて英語の一部になってしまっているからには 1～4 のように表現しなくてはならない。

英語を書くとき，つづりが確かでなければ，必ず辞書でつづりをチェックしましょう。
　If you are not sure of the spelling when writing English, be sure to check it in the dictionary.
　If you are not sure of the spelling when writing English, be sure to consult the dictionary.

単語によっては発音しない文字を含んでいるものもあります。
　Some words have letters that are not pronounced.
　Some words have letters that are silent.
　Some words have silent letters.

発音しないつづり字について説明しましょう。
　Let tell us about silent spellings.
　Let explain about spellings that are not pronounced.

climb の b は黙字で，発音しません。
> The *b* of *climb* is a silent letter, so you don't pronounce it.
> The *b* of *climb* is a silent letter, so it isn't pronounced.

[nálidʒ] のつづりはどうですか。
> What is the spelling of [nálidʒ]?
> How do you spell [nálidʒ]?

[mìsisípi] には，s と i がいくつありますか。
> How many *s*'s and *i*'s are there in [mìsisípi]?
> How many *s*'s and *i*'s does [mìsisípi] have?

イギリス英語では [θíətə] を theatre とつづりますが，アメリカ英語ではどのようにつづりますか。
> In British English, [θíətə] is spelled t-h-e-a-t-r-e, but how do you spell it in American English?

ph で始まる言葉を4つ書きなさい。
> Write four words that begin with *ph*.

ph で終わる言葉を3つ書きなさい。
> Write three words that end with *ph*.

r が1つではなくて，2つあるはずです。
> There should be two *r*'s, not one.

s と r の間に，t が必要です。
> You need a *t* between *s* and *r*.
> There should be a *t* between *s* and *r*.

d の代わりに g があるはずです。
> There should be a *g* instead of a *d*.

pとhの文字が抜けています。
Both *p* and *h* are missing.

2つの語の間に，ハイフンが必要です。
You need a hyphen between the two words.

その単語にはハイフンが付いています。
The word is hyphenated.
　　外国系のアメリカ人を hyphenated American ということがある。Japanese-American, German-American などがそうである。

そこに入る単語はpで始まります。
1. **The word that goes there begins with *p*.**
2. **The word to be filled in there begins with *p*.**
　　1の方が2よりもよい。2の there は省略することもできる。

そこに入る単語はlで終わります。
The word to be filled in there ends with *l*.

最初の文字は大文字です。
1. **The first letter is a capital letter.**
2. **The initial letter is a capital letter.**
　　1の方が普通の言い方である。2の initial という語はこのような簡単な説明文では不釣り合いな感じがする。written あるいは technical なニュアンスがある。

それは分けて書きなさい。
Write it separately.

それは1語に書きなさい。
Write it together.

それは小文字で書きましょう。
　　Let's spell it in small letters.
　　Let's spell it with small letters.

つづりが正しいかどうか見てみましょう。
　　Let's see if you've spelled it correctly.
　　Let's see if you've spelled it right.

つづりを間違えないようにしなさい。
　　1. Be careful not to make spelling mistakes.
　　2. Watch your spelling.
　　3. Be careful about making spelling mistakes.
　　4. Pay attention to spelling.
　　　　2, 4には「間違い」に相当する言葉は出てこないが, いずれももとの日本文に近い意味合いで使われる。

書き終わったら, つづりをチェックしなさい。
　　Check your spelling when you finish.
　　Doublecheck your spelling when you finish.

つづりに何か間違っているところがありますか。
　　Is there anything wrong with the spelling?

あなたの作文に, つづりの間違っている語が4つあります。
　　There are four misspelled words in your composition.
　　There are four words you've spelled wrong in your composition.
　　Your composition has four misspelled words.
　　　　アメリカ英語では spelled, イギリス英語では spelt のようにつづる。

このつづりの間違いをだれか訂正できますか。
　　Can anybody correct this misspelt word?

後ろの人はこの単語のつづりがはっきりとわかりますか。
　　Can people in the back see the spelling of this word clearly?
　　Can people at the back see the spelling of this word clearly?

その言葉はどうつづりますか。
　　1. How do you spell that word?
　　2. How do you spell that?
　　3. How is that (word) spelled?
　　4. What's the spelling of that (word)?
　　5. How do you spell the word?
　　6. What is the spelling of the word?
　　　that word と言っても that と言ってもよい。that の方が口語的である。最もスタンダードな表現は1である。
　　　5と6で the word が使われているが，the word では意味がわかりにくい。話し手がどの言葉についていっているのかわかる場合には可能である。6は stilted なニュアンスのある表現である。

来週のこの時間は，これらの単語のつづりのテストをします。
　　Next week this hour, I'm going to give you a spelling test on these words.
　　Next week at this hour, I'm going to give you a spelling test on these words.
　　Next week at this period, you'll be tested on the spelling of these words.
　　Next week at this hour, you'll have a test on the spelling of these words.
　　　Next week at this hour の at は省略可能である。

▶**よくつづりの間違いをします。**
　　I often make mistakes in spelling.
　　I often make spelling mistakes.

▶私は英語のつづりは苦手です。
1. **I am weak at spelling English words.**
2. **I am not good at spelling English words.**
3. ***I am weak at spelling English.**
4. ***I am not good at spelling English.**

　　3と4では... spell の目的語が English になっている。つまり，「"English" をつづる」という関係になっているからおかしい。English のつづりくらいならだれでもできる。1や2のように，English words としなくてはならない。

▶つづりはどのようにしてマスターしたらよいのでしょうか。
How can we master spelling?

▶英語の単語はなぜつづりが難しいのですか。
1. **Why are English words difficult to spell?**
2. **Why is the spelling of English words difficult?**
3. ***Why are the spellings of English words difficult?**

　　ほとんどの単語には1つしかつづりがないので，3のように言うのはおかしい。

▶ refrigerator という言葉はどのようにつづりますか。
How do you spell the word *refrigerator*?

　　この refrigerator は冗長で発音も難しいことから，略して fridge とも言う。
　　アメリカ英語では refrigerator を icebox と呼ぶこともある。

▶ [bjúːtəfəl] は，どのようにつづりますか。
How do you spell [bjúːtəfəl]?
Would you tell me how to spell [bjúːtəfəl]?
Will you tell me how to spell [bjúːtəfəl]?

▶ [kɔ́ːɾtəsi] のつづりを書いてください。
Please spell [kɔ́ːɾtəsi] for me.

▶ [spéiʃəs] という単語のつづりを黒板に書いてください。
  1. **Could you write [spéiʃəs] on the board?**
  2. **Could you spell out the word [spéiʃəs] on the board?**
  3. **Could you write out the word [spéiʃəs] on the board?**
  4. **Could you write the spelling of the word [spéiʃəs] on the board?**

   1が簡潔で最も普通な言い方である。4はやや冗長な表現である。

▶ [pǽrəlèl] はどのようにつづりますか。
  How do you spell [pǽrəlèl]?
  How is [pǽrəlèl] spelled?

▶「パラレル」のつづりを教えてください。
  Could you tell me how to spell [pǽrəlèl]?

▶「パラレル」の正しいつづりは何ですか。
  What is the correct spelling of [pǽrəlèl]?

▶2番目の字は何ですか。
  What is the second letter?

▶最後の単語の後ろから2番目の字は何ですか。
  What is the second to the last letter of the last word?

▶単語のスペリングがわかりません。
  1. **I don't know how to spell this word.**
  2. **I don't know how to spell that word.**
  3. ***I don't know how to spell the word.**

   単語の一部が書かれたペーパーなどを指さしながら言う場合には1のように this を使う。
   教師が説明した単語に言及する場合は2のように通例 that を使う。
   3では the という形が使われているが、この使い方にはやや

impolite, complaining あるいは argumentive tone がある。文法的には this や that の位置に来そうであるが，この場合には the で置換することはふさわしくない。1や2のように言いたい。

▶先生が今おっしゃった単語のつづりは何ですか。
What is the spelling of the word you mentioned a minute ago?

▶山崎先生，単語のつづりが間違っているのではないでしょうか。
1. **Mr. Yamasaki, I'm afraid you've spelled that word incorrectly.**
2. **Mr. Yamasaki, I'm afraid you've spelled that incorrectly.**
3. **Mr. Yamasaki, I'm afraid you've spelled it incorrectly.**
4. **Mr. Yamasaki, I'm afraid you've spelled the word incorrectly.**

　だれかが，黒板に書かれたつづりの違う単語を指さしながら言うような場合には，1のように that word を使うか，2のように that を使う。

▶小川先生，スペリングが間違っています。
Mr. Ogawa, is this spelling OK?

　直訳的に This spelling is not correct. とすると，生徒同士ではよいとしても，生徒から先生に対しては少し直接的過ぎる。疑問文の形にすると，柔らかいニュアンスになる。

▶山崎先生，黒板の単語のつづりが間違っているのではないでしょうか。
1. **Mr. Yamasaki, is the word you wrote on the board misspelled?**
2. **Mr. Yamasaki, is the word you wrote on the board all right?**
3. ***Mr. Yamasaki, is the word you wrote on the board wrong?**

3 は強い響きをもっているのでふさわしくない。

▶ k が抜けています。
1. **There's a *k* missing.**
2. **A *k* is missing.**
3. ***K* is missing.**

　2 では a k のように不定冠詞の a が付いているが，3 では不定冠詞の a が付いていない。状況によって，不定冠詞を付けても付けなくてもどちらでもよい場合があり得る。

C　句読点

句読点がないために，読者がわからないこともあります。
1. **Omission of punctuation may sometimes confuse readers.**
2. **Omission of punctuation may sometimes lead readers astray.**
3. **Lack of punctuation may sometimes confuse readers.**
4. **Lack of punctuation may sometimes lead readers astray.**

　1〜4 はいずれでもよいが，1, 2 が最もよい。
　lead という動詞は，
　　This road will lead you to the village.
　　（この道を行けば，その村に行きます。）
のように，lead 〜 to と用いることがある。4 の文も，
　　*Lack of punctuation may sometimes lead readers to astray.
と to を付けたくなるが，astray は名詞でなく「（道に）迷って」という意味の副詞であり，前置詞の to では誤りとなる。

句読点にも注意して，英文を書いてください。
1. **When you write English sentences, pay attention to punctuation.**

2. **When you write English sentences, be careful about how you punctuate.**
3. **Write English sentences, paying attention to punctuation.**

　　1，2と3とは少しニュアンスが異なる。前者は，「英文を書くときに，句読点に注意しなさい」という意味である。つまり，1つのことに注意しなさいということである。後者は，「英文を書きなさい。そのとき，句読点にも注意しなさい」という意味である。2つのことを命じている点が異なる。

however が文の最初に来ると，その後にコンマを打つのが普通です。
When the word *however* comes at the beginning of a sentence, a comma is usually placed after it.

ピリオドが抜けています。
1. **The period is missing.**
2. **A period is missing.**
3. **You forgot the period.**
4. **You left out the period.**
5. **There's no period.**

　　1～4は standard，5はやや informal な表現である。
　　アメリカ英語ではピリオドのことを period や point ということが多いが，イギリス英語では full stop を用いる傾向がある。

ここはセミコロンの代わりにコロンを使わなくてはいけません。
We have to use a colon instead of a semicolon here.

　　コロンは句読点の1つで，ピリオドよりは弱く，コンマやセミコロンよりは強い切れ目を表す。

▶コロンとセミコロンとの違いは何ですか。
1. **What is the difference between how colons and semicolons are used?**

2. **What is the difference in the usage of colons and semicolons?**
3. **What is the difference between a colon and a semicolon?**

　　1と2は明確であるが、3はやや曖昧な表現である。

▶句読点の用法がよくわかりません。
I don't understand how to use punctuation.

▶句読点について説明していただけませんか。
1. **Could you explain how to punctuate sentences?**
2. **Could you give us some pointers on punctuation?**
3. **Could you give us some punctuation tips?**
4. **Could you explain how to use punctuation?**

　　1は standard, 2〜3はやや informal, 4は不自然である。

▶アポストロフィーの使い方がよくわかりません。
1. **Could you tell me how to use an apostrophe?**
2. **I don't know how to use an apostrophe.**

　　1の方が丁寧な質問である。
　　アポストロフィー（'）には、およそ3つの働きがある。
　①文字・数字の省略を示す。
　　He can't do it.
　　（彼にはそれができない。）
　　I won't do it.
　　（私はそれをするつもりはない。）
　　She'll be back in ten minutes.
　　（彼女は10分したら戻ってくるでしょう。）
　　4/9/'92
　　（1992年4月9日）
　　最近では、4/9/92のように、アポストロフィー（'）を使わないことが多い。
　　アメリカ英語では月を先に日を後に言うが、イギリス英語では日を先に月を後に言う。したがって、イギリス英語では 4/9/92

> **句読点のいろいろ**
>
> | 記号 | 名称 |
> |---|---|
> | . | period（英 full stop） |
> | , | comma |
> | ? | question mark |
> | ' | apostrophe |
> | " " | quotation marks |
> | ( ) | parentheses |
> | [ ] | brackets |
> | { } | braces |
> | ! | exclamation point（米），exclamation mark（英） |
> | ; | semicolon |
> | : | colon |
> | - | hyphen |
> | — | dash |
> | / | slash |
> | * | asterisk |

は，「1992年9月4日」ということになる。

②所有格を示す。

　Tom's house is gigantic.
　Tom's house is huge.
　（トムの家はとてつもなく大きい。）
　Jill is a friend of Sandy's.
　（ジルはサンディーの友人の1人です。）
　The house over there is Mr. Johnson's.
　（あそこの家はジョンソン氏の家です。）

③文字・数字・符号などの複数形を示す。

　There are two l's in the word *yellow*.
　（yellow という語には l が2つある。）
　I saw a few MP's on the plane.

（私は飛行機の中で数人の国会議員を見た。）
MP は Member of Parliament の省略である。
Dot the i's.
（i には点を打ちなさい。）
I think he was born in 1950's.
（彼は 1950 年代に生まれたと思う。）

1. Don't use too many exclamation points in your composition.
2. Don't use too many !'s in your composition.

（作文で，感嘆符を使い過ぎないようにしなさい。）
1 の方が 2 よりもよい。

▶この文の句読点の打ち方がわかりません。
I don't know how to punctuate this sentence.

▶この場合，コンマは必要ですか。
1. **Do you need a comma in this case?**
2. **In this case do you need a comma?**

1 の方が 2 よりもより自然である。

5　作文

A　英作文

英文がすらすら書けますか。
Can you write English with ease?
Can you write English without any trouble?
Can you write English effortlessly?
Can you write English without any effort?

書けば書くほどうまくなりますよ。
1. **The more you write, the better you will write.**
2. **The more you write, the better writer you will be.**
3. **The more you write, the better writer you will become.**
4. **The more you write, the better you will be at writing.**
5. ***The more you write, the better you will be.**

　　1，2，3は自然な言い方である。5のように，... will be とすると，the better person you will be. の意味になってしまう。

英作文があまり得意でない人はいますか。
Are there any of you who are not good at English composition?

Are there any students who are not good at English composition?

Are there any of you who are weak at writing English sentences?

英語で日記をつけたことがありますか。
Have you ever kept a diary in English?

　　生徒に，「私はこれまでに，英語で日記をつけたことがあります」という日本語を英語に直しなさいと言うと，次のように誤ることが多い。
　　　　*I have ever kept a diary.
　　肯定文に ever を付ける誤りは，日本語的な発想に起因する。「私はこれまで〜」という表現は，日本語においては極めて普通に見受けられる表現であるからである。最上級を修飾する形容詞節などの中では，
　　　　This is the longest letter I have ever written.
　　（これは私がこれまで書いたうちで一番長い手紙です。）
のように，ever を使うことができるが，それ以外には肯定文では ever は使えないと指導したい。
　　ever が抵抗なく使えるのは，《疑問文》《否定文》《条件文》である。

英作文が上達するには，絶えず英語の文章を書くことが大切です。

1. If you want to improve your writing skills, you should keep writing English sentences.
2. If you want to improve your writing skill, you need to keep on writing.
3. If you want to improve your writing skills, you have to keep on writing.
4. If you want to improve your writing skills, you always have to practice writing English sentences.
5. *If you want to improve your writing skills, you always have to write English sentences.
6. *If you want to improve your writing skills, you always have to keep on writing.

　1では skills，2では skill となっている。skills という場合には，penmanship よりも，ability や creativity に力点がある。skill の場合には penmanship に力点がある。上記の場合には，skills を使った方が文意に合う。

　5のように always を使うと，

> You're not allowed to eat, sleep, wash, attend other classes, or have a personal life.

というような意味に取れるのでふさわしくない。

　6のように，keep on 〜の形を使う場合には，always の意味合いは薄れるが，on に《継続》の意味があるから重複するので，避けた方がよい。

書く力をつけるには，立派な英語を読むことが大切です。

In order to improve writing ability, it is important to read good English.

In order to improve your writing ability, it is important to read good English.

英語を上手に書くためには，大きな声でいい英語の文章を何度も読むことも効果があります。
In order to be able to write good English, it is also useful to read good English sentences aloud many times.
In order to be able to write good English, it is also helpful to read good English sentences aloud many times.

ペンパルと英語で文通することは，英語がうまくなるいい方法です。
Corresponding with pen pals in English is a good way to improve your English.
Writing to pen pals in English is a good way to improve your English.

英語がうまく書けるようになるためには，文法をマスターすることが大切です。
It is important to master grammar if you want to be a good writer of English.
It is important to master grammar in order to be a good writer of English.
It is important to master grammar if you want to write English well.

立派な英語が話せたら，立派な英語が書けるはずです。
If you can speak good English, you should be able to write good English.

立派な英語が書けたら，必ず立派な英語が話せるはずです。
If you can write good English, you'll surely be able to speak good English.

英作文をすると文法の力がわかります。
1. We can see in your compositions how well you've mastered English grammar.

2. **We can tell by your compositions how well you've mastered English grammar.**
3. **If you write in English, your grammatical ability will be revealed.**
4. **We can see how well you've mastered English grammar in your compositions.**
5. ***English composition will reveal one's grammatical knowledge.**

　　4 は，We are able to determine the level of grammar you've mastered in your composition. という意味であるから，1～3 の方がもとの日本文の意味に近い。

　　5 は awkward である。また，knowledge と ability とは同一のものではない。ときに相反することもある。

いつもわかりやすい英語を書くように心がけてください。
1. **Always try to write in plain English.**
2. **Always try to write plain English.**
3. ***Try to write in plain English always.**
　　副詞の位置は比較的自由であるが，3 のように always を文尾に置くのはあまり自然ではない。

▶全く英語が書けません。
I cannot write English at all.

▶なぜそういう表現をするのですか。
Why is that kind of expression used?
Why is an expression like that used?
Why do you use that kind of expression?
Why do you use an expression like that?
Why do you use such an expression?

▶どうしたら書く力がつくでしょうか。
How can I improve my writing skill?

▶どうしたら英語がうまく書けるようになるのでしょうか。
  How can I be a good writer of English?

▶英語の手紙の書き方を教えてください。
  1. Please tell me how to write a letter in English?
  2. Could you tell me how to write a letter in English?
  3. Please tell me how to write English letters?
  4. Could you tell me how to write English letters?
     3と4では,「英語のABCを手伝ってほしい」という意味にも解釈できるので,「英語で手紙を書くのを手伝ってほしい」と言う意味を明確に伝えるには,1と2の方がよい。

▶辞書を引けば,多少英語を書くことはできます。
  If I use a dictionary, I can write a little English.

▶英語を書く上で参考になる辞書を教えてください。
  Could you tell me what dictionaries are helpful for writing English?

▶英語を書く力と,話す力とは大いに関係がありますね。
  Writing English has a lot to do with speaking English.

▶英語を書くことと,話すことはあまり関係がありませんね。
  Writing English has little to do with speaking English.

あなたの将来について英作文をしなさい。
  Write an English composition on your future.

「私の将来」というタイトルで英作文をしてください。
  Please write an English composition entitled "My Future".

何でも好きなことについて書いていいですよ。
  You can write about anything you like.

You can write about anything you want.
You can write about anything you wish.
*You can write anything you like.
*You can write anything you want.
*You can write anything you wish.

　日本文からして，この場合 write about のように，前置詞の about を入れるべきである。about を入れず You can write anything ... にすると，「何を書いてもよい」という意味になる。例えば，ABC を逆に 100 回書くことも許されることになる。write about とすると，「〜について書く」ということになる。

この話題について時間内に知っているだけ書きなさい。

1. **Write as much as you can about this topic within the time limit.**
2. ***Write as much as you know about this topic within the time limit.**

　as 〜 as ... can は「できるだけ〜」という表現であるから，1 の表現は何ら抵抗はない。

　as much as 〜 には「〜と同量の」という意味があり，2 の文は「知っている（量・こと）だけ〜」と解釈される。「多く書くように」と量を強調する場合は，1 の方が自然である。

作文の題は君たちに任せます。

1. **I will leave the title of the composition up to you.**
2. **I will leave it to you as far as the title of the composition is concerned.**

　2 は正確ではあるがあまりにも wordy である。1 の方が簡潔でよい。

辞書を見ないで作文してごらんなさい。

Write a composition without using your dictionary.

318 Ⅳ 授業内容

英作文は，1000 語以内でまとめてください。
　Write your English composition in 1,000 words or less.
　Write your English composition within 1,000 words.
　　「〜以内で」という日本語にとらわれると within を使いたくなるが，in 〜の方が普通である。

今回は，長さについては制限はありません。
　1. This time around, there are no restrictions on the length.
　2. This time around, there are no restrictions as to the length.
　　1 の方が自然である。

今回は，字数制限はありません。
　1. This time around, there is no word limit.
　2. This time around, there is no limit to the number of words you can use.
　3. This time around, there is no limit to the number of words to be used.
　4. This time around, there is no limit on the number of words you can use.
　5. This time around, there is no limit on the number of words to be used.
　　1 が最もよい。

もし余分な時間があれば，間違いがないかどうか読み直してみてください。
　If you have extra time, why don't you look it over to see if you have made any mistakes.
　If you have extra time, why don't you look your paper over to see if you have made any mistakes.

文章ができあがった人は，黒板に出てそれを書きなさい。
　1. Those who have written the sentences, please come here

and write them on the board.
2. **Those who have written the sentences, please come up and write them on the board.**
3. ***For those who have written the sentences, please come here and write them on the board.**

　　... come here ... でも ... come up ... でもよい。

　　3 の For those who ... の for は不要である。For those who ... の形が許されるのは次のような場合である。

　　　For those who ... , there is a special treat.
　　（There is a special treat for those who ...）

作文を書き終えた人は，今提出してください。
If you are through with your composition, please hand it in now.
If you have finished your composition, please hand it in now.
Those who have finished writing their composition, please turn it in now.

▶**何について書いてもいいのですか。**
Can we write about anything we want?
Can we write about anything we wish?

　　want の方が欲する気持ちが強い。この場合は，want の方が wish よりも自然である。

▶**書くことが何もありません。**
I have nothing to write about.

▶**辞書を使ってもいいのですか。**
1. **May I use a dictionary?**
2. **May I use my dictionary?**
3. **May I use my dictionaries?**

　　1 冊の辞書であれば 1 や 2，何冊か使うのであれば 3 の英文と

▶どれくらい書いたらいいのでしょうか。
How long should our compositions be?

▶どれくらいの長さにまとめたらいいのですか。
1. What length do you want our compositions to be?
2. How long should our compositions be?
3. How many words should our compositions be?
4. How many words do you want us to write?
5. *Within how many words are we supposed to write?

　　日本語の「何語以内」に引かれて within how many words ... と直訳すると，awkward な英文になる。1〜4のように言うべきである。そうすれば，教師から具体的な答えを引き出すことができる。

▶英作文は，手書きでも構いませんか。
1. Is it all right if I do the English composition in my handwriting?
2. Is it OK to write the English composition in my handwriting?
3. *Can we write the English composition by hand?
4. *Is it all right if you hand write the English composition?

　　1と2は正しいが，3と4は不自然である。

▶時間の制限はありますか。
Is there a time limit?

▶書くのが遅いので時間が足りません。ちょっと待ってください。
1. Since I am a slow writer, I need more time. Could I have a little longer?
2. Since I am a slow writer, I need more time. Could you

give me a little more time?
3. Since I am a slow writer, I need more time. Could you wait for a minute?
4. Since I am slow in writing, I need more time. Could you wait for a second?

  日本語の「ちょっと待ってください」を直訳的に Wait for a minute. や Wait for a second. に直すとネイティブスピーカーには心理的にいい印象を与えない。1 と 2 の方が 3 と 4 よりも丁寧な表現である。

▶紙が足りません。裏に書いてもいいですか。
I ran out of paper. Can I write on the back?
I ran out of paper. Is it all right to write on the back?

▶できあがったら，提出してもいいのですか。
May those who are through writing turn it in?
May those who are finished writing turn it in?
Can those who are through writing turn it in?
Can those who have finished writing turn it in?
  イギリス英語では，このような意味合いで through を使うことはない。

▶締め切りはいつですか。
When is it due?
What is the due date?
By when are we supposed to turn it in?
When are we supposed to turn it in?
By when should we hand it in?
When should we hand it in?
By when do we have to submit it?
When do we have to submit it?
  「～まで」に相当する英語の by は省略可能である。

▶私の書いたものを添削していただけませんか。
Could you correct what I wrote?

B 和文英訳

全体の意味を考えながら和文を英訳することが大切です。
1. It is important to bear in mind the meaning of the complete sentence when translating Japanese into English.
2. *It is important to translate the Japanese sentence into English, bearing in mind the whole sentence.

　　1 は standard であるが，2 は不自然な表現である。

和文英訳するには文法の知識も必要です。
1. A good knowledge of grammar is also necessary when translating Japanese into English.
2. *Knowledge of grammar is also necessary to translate Japanese into English.

　　1 は standard な表現であるが，2 は不自然な表現である。

和文英訳はひとつの正しい答えに限られているわけではありません。
1. There is more than one way of putting Japanese into English.
2. *Putting Japanese into English is not restricted to just one correct answer.

　　1 は standard な表現であるが，2 は不自然である。

いろいろな和文英訳が可能です。
It is possible to translate Japanese into English in many ways.

AもBも正解ですが，Bの方がより自然な英語です。
Both A and B are correct, but B is more natural.

Both A and B are correct, but B sounds more natural.
Both A and B are correct, but B sounds better.
　　いずれも standard な表現である。

これも正解です。
　　This is also correct.

▶和文英訳は試験に出ますか。
　　Are we going to have Japanese-English translation on the exam?

▶日本語の「失礼しました」は英語で何と言ったらよいのでしょうか。
　　How do you say the Japanese sentence *shitsureishimashita* in English?

6　読解

A　語句の理解

熟語は逐一訳しても意味をなしません。
　　Idiomatic expressions do not make much sense if they are translated word for word.

文脈が言葉の意味を与えます。
　　The context will clarify the meaning of the word.
　　The context will show you the meaning of the word.

文脈から言葉の意味がわかります。
　　The context helps us understand the meaning of the word.
　　You can understand the meaning of the word from the con-

text.
You can get the meaning of the word from the context.

deliberate とはどんな意味ですか。
　What is the meaning of *deliberate*?
　What do you mean by *deliberate*?
　What does *deliberate* mean?

deliberate という単語の意味を知っていますか。
　Do you know the meaning of the word *deliberate*?
　Do you know what the word *deliberate* means?

deliberate という単語の意味を言ってください。
　Please tell me the meaning of the word *deliberate*.

deliberate という単語の意味を言うことができますか。
　Can you tell me the meaning of the word *deliberate*?
　Can you tell me what the word *deliberate* means?

delicious は日本語ではどう言いますか。
　What's *delicious* in Japanese?
　What is the Japanese for *delicious*?
　How do you say *delicious* in Japanese?

principal の意味は何ですか。英語でも日本語でもかまいません。
　What does *principal* mean? Either English or Japanese will be OK.

sea と ocean の意味の違いを言ってください。
　Tell me the difference in meaning between *sea* and *ocean*?
　Can you tell me the difference in meaning between *sea* and *ocean*?

desk と table の意味の違いは何ですか。
　What is the difference in meaning between *desk* and *table*?
　Could you tell me the difference in meaning between *desk* and *table*?

gift という語には，「贈り物」という意味のほかに，「才能」という意味もあります。
　1. **The word *gift* means *ability* as well as *present*.**
　2. **The word *gift* means not only *present* but also *ability*.**
　3. **The word *gift* has the meaning *ability* as well as *present*.**
　　1と2は自然だが，3はやや stilted な感じがする。

since と as は，だいたい同じ意味をもっています。
　***Since* and *as* have more or less the same meaning.**
　　《理由》を表すときには since と as とをほぼ同じように使うことができるが，「～以来」のように《時》に言及する場合に as を使うことはできない。

street と road は日本語に訳すと同じ意味になりますが，英語では使い分けなくてはなりません。
　***Street* and *road* have the same meaning when translated into Japanese, but you have to use them properly in English.**

small と little は共に「小さい」という意味ですが，2つの違いは何でしょうか。
　Both *small* and *little* mean "chiisai", but what is the difference between the two?

large と big は，共に「大きい」という意味ですが，どのような違いがありますか。
　Both *large* and *big* mean "ookii", but what is the difference between the two?

get や take などは，いろいろな意味をもっています。
Words like *get* and *take* have many meanings.

その単語の意味を簡単な英語で説明してごらんなさい。
Try to explain the meaning of the word in plain English.

"It never rains but it pours." とは，「降れば土砂降り」という意味です。
"It never rains but it pours." means "Once it begins to rain, it rains a lot."
"It never rains but it pours." means "Once it begins to rain, it rains hard."

"This is a big apple." は，"This apple is big." とも言うことができます。
"This is a big apple." has more or less the same meaning as "This apple is big."

　　big apple を大文字で Big Apple と言えば，ニューヨーク市のニックネームである。これは，Johnny Appleseed（1774-1845）という園芸家が，Pennsylvania から Ohio にリンゴの種をまいて普及につとめた歴史上の事実によるらしい。

ここではその言葉はどのように使われていますか。
How is the word used here?

ここではその言葉はどんな意味で使われていますか。
In what sense is the word used here?

意味のわからない単語がありますか。
Are there any words that you don't understand?
Do you have any words you don't understand?

この単語と同じ意味を持っている単語が文中にありますか。
　Are there any words that have the same meaning as this?

have と同じ意味を持つ単語を１つ探しなさい。
　Find a word that has the same meaning as *have*.

beauty と同じ意味を表す英語を本文の中から選びなさい。
　Find a word in the text that has the same meaning as *beauty*?

本文を読めば，その言葉の意味がわかります。
　The text will show you the meaning of the word.

意味がはっきりしましたか。
　Is the meaning clear to you?

その辞書に載っている意味はここでは不適当です。
　The meaning given in the dictionary does not fit in this case.
　The meaning given in the dictionary does not apply in this case.

ここでは辞書の中の３番目の意味がいいでしょう。
　The third meaning given in the dictionary will apply in this case.
　The third meaning given in the dictionary applies here.
　The third meaning given in the dictionary is good here.
　The third meaning given in the dictionary fits here.
　　　助動詞の will はなくてもよい。

文脈からその単語の意味を想像してみなさい。
　From the given context, try to imagine the meaning of the word.

この２つの言葉は同じ意味を持っていますか，それとも異なる意味を持っていますか。
  Do these two words have the same meaning or different meanings?

ここでは引用句が比喩的な意味で使われています。
  The quoted phrase is used figuratively here.

この表現はよく使われるので覚えましょう。
  1. **Since this expression is often used, let's learn it.**
  2. *__Since this expression is often used, let's memorize it.__
     memorize の目的語には次のようなものが可能である。
         memorize a poem
         memorize a short story
         memorize a page of expressions
         memorize a list of expressions
     しかしながら，
         *memorize an expression
     ということはできない。目的語に expression をとる場合には，
         learn an expression
     と言わなくてはならない。

▶ video とはどんな意味ですか。
  What does *video* mean?

▶ recede の意味を簡単な英語で説明してください。
  Could you explain the meaning of the word *recede* in plain English?

▶ desk と table の単語の意味の違いは何ですか。
  What is the difference in meaning between *desk* and *table*?

▶ desk と table の単語の使い方の違いを教えてください。
　Could you tell me the difference in usage between the words *desk* and *table*?

▶ YMCA は何の略ですか。
　What does *YMCA* stand for?

　　日本語では英語の語群を省略するとき，言葉の一部分を使って略語を作ることが多いが，英語ではそれぞれの単語の頭文字を使って省略することが多い。例えば，San Francisco という地名を日本語ではシスコと言うが，英語で省略する場合には S.F. のように言う。Los Angeles は日本語ではロスとなり，英語で L.A. のように言う。
　　ＹＭＣＡは，Young Men's Christian Association の略である。

▶ その言葉はどのように使いますか。
　How can we use the word?

▶ その言葉はどのような場合に使われるのですか。
　In what case can we use the word?

▶ どうして as という言葉をこの場合使ってはいけないのですか。
　Why can't we use the word *as* in this case?

▶ なぜ，こういう表現をするのですか。
　Why do you use this expression?
　Why is this expression used?
　Why is this expression possible?

▶ そのほかにどういう表現がありますか。
　What other expressions do you have?
　How can you say it another way?
　On top of that, what expressions do you have?

▶ hindrance という単語の意味がわかりません。
I don't know the meaning of the word *hindrance*.

▶ hindrance とはどんな意味ですか。
What does *hindrance* mean?
What is the meaning of *hindrance*?
What do you mean by *hindrance*?

▶ この単語の意味は何ですか。
What is the meaning of this word?

▶ この場合，辞書の２番目の意味でよいのでしょうか。
Will the second meaning in the dictionary be all right in this case?

▶ ５ページに，意味のわからない単語が３つあります。
There are three words I am not familiar with on page 5.
There are three words I don't know on page 5.

▶ ３番目の段落では，miss という言葉はどんな意味で使われていますか。
In what sense is the word *miss* used in the third paragraph?

▶ 25 ページの７行目の，envoy という言葉の意味がわかりません。
I don't know the meaning of the word *envoy* on line 7 on page 25.

▶ 上から５行目の stationary という言葉の意味がわかりません。
I don't know the meaning of the word *stationary* on the 5th line from the top.

▶アメリカでまだこのような表現が使われているのでしょうか。
　Are these expressions still used in America?

▶その単語は，まだ習っていません。
  1. **We haven't learned the word yet.**
  2. **We haven't learned that word yet.**
  3. **We haven't had that word yet.**
　　　1は，生徒が最も普通に使う表現である。
　　　3の言い方は頻度から言えばあまり高くはない。

B　文・文章の理解

Aの文とBの文との違いは次の通りです。
　The difference between sentence A and sentence B is as follows.
　　　書き言葉では，as follows という表現の次にはコロン（：）を使うことが多い。

Aの文とBの文との違いがわかりますか。
　Do you understand the difference between sentence A and sentence B?

2つの文の意味の違いについて説明してごらんなさい。
　Explain the difference in meaning between the two sentences.
　Explain how these two sentences differ in meaning.
　Explain how these two sentences are different in meaning.
　　　「違う」という日本語は，英語表現では名詞の difference，形容詞の different，あるいは動詞の differ を使って表すことができる。

Aの文とBの文との間には大差はありません。
　There is no big difference between sentence A and sentence B.

その文の意味を，できるだけ易しい英語で説明しなさい。
　Explain the meaning of the sentence in as plain English as possible.
　Explain the meaning of the sentence in as plain English as you can.

この章の内容を理解するのはそれほど難しいことはないはずです。
　It shouldn't be so difficult to understand this chapter.

▶この文の意味は何ですか。
　What's the meaning of this sentence?
　What does this sentence mean?

▶この文の意味がわかりません。
　I can't understand the meaning of this sentence.
　I can't understand what this sentence means.

▶文AとBとの違いについて説明してください。
　Could you explain the difference between Sentence A and Sentence B?
　Could you tell us the difference between Sentence A and Sentence B?

▶6ページの3行目の文の意味は何でしょうか。
　What is the meaning of the third line on page 6?

▶6行目の文の意味は全くチンプンカンプンです。
　The meaning of the sixth line is Greek to me.

この話の内容が理解できましたか。
1. **Did you understand what this story is about?**
2. **Did you understand the content of this story?**

　　1 の方が 2 よりも自然である。
　　content「内容」に類似した単語に context がある。後者は「文脈」や「文の前後関係」という意味である。

まだ，このページの内容がよく飲み込めない人はいますか。
1. **Are there any students who still don't understand this page well?**
2. **Are there any students who have not understood this page well?**

　　1 の方がより自然な表現である。

(記事の) 内容が難しすぎますか。
Is the story too difficult for you?
Is the content too difficult for you?

この章の内容が理解できましたか。
1. **Did you understand this chapter?**
2. **Did you understand what the chapter was about?**
3. **Do you understand what the chapter is about?**
4. **Did you understand what was in this chapter?**
5. ***Did you understand the content of this chapter?**
6. ***Did you understand the contents of this chapter?**
7. ***Did you understand what the chapter is about?**

　　7 の is という形は不自然である。2 のように Did 〜 was ...? とするか，3 のように Do 〜 is ...? とするのが自然である。
　　「内容」という日本語を content あるいは contents という英語に無理に訳すと不自然な文になる。

第3章の内容は，第2章の内容と類似しています。
　The contents of Chapter 3 are similar to those of Chapter 2.

Chapter 3 is similar to Chapter 2 in content.
「(容器の) 中身」や「本の目次」などについて言うときにも，
　　　the contents of a pocket　ポケットの中身
　　　the contents of a book　本の目次
のように，content に《複数の -s》を付ける。

この文章が何を言っているのか，簡単に説明してください。
Could you briefly tell me what this sentence is saying?
Could you briefly tell me what this sentence means?

この本の内容を，ノート3ページ以内にまとめてごらんなさい。
1. **In your notebook, sum up the book in three pages or less.**
2. **Sum up the book in three notebook pages or less.**
3. **Sum up this book in your notebook, in 3 pages or less.**
4. **Sum up the contents of this book in your notebook, in 3 pages or less.**
5. **Sum up this book within 3 pages in your notebook.**

　　1 が最も自然である。5 のような within の使い方はあまり自然ではない。

▶だいたい，わかりました。
1. **I caught the gist of it.**
2. **I roughly understood.**
3. **I understood more or less.**

　　1〜3 はどれでもよいが，1 は最も自然な口語表現である。

▶いいえ，まだ，この章がよくわかりません。
No, I don't. I don't understand this chapter well.

▶いいえ。説明していただけますか。
No, I don't. Could you explain it?

新出単語が多いので，少し内容を理解するのが難しいかもしれません。
1. Since there are many new words, you may have a little difficulty understanding the content.
2. Since there are many new words, you may have a little difficulty in understanding the content.
 1の方がよく使われる。

この段落の内容を，だれかわかりやすく説明してください。
 Somebody explain the meaning of this paragraph in plain terms.
 Somebody explain the content of this paragraph in plain terms.
 content には formal で literary なニュアンスがある。

この段落の内容を，おおまかに説明してください。
 Please explain briefly what this paragraph is about.

筆者が言いたいことをノートに書きなさい。
 Write in your notebooks what the author wants to say.
 Write in your notebooks the author's main point.
 日本語の意味だけに注意してこの文を英訳すると，Write what the author wants to say in your notebooks. のような文も考えられる。しかし，このような語順にすると，in your notebooks が the author wants to say という節の一部であるかのような印象を一瞬与えるかもしれない。

2番目の段落のおおよその意味を言いなさい。
 Sum up the second paragraph.

難しい語句のほとんどは，注に説明されています。
1. Most difficult words are defined in the footnotes.
2. Most of the difficult words are defined in the footnotes.

3. **Difficult words are mostly defined in the footnotes.**
4. **Difficult words are mostly explained in the footnotes.**
5. **Difficult words are mostly accounted for in the footnotes.**

　　1, 2は「難しい語句のほとんどが,注に説明されている」という意味にしか取れないが, 3, 4, 5はこの意味のほかに,「難しい語句は,ほとんど注で説明されているが,注以外のところで説明されているものもある」という意味にも取れる。1, 2の方が3, 4, 5よりもまぎらわしくなくてよい。こうした意味の違いは mostly という副詞の使い方と位置に起因する。

本文は私にとっても難しいので,わからなくても気にする必要はありません。
As the text is difficult for me, don't worry even if you don't understand it.
As the text is difficult for me, don't worry even if you don't understand.
　　いずれも正しい。

次の課は,この課よりも少し難しくなっています。
The next lesson will be a bit more difficult than this lesson.
The next lesson is a bit more difficult than this lesson.
　　「次の〜」という場合,定冠詞の the が必要である。

次の課は,この課よりも簡単です。
The next lesson will be easier than this lesson.
The next lesson is easier than this lesson.

この課の内容を,英文でまとめなさい。
Sum up this lesson in English.

▶まだ意味がはっきりしません。
The meaning is not clear, yet.

▶単語の意味はすべてわかりますが，内容が理解できません。
I know every word but, I cannot understand what is written.

▶問題の意味がわかりません。
I don't understand the question.

▶8ページの 16 行目から9ページの3行目までの意味がわかりません。
I don't understand the meaning of the passage from line 16 on page 8 to line 3 on page 9.

▶この文がどこにかかるかがわかりません。
I don't know what this word modifies.

▶この段落の内容が理解できません。
I don't understand the contents of this paragraph.

▶もっとわかりやすく説明してください。
Could you explain that in simpler terms?

　　上記の代わりに，Could you make this easier to understand? Could you elaborate on that? などと表現してもよい。

▶具体的な例をあげて説明してください。
Could you give me some examples?

▶それについてどのように考えればいいのでしょうか。
How should we go about it?

C 和訳

この文は日本語で何と言いますか。
  What is this sentence in Japanese?
  How do you say this sentence in Japanese?

この文は，日本語でどのように訳しますか。
  How would you translate this sentence into Japanese?

この文では，こういう訳し方は適当ではありません。
  For this sentence, this kind of translation is not suitable.

文全体の意味を考えなくてはいけません。
  You have to think about the complete meaning.
  You have to think about the meaning of the whole sentence.

　　whole は「全体の」という意味であり，every や all と意味上混同しやすい。whole は単数の可算名詞を修飾する。all は可算・不可算名詞のいずれをも修飾することができる。定冠詞の the がある場合には，the whole ..., all the ... の順序になる。
　　every の場合には the と共に使うことはできない。

自分で日本語に訳したところの意味がよくわかりますか。
  1. Do you understand well what you've translated into Japanese?
  2. Do you understand what you've translated into Japanese well?
  3. Do you understand well the English sentence you've translated into Japanese?
  4. Do you understand the English sentence you've translated into Japanese well?

　　1〜4 はいずれも standard な表現である。3, 4 は，what の

代わりに the English sentence と置き換えているが、この方がより明確である。

だれか hostility を日本語で何というか知っている人はいますか。
　Does anyone know how to say *hostility* in Japanese?

予習をしていないと，訳はわかりませんよ。
　If you don't prepare beforehand, you won't be able to translate.

教科書に訳を書いてはいけません。
　1. Don't write the translation in your textbooks.
　2. Don't write the translation out in your textbooks.
　　　1の方が2よりもよい。

D　文学作品

この小説の著者はだれですか。
　Who is the author of this novel?
　Who wrote this novel?

この作者の小説を何か読んだことがありますか。
　1. Have you ever read any novel written by this author?
　2. Have you ever read any novel written by this writer?
　　　author と writer のどちらでもよいが，author の方が品格のある語とされるので、1の方を好む人がいる。

作者はいつ頃活躍しましたか。
　About when was the author active?

この小説は1986年に書かれました。
　This novel was written in 1986.

この随筆は 17 世紀初頭に書かれました。
1. This essay was written at the beginning of the 17th century.
2. This essay was written in the early 17th century.
3. This essay was written in the beginning of the 17th century.

  1 と 2 はよいが，3 は不自然に感じるネイティブスピーカーがいる。

この作者と同時代の人に，どんな人がいますか。
Who are some contemporaries of the author?

この悲劇は日本の神話からヒントを得ています。
1. This tragedy is based on a Japanese myth.
2. This tragedy is based on Japanese mythology.
3. *This tragedy is based on a Japanese mythology.

  1 と 2 は正しいが，3 は誤りである。mythology は不可算名詞である。

小説には，どんなジャンルがあるのですか。
What genres of novels are there?
What genres are novels classified into?

  ここでは classified という語はやや formal な響きがする。
  genre [ʒɑ́ːŋrə] はもともと「(芸術品の) 品種，様式」という意味のフランス語。元来英語には語頭に [ʒ] の音が来ることはなかった。

これらはどういう種類の小説ですか。
What kinds of novels are these?

作者がここで最も言いたいことは何ですか。
What point does the author most want to make here?
What is the main thing the author wants to say here?

What is the main point of the author's argument?

ここで，作者は何を言おうとしているのでしょうか。
What is the author trying to say here?
What is the author driving at here?

> drive at は「～を意図する」「(～を言う) つもりである」という意味の熟語的表現であるが，通例進行形で使う。
>
> > What are you driving at?
> > (あなたは何を言おうとしているのですか。)
>
> ただし，you とともに drive at という語句を用いるときには非常に rude, angry なニュアンスがあるので注意が必要である。第三者に言及する場合は drive at という言い方をしても問題はない。

この作品における主人公の敵対者はだれですか。
Which character in this book has the role of antagonist?
Which character in this book plays the role of antagonist?

63ページの上から7行目の文は，何を暗示しているのでしょうか。
1. **What does the seventh sentence from the top of page 63 imply?**
2. **What does the seventh sentence from the top, on page 63 imply?**

> 1, 2 のいずれでもよいが，2 のように言うときには，... from the top, on page ... のようにポーズが必要である。

▶作者が言おうとしていることがよくわかりません。
1. **I cannot understand clearly what the author wants to say.**
2. **I don't understand clearly what the author wants to say.**
3. **I don't understand clearly what the author is driving at.**
4. **I don't understand what the author is getting at.**

> 1, 2 は標準的な表現，3, 4 は口語的な表現である。
> 日本語に引かれて英訳すると，

*I don't understand what the author is driving at so well.
　　　*I don't clearly understand what the author wants to say so well.

などの文が考えられそうであるが，いずれも不自然である。

▶作者が言いたいことは自然への畏敬(いけい)ということでしょうか。

1. **Is the author trying to express his respect for nature?**
2. **Does the author want to point out the awesomeness of nature?**
3. **Does the author want to point out his reverence for nature?**
4. **Does the author want to point out that he stands in awe of nature?**
5. **Is it that what the author wants to do is express his reverence towards nature?**
6. **Is it that what the author wants to point out is his reverence for nature?**

　　　5と6はやや冗長な表現であるから，1〜4の方がよい。

▶要するに，作者は神を畏敬しているということでしょうか。

1. **In short, does the author stand in awe of God?**
2. ***In short, is the author in awe of God?**

　　　1の方が2よりもよい。2はやや "off" な感じ。
　　　「神」というとき，god のように小文字でつづると多神教を表し，God のように大文字でつづると一神教を意味する。キリスト教は一神教であるから，その意味なら God のようにつづらなくてはならない。

▶この本はどういう点に注意して読んだらいいのでしょうか。

What points should we pay attention to when reading this book?

▶この作品は何にヒントを得ていますか。
  1. **What gave rise to this work?**
  2. **What gave hints to this work?**
     もとの日本文には2の方が近いが，1の方が意味がわかりやすい。

▶この本は事実に基づいて書かれていますか。
  Is this book based on actual fact?
     「書かれている」を無理に訳して，
        *Is this book written based on facts?
     のように言うと，やや不自然である。
     ついでながら，fact には true の意味があるから，*a true fact のような言い方はできない。

▶作者と作品の主人公とは大いに関係がありますか。
  1. **Is there a close relationship between this book's author and his hero?**
  2. **Is there a strong correspondence between this book's author and her heroine?**
  3. **Does the author have a lot to do with the hero of the book?**
     2の correspondence には，
        ① relationship
        ② letter-writing activity
     の2つの意味があり，まぎらわしい。
     3の意味は不明瞭である。... have a lot to do with ... にはいろいろな解釈が成り立つ。
        ① Does the author pay much attention to the hero?
        ② Has the author been able to create much activity for the hero's part in the story?
        ③ Is the hero in some way connected with the author's life and experiences?

▶この作品の著者はどういう経歴の持ち主ですか。
  1. **What is the background of the author of this book?**
  2. **What background does the author of this book have?**
  3. **What is the career of the author of this book?**
  4. **What career does the author of this book have?**
    3，4 はあまり自然な表現ではない。
    career [kəríər] の発音に注意すること。日本語のキャリアはこの語に由来する。

▶この作品の著者はどのような時代に生まれ育ったのですか。
  In what era was the author of this book born?
  In what period was the author of this book born and raised?

▶この話には難しい単語が多くて速く読めません。
  1. **There are many difficult words in this story, so I can't read it fast.**
  2. **There are many difficult words in this story, so I can't go very fast.**
  3. ***There are many difficult words in this story, so I can't read fast.**
    3 の can't read fast という言い方は，total reading ability (for all reading material) has been slowed down という意味合いが強いから，この場合には 1 や 2 の方がよい。

▶何が文学のよしあしを決めますか。
  What determines the quality of literature?

▶私は語学よりも文学の方が好きです。
  I like literature better than linguistics.
  I prefer literature to linguistics.

7　単語・語い

英語がうまくなるには語いを増やすことが大切です。
   It is important to increase your vocabulary in order to become a good speaker of English.

内容を理解するには，語いの力が不可欠です。
   1. You need to have a rich vocabulary in order to grasp the contents.
   2. You have to have a rich vocabulary in order to grasp the contents.
   3. You need to have rich vocabulary in order to grasp the content.
   4. You have to have rich vocabulary in order to grasp the content.

　　　need の方が have to よりも丁寧で，自然である。1，2，3 は a rich vocabulary となっているが，4 は rich vocabulary のように冠詞が付いていない。a がある方が普通の言い方である。

単語は単語だけ切り離して暗記するよりも，文脈の中で覚える方が覚えやすいと思います。
   I think it is better to learn words in context rather than to memorize them independently.

語いを増やす一番いい方法はできるだけ多くの本を読むことです。
   The best way to increase your vocabulary is to read as many books as you can.
   The best way to increase your vocabulary is to read as many books as possible.
   The best way to increase your vocabulary is to read extensively.

いずれも standard な表現である。

単語は意味を理解するばかりでなく，つづりも書けるようにしておきなさい。
Please try to be able to not only understand the meaning of words, but also write them.

必ず新出語いの意味は調べておきなさい。
Be sure to check the meaning of the new vocabulary.

Be sure to check the meanings of the new vocabulary items.

Be sure to check the meanings of the new words and phrases.

いずれも standard な表現である。

月曜日に語いのクイズをします。
You are going to have a vocabulary quiz on Monday.

月曜日の語いのクイズの範囲は 34 ページから 38 ページまでです。
1. The quiz on Monday will cover pages 34 through 38.
2. The quiz on Monday will cover from page 34 through 38.
3. The quiz on Monday will cover from page 34 to page 38.
4. The quiz on Monday will cover pages 34 to 38.

「～から ... まで」に相当する英語に from ～ to ... があるが，この形は不明瞭である。上記の場合を考えると，たとえば，page 38 が含まれるのかどうかということである。page 38 を明確に含むには 1 や 2 のように言った方がよい。

from ～ to ... の from は，4 のように省略することも可能である。

import の反意語は何ですか。
What is the antonym of *import*?
What is the opposite of *import*?

sure の同義語は何ですか。
What is a synonym of *sure*?

日本語の「始発列車」に当たる英単語は何といいますか。
1. **How do you say *shihatsuressha* in English?**
2. **What is the English equivalent of the Japanese word *shihatsuressha*?**
3. **What is *shihatsuressha* in English?**
4. **What is the English for the Japanese word *shihatsuressha*?**

　　1 は standard, 2 は formal, 3 は informal, 4 はやや不自然な表現である。

この言葉の反意語と類義語を言いなさい。
1. **Please tell me the antonym and some synonyms for this word.**
2. **Please give me the antonym and some synonyms for this word.**
3. **Please tell me some words that mean the same as this word, and also give me its opposite.**
4. ***Please tell me the opposite of this word and some other words with the same meaning.**

　　synonyms に複数形の s が付いているのは, 類義語にはふつう 2 つ以上あることが多いからである。
　　4 の意味は不明瞭である。反義語と同じ意味を持つ語を尋ねているようなニュアンスがある。

▶私の語いはとても貧弱です。
1. **My vocabulary is very limited.**
2. **My vocabulary is very poor.**
3. **My vocabulary is very small.**

　　1～3 はいずれも正しいが, 1 が 2 よりも, 2 が 3 よりもよい。

▶この単語を使った熟語を教えてください。
1. Could you give us some idioms using this word?
2. Could you show us some idioms that include this word?
3. Could you show us some idioms with this word?
4. Could you give us some idioms that use this word?
5. Could you give us some idioms that have this word in them?
6. Could you show us some idioms with this word in them?
7. Could you give us some idioms containing this word?
8. Could you show us some idioms containing this word?
9. *Could you show us some idioms with this word in it?
10. *Could you show us some idioms having this word in it?

　　1〜6 は standard, 7〜8 はやや informal, 9 と 10 は正しくない。
　　9, 10 の ... in it? の代名詞 it が them であれば正しくなる。

▶この単語はもともとフランス語から来ているのでしょうか。
Is this word derived from French?

▶follow one's nose という熟語は、どのようにして使うのですか。例をあげて説明してください。
How can we use the idiom *follow one's nose*? Could you show us some examples of how it is used?

8 　文法

A 　主語

主語は大文字のSで表します。
　　Subjects are indicated by capital S's.

The subject of a sentence is indicated by a capital S.
Subjects are shown by capital S's.
The subject of a sentence is shown by a capital S.
The subject of a sentence is marked by a capital S.
いずれでもよい。

日本語では主語をよく省略しますが，英語ではほとんどの場合において主語が必要です。
In Japanese the subject is often deleted, but in English it is almost always necessary.

その場合には，主語は we でも you でもかまいません。
In that case, the subject can be either *we* or *you*.

英語では，「天候」や「時刻」などについていう場合は，非人称の it を主語にします。
In English, the impersonal *it* is used as a subject when referring to weather or time.

英語では，動詞は主語の人称と数に一致します。
In English, the verb agrees with the subject in person and number.

命令文では主語の you を省略することが多いのですが，省略しない場合もあります。
In imperative sentences the subject *you* is usually deleted, but in some cases it is not.

肯定文では，主語は動詞の前に置かれます。
In affirmative sentences the subject is placed in front of the verb.

複文では，従属節で主語と動詞の位置が変わる場合があります。
1. **In complex sentences, the order of the subject and the verb in subordinate clauses is sometimes reversed.**
2. ***In complex sentences, the order of the subject and the verb in subordinate clauses is sometimes changed.**

　　1 では reversed が使われ，2 では changed が使われている。change はこのような状況ではあまり使われない。

受動態では，能動態のときの目的語が主語になります。
In passive sentences, the object of the active sentence becomes the subject.

代名詞が主語になる場合には，ふつう強勢はありません。代名詞は機能語の1つだからです。
1. **When the pronoun becomes the subject, it is usually not accented. That is because the pronoun is a function word.**
2. ***When the pronoun becomes the subject, it is usually not accented. It is because the pronoun is a function word.**

　　2 では … it is because … となっているが，1 のように … that is because … としたい。that は前述した事柄の理由を説明する機能があるが，it では指す内容が不明瞭である。it を使うと，"off" あるいは "foreign" な感じがする。しかし，it は次のような場合には that と同じ働きをする。

　　　　I'm sleepy this morning. It's because I didn't get much sleep last night.

主語を強調すると，どんな文に書き直すことができますか。
1. **If you want to stress the subject, what kind of sentence can you put it in?**
2. **If you want to stress the subject, what kind of sentence can you rewrite it into?**

　　1 の方が 2 よりもよい。

主語を強調すると，どんな文が可能ですか。
　If the subject is emphasized, what kind of sentence will be possible?

この文の主語は何ですか。
　What is the subject of this sentence?

この文の主部はどこからどこまでですか。
　1. What is the subject of this sentence?
　2. What comprises the subject of this sentence?
　3. What makes up the subject of this sentence?
　4. *From where to where is the subject of this sentence?
　　「どこからどこまで」を英語に直訳して From where to where ... とすると，英文として viable でなくなる。2 や 3 でもよいが，convoluted すぎる。1 のように簡潔に言いたい。

この文を受動態にすると，主語はどうなりますか。
　If this sentence is changed to the passive, what will happen to the subject?

この文の主語は単数ですかそれとも複数ですか。
　Is the subject of this sentence singular or plural?

その文の主語を複数形にして，全体の文を書き直してください。
　1. Rewrite the sentence, changing the subject to the plural form.
　2. Rewrite the sentence, making the subject plural.
　3. Change the subject of the sentence into the plural form and rewrite the sentence.
　4. Make the subject of the sentence plural and rewrite the sentence.
　　1 と 2 は直接的な表現である。

どんな場合に主語を省略することができますか。
　In what case can you delete the subject?
　In what case is it possible to omit the subject?
　Under what condition can you omit the subject?

▶主語とは何ですか。
　What is a subject?

▶文章の主語にはどんな品詞がなれるのですか。
　What parts of speech can be the subject of a sentence?

▶命令文では例外なく主語を省略するのですか。
　In imperative sentences, can you delete the subject without exception?
　In imperative sentences, can you always delete the subject?

▶命令文ではいつも主語を省略することが可能なのですか。
　Is it always possible to omit the subject in an imperative sentence?

▶この文の主語はどれでしょうか。
　What is the subject of this sentence?

▶この it は仮主語ですか。
　Is this *it* a tentative subject?

▶この it は何を指しているのでしょうか。
　What does this *it* refer to?

▶主語の it の用法は何ですか。
　1. What is the subject *it* used?
　2. What is the use of the subject *it*?
　　　2の What is the use of ...? の意は，口語では "What good is ...?"

(〜は何の役に立つのですか)ということである。それゆえ,人によっては "No use, that I can see!" といったような flippant な応答も考えられる。1のように言いたい。

▶この文で主語を複数にすると文全体はどのように変わりますか。
  1. **If the subject of this sentence is changed to the plural, how will the sentence change?**
  2. **If the subject of this sentence is changed to the plural, what will happen to the whole sentence?**

  1の方が2よりもよい。

▶この文で主語は省略できますか。
Can you omit the subject from this sentence?
Can you omit the subject of this sentence?
Can you omit the subject in this sentence?

  She omitted his name on [in] the list.
  (彼女は彼の名前を名簿に載せなかった。)
  omit は「〜を落とす」という意味で,このような文にも使うことができる。この文の場合,
   ① 彼女は(故意に)彼の名前を名簿に載せなかった。
   ② 彼女は(うっかりして)彼の名前を名簿に載せなかった。
の両方の意味が可能である。どちらの意味であるかは文脈によって判断するしかない。

▶なぜ主語がこの位置に置かれているのですか。
Why is the subject placed in this position?

▶この場合,何を主語にして英作文をしたらいいのでしょうか。
What subject do I need in this case to make an English sentence?
In this case, what subject do I need to make an English sentence?
In this case, what subject should I have to make an English

sentence?
　　英作文をする場合，何を主語にしてよいか迷うことが多い。主語が決まればそれを受ける述語やそのほかの関係がわかる。

▶ you の代わりに，they を主語にすることも可能ですか。
Can we use *they* instead of *you* as a subject?

▶ 18 ページ，上から 5 番目の文の主語は何ですか。
What is the subject of the fifth sentence from the top on page 18?

B　述語

述語は大文字の V で表します。
　Verbs are indicated by capital V's.
　Verbs are shown by capital V's.

主語と述語の関係を説明してください。
　Could you explain the relationship between the subject and the predicate?

状況から文脈が判断できる場合には，述部を省略することもあります。
　When the context is understood from the given situation, the predicate is occasionally deleted.

be 動詞が述部にある場合には，be 動詞を前に出して疑問文を作ります。
　When you have a *be*-verb in the predicate, the question sentence is made by putting the *be*-verb in front.

この文の述語はどれですか。
　What is the predicate of this sentence?

この文で，主語と述語は何ですか。
　What are the subject and the predicate of this sentence?
　What is the subject and what is the predicate of this sentence?
　What are the subject and the predicate in this sentence?
　What is the subject and what is the predicate in this sentence?
　　... the predicate of this sentence でも ... the predicate in this sentence でもよいが，of の方が smooth である。

この文の述部はどこからどこまでですか。
　What is the predicate of this sentence?

黒板に書いた文の主語と述語を指摘してごらんなさい。
　Point out the subject and the predicate of the sentence on the board.

24ページの下から6行目の文の述語は何ですか。
　1. What is the predicate of the sixth sentence from the bottom of page 24?
　2. What is the predicate of the sixth sentence from the bottom, on page 24?
　　1の方が2よりもよい。

▶述語とは何ですか。
　What does predicate mean?
　What is a predicate?

▶述語を文頭に置くこともあるんですか。
　1. Do you sometimes place the predicate at the front of a

sentence?
2. **Do you sometimes place the predicate in the front part of a sentence?**
3. **Do you sometimes place the predicate at the head of a sentence?**
4. ***Do you sometimes place the predicate in the front of a sentence?**

　前置詞と front という名詞との間には次のような関係がある。
　　in front of ～
　　at the front of ～
　つまり，前置詞 at を使う場合は front の前に定冠詞 the が必要である。
　2 では front が part にかかる形容詞として使われている。

▶どんな品詞でも述語になれますか。
Can any part of speech be a predicate?

▶文の述語にはどんな品詞がなれるのですか。
What parts of speech can be the predicate of a sentence?

▶述語になれない品詞にはどんなものがありますか。
What are the parts of speech that cannot be a predicate?

C 目的語

目的語は大文字のOで表します。
　Objects are indicated by capital O's.
　Objects are shown by capital O's.

自動詞は，目的語をとることはできません。
　1. **An intransitive verb does not take an object.**
　2. **An intransitive verb cannot take an object.**

1の方が2よりも自然である。

目的語をとる動詞を他動詞といいます。
　A verb that can take an object is called a transitive verb.

目的語には直接目的語と間接目的語の2種類があります。
　There are two kinds of objects : direct objects and indirect objects.

動詞の中には，目的語を2つとるものがあります。
　1. There are verbs that can take two objects.
　2. Some verbs can take two objects.
　3. Among verbs there are verbs that can take two objects.
　　1や2の方が3よりもより自然な表現である。

他動詞を含む文は，受動態に変えることができます。
　Sentences containing a transitive verb can be changed into the passive.
　Sentences that contain a transitive verb can be changed into the passive.

間接目的語を直接目的語の後に置くと，前置詞が必要です。
　A preposition is required when an indirect object is placed after the direct object.

日本語と英語とでは，目的語の位置が異なります。
　The position of objects differs between Japanese and English.
　Japanese and English differ in their placement of objects.
　Japanese and English differ in the placement of objects.

目的語とは何ですか。
　What is an object?

目的語に相当する英語 object は可算名詞であるから,「目的語は何ですか」というような文においても可算名詞の扱いを念頭に入れなくてはならない。「美とは何か」というような文では, beauty が不可算名詞であるから, What is beauty? のように不定冠詞を付さないことになる。

bought の目的語はどれですか。
  What is the object of *bought*?

bought の目的語はどの言葉ですか。
  Which word is the object of *bought*?

どちらが間接目的語で,どちらが直接目的語ですか。
  Which word is the indirect object and which word is the direct object?
  Which one is the indirect object and which one is the direct object?

▶目的語になれる品詞にはどんなものがありますか。
  What parts of speech can be an object?

▶自動詞は目的語をとることはないのですか。
  Don't intransitive verbs take an object?

▶直接目的語と間接目的語との違いは何ですか。
  What is the difference between a direct object and an indirect object?

▶間接目的語と直接目的語の位置を入れ替えたら,どんな前置詞が必要ですか。
  If you reverse the direct and indirect objects, what kind of preposition will you need?
  If you exchange the position of the indirect object and the

direct object, what kind of preposition will you need?
If you exchange the position of the indirect object and the direct object, what preposition will you need?

▶ 7行目の文の目的語は何ですか。
1. **What is the object in the seventh sentence?**
2. **What is the object for the seventh sentence?**
3. **What word is the object of the seventh sentence?**
4. *****What is the object of the seventh sentence?**
    4は日本語の意味に合わない。以下の2つの意味に解釈される。
    ① What is the seventh line trying to achieve?
    ② What is its purpose?
    1〜3の方がよい。

▶ どれがこの文の目的語であるかわかりません。
I don't know what the object is in this sentence.
I don't know what word is the object in this sentence.
I don't know what word is the object of this sentence.

D 補語

補語は動詞の意味を補って文を完成させます。
1. **A complement completes a sentence by supplying a meaning to a verb.**
2. **Complements complete sentences by supplying some meaning to verbs.**
    1の方が2よりもよい。

補語とは，それだけでは完全な意味を表さない動詞の意味を補う語です。
1. **A complement is a word that completes the meaning of the verb it follows.**

2. **A complement is a word that can make up for the meaning of a verb that cannot convey a complete meaning.**

 2は日本文に近いがやや wordy である。端的に1のように言ってもよい。

補語は大文字のCで表します。
 Complements are indicated by capital C's.
 Complements are shown by capital C's.

動詞の中には補語をとるものがあります。
 Some verbs require complements.

補語には2種類あります。
 There are two kinds of complements.

補語には主格補語と目的格補語という2種類の補語があります。
 There are two types of complement: a subjective complement and an objective complement.

主格補語は主語と関係があり，目的格補語は目的語と関係があります。
 The subjective complement has to do with the subject and the objective complement has to do with the object.

述部の中で，be 動詞の次に来るものを主格補語といいます。
 What comes after the *be*-verb in the predicate is called a subjective complement.

目的語の次に来る補語を，目的格補語と呼びます。
 A complement coming after the object is called an objective complement.

この文で補語はどれですか。
　What is the complement in this sentence?

補語とは何ですか。簡単に説明しなさい。
　1. **What is a complement? Please explain it briefly.**
　2. **What is a complement? Please explain briefly.**
　　　1 では代名詞の it が使われているが，この代名詞は 2 のように省略した方がよいと考えるネイティブスピーカーもいる。

補語にはどんなものがありますか。
　1. **What kinds of complements are there?**
　2. **What kinds of complements do you have?**
　　　1 の方が 2 よりもよい。

主格補語の例をあげてごらんなさい。
　Show me some examples of subjective complements.

目的格補語をとる動詞に，どんなものがありますか。
　What kinds of verbs do you have that can take an objective complement?

補語を省略すると文はどうなりますか。
　1. **If you take the complement out of the sentence, what will happen to the rest of the sentence?**
　2. **If you take a complement out of the sentence, what will happen to the rest of the sentence?**
　3. **If you take a complement out of the sentence, what will happen to the sentence?**
　4. ***If you take a complement out of the sentence, what will happen to the whole sentence?**
　　　補語を省くと，その後に残る文はもはやもとの文とは異なってしまう。したがって，4 のように ... what will happen to the whole sentence? という言い方はおかしい。the whole sentence

の代わりに，1や2のように the rest of the sentence とすべきである。3では the rest of the sentence ではなく the sentence となっているが，この言い方も可能である。

the complement は特定の状況，a complement にすると一般的な状況になる。

「補語」と「お世辞」のつづりを間違えないようにしなさい。
1. **Be careful not to confuse *complement* with *compliment*.**
2. **Be careful not to confuse the spelling of *complement* with that of *compliment*.**
3. **Be careful not to make a spelling mistake between *complement* and *compliment*.**

1や2の方が3より自然な英語表現である。

confuse という動詞を使うとき，with という前置詞を相関的に使うことに注意すること。

91ページの上から8行目の文には補語がありますか。
1. **Is there a complement in the eighth sentence from the top of page 91?**
2. **Does the eighth sentence from the top of page 91 have a complement?**
3. ***Is there any complement in the eighth sentence from the top on page 91?**

3の any complement, from the top on page 91 は，1のように，それぞれ a complement, from the top of page 91 とすべきである。

▶ 「補語」の英語を教えてください。
Please tell us the English word for *hogo*.

▶ 「補語」はどのように英語でつづりますか。
How do you spell the English word for *hogo*?

▶どうして補語は大文字のCで表すのですか。
Why do you use a capital C to show *hogo*?
*Why do you use the capital C to show *hogo*?
　　the capital C とすると，どの大文字のCかと読者を distract させる。a capital C とすべきである。

▶補語がまだよくわかりません。
I am not familiar with complements yet.

▶補語は文中でどんな働きをしているのですか。
What role do complements play in a sentence?

▶補語にはどんな品詞がなれるのですか。
What parts of speech can complements be?
What parts of speech can be complements?

▶どんな動詞が補語をとることができますか。
What kinds of verbs can take complements?
What kinds of verbs take complements?
What kinds of verbs have complements?

▶補語と目的語とはどのように異なるのですか。
What is the difference between complements and objects?

▶補語には何種類あるのですか。
How many kinds of complements are there?

▶主格補語と目的格補語との違いは何ですか。
What is the difference between subjective complements and objective complements?

▶ 19ページの下から2行目の文にある beautiful という語は補語ですか。
Is the word *beautiful* in the second sentence from the bottom of page 19 a complement?
Is the word *beautiful* in the second sentence from the bottom on page 19 a complement?

　on page も of page もいずれも可能であるが，on page と言う場合には直前にポーズを置くべきである。そうでなければ from the bottom of page 19 とする。top of 〜 や bottom of 〜 という言い方の場合には，top や bottom と前置詞 of との結び付きが非常に強いからである。

E 文型

英語には5つの基本的な文型があります。
There are five basic sentence patterns in English.

S，V，O，Cはそれぞれ主語，動詞，目的語，補語の意味です。
S, V, O, and C mean subject, verb, object and complement, respectively.

最も簡単な文は，SVから成ります。
The simplest sentence consists of an S and a V.
The simplest sentence consists of a subject and a verb.

この文は第3文型です。
1. This sentence falls into the third sentence pattern.
2. This sentence belongs to the third sentence pattern.
3. This sentence is in the third sentence pattern.

　1〜3のいずれでもよいが，2はやや formal, 3はやや informal な感じがある。

▶この文は第何文型ですか。
  1. **What sentence pattern does this sentence fall into?**
  2. ***What sentence pattern is this sentence?**
     日本文には 2 の方が近いが，あまり自然な表現ではない。

F　名詞

名詞とは何ですか。例をあげて簡単に説明しなさい。
  What is a noun? Explain, using some examples.
  What is a noun? Explain, giving some examples.

英語の名詞は，可算名詞と不可算名詞に大別できます。
  English nouns can be divided into two main categories: countable nouns [countables] and uncountable nouns [uncoutables].

可算名詞とは数えることができると名詞という意味で，不可算名詞とは数えることができない名詞という意味です。
  1. **Countable nouns refer to things that can be counted, and uncountable nouns refer to things that cannot be counted.**
  2. ***Countable nouns mean that they can be counted, and uncountable nouns mean that they can not be counted.**
     1 は正しいが，2 は正しくない。名詞そのものが数えられるわけではなく，名詞が言及するものが数えられるからである。

可算名詞は普通名詞と集合名詞に分類できます。
  Countable nouns are divided into common nouns and collective nouns.

集合名詞は，いくつかのもの，あるいは複数の人から成り立ってい

る集合体を表す名詞です。
Collective nouns are nouns that show a collective entity consisting of some things or some people.

不可算名詞には，固有名詞，抽象名詞，物質名詞があります。
Uncountable nouns consist of proper nouns, abstract nouns and material nouns.

固有名詞は特定のものや人を表す名詞で，最初の文字は大文字にします。
Proper nouns are nouns that refer to specific things or people, and they begin with a capital letter.
Proper nouns are nouns that refer to specific things or persons, and they begin with a capital letter.
　　People という言葉は日々の会話でよく使われるが，person は法律の文書などでしばしば使われる。

抽象名詞は事柄やものの状態・性質・動作などを表す名詞です。
Abstract nouns are nouns that refer to the state, character, motion, etc. of things.

抽象名詞に属する名詞は，形が定まっていないので，数えることができません。
1. Abstract nouns do not take a finite form, and they are uncountable.
2. Nouns that fall into abstract nouns do not take a finite form, and they can not be counted.
　　1 は自然であるが，2 はあまり自然な言い方ではない。

kindness, happiness などの言葉は抽象名詞です。
Words like *kindness* and *happiness* are abstract nouns.

beauty は何という種類の名詞ですか。
  What kind of noun is *beauty*?

物質名詞は，ふつう，特定の形をしていなくて，しばしばものを作る材料などを表す名詞をいいます。
  Material nouns refer to things that are usually shapeless and that are often used as materials to make something.
  Material nouns usually refer to shapeless things that are often used as materials to make something.

この文で名詞はどれですか。
  What are the nouns in this sentence?

この red は名詞ですか形容詞ですか。
  1. Is the word *red* a noun or an adjective?
  2. Is this *red* a noun or an adjective?
    1の方が明確である。2は informal な表現。

ふつう，名詞の複数形には -s や -es を付けますが，このルールに従わないものもあります。
  Usually, the plural form of a noun is made by adding *-s* or *-es*, but there are some nouns that do not follow this rule.

knife の複数形は何ですか。
  1. What is the plural form for *knife*?
  2. What is the plural form of *knife*?
    for knife でも of knife でもよい。

data の単数形を知っていますか。
  Do you know the singular form of *data*?

このような場合，この単語はふつう，複数形で使います。
  1. In such case, this word is used in the plural.

2. **In cases like this, the word is usually pluralized.**
3. **In this case, the word is usually pluralized.**
　　1と2の方が3よりもよい。3のように in this case というと、「今回が例外である」というニュアンスが強くなるからである。

名詞は意味を持っている内容語なので、強く発音します。
1. **As nouns are content words that carry meaning, they are stressed when pronounced.**
2. **As nouns are content words that carry meaning, they receive vocal stress.**
3. **As nouns are content words that carry meaning, they are pronounced strongly.**
　　3はもとの日本文の意味にぴったりしない。1や2のように言った方がよい。

単語によっては、名詞形と動詞形とが同じものがあります。
1. **Some words function as both nouns and verbs.**
2. **Some words can function as both nouns and verbs.**
3. ***Some words are both nouns and verbs.**
　　3の意味は不明瞭である。1や2のように言うべきである。

名詞形と動詞形のスペリングが同じ単語があります。
The noun and verb forms of some words have the same spelling.

The noun and verb forms of some words are spelled in the same way.

-tion や -cy などは、名詞を作る接尾辞です。
-tion and *-cy* **are suffixes that can make nouns.**

young の名詞形は何ですか。
What is the noun form of *young*?

▶名詞にはどんなものがありますか。
1. **What kinds of nouns are there?**
2. **What are the kinds of nouns?**
3. **What kinds of nouns do you have?**
    3 はこの場合あまり自然な響きがしない。

▶名詞にはいろいろあるんですか。
Are there many kinds of nouns?
    「名詞には」という日本語の表現としては前置詞は in がふさわしく思われるが，kinds を使うと of を使わなくてはいけない。
    ＊Are there many kinds in nouns?

▶名詞は大別すると何種類くらいありますか。
How many major categories of nouns are there?
How many major kinds of nouns are there?
How many kinds of nouns do you have if you put them into main categories?
How many kinds of nouns do you have if you group them in main categories?

▶抽象名詞とは何ですか。
What is an abstract noun?

▶叙述名詞について詳しく説明してください。
Could you explain predicative nouns in detail?
    He is a pilot.
    (彼はパイロットだ。)
    このように，補語として用いられた名詞を述部名詞［叙述名詞］という。

▶英語の名詞の複数形について説明してください。
Could you explain the plural forms of English nouns?

▶名詞を作る接辞について説明してください。
Please explain affixes that form nouns.

▶英語では名詞と動詞とではどちらが重要ですか。
Which are more important in English, nouns or verbs?

▶どんな動詞が名詞と同じ形をしていますか。
What are some verbs that have the same forms as nouns?
What are some words that can function both as a noun and as a verb?

▶この名詞は単数形ですかそれとも複数形ですか。
Is this noun singular or plural?

▶この名詞の複数形は -s を付ければいいのですか。
Are we supposed to add an *-s* to form the plural?

G 代名詞

代名詞とは，すでに話題にのぼった名詞の代わりをする言葉です。
1. Pronouns are words used in place of nouns that have already been mentioned.
2. Pronouns are words used instead of nouns that have already been talked about.
　　1の方が2よりもよい。

例えば，it や they などは代名詞です。
1. For example, *it*, *they* and so on are pronouns.
2. For example, *it* and *they* etc. are pronouns.
　　1の方が2よりもよい。

代名詞には，関係代名詞・疑問代名詞・再帰代名詞・指示代名詞・所有代名詞・不定代名詞・人称代名詞などがあります。
　Among pronouns are relative pronouns, interrogative pronouns, reflexive pronouns, demonstrative pronouns, possessive pronouns, indefinite pronouns and personal pronouns.

代名詞はふつう強く発音しません。
　Pronouns are in general not pronounced strongly.
　Pronouns are in general not stressed.

命令文では代名詞の you をしばしば省略します。
　The pronoun *you* is often deleted in an imperative sentence.

英語で天気や時について述べるときには，しばしば代名詞の it が使われます。
　When they talk about weather or time in English, they often use the pronoun *it*.
　When we talk about weather or time in English, we often use the pronoun *it*.

この代名詞は，何を指していますか。
　What does this pronoun refer to?

この it は，どういう it ですか。
　1. What kind of *it* is this?
　2. What kind of *it* is this *it*?
　　　1 の方が 2 よりもよい。

▶代名詞はどんなときに省略できますか。
　In what cases can you delete pronouns?

▶この代名詞が何を指しているかわかりません。
I don't understand what this pronoun refers to.

H　関係代名詞

関係代名詞には，that, which, what などがあります。
Among relative pronouns are *that*, *which* and *what*.

関係代名詞は省略できるときと，省略できないときがあります。
Relative pronouns can be deleted in some cases, and cannot be deleted in other cases.
Relative pronouns can be deleted in some cases, but not in other cases.
Relative pronouns can be deleted in some cases, but not in others.

目的格の関係代名詞は省略できます。
An objective relative pronoun can be omitted.
A relative pronoun used as an object can be omitted.

関係代名詞の what は先行詞を含んでいます。
The relative pronoun *what* includes an antecedent.

この関係代名詞は何を指していますか。
What word does this relative pronoun refer to?

この関係代名詞の先行詞は何でしょうか。
What is the antecedent of this relative pronoun?

どこに関係代名詞の省略がありますか。
1. Where was a relative pronoun omitted?
2. *Where is the omission of a relative pronoun?

1 は自然な表現である。2 は日本語の直訳的で，英語としては不自然である。

▶**関係代名詞の用法がまだわかりません。説明していただけませんか。**
I don't understand how to use relative pronouns yet. Could you tell me how to use them?

I　動詞

今から動詞について説明します。
　I'll explain the verbs, starting now.
　Let me start explaining the verbs, starting now.
　I'll start explaining the verbs now.
　Let me start explaining the verbs now.
　Let me start talking about verbs now.
　*Let me explain verbs from now.
　　　「今から」という日本語を from now と訳すことはできない。

動詞は自動詞と他動詞に分けられます。
1. Verbs are divided into transitive verbs and intransitive verbs.
2. Verbs are divided into intransitive verbs and transitive verbs.
　　　1 のように transitive verbs and intransitive verbs という語順にした方が自然である。

動詞も内容語ですから，名詞と同じように強く読みます。
1. Verbs are also content words, so they are stressed just like nouns are.
2. Verbs are also content words, so they are stressed, the same as nouns.

3. **As verbs are also content words, they are stressed along with nouns.**
4. **As verbs are also content words, they are stressed as well as nouns.**
5. **Verbs as well as nouns are stressed since they are content words.**
6. **Verbs as well as nouns are stressed as they are content words.**

　　5と6はあまり自然な英文ではない。

do は時として動詞の代わりをします。
Do sometimes behaves like a verb.
Do can sometimes be used as a verb.

　　do には助動詞としての用法もあるので，このような文も可能である。もちろん do には動詞としての用法もある。ここでは代動詞としての用法についてである。

三人称単数現在の形では，動詞に s が必要です。
If the subject is a singular, third person pronoun, and present, you need to add an *s* to the verb.

be 動詞は，本動詞の現在分詞，不定詞，過去分詞のどれかと結合します。
be-verbs combine with a present participle, infinitive or past participle.

動詞の語尾の発音に気をつけてください。
1. **Be sure to pronounce verb endings.**
2. **Be sure to pronounce the ending of a verb.**
3. **Be careful of the pronunciation of the ending of a verb.**

　　1 > 2 > 3 の順で自然な表現である。

-en は，いくつかの名詞を動詞にすることができる接尾語です。
  1. *-en* is a suffix that can change certain nouns into verbs.
  2. *-en* is a suffix that changes certain nouns into verbs.
  3. **-en* is a suffix that will turn a noun into a verb.
     3 は，-en がすべての名詞を動詞に変えることができるという意味になってしまうのでふさわしくない。1 や 2 のように表現すべきである。

不規則動詞にはどんなものがありますか。
  What kinds of irregular verbs are there?

discovery の動詞形は何ですか。
  What is the verb form of *discovery*?

この動詞はどのように活用させますか。
  How do you conjugate this verb?

study はどのように活用しますか。
  How do you conjugate *study*?

動詞 study の活用を書きなさい。
  Write the conjugation of the verb *study*.

quit の過去分詞形は何ですか。
  What is the past participle of *quit*?

lay の過去形と過去分詞形は何ですか。
  What are the past and the past participle of *lay*?

fit は規則動詞ですか，それとも不規則動詞ですか。
  1. **Is *fit* a regular or an irregular verb?**
  2. **Is *fit* a regular verb or an irregular verb?**
     1 の方が 2 よりもよい。

この長い文の動詞はどれですか。
1. **What is the main verb of this long sentence?**
2. **What is the main verb in this long sentence?**

　　1では前置詞に of が，2では in が使われている。どちらでもよい。「彼は飛行機に乗っている」というとき，前置詞は，
　　　　He is on the plane.
　　　　He is in the plane.
のように，on でも in でもよい。ときによって2つ以上の前置詞を使うことができる場合がある。

and の後で動詞が省略されていることに気が付きましたか。
1. **Did you notice that the verb was omitted after *and*?**
2. **Did you notice that the verb is omitted after *and*?**

　　2では is omitted という形が使われているが，is にすると「and の後ではいつも動詞が省略される」という印象を与えてしまう。

この中で，不定詞をとらない動詞はどれですか。
1. **Which of these verbs can't take the infinitive form?**
2. ***Which of these verbs can't take an infinitive form?**

　　不定詞には何種類もないので，1のように the infinitive とする。2の an infinitive という言い方は誤りである。

どんな動詞を使ってこの日本語を英語に直したらいいでしょうか。
What verb should I use in order to put this Japanese sentence into English?

▶動詞とは何ですか。
What is a verb?

▶動詞にはどのような種類がありますか。
1. **What verb categories are there?**
2. **What kinds of verbs are there?**
3. **What kinds of verbs do you have?**

英語の動詞について全く知識がない場合には3のように ... do you have? という形もおかしくはないが，1や2のように ... are there? とした方が自然である。

▶どんな場合に動詞を省略することが可能なのでしょうか。
　On what occasion can you delete verbs?
　*In what occasion can you delete verbs?
　　　occasion という語は前置詞の on と結び付く。

▶動詞を重ねて使うこともあるのですか。
　Can verbs be used in succession?
　Are verbs sometimes used in succession?
　Do you sometimes use verbs in succession?

▶動詞はふつう強く発音するのですか。
　Do you usually stress verbs?
　　　動詞は内容語の1つであるから，ふつうストレスを置いて発音する。

▶ be 動詞と become はどのように違うのでしょうか。
　How are *be*-verbs different from *become*?

▶ hand という言葉には動詞用法もありますか。
　Can the word *hand* be used as a verb?

▶ hang という動詞の活用を教えてください。
　Will you tell me the conjugation of the verb *hang*?

▶ drank という語は口語的アメリカ英語では過去分詞として使うこともあるんですか。
　Is the word *drank* sometimes used as a past participle in colloquial American English?
　Do you sometimes use the word *drank* as a past participle

in colloquial American English?

drink という動詞はふつう，drink-drank-drunk のように活用する。しかし，アメリカ英語では口語的表現として drank を過去分詞として用いることがある。

▶ finish の次には to が来れますか。
Can *finish* be followed by *to*?

▶ この動詞は他動詞ですか，それとも自動詞ですか。
  1. **Is this verb transitive or intransitive?**
  2. **Is this verb a transitive verb or an intransitive verb?**
     1の方が2よりも簡潔でよい。

J　助動詞

助動詞にはいくつかの特徴があります。
  1. **Auxiliary verbs have their own characteristics.**
  2. **There are some characteristics of auxiliary verbs.**
     1は自然であるが，2はあまり自然な言い方ではない。

auxiliary という語の代わりに，しばしば aux という略語を使います。
The abbreviated word *aux* is often used instead of the word *auxiliary*.

文法的には，助動詞は本動詞の原形と一緒に使います。
Grammatically, an auxiliary verb is used together with the original form of a verb.
Grammatically, an aux is used together with the original form of a verb.
Grammatically, a helping verb is used together with the root form of a verb.

助動詞の特徴のひとつは，三人称単数現在の s をつけないことです。
One of the characteristics of an auxiliary verb is that it does not take a third-person-singular *s*.

助動詞は to のない不定詞と結合します。
Auxiliary verbs combine with an infinitive without inserting *to*.

語形変化が完全な have，do，be などのような助動詞と，語形変化が不完全な will，can，must，may，dare などがあります。
There are auxiliary verbs that conjugate perfectly such as *have*, *do* and *be*, and those that conjugate imperfectly as in *will*, *can*, *must*, *may* and *dare*.

have や do のように，助動詞の中には本動詞として使われるものもあります。
Some auxiliary verbs such as *have* and *do* are used as verbs.

英語には日本語のような丁寧語はありませんが，しばしば can, may, will などの助動詞の過去形で丁寧さを表します。
1. There are no honorific expressions in English as there are in Japanese, politeness is often expressed with auxiliary verbs such as *can*, *may*, and *will*.
2. There are not courteous language in English as in Japanese, politeness is often expressed with auxiliary verbs such as *can*, *may*, and *will*.
　　1 は自然であるが，2 はあまり自然な言い方ではない。

助動詞に対して，普通の動詞を本動詞と言います。
Ordinary verbs are called main verbs as opposed to auxiliary verbs.

音声的には，助動詞はふつう強く発音しません。
  Phonologically, auxiliary verbs are not usually pronounced strongly.

Yes, I can. などのように，文が助動詞で終わる場合には，助動詞を強く発音します。
  When a sentence ends with an auxiliary verb such as "Yes, I can.", the auxiliary is pronounced strongly.

K 形容詞

形容詞は名詞を修飾することができます。
  Adjectives can modify nouns.

英語では一般に形容詞はそれが修飾する名詞の前に置きます。
  1. In English, adjectives are generally placed in front of the nouns they modify.
  2. In English, adjectives precede the nouns they modify.
    1と2はいずれでもよいが，2は formal な表現である。

多くの形容詞が1つの名詞を修飾する場合には，おおよその順序が決まっています。
  When many adjectives modify a noun, there is a rough rule determining their order.
  When many adjectives modify a noun, there is a rough rule as to their order.

形容詞が名詞を修飾する場合には，数［冠詞・指示詞］，判断，大きさ，年齢，色，材料を表す形容詞が名詞の前にこの順序で置かれます。
  1. The order to follow when several adjectives modify a noun is adjectives denoting number [article, demonstra-

tive], judgement, size, age, color and material.
2. **When adjectives modify a noun, adjectives denoting number [article, demonstrative], judgement, size, age, color and material are placed in the preceding order.**

　　1の方が2よりも自然で明確な表現である。

-thing で終わる名詞の場合は，形容詞を後ろに置いて修飾させます。
1. **When a noun ends in -*thing*, the modifying adjective is placed after it.**
2. **When a noun ends in -*thing*, any modifying adjectives are placed after it.**
3. **When a noun ends in -*thing*, adjectives follow, rather than precede it.**
4. ***When a noun ends with -*thing*, adjectives are placed after and modify it.**

　　1と2が最もよい。3は2を強調した表現である。anything, something, everything などが該当する名詞である。
　　　anything useful
　　　something good
　　　everything expensive

形容詞は何を修飾するのですか。
　What do adjectives modify?

形容詞にはどんな種類がありますか。
　What kinds of adjectives are there?

形容詞には，2通りの比較級と最上級の作り方があります。
　There are two ways of making comparative and superlative forms of adjectives.

polite の比較級は more polite, politer のいずれでもかまいません。
　The comparative degree of *polite* can be either *more polite*

or *politer*.

best は形容詞の最上級としても使われます。
Best is also used as the superlative degree of an adjective.

副詞の最上級と形容詞の最上級の違いは何ですか。
What is the difference between the superlative form of the adverb and that of the adjective?

fast は形容詞でもあり，副詞でもあります。
Fast can be both an adjective and an adverb.

enjoy という動詞の形容詞形は何ですか。
What is the adjective form of the verb *enjoy*?

それは名詞を修飾していますから形容詞です。
1. **It modifies a noun, so it is an adjective.**
2. **As it modifies a noun, it is an adjective.**
3. **As it modifies the noun, it is an adjective.**

　　1と2ではa noun，3ではthe nounという形が使われている。the nounの場合には特定の名詞に限定されてしまうので，a nounと言った方がよい。

▶形容詞の役割は何ですか。
What is the role of an adjective?

▶述部形容詞とは何ですか。
What is a predicative adjective?

　　　　She is tall.
　　　　（彼女は背が高い。）
　　　　The news made me sad.
　　　　（そのニュースで悲しくなった。）
　　これらのような文における tall や sad のように，補語として用

いられた形容詞を述部形容詞［叙述形容詞］という。

▶定冠詞や不定冠詞も形容詞の１つですか。
Are the definite article and the indefinite articles kinds of adjectives?

▶いくつもの形容詞が名詞を修飾する場合，どんな順序になりますか。
When there are some adjectives modifying a noun, what order do they go in?
When there are some adjectives modifying a noun, in what order should they be arranged?

▶形容詞の最上級にはいつも定冠詞の the を付けるのですか。
Do you always have to add the definite article *the* to the superlative of an adjective?

▶形容詞を作る接辞にはどんなものがありますか。
What affixes are there to make adjectives?

▶ polite の比較級と最上級は何ですか。
What are the comparative and superlative forms of *polite*?
　　日本語の意味だけを考えると，
　　　*What is the comparative and superlative form of *polite*?
のように be 動詞は is という単数形が使えそうであるが,「比較級」と「最上級」という２つの《複数》の補語があるので，be 動詞は are という形を使わなくてはいけない。

▶ well は形容詞ですかそれとも副詞ですか。
Is *well* an adjective or an adverb?

▶ spirit という名詞の形容詞形は何ですか。
What is the adjective form of the noun *spirit*?

▶ insist という動詞の形容詞形は insistent でいいのでしょうか。
Is the adjective form of the verb *insist* *insistent*?

▶ natural という形容詞は何を修飾しているのですか。
What does the adjective *natural* modify?

L　副詞

副詞は，形容詞，動詞，それにほかの副詞を修飾することができます。
Adverbs can modify adjectives, verbs, and other adverbs.

副詞の位置は比較的自由です。
The position of adverbs is comparatively flexible.
The position of adverbs is comparatively free.
　　　comparatively の発音は，[kəmpǽrətivli] である。ストレスの位置に注意。

副詞は -ly で終わるものが多いのです。
Many adverbs end with *-ly*.

関係副詞とは何ですか。
What is a relative adverb?

関係副詞は，副詞と接続詞のふたつの役割をします。
Relative adverbs act as an adverb and a conjunction.

関係副詞には，when, where, why, how などがあります。
Among the relative pronouns are *when, where, why* and *how*.

疑問副詞とは何ですか。
　What is an interrogative adverb?

副詞も形容詞と同じように，比較級，最上級があります。
　Adverbs, as well as adjectives, have comparative and superlative degree.

副詞の最上級には the を付けません。
　1. *The* is not used with superlatives of adverbs.
　2. *The* is not attached to superlatives of adverbs.
　　　1 の方が 2 よりも自然な言い方である。
　　　attach のつづりは atatch などのように間違うことがある。[tʃ] の音が tch，ch などによって表記されるからである。

副詞は内容語なので強勢を受けます。
　Adverbs are content words, so they get accented.

up は，しばしば副詞として使われます。
　Up is often used as an adverb.

この good は形容詞ですか，それとも副詞ですか。
　Is this *good* an adjective or an adverb?

この形容詞の副詞形は何ですか。
　What is the adverbial form of this adjective?

yesterday という副詞は，この場合どこに置くのが一番自然ですか。
　In this case, what do you think is the most natural place for the adverb *yesterday*?
　*In this case, what do you think is the most natural place of the adverb *yesterday*?
　　　place という名詞と前置詞との間には，次のような関係がある。
　　　　a place of terror

  a place of rest
  a place for resting
  a place for you
  a place for my hat
  a place for the adverb

well という副詞の比較級は何ですか。
 What is the comparative form of the adverb *well*?

87 ページの 5 行目の文で，副詞はどれですか。
 What is the adverb in the fifth sentence on page 87?

only という言葉はどこにかかっていますか。
 What does the word *only* modify?

▶ 副詞はどんな働きをするのですか。
 What is the role of adverbs?

▶ 副詞にはどんなものがありますか。
 What kinds of adverbs are there?

▶ 副詞はどの位置に置くのが一番いいのですか。
 Where is the best place to put adverbs?
 What is the best place to put adverbs?

▶ 副詞は活用をするのですか。
 1. **Can adverbs be conjugated?**
 2. ***Do adverbs conjugate?**
  2 のように conjugate を自動詞的に使うと weird な感じがする表現になる。

▶ -ly が付く語はいつも副詞なのですか。
 Are words ending with *-ly* always adverbs?

おおよそにおいて -ly で終わる語は副詞と見なしてよいが，たまに -ly という接尾辞で終わりながら形容詞であるものがある。
(例) friendly　　親しい
Those kids are very friendly.
(あの子たちは大変親しい。)

▶副詞と形容詞とはどんな違いがあるのでしょうか。
What is the difference between adverbs and adjectives?

▶副詞はほかの副詞を修飾することができますか。
Can adverbs modify other adverbs?

▶副詞はいくつも一緒に使っていいのですか。
Can you use some adverbs together?

▶副詞は強く読むのですか。
Are we supposed to read adverbs strongly?

▶ good は形容詞ですか，それとも副詞ですか。
Is *good* an adjective or an adverb?

▶ last time は文尾でも文頭でもよいのですか。
1. **Can you put *last time* either at the end or at the beginning of a sentence?**
2. **Can you put *last time* either at the end or the beginning of a sentence?**
3. ***Can you put *last time* at both the end of a sentence and at the beginning of a sentence?**

3 のように both を使うと，同じ文で last time を2度使う意味になってしまうのでふさわしくない。

▶ very と much はどのように違うのですか。
How is *very* different from *much*?

M　前置詞

前置詞は機能語です。
　　Prepositions are function words.

それぞれの前置詞には多くの用法があります。
　　Each preposition has many uses.
　　There are many uses for each preposition.

前置詞の使い方については決まった規則がないので，使い方に慣れるしか方法がありません。
　　There are no definite rules as to how to use prepositions, so you simply have to be familiar with their usage.
　　There are no definite rules on how to use prepositions, so you simply have to be familiar with their usage.

前置詞を制するものは英語を制するといいます。
　　It is said that those who master prepositions can master English.
　　　日本語の「制する」に影響されて govern を使うと，英文としては不自然になる。

大学入試では，よく前置詞についての問題が出ます。
　　In the college entrance exam, questions involving prepositions are often asked.
　　For the college entrance exam, questions involving prepositions are often asked.

前置詞は英語の中でマスターするのが最も難しいものの1つです。
　　Prepositions are one of the most difficult things to master in English.

ときには2つの前置詞が続いて現れることがあります。
From time to time, two prepositions appear in succession.

例えば2つの前置詞が次のような文に現れる。

A white cat suddenly appeared *from under* a hedge.
(垣の下から突然，白い猫が現れた)
The store is *across from* the bank.
(その店は銀行の反対側です)
A child dashed out *from behind* the wall.
(子供が壁の後ろから飛び出した)

前置詞は機能語ですから，ふつう強勢は受けません。しかし，文脈上大切な働きをする場合には強勢を受けます。

1. Prepositions are function words, so they are usually not accented. They receive stress when they play an important role in the context, however.
2. Prepositions are function words, so they are usually not accented. They are stressed when they play an important role in the context, however.
3. Prepositions are function words, so they are usually not accented. They are accented, however, when they play an important role in the context.
4. As prepositions are function words, they are usually not accented. When they play an important role in the context, however, they are stressed.
5. As prepositions are function words, they are usually not accented. But when they play an important role in the context, they are stressed.
6. *As prepositions are function words, they are usually not accented. But when they play an important role in the context, they are subject to stress.

文章の書き出しは but で始めない方がよいとする意見がある。5 よりも，1～4 の方が無難な表現である。

6 では be subject to stress という形が使われているが，この表

現は be subject to strain の意味で "set phrase" 的に広く使用されている。したがって 6 の文は,

> "They may get upset or have a nervous breakdown when they play an important role ..."

という具合に, ネイティブスピーカーには leap out (心に浮かぶ) しがちである。

場合によっては, in でも at でも for でもよいこともあります。
In some cases, you can use any of *in*, *at*, or *for*.

例えば「彼は九州銀行で働いています」というとき,

① He is working in the Bank of Kyushu.
② He is working at the Bank of Kyushu.
③ He is working for the Bank of Kyushu.

のように, 前置詞は in, at, for のいずれでもよい。ただし, ①, ②, ③の間には厳密には意味の違いがある。

①は He is working inside the bank. という意味である。したがってこの場合の He は, 九州銀行の中で工事をしている配管工であることも考えられる。彼は, この工事をすませたら次は丸ビルの工事に取りかかることになっているかもしれない。

②の He は, やはり full-time employee ではないかもしれない。あるところから派遣されて仮に九州銀行で働いているという含みもある。He is working there (at the bank). というのが②の文の意味である。これは前置詞の at の使い方と, working という動詞 work の現在分詞の影響にほかならない。

> "Where is your husband working now?"
> "Well, he's working at the Bank of Kyushu, but next month we're moving to Hokkaido, and he's going to go into business for himself."

などのケースが容易に考えられる。③は He is definitely a Bank of Kyushu employee. の意味である。

もし, ①, ②, ③の代わりに,

a. He works in the Bank of Kyushu.
b. He works at the Bank of Kyushu.

c. He works for the Bank of Kyushu.
という文であれば，上記のような意味の違いは生じにくくなる。
a はやはり意味はややあいまいであるが，b と c は同じになり，
いずれも He is a Bank of Kyushu employee. という意味になる。

be interested の次には，どんな前置詞が来ますか。
What preposition do you need after *be interested*?

この空欄にはどんな前置詞が当てはまると思いますか。
What preposition do you think will fit into this blank?

▶前置詞には何種類くらいあるのでしょうか。
How many kinds of prepositions are there?

▶しばしば前置詞の使い方を間違えます。どのようにしてマスターしたらいいでしょうか。
I often make mistakes in the use of prepositions. How can I master prepositions?

▶なぜ前置詞は聞き取りにくいのでしょうか。
Why are prepositions difficult to catch?
Why are prepositions difficult to hear?

▶前置詞の in の代わりに at を使うことができますか。
1. **Can you use the preposition *at* instead of the preposition *in*?**
2. **Can you use the preposition *at* instead of *in*?**
3. ***Can you use the preposition *at* instead of the *in*?**

　　3 では ... the in? となっているが，このままでは誤り。1 か 2 のように変えなくてはならない。

▶ on the plane と in the plane とはどのように意味が違うのでしょうか。
What is the difference in meaning between *on the plane* and *in the plane*?

▶ He asked about a hotel to stay at. の文で，どうして文の最後に前置詞の at があるのでしょうか。
1. Why is the preposition *at* at the end of the sentence *"He asked about a hotel to stay at."*
2. What is the purpose of the preposition at at the end of the sentence *"He asked about a hotel to stay at."*

   1 は preposition，2 は purpose についての英文である。

▶ give up などの表現において，up は前置詞でしょうか，それとも副詞でしょうか。
Is *up* in the expression *give up* a preposition or an adverb?

N 冠詞

冠詞には a, an, the の3つがあります。
There are three articles : *a, an,* and *the*.

「3つ」を three kinds of articles とすると，誤解を招きやすい。a と an は，次に来る語の語頭音が母音か否かという音韻上の問題できまるので，同一の種類とみなされる。the は a や an とは別の種類である。前者は不定冠詞，後者は定冠詞である。したがって冠詞は2種類しかない。

冠詞は定冠詞と不定冠詞に分類できます。
Articles are classified in two categories : definite and indefinite articles.
Articles are divided into two categories : the definite articles and the indefinite articles.

Articles are classified as definite articles or as indefinite articles.

冠詞は日本語にないので難しく思われますが，ルールで説明できることが多いのです。
Articles seem to be difficult as they do not exist in Japanese, but they are often accounted for in terms of rules.

母音の前では a は an となります。
1. *A* becomes *an* in front of a vowel sound.
2. *A* becomes *an* in front of a vowel.

　　a union / *an union

の関係からもわかるように，u の前では常に an とは限らない。a と an との関係はあくまで発音に起因する問題である。1 も 2 も正しいが，vowel には「母音」のほか「母音字」の意味もあるので，1 のように in front of a vowel sound としたい。

どんな場合に a の代わりに an を使うのですか。
1. **On what occasion do you use *an* instead of *a*?**
2. ***In what occasion do you use *an* instead of *a*?**

　　学生は機械的に「母音の前では a の代わりに an を使う」と覚えていることが多いので，つづり字に惑わされて不定冠詞の使い方を誤ることがある。例えば，
　　① *He has a M.A. in linguistics.
　　② He has an M.A. in linguistics.
　　（彼は言語学で M.A. を持っている。）
という文において，M.A.（Master or Arts）の M が子音と思い込んで①のような誤文を書いてしまいがちである。M の発音は [em] であるから，母音の [e] に影響されて不定冠詞は a ではなくて an を使うことになる。a と an の問題はつづりではなく，あくまでも発音であることを学生に徹底させたい。

不可算名詞でも限定される場合には the が付きます。
  Even an uncountable noun will have *the* before it when it is restricted.

固有名詞に the が付く場合もあります。
  There are cases in which even proper nouns require *the*.

「総称を表す」場合には，定冠詞を使うことができます。
  In generic use, a definite article can be used.
  In generic use, the definite article can be used.

名詞が本来の目的で使われた場合には，普通名詞にも冠詞が付かないことがあります。
  There are cases where even common nouns are free from articles when they are used in their original meaning.
    go to school, go to church などがこの例である。

冠詞の用法は，イギリス英語とアメリカ英語とでは異なることがあります。
  The use of articles sometimes differs between British English and American English.

冠詞の使い方について何か質問はありますか。
  Are there any questions on the use of articles?
  Do you have any questions on how to use articles?

この場合には定冠詞と不定冠詞とどちらがいいと思いますか。
  In this case which do you think is better, a definite article or an indefinite article?

冠詞は弱く発音されるので，アメリカ人やイギリス人でも聞き取れないことがあります。
  Since articles are weakly pronounced, there are times when

even Americans and British people cannot catch them.

the の強形は [ðiː] と発音します。
　The strong form of *the* is pronounced as [ðiː].

本文の冠詞にすべて下線を引いて，用法がわからないものがあれば質問しなさい。
　Underline all the articles in the text. If there's anything you don't understand, please ask me.
　Underline all the articles in the text. If you have anything you don't understand, please ask me.

この文では冠詞が1つ抜けています。
　1. An article is missing in this sentence.
　2. This sentence lacks an article.
　3. You need one more article in this sentence.
　　　1〜3のいずれでもよいが，2 は formal，3 はやや informal である。

▶冠詞をよく理解するにはどうしたらいいでしょうか。
　1. What should I do in order to understand articles better?
　2. *What should I do in order to master articles?
　　　1 はよいが，2 の使い方はふさわしくない。
　　　日本語で「冠詞をマスターする」といってもそれほど違和感はないが，英語で master articles と言うと，現在の状態から一挙に（魔法でも使うように）力をつけるような印象を与えがちである。ただし，次のように master を使うのはよい。
　　　　"I'm absolutely determined that, one way or another, I'm going to keep trying until I master articles."

▶不定冠詞にストレスを置くとどのように発音するのですか。
　How do you pronounce indefinite articles when they are stressed?

▶冠詞の使い方がまだよくわかりません。
　I don't quite understand how to use articles.
　I am still not familiar with the use of articles.

▶冠詞の使い方について説明してください。
　1. Please tell us how to use articles.
　2. Please tell us about the usage of articles.
　3. Could you explain how to use articles?
　4. Could you give us an explanation on the use of articles?
　5. *Could you make an explanation on the use of articles?
　　　「〜について」「〜に関して」という意味合いで前置詞の on が使われることがあるが，
　　　　*Please tell us on the use of articles.
　　　　*Could you explain on the use of articles?
　などは誤りである。on を使うためには，その直前に名詞が必要である。4 の文はやや冗長であるが，an explanation on the use of ... では，an explanation という名詞があるので正しい on の用法となっている。しかし，1〜3 の方が自然ではある。日本語だけに引かれて英訳すると，上記の誤文のような文を作りがちである。また 5 は不自然である。

▶この場合，なぜ a ではなくて the になるのですか。
　In this case, why do you have to use *the* instead of *a*?

▶固有名詞に the が付くときの用法がよくわかりません。
　I don't understand the use of *the* for proper nouns.

▶ school は普通名詞なのに，なぜ go to school のようになるのですか。冠詞は school の前に必要ないのですか。
　School is a common noun, but why do you say *go to school*. Don't you need an article in front of *school*?

▶ beauty は抽象名詞なのに，なぜ 75 ページの上から 3 行目では beauty の前に a が付いているのでしょうか。
Beauty is an abstract noun, but why is there *a* in front of *beauty* on the third line from the top on page 75?

▶ 辞書に be in hospital と be in the hospital の両方の形がありました。the があるのとないのとでは，どのように意味が異なるのでしょうか。
My dictionary has both *be in hospital* and *be in the hospital*. What is the difference between the two in meaning?

O 接続詞

口語では接続詞の that はしばしば省略されます。
In colloquial English, the conjunction *that* is often omitted.

文章語では，that を省略しないことがあります。
In written English there are cases where *that* is not deleted.

接続詞の and so は，and あるいは so だけ使うこともできます。
1. The conjunction *and so* can be used in place of *and* or *so*, alone.
2. *The conjunction *and so* can be used as *and* or *so* alone.
   2 の意味は不明瞭。

either 〜 or は，相関接続詞と呼ばれています。
Either ... or is called a correlative conjunction.

セミコロンには，等位接続詞の働きもあります。
A semicolon functions as a coordinate conjunction.

等位接続詞でつないだ文を重文といいます。
A sentence containing a coordinate conjunction is called a compound sentence.

群接続詞とは，2つ以上の語が集まって1つの接続詞と同じ働きをするものを言います。
A group conjunction is a conjunction in which two or more words function together as a conjunction.

since などは，副詞や前置詞として使われますが，接続詞としても使われます。
1. **Words like *since* are used both as adverbs and as prepositions, but they are also used as conjunctions.**
2. **Words like *since* can be used either as an adverb or as a preposition, but they can also be used as a conjunction.**
3. ***Words like *since* are both used as adverbs and as prepositions, but they are also used as conjunctions.**

   3 では both が used の直前に置かれているが，both は副詞か形容詞を修飾するので，1のように ... are used both as ... のようにしたい。

after や before なども，since と同じように接続詞としても使われます。
***After*, *before* and the like are used as conjunctions, just as *since* is.**
***After*, *before* and the like are used as conjunctions, in the same way as *since*.**

   上記の英文で，「接続詞として」というときの英文は，as a conjunction ではなく，as conjunctions と複数形であることに注意。主語が after, before and the like のように複数形であるから，それに呼応して as conjunctions のようになる。

I think that ... などの文では that は接続詞ですから，that の前で息継ぎをします。
  As *that* in sentences like "*I think that ...*" is a conjunction, you have a pause before *that*.

この場合の that は接続詞ですか，それとも関係代名詞ですか。
  In this case is *that* a conjunction or a relative pronoun?

この that 節は，どこまでかかるんですか。
  What does this *that*-clause govern?

この文には，接続詞がいくつありますか。
  How many conjunctions are there in this sentence?
  How many conjunctions do you have in this sentence?

この文では，どこで接続詞の that が省略されていますか。
  Where in this sentence is the conjunction *that* omitted?

I don't think that that that that that man used in that sentence is correct. と言うときの，それぞれの that の用法について説明してごらんなさい。
  Could you explain the usage of each that in the sentence "*I don't think that that that that that man used in that sentence is correct*"?

　　I don't think that ① that ② that ③ that ④ that ⑤ man used in that ⑥ sentence is correct.
　　①の that は接続詞，②・⑤・⑥の that は指示形容詞，③の that は that という語，④の that は関係代名詞を表す。このそれぞれの that の用法がすぐわかれば，学生にかなりの英語の力があるとみてよかろう。答えを説明したあとで，この文の意味がわかるように英文を読ませるのもおもしろい。ちなみにこの文の意味は「あの男があの文で使ったあの that は正しいとは思わない」となる。

▶接続詞にはどんなものがありますか。
What kinds of conjunctions do you have?
What kinds of conjunctions are there?

▶接続詞が文頭に来ることはよくありますか。
Do conjunctions come at the beginning of a sentence?
Can conjunctions come at the beginning of a sentence?

▶接続詞を使わないで2つの文章をつなぐ方法はありますか。
Is there any way to connect two sentences without using a conjunction?

▶ however はどの位置に置いてもいいのですか。
Can you place *however* any place in the sentence?
Can you place *however* anywhere in the sentence?

▶ however と but の意味の違いは何ですか。
What is the difference in meaning between *however* and *but*?

▶ I think that he is coming to Japan next year. と言うとき, that の前で切って読むのですか, それとも that の後で切って読むのですか。
When you say *"I think that he is coming to Japan next year"*, do you pause before *that* or after *that*?

▶ and so と so はどのように使い分けるのですか。
How do you make a distinction between *and so* and *so*?

▶ 81 ページの下から6行目の that は接続詞ですか。
Is the *that* on the sixth line from the bottom on page 81 a conjunction?

▶この that 節はどこにかかるんですか。
What does this *that-clause* modify?

P　間投詞

間投詞はほかの語句とは関係なく，文中に投入されている品詞のことです。
　Interjections are parts of speech that are thrown into a sentence and are independent of other words or phrases in the sentence.

well, ah などは，間投詞の例です。
　Words like *well* and *ah* are examples of interjections.

間投詞とはどんな品詞でしょうか。
　What part of speech is *kantoshi*?

間投詞の例をいくつか言ってごらんなさい。
　Show us some examples of *kantoshi*.
　*Show us some of the examples of *kantoshi*.

9課の中から間投詞をすべて選んでごらんなさい。
　Find all the interjections from lesson 9.

▶間投詞とは何ですか。
　What is an interjection?

▶間投詞の定義は何ですか。
　1. How do you define an interjection?
　2. What is the definition of an interjection?
　3. Define interjections.
　　　interjection は可算名詞であるから，1～3のいずれも正しい。

▶間投詞の例をいくつか示してください。
Could you show us some examples of interjections?

▶アメリカ人はどんなとき間投詞を使うのでしょうか。
1. When do Americans use interjections?
2. Under what circumstances do Americans use interjections?
3. *On what occasions do Americans use interjections?

　「どんなとき」の英訳として on what occasions でもよさそうであるが，occasion は specific times, specific dates などを暗示させる言葉なので，

　　"On what occasions do Americans eat turkey?"
などのように使ったときの応答は，

　　"Mainly on Thanksgiving and Christmas."
などになろう。したがって，上記の場合，occasion は使いにくい。1や2のように言うべきである。

▶58ページに間投詞はありますか。
Are there any interjections on page 58?

Q　語順

英語の基本的な語順はSVOです。
The basic word order in English is SVO.

受動態にすると，語順が変わります。
1. In passive sentences, the basic word order changes.
2. *In passive sentences, the word order is subject to change.

　　be subject to change は，
　　　it can change ; it may or may not ; changing is optional ; it
　　　doesn't have to change

という意味合いになる。したがって，2は正しくない。

be 動詞を含む文では，疑問文にすると主語と動詞の位置が逆になります。

1. **In a sentence including a *be*-verb, the order of the subject and the verb is reversed to form a question sentence.**
2. **In a sentence including a *be*-verb, the order of the subject and the verb is reversed to form an interrogative sentence.**
3. **In a sentence including a *be*-verb, the order of the subject and the verb is reversed when the sentence is changed into a question.**
4. ***In a sentence including a *be*-verb, the word order of the subject and the verb is inverted when changed into a question sentence.**

　　4は convoluted なうえ，あたかも the subject and verb が question sentence に変えられるかのような印象を与えるからふさわしくない。1，2，3のように言うべきである。

強調のために never を文頭に出すと，have I ... のような語順になります。

1. **If *never* is put at the beginning of a sentence for emphasis, the word order becomes like *have I* ....**
2. **If *never* is put at the beginning of a sentence for emphasis, the order of the words becomes like *have I* ....**
3. ***If *never* is put in front of a sentence for emphasis, the order of words becomes like *have I* ....**

　　in front of ～については p. 356 を参考のこと。

　　3の the order of words は正しくない。この場合，words は a sentence に現れる語であるから，1のように the word order とするか，2のように the order of the words のように words に定冠詞を付さなければならない。

AとBはどちらの語順が正しいと思いますか。
Which word order is correct, A or B?

この文の語順について，何か質問はありませんか。
1. **Do you have any questions about the word order in this sentence?**
2. **Are there any questions about the word order in this sentence?**
3. **Don't you have any questions about the word order in this sentence?**

英文としては3のように否定文で聞くよりも，1や2のように肯定文の形で聞く方が普通である。もちろん，教師が "Do you have ...?" と何度も聞いたあとであれば，"Don't you have ...?" と否定文で聞くのはおかしくない。

その文の語順は正しくありません。
1. **The word order in that sentence is not correct.**
2. **The order of the words in that sentence is not correct.**
3. ***The word order in that sentence is wrong.**

3の is wrong は強い響きを持つ表現であるから避けた方がよい。

語順に注意して訳してごらんなさい。
Translate into Japanese, paying attention to the word order.

▶英語の基本的な語順は何ですか。
What is the basic word order used in English?

▶一般疑問文の基本的な語順は何ですか。
What is the basic word order of a general question?

▶ be 動詞を含む文を疑問文にするには，いつも be 動詞を文頭に置くだけでいいのですか。
Is it all right to place the *be*-verb at the beginning of a sen-

tence when changing a sentence including a *be*-verb into a question?

▶能動態を受動態に直すと，どんな語順になりますか。
When I change an active sentence into a passive sentence, what will the word order be?
When changing an active sentence into a passive sentence, what will the word order be?

▶英語を話していると，語順がわからなくなってきます。
1. When I am speaking English, I have trouble with the word order.
2. When I am speaking English, word order is a big problem.
3. When I am speaking English, I get stuck with the word order.
　　3 は日本語に近いが，1 や 2 の方が自然な英語である。

▶いくつもの形容詞が名詞を修飾するとき，決まった語順がありますか。
1. When several adjectives modifying a noun, is there any set word order?
2. When there are several adjectives modifying a noun, is there any specific word order?
3. When more than one adjectives modifies a noun, is there any set word order?
4. *When there are some adjectives modifying a noun, is there any specific word order?
　　4 は不自然な表現である。1 ～ 3 のように言いたい。

▶どうして so が文頭に来ると So did I. のような語順になるのですか。
Why is the word like "*So did I.*" when *so* comes at the be-

ginning of a sentence?
Why do you have a word order like *"So did I."* when *so* comes at the beginning of a sentence?

R 疑問文

疑問文にはいくつかの種類があります。
There are some kinds of questions.

be 動詞のある文では, be 動詞を文頭に置いて疑問文を作ります。
1. If there is a *be*-verb in a sentence, the question is made by placing the verb at the beginning of the sentence.
2. If there is a *be*-verb in a sentence, the question is made by placing the verb at the head of the sentence.
3. *If there is a *be*-verb in a sentence, the question is made by placing the verb in front of the sentence.

　1 と 2 は standard な表現であるが, 3 はふさわしくない。in front of の使い方が正しくない。p. 393 の 1. *A* becomes *an* in front of a vowel sound.　2. *A* becomes *an* in front of a vowel. の 2 つの文の場合には, 不定冠詞の an は a vowel sound あるいは vowel の一部ではない。しかし, 上記の 3 の文においては, be 動詞は a sentence の中にあって, その一部であり, このような場合は, 3 のように言うことはできない。

　in front of は, There is a car in front of the bus. のように, in front of の前に置くものと, 後に置くものとが別個のものであることを暗示させる語句である。

肯定文でも, 文尾を上げると疑問文になります。
Even an affirmative sentence can be a question sentence if it has rising intonation at the end.

WH言葉を使った疑問文は yes, no では答えられません。
　In question sentences in which *WH*-words are used, you cannot answer using *yes* or *no*.

42ページの上から5行目の文を疑問文にするとどうなりますか。
　How can you make the fifth sentence from the top of page 42 into a question?

S　付加疑問文

付加疑問文には2通りの読み方があります。文尾を上げる読み方と, 文尾を下げる読み方です。
　1. There are two ways to read tag questions : One is to read them with rising intonation and the other is to read them with falling intonation.
　2. There are two ways of reading a tag question : One way is to read it with rising pitch and the other is to read it with falling pitch.
　　　1, 2いずれでもよい。tag questions とするか a tag question にするかによってその語の代名詞の扱いが異なってくる。

文尾でピッチを上げると, 疑問の意味が強まります。
　If you raise the pitch at the end of a sentence, you will increase the feelings of doubt.
　If you raise the pitch at the end of a sentence, you will increase the feelings of uncertainty.

文尾を下げると, 確認の意味が暗示されます。
　If you have falling intonation at the end of a sentence, confirmation is implied.

文尾を下げると，自信の意味が暗示されます。
　If you have falling intonation at the end of a sentence, confidence is implied.

Let's で始まる文の付加疑問文は，shall we? の形になります。
　A tag question beginning with *Let's* ends with *shall we*?

付加疑問文の作り方はわかりますか。
　Do you know how to make tag questions?

付加疑問文の作り方を大体説明しなさい。
　Explain briefly how to make tag questions.

命令文の付加疑問文はどうなりますか。
　How can you make a tag question out of an imperative sentence?

▶付加疑問文とは何ですか。
　What is a tag question?

▶付加疑問文の作り方を説明してください。
　1. Could you tell us how to make tag questions?
　2. Could you explain as to how to make tag questions?
　　　1の方が2よりもよい。

▶付加疑問文では，どのような場合に抑揚を上げるのでしょうか。
　For a tag question, in what case do you have to have rising intonation?
　With a tag question, in what case do you need to have rising intonation?
　　　for の場合には in order to have, with の場合には in the case of ; when we're working with というニュアンスの違いがある。

▶付加疑問文のイントネーションはどんなとき上がって，どんなとき下がるのでしょうか。
In tag questions, when do you have rising intonation and when do you have falling intonation?

▶付加疑問文にはどんなニュアンスがあるのですか。
1. **What nuance do tag questions give?**
2. **What nuance do tag questions have?**
　日本語の「ある」は，give よりも have の方がよい感じがするが，英語としては 1 のように give を使った方がより自然である。

▶付加疑問文は目上の人にも使っていいですか。
1. **Can we use a tag question with people who rank higher than we do?**
2. **Can we direct a tag question to people who rank higher than we do?**
3. ***Can we use a tag question to people who rank higher than we do?**
　1 のように動詞 use を使えば，前置詞は with をとる。3 のように to を使うのは誤り。
　2 のように動詞 direct を使えば，前置詞は to を伴う。

T　態

受動態の文では，能動態の文の目的語が主語になります。
In a passive sentence, the object of the active sentence becomes the subject.

受動態は改まった文章でよく使われます。
The passive voice is often used in formal sentences.

受動態の文では，能動態の主語が省かれることがあります。
　In passive sentences, the subject of an active sentence is sometimes deleted.
　In passive sentences, the subject of an active sentence is sometimes omitted.

能動態と受動態はどのように違うかわかりますか。
　Do you know how the active voice is different from the passive voice?
　Do you know the difference between the active voice and the passive voice?
　Could you tell me the difference between the active voice and the passive voice?
　　いずれも standard な表現である。

次の受動態の文で，省略されている主語を指摘してください。
　In the following passive sentences, point out the missing subjects.

これを受動態で書き直すと，どうなりますか。
　How would you change this sentence into the passive voice?
　How can this sentence be changed into the passive voice?

▶能動態と受動態のニュアンスの違いは何ですか。
　What is the difference in nuance between the active voice and the passive voice?

▶この受動態の文には主語がありませんが，何が省略されているのでしょうか。
　1. There is no subject in this passive sentence. What is the deleted subject?
　2. What is the missing subject in this passive sentence?

1と2はいずれでもよい。

U　時制

時制とは，動詞の表す動作や作用の時間的な関係を表す文法上の言葉です。
　The word "tense" is a grammatical term showing a relation in time that a verb expresses an action or condition.

現在形・過去形・過去分詞形を三主要形と言います。
　The present form, past form, and past participle form are called the three principal parts.

時制の一致とは，主節の動詞と従属節の動詞の時制を合わせることです。
　Tense agreement is making the tense of a main clause and that of a subordinate clause agree.
　Tense agreement is having the tense of a main clause and that of a subordinate clause agree.

述部の時制に注意しなさい。
　Pay attention to the tense of the predicate.

▶現在完了と過去完了とは，どのように違うのですか。
　What is the difference between the present perfect tense and the past perfect tense?

▶この文は過去時制にしなくてはいけないのですか。
　Do we have to write this sentence in the past tense?

▶その文を過去時制で言うと，どうなりますか。
　How can you change the sentence to the past tense?

V 話法

話法には直接話法，間接話法という２つの種類があります。
  1. There are two types of narration: direct and indirect.
  2. There are two types of narration: a direct narration and an indirect narration.
     1，2のいずれでもよいが，2の方が簡潔で，自然である。

直接話法は，ほかの人が言ったことをそのまま伝える方法です。
  A direct narration is a direct quotation of what someone says.
  A direct narration shows someone's exact wording.

直接話法では引用符を用います。
  Quotation marks are used in direct narrations.

間接話法は，ほかの人が言ったことを間接的に伝える方法です。
  An indirect narration is a way of conveying what someone says without using his exact words.
  An indirect narration is a way of conveying what someone says without using his exact wording.

間接話法は，ほかの人が言ったことを話し手の言葉に言い換えて伝える方法です。
  An indirect narration is a way of conveying what someone says in the speaker's way.
  An indirect narration is a way of conveying what someone says in the speaker's own words .

間接話法で使われる that はしばしば省略されます。
  1. *That*, used in a direct narration, is often deleted.
  2. *That*, which is used in a direct narration, is often deleted.

1，2のいずれでもよいが，2の方が簡潔である。

直接話法を間接話法に言い換えなさい。
　Change this direct quote into an indirect quote.

▶直接話法を間接話法に換えるやり方がわかりません。
　1. I don't understand how to change from direct discourse to indirect discourse.
　2. I don't understand how to go from direct narration to indirect narration.
　　　1，2のいずれでもよいが，2の方がよいという人がいる。

W　その他，文法に関して

文法を理解していると，複雑な英文を訳すことができます。
　You will be able to translate complex English sentences if you are familiar with grammar.
　You are able to translate complex English sentences if you are familiar with grammar.

訳すのが苦手な人は，文法を理解する必要があります。
　Those who are not good at translating need to work on their grammar.

解釈の力を向上させるには，文法力をつけるのと，単語力をつけることが必要です。
　1. In order to improve your comprehension of English, it is necessary to work on your grammar and vocabulary.
　2. In order to improve your comprehension of English, it is necessary to increase your grammar and word power.
　　　1 はやや formal な表現である。

英単語は機能語と内容語に大別できます。
English words can be divided into function words and content words.

この文の内容語を指摘しなさい。
Point out the content words in this sentence.
Point out the content words of this sentence.

  英語の文は内容語と機能語とに大別できる。内容語とは動詞・名詞・形容詞・副詞などのように，それ自身で意味を持つ語のことをいう。機能語とは文法的に必要であるが，それ自身ではさほど大きな意味を持たない語をいう。英語の文を読むときには，概して，内容語は強く，機能語は弱く発音することになる。日本語ではすべての単語を同一のストレスで読みがちであるから，この点に留意しなくてはならない。日本語式の発音で英文を読むと，日本語訛りが強い英語として響いたり，場合によっては英語を母語とする人々に通じないことになる。

この単語の品詞は何ですか。
1. What part of speech is this word?
2. What's the part of speech of this word?

  もとの日本語には2が近いが，英文としては1の方が自然である。

ここでは，何が省略されてますか。
What is omitted here?
What was omitted here?
What is left out here?
What was left out here?

  be 動詞は現在形でも過去形でもよい。

ここではどんな言葉が省略されていますか。
What word is deleted here?

この文を短くするとどうなりますか。
1. **How do you think this sentence will change if it is shortened?**
2. **What do you think will happen to this sentence if it is shortened?**
3. ***What do you think will become of this sentence if it is abbreviated?**

　　abbreviate は words を短縮するときに使う言葉である。文を短くする場合に使うのはおかしい。文の場合には shorten を使うべきである。

下線部を別の言い方で表すとどうなりますか。
How can we express the underlined expression in a different way?

▶文法がよくわかりません。
I don't know grammar very well.

▶この文の構造がよくわかりません。
1. **I don't understand the construction of this sentence.**
2. **I don't understand how this sentence is constructed.**
3. ***I don't understand what the construction of this sentence is.**

　　1と2がよい。3の意味は不明瞭である。

▶その文を文法的に解釈すると，どうなりますか。
1. **How would you explain that sentence from a grammatical point of view?**
2. **Please explain what is going on grammatically in that sentence.**
3. **What would be the grammatical interpretation of that sentence?**

　　3はぎこちない。

▶この最上級の文の意味を変えないで比較級で表すには，どうしたらいいでしょう。
How can we change this superlative sentence into a comparative sentence without changing the meaning?
How can we change this superlative sentence to its comparative form without changing the meaning?
How can we change this superlative sentence into its comparative form without changing the meaning?

▶私たちは，まだこの文法事項を学んでいません。
We have not learned this grammatical item yet.

▶この文には，どのような構文が含まれていますか。
1. What sentence structures are included in this sentence?
2. What sentence structures does this sentence contain?
3. *What sentence structure is included in this sentence?
　　3はおかしい。What sentence structure というと，ただ1つの文しか含まれていない印象を与える。しかし，included というといくつかのものが含まれている印象を与えるから矛盾する。1や2のように言うべきである。

▶それは省略できますか。
Can we delete it?
Can we omit it?
Can we leave it out?
Can we drop it?

▶AとBの文では，どちらがより口語的ですか。
Which is more colloquial, sentence A or sentence B?

V 英語の学習について

1 学習方法について

努力次第で，英語の成績はどんどんよくなります。
　Your English score will improve a lot better, depending on how hard you try.
　Your English score will become a lot better, depending on your efforts.
　　1の方がよい。

一生懸命にすればするほど，あなたの英語の成績はよくなります。
　The harder you try, the better your English score will become.

詰め込み勉強では英語はうまくなりません。
　You cannot improve your English by cramming.

長時間だらだら勉強するよりは，短時間でも集中した方が効果があがります。
　1. Concentrating for a short time is more effective than doodling for a long time.
　2. You can get good results by concentrating even for a short time rather than doodling for a long time.
　3. Short-time concentration is more effective than long-time doodling.

4. *You can get a good result by concentrating even for a short time than doodling for a long time.

　　1が最も自然な表現である。2もよい。3は簡潔な表現である。4は正しくない。

しっかり勉強しないと，授業についていけないぞ。
Unless you study hard, you will not be able to keep up with the class.

　　keep up with は，「〈人・流行・勉強・国際情勢などに〉（遅れないで）ついていく」という意味である。これに類似した表現に catch up with ～ があるが，これは「追い付く」という動作を表す表現である。生徒の勉強がすでに遅れをとっているのであれば，こちらがふさわしい。

文法力は英語の成績に大きく影響します。
Grammar plays a big role in developing English ability.
Grammar plays a big role in improving English ability.

文法力は英語を話したり，読んだりする力に大きく影響します。
Grammar plays a big role in developing your ability to speak and read English.
Grammar plays a big role in improving your ability to speak and read English.

単語をしっかり覚えて文法の力をつければ，英語の成績はよくなります。
Your English will become much better if you memorize words and improve your grammatical ability.

英語がうまくなるためには，基本的な文法を理解し，少しずつ語いを増やしていくことが大切です。
To speak English well, you should master basic grammar and build up your vocabulary little by little.

1 学習方法について　*419*

- To be proficient in English, you should master basic grammar and build up your vocabulary little by little.
- To become a good speaker of English, you should master basic grammar and build up your vocabulary little by little.

英語がうまく話せるようになりたいなら，英語の音が聞き取れるように，よく英語を聞くことも大切です。
1. If you want to be a good speaker of English, it is also important for you to listen to English so that you can understand what is being spoken well.
2. If you want to be a good speaker of English, it is also important for you to listen to English so that you can build up your listening skills.
3. If you want to be a good speaker of English, it is also important for you to listen to English so that you can understand it well.

　　3 もよいが，1 と 2 の方がより正確である。

予習をすると英語がよくわかるようになります。
1. Study the lesson before class, and you'll come to understand English well.
2. Study the lesson before class, and you'll get to understand English well.
3. Prepare well for class, and you'll come to understand English well.
4. Prepare well for class, and you'll get to understand English well.
5. Prepare your lessons well, and you'll come to understand English well.
6. Prepare your lessons well, and you'll get to understand English well.

　　「予習をする」に相当する表現はいろいろ可能であるが，1 と 2

が最もよい。study と prepare には次のような基本的な使い方がある。
>A teacher prepares a lesson in order to teach it.
>The student studies a lesson before class, in order to prepare for class.

英語がうまくなるためには，学んだことをしばしば復習することです。

1. **To be a good speaker of English, it is recommended that you often review what you have learned.**
2. **To be a good speaker of English, frequent review of what you have learned is recommended.**
3. **It would be nice to review often what you have learned to be a good speaker of English.**

1 は standard，2 はやや formal，3 はやや不自然な表現である。It would be nice ... は，主としてだれかにどのように振る舞うかを勧めるようなときによく使う。たとえば，
>It would be nice to give her something in return.
>It would be nice to call your host family if you will be late for dinner.
>It would be nice to write them a thank-you letter.

チャンスを見つけて，できるだけ外国人と英語で話すようにしなさい。
Try to find as many chances to talk with foreigners as possible.

日本語に引かれて直訳的に，
>*Try to find a chance and talk to foreigners as much as possible.

などとすると誤りの文となる。

1 学習方法について

日ごろから，できるだけ外国の雑誌や新聞などを読むようにしておきなさい。
1. **Always try to read as many foreign magazines and newspapers as possible.**
2. **Always try to read as many foreign magazines, newspapers and the like as possible.**
3. **Always try to read as many foreign magazines, newspapers and what not as possible.**

このようにいろいろな表現のしかたが可能であるが，自然な形としては1＞2＞3の順である。

foreign magazines and newspapers の代わりに，foreign magazine and newspaper articles と表現してもよい。

英語のことで何か質問があったら，いつでも私のところに来なさい。
Whenever you have a question about English, please come to me.
Whenever you have questions about English, please come to me.
Whenever you have a question about English, please see me.
Whenever you have questions about English, please see me.
Any time you have a question about English, please come to me.
Any time you have questions about English, please come to me.

▶**英語はどうも苦手です。**
I am not good at English.

▶**まだ，英語をどのようにして勉強してよいのかわかりません。**
I don't know how to study English yet.

V 英語の学習について

▶英語はどのようにしたらうまくなるのでしょうか。
How can we improve our English?

▶英語がうまくなるためには、どのような勉強をしたらいいですか。
1. How should I study to be a good speaker of English?
2. How should I study to become a good speaker of English?

  1, 2 とも standard な表現である。

▶英語が上達する方法を教えてください。
Could you tell me how to be a good speaker of English?

▶英語をマスターするにはどのような勉強をすればよいのでしょうか。
How should we study in order to master English?

▶英語がわかるには、どうしたらよいのでしょう。
What should I do if I want to be able to understand English?

▶語いを増やすには、どのようにしたらいいのでしょうか。
How can we increase our vocabulary?
In what way can we expand our vocabulary?

▶単語や熟語はどのようにして覚えたらいいのでしょうか。
1. What's a good way for us to memorize words or fixed expressions?
2. What can we do to memorize words or fixed expressions?
3. *How should we memorize words or fixed expressions?

  1, 2 は正しいが、3 はふさわしくない。1 が最もよい。
  日本語では相手を敬う気持ちから、つい、3 のように言いがちであるが、このような表現は避けるべきである。How should ...? は（自分で努力をせずに）すべての助けを相手に求めているニュ

アンスがあるので，"You should put some effort into it and not be lazy [lackadaisical]!"というような感情を相手に抱かせかねない。次のような状況での should は自然な使い方である。

"I'm not really very good at memorizing. I tend to forget so quickly. I'd like to do better. What should I do in order to memorize and retain what I have learned?"

この場合には，努力をした結果，どうしても要領を得ないので助けを求めている気持ちが相手に伝わるからである。

should は次のような場合にも使うことができる。

① A : How should I tie my tie?
　B : You should tie it like this.
　（B は実際にネクタイの結び方を教える）
② A : How should I fold my paper?
　B : Fold it in half, this way.
　（B は紙を折ってみせる）
③ A : What size notebook should I buy?
　B : A B-5 size notebook would be the best.
　B : A B-5 size notebook would be best.

①②③はいずれも，opinion about the right way を尋ねている。

▶いくらやっても単語を覚えることができません。

1. **No matter how hard I try, I can't memorize words.**
2. **I can't memorize words no matter how hard I try.**

　　1 と 2 は基本的には同じ文であるが，1 の方が 2 よりも自然である。

▶英会話は苦手です。

I'm poor at English conversation.

　　be poor at 〜 のかわりに，be weak in 〜 や be not good at 〜 も使うことができる。

▶英会話がうまくなりたいのですが。

I would like to be a good speaker of English.

▶英語はある程度読めますが，話すのは苦手です。
I can read English to some degree, but I'm not good at speaking.

▶どうしたらペラペラしゃべれるようになるんでしょうか。
How can I become a fluent speaker of English?
How can I become fluent in English?

▶英語で質問したいんですが，どのように言ったらよいのかわかりません。
I would like to ask questions in English, but I don't know how to phrase them.

▶外国人に話しかけようとすると，胸がドキドキし始めます。
1. When I try to talk to foreigners, I get butterflies in my stomach.
2. When I try to talk to foreigners, my heart begins to pound.
3. When I try to talk to foreigners, my heart begins to beat fast.
4. *When I try to talk to foreigners, my heart begins to beat.

　「蝶々（ちょうちょう）」を意味する butterfly は，butterflies という複数の形で「(不安で) どきどきする様子」の意味がある。
　1 > 2 > 3 の順でよい。4 の ... begins to beat. はおかしい。心臓が beat していなければ死んでいるはずであるからである。

▶なぜ私は8年間も英語を勉強していてうまく話せないのでしょうか。
Why can't I speak English well in spite of the fact that I've been studying English for eight years?

▶「英語を聞いて話せる」ようになるには，何年くらいかかります

か。
How long will it take to be able to understand and speak English?
How long will it take in order to be able to understand and speak English?

▶僕の英語はアメリカで通じるでしょうか。
Do you think Americans will understand my English?
Do you think Americans will be able to understand my English?

▶アメリカで英語が通じるくらいになるまで，どれくらい英語を勉強しなければならないのでしょうか。
How long do we have to study English in order to be able to make ourselves understood in the U.S.?

▶自然な英語の発音を身につけるにはどうしたらよいのでしょう。
What should I do in order to master natural English pronunciation?

▶ネイティブのような英語の発音を身につけるにはどうしたらよいのでしょう。
What should I do in order to master English pronunciation like native speakers of English?

▶発音が悪いために，ときどき相手に通じません。
I cannot make myself understood to others because of my bad pronunciation.

▶洋画を見ることは本当にヒアリング力を高めることになるのでしょうか。
Can we improve our listening ability by watching English movies?

▶英語が速く読めるようになりたいのですが。
  I'd like to be able to read English fast.
  「読み」についての詳細は p. 290 参照のこと。

▶どんな英語の本を読んだらよいのでしょうか。
  What English books shall we read?
  What kinds of English books shall we read?
  英語を母語とする人々が日本人の英語を批評して,「日本人はWhat kind of ～という表現を多用しすぎる」ということがある。

▶英語を書くと,いつも間違いをたくさんします。
  Whenever I write English, I make lots of mistakes.

▶アメリカに２年間いれば,英語がペラペラになるのでしょうか。
  If we stay in America for two years, will we be able to speak English fluently?

2　英語を学ぶ意義

英語は世界で使われている言葉です。
  1. **English is a world language.**
  2. **English has been used all over the world.**
  3. **English is the language used in the world.**
  4. **English is a language that has been used all over the world.**
  5. **English is a language that has been used in the world.**
  1 は standard な表現である。world language と同じ意味合いで,少し formal は言い方ではあるが lingua franca という語も English is the lingua franca in business. のように使われる。2 は標準的な表現。3 や 4 でもよいが,5 はやや曖昧な表現である。

英語は，世界のいろいろな地域で話されています。
English is spoken in many parts of the world.

英語が使えれば，世界の多くの人との意思疎通ができます。
1. If you can use English, you will be able to communicate with people from all over the world.
2. If you can use English, you will be able to communicate with many people in the world.

　1 も 2 もよいが，1 の all over the world という表現の方が意味合いが強い。

英語が読めれば，世界の多くの情報に接することができます。
1. If you can read English, you will be able to gain access to various kinds of information from all over the world.
2. If you can read English, you will be able to get various kinds of information from all over the world.
3. If you can read English, you will be able to get a lot of information of the world.

　1 〜 3 はいずれも正しいが，1 が最もよい。3 はやや大人しい表現である。

英語を学習することで，新たな世界が広がります。
1. Studying English will open up a whole new world for you.
2. By studying English, a new world will broaden.

　broaden には「広がる」という意味の自動詞としての用法があるが，2 の使い方には不自然さを感じるネイティブスピーカーがいる。

英語を学ぶことによって，視野を広げることができます。
1. Studying English will help you broaden your horizons.
2. By studying English, you can broaden your horizons.
3. Studying English will broaden your horizons.

1～3のいずれでもよいが，1が最も好まれる。

いろいろな事柄が英語を通して知らされます。
1. **You can get to know a variety of things through English.**
2. **You can learn a variety of things through English.**
3. ***A variety of things will be known through English.**

　　1と2は自然である。3の will be known という言い方がもとの日本語には近いが不自然である。

インターネットの情報の多くは英語で伝えられます。
1. **Much of the information on the Internet is in English.**
2. **A lot of information on the Internet is passed on through English.**

　　1は端的な表現，2はやや formal な表現である。

英語はアジアの人たちとコミュニケーションをはかるには，一番よい言語です。
1. **English is the best language for us to communicate with people in other Asian countries.**
2. **English is the most convenient language for Asians to communicate with people from other Asian countries.**
3. **English is the most convenient language for Asians to communicate with other Asians.**
4. **English is the best language to communicate with people in Asia.**

　　1は最も standard な表現である。日本はアジアの国のひとつであるから，other Asian countries のように使うのがよい。2もよいが，少し意味合いが異なる。3は端的であるが，やや意味が不明瞭である。4は日本がアジアの国のひとつであるということは不明瞭である。

英語はこれからますます重要になってくるでしょう。
English will become more and more important from now

on.

これからは，少しは英会話ができるようにしましょう。
  Let's try to carry on, at least, a simple conversation in English.
  Let's develop an ability to carry on a simple conversation in English.

これからは聞いて話せる英語がますます重要になってきます。
1. From now on aural and oral English will become more important.
2. From now on, aural and oral English will become more important.
3. From now on, listening and speaking English will become more important.
4. From now on, listening to English and speaking it will become more important.

    1のように from now on のあとにコンマを付さなくても，2〜4のようにコンマを付してもよい。

外国語を学ぶことで母語に対する感覚も磨かれます。
1. Foreign language study will help you use your native language more effectively.
2. By learning a foreign language, you will be able to brush up your native language skills.
3. By learning a foreign language, you will be able to use your native language more effectively.
4. Foreign language study will enhance your native language skills.
5. By learning a foreign language, you will be able to polish a sense of your native language.

    1は最も好まれる言い方である。2〜4もよい。5はもとの日本語に近い表現であるが，あまりしっくりとこないと感じるネイ

ティブスピーカーがいる。

▶英語はこれからますます大切になってくるでしょうか。
Do you think English will become more and more important from now on?

3 英語や英語文化に関する知識

英語はインド・ヨーロッパ語族に属します。
English belongs to the Indo-European language family.

英語は世界の多くの国で公用語として使われています。
English is used as an official language in many countries in the world.

英語には多くの変種があります。
There are many varieties in English.

アメリカ英語には北東部方言，南部方言などがあります。
1. There are dialects such as the New England and Southern dialects in American English.
2. American English has dialects such as the New England and Southern dialects.
    1, 2 いずれの言い方でもよい。

英語はそもそも大ブリテン島のイングランド（地方）で話されていました。
English was originally spoken in England in Great Britain.

3 英語や英語文化に関する知識   *431*

大ブリテン島では English, Welsh, Scottish という３つの異なる言語が話されていました。
Three different languages such as English, Welsh and Scottish were spoken in Great Britain.

BBC 英語を話す英国人は，人口のわずか３％と言われています。
1. **It is said that only three percent of the British population speaks BBC English.**
2. ***It is said that British people who speak BBC English are only 3 percent of the population.**

　　1 は自然な言い方であるが，2 は不自然である。

歴史的に英語は古英語，中期英語，現代英語の３期に分けられます。
Historically, English can be divided into Old English, Middle English and Modern English.

ドイツ語は英語に近い言語です。
1. **German is a language closely related to English.**
2. **German is a language close to English.**

　　1 は standard な言い方であるが，2 はやや不明瞭である。

英語はラテン語の影響を大きく受けています。
English has been greatly influenced by Latin.

英語は世界の言葉の多くの語を含んでいます。
1. **Many English words come from various languages.**
2. **Many English words are derived from other languages.**
3. **English contains a lot of words from other languages.**
4. **Many English words come from other languages.**
5. **English contains a large number of words from languages in the world.**
6. ***English contains a lot of words in world languages.**

　　1 〜 3 は standard な言い方である。4 は informal, 5 は不明

瞭である。

日本語の多くのカタカナ語は英語に由来します。
Many of the Japanese words written in *katakana* come from English.

日本語の多くの語も英語の語になっています。
1. **A large number of Japanese words have become English words.**
2. **A large number of Japanese words have been assimilated into English.**

  1 は standard, 2 は formal な表現である。

▶英語は世界のどれくらいの国々で話されているのですか。
In how many countries of the world is English spoken?

▶世界の人口の何割くらいが英語を話しているのでしょうか。
What percent of the total population of the world speak English?

  percent はイギリス英語では，per cent と２語に分けてつづることもある。
  percent は単数・複数が同じ形をとるが，可算名詞の扱いをする。
   Fifty percent of the students were present at the meeting.
  （学生の 50 パーセントはその会合に出席していた。）
  「学生の 50 パーセント」は複数であるから，動詞は were という形を使わなくてはいけない。

▶イギリス英語とアメリカ英語の違いは何ですか。
What is the difference between British English and American English?

  両者の違いは多いし，複雑でもある。こんな話があった。あるとき，１人のイギリス人から，アメリカ英語について barbarous use of grammar ということで読売新聞に投書があった。この記

事に対して，指摘された文法のポイントに詳しいアメリカ人から，「イギリスからアメリカに入植者たちがやってきたころはそうした英語を使っていた」という反論があった。アメリカに伝えられたイギリスの英語は変化しなかったが，本国のイギリス英語が変わってしまったというわけである。

文法，発音，つづり，語いで違いがあるが，特に語いについてはかなりの違いがある。

▶イギリス英語とアメリカ英語のどちらをマスターしたらよいのでしょうか。
Which variety of English should we master, British English or American English?

▶英語にも方言はあるのですか。
Are there any dialects in English?

▶アメリカのそのほかの習慣を教えてください。
Could you tell us about some other American customs?

customs とは what a group of people generally do であり，habit とは what an individual generally does ということである。

▶英語のジョークを教えてください。
Please tell us some English jokes.

英語文化では，地口の類はあまり好まれない。

VI テスト・試験

1 試験前後

A 試験の予告

試験が近づいてきました。しっかり勉強していますね。
The exam is just around the corner. I hope you are studying very hard.

中間テストは来週の月曜日から始まります。
Midterm exams will begin next Monday.

> exam は examination の省略形である。「期末テスト」は final exams という。アメリカの大学では非常にしばしば試験を行う。簡単な試験は quiz といい, 大きなものは exams という。

2週間後に英語の試験を行います。
You are going to have an English test two weeks from now.
You are going to have an English test in two weeks.

2週間後の月曜日に, 英語の試験をします。
Two weeks from Monday, you are going to have an English test.
Two weeks from Monday, you are going to have an English quiz.

> アメリカの大学などでは, quiz がしばしば出される。quiz と

は小さな test のことで，不意に出されるものを特に pop quiz と言う。

来月の第2水曜日の3時間目に英語の試験をします。
You are going to have an English test third period on the second Wednesday next month.

During third period on the second Wednesday next month, you are going to have an English test.

教科書の35ページから64ページまでを，今度の試験範囲にします。
1. **The next exam will cover from page 35 through page 64 in your textbook.**
2. **The next exam will cover page 35 through page 64 of your textbook.**

　　1の方が2よりもよい。

試験の範囲については，来週のこの時間に詳しく説明します。
I am going to tell you about the exam in detail in this class next week.

　　in this class は省略可能である。

ここは試験に出そうなので，よく復習しておくように。
1. **This may appear on the test, so please review it well.**
2. **This may appear on the test, so please revise it well.**

　　1はアメリカ英語，2はイギリス英語。revise はアメリカ英語では change や rearrange の意味で使われる。

今度のテストは，教科書16ページの練習問題とそっくり同じ問題を出します。
1. **The test coming up will be exactly the same as the exercises on page 16 in your textbook.**
2. **The test coming up will consist of the exercises on page 16 in your textbook.**

3. **The test coming up will be on the exercises on page 16 in this textbook.**
4. **The exercises on page 16 will be on the coming test.**

　　文法や練習問題に関しては,「問題」に相当する語は problems とは言わない。exercises を使う。数学などでは problems という語を使うことができる。

　　4 は, ほかの事柄もテストに出ることを暗示させる。

試験の範囲は Lesson 6 から Lesson 10 までです。
1. **The exam will cover from Lesson 6 through Lesson 10.**
2. **The exam will cover from Lesson 6 to Lesson 10.**

　　1 の方が 2 よりもよい。2 は Lesson 10 が含まれているかどうかわからない。through を使うと, Lesson 10 は含まれる。

来週の試験は辞書を持ち込んでもかまいません。
1. **You can use your dictionary during the exam next week.**
2. **You can use your dictionary while taking the exam next week.**
3. **You can use your dictionary in the exam next week.**

　　アメリカ英語では, 1, 2 が普通。

今度の中間テストは再試験は行わないので, しっかり勉強しておくように。
There will be no make-up exam for the next midterm exam, so study hard.

今回の試験結果は親に連絡をします。
The results of this exam will be sent to your parents.
The results of these exams will be sent to your parents.
The results of the exams will be sent to your parents.
The results of exams will be sent to your parents.

補講日の２日目に英語の追試を行います。
　You are going to have an English make-up exam on the second day of the make-up period.

今度の試験は平常の教室ではなく，CALL 教室で行うので間違えないようにしなさい。
1. The next exam will take place in the CALL, not in our ordinary classroom, so be sure to go to the right room.
2. The next exam will take place in the CALL, not in our ordinary classroom, so don't make a mistake about where to go.
3. The next exam will take place in the CALL, not in our ordinary classroom, so be careful not to make a mistake that day.
4. The next exam will take place in the CALL, not in our ordinary classroom, so please don't make a mistake about the place.
5. The next exam will take place in the CALL, not in our ordinary classroom, so please be careful not to make a mistake about the place.
6. *The next exam will take place in the CALL, not in our regular classroom, so please be careful.
7. *The next exam will take place in the CALL, not in the regular classroom, so please be careful.
　　６と７では be careful が qualifiers（修飾語句）を伴わずに単独に使われている。Please be careful. のように使う場合には，通例，Watch your step. や Look out. の意味である。このような理由から６と７はふさわしくない。誤解を避けるために１〜５のように具体的に述べるべきである。

▶**中間テストはいつからですか。**
　When are midterm exams going to start?
　When will our midterms start?

When will the midterms start?
When are the midterms?
 日本語に引かれて英訳すると,
  *From when are we going to have the midterm exams?
のように from を入れがちであるが, from を入れると不自然な英文になる。

▶期末試験はいつですか。
When are finals?
When are the finals?
When are the final exams?
When are we going to have the final exams?

▶英語の試験はいつですか。
When are we going to have the English test?

▶英語の試験は2週間後にありますか。
Are we going to have the English test two weeks from now?

▶英語の試験はあと何回ありますか。
 1. **How many more English tests are we going to have?**
 2. **How many more times will we have English tests?**
  1の方が2よりも自然な英語表現である。

▶今度はどんな試験ですか。
What type of test are you going to give us this time?
What type of test will you give us this time?
What kind of test are you going to give us this time?
What kind of test will you give us this time?

▶今度の英語の試験はどんな試験ですか。
What kind of English test are we going to have this time?

▶今度の試験では，教科書だけ勉強してもいい点が取れますか。
Can we get a good score in the next test even if we study only our textbook?
Can we get a good score on the next test even if we study only our textbook?
Do you think we can get a good score on the next test even if we only study our textbook?
Do you think we can get a good score on the next test even if we only study our textbook?

▶テストは主にどこが出るんですか。
What area will the test mainly cover?
What will the test mainly cover?

▶試験は前回と同じようなものですか。
1. Is the test like the one we had last time?
2. Will the test be like the one we had last time?
　　試験の問題用紙が配布されていれば1，まだ配布されていないのであれば2のようになる。

▶テストは易しくしてください。
Please make the test easier.
Please make an easy test.

▶今度の試験は前回よりも易しくしてください。
1. Could you please make the test easier than before?
2. Could you please make the test simpler than before?
　　simpler とは less complicated の意味である。形の上では単純になっても，内容的にはより難しい場合も有り得るから，厳密な意味では1の方が2よりもっと日本文に近い。

▶ヒントを教えてください。
Could you give us some hints?

▶試験に落ちたら，追試験もありますか。
1. **Could you give us a make-up exam if we fail the test?**
2. **Could you give us a make-up exam if we fail in the test?**
   fail が「〈学科試験などに〉落ちる」という意味の自動詞として使われるときには，2 のように前置詞 in が使われる。しかし，現代用法では 1 のように使うことが多い。

▶この試験で何点くらい取ったらいいのですか。
1. **What's the passing score in this test?**
2. **How many points are we supposed to score in this test?**
   日本語を直訳すると 2 に近いが，1 の方がより自然な英語表現である。

▶成績は試験だけで決まるのではありませんね。
1. **Our grade won't be based on this one exam, will it?**
2. **The exam is not everything, is it?**
   日本語の直訳は 2 であるが，試験だけでなく，平素の学習ぶりも成績をつける上で考慮に入れてもらえるかどうかを尋ねる場合には 1 の方がわかりやすい。

▶試験の結果は親に知らせるのですか。
Are you going to let our parents know the results of the tests?

B 試験の注意事項

机と机の間をもっと広げなさい。
1. **Try to leave more space between the desks.**
2. **Try to have more space between the desks.**
   1 の方が 2 よりもよい。

辞書を見てもいいですよ。
You can use your dictionary.

今回は辞書を使ってもかまいません。
This time, you can use your dictionary.

このテストでは，何を参考にしてもかまいません。
In this test, you can refer to anything you want.

カンニングをしないように！
Don't cheat!

　　実際，ある学生がカンニングを行っているような状況で使う表現である。
　　日本語の「カンニング」は cunning という英語の直訳である。もともとの意味は「ずるい」ということであるが，このような状況で使うことはできない。cheat を使うことに注意。

できる範囲内でやりなさい。
Do your best.

鉛筆を忘れた人はこれを貸してあげます。
1. **If you forgot to bring your pencil, I will let you use one of these.**
2. **If you forgot to bring your pencil, I will let you use this one.**

　　鉛筆を忘れた人が 1 人以上いれば，代替の鉛筆は当然 1 本以上必要になってくる。2 の this one は this pencil の意味であるから，代替の鉛筆が 1 本しかないことになる。

ここに鉛筆が何本かあります。
Here are some extra pencils.

今から試験問題を配布します。筆記用具以外は片付けてください。

I am going to give you your test papers. Please put your things away, except writing materials.

I am going to give you your test papers. Please put your stuff away, except things necessary for writing.

I am going to hand out the test papers. Please put your things away, except writing materials.

I am going to hand out the test papers. Please put your stuff away, except things necessary for writing.

今からテスト問題を配布します。鉛筆と消しゴム以外はしまってください。

I am going to give you your test papers now. Please put your things away, except for your pencil and eraser.

give は2つの目的語をとる動詞であるから，you，your ～ と続くことになる。間接目的語の you を省くと自然な英語ではない。

*I am going to give your test papers now.

答案用紙は全部で3枚あります。

You should have three pages in all.

You should have three pages to your test.

Your test should have three pages in all.

紙を数えるとき，a sheet of paper とか a piece of paper という言い方がある。sheet は定形の紙を数えるとき，piece は不定形の紙を数えるときに使う。答案用紙は印刷されたものであるから pages がふさわしい。

答案用紙が2枚，解答用紙が1枚，合計3枚あるはずです。

You should have three pages in all : two test pages and one answer sheet.

ミスプリントがあります。

There is a misprint.

misprint には,「印刷を誤る」という動詞用法もあれば,「誤植」という名詞用法もある。

合図するまで,問題用紙は伏せておいてください。
1. **Please don't turn over your test paper(s) until I say "Start".**
2. **Please don't turn over your test paper(s) until I say "Begin".**
3. **Please keep your test paper(s) turned until I say "Start."**

1,2の方が3よりもよい。3は明確でない。

合図をするまで,問題を解いてはいけません。
1. **You cannot begin answering the questions until I tell you to start.**
2. **You cannot answer the questions until I tell you to start.**

1の方が状況にぴったりした言い方である。

「始め」と言うまで待っていてください。
Wait until I tell you to start.

「始め」と言うまで何も書いてはいけません。
Don't write anything until I tell you to start.

合図をするまで始めてはいけません。
Don't start until I tell you to.

まず,最初に名前と出席番号を記入してください。
First, write down your name and number.

忘れないうちに,番号と名前を書いておいてください。
1. Before you forget, make sure you write your number and name down.
2. Before you forget, be sure to write your number and

name down.
3. **Before you forget, make sure you write your number and name down.**
4. **Before you forget, be sure to write your number and name down.**

英語としては your name and number という言い方が普通であるから，1や2の方が3や4よりもよい。ちょうど，black and white, bread and butter, ladies and gentlemen という語順が定着しているのと同様である。ただ，実際に試験の答案用紙に number が先にあり，name が後になっていれば3や4のように your number and name と言ってもおかしくはない。

Before you forget, make sure ... は redundant であると考えるネイティブスピーカーもいる。Before you forget か make sure の一方を使ってもよい。

今日の日付も答案用紙に書いておきなさい。
Write today's date on your test paper, too.

今からそれについて説明します。
I'm going to explain it.

explain は他動詞的に使う方が普通である。

後ろの人たちは，私の言うことが聞こえますか。
Can the people sitting at the back hear me?

「後ろの人たち」という場合には，状況からどこに座っている人々であるか明白であるから，定冠詞の the を必要とする。

今の説明でわからなかった人はいますか。
Is there anyone who is still lost?
Is there anyone who still can't get me?
Is there anyone who did not understand my explanation?

anyone の次に否定語を置くことはできない。したがって，

*Anyone cannot attend the meeting.

(だれも会合には出席できない。)
のような英文は誤りである。これを正しい文にするには,
> None can attend the meeting.

としなければならない。ただし, anyone の後に関係詞が続く場合には, 否定語を置くことができる。
> Anyone who is unwilling to study English may not be able to pass the entrance exam.

今の説明でわからなかった人はいませんか。
1. **Isn't there anybody who is still lost?**
2. **Isn't there anybody who still doesn't get it?**
3. **Isn't there anybody who still can't understand me?**
4. **Isn't there anybody who did not understand my explanation?**
5. *****Isn't there anybody who still can't get me?**

2 の doesn't get it は set expression であるが, 5 の can't get me は garbled な感じがする。避けた方がよい。2, 3, 4 は文法的には正しいが, double negative (二重否定) であるから文型的にはあまりよくない。

anybody を anyone で言い換えることは可能である。

テスト中は私語をしてはいけません。
Don't talk with your neighbor during the test.
You cannot whisper during the test.

テスト中は, 友だちからものを借りてはいけません。
1. **You cannot borrow anything from your friends during the test.**
2. **You cannot borrow anything from your friend during the test.**

1 の your friends はクラスに友人が何人かいることを, 2 の your friend はクラスに友人がたった1人しかいないことを presuppose させる。通常は, ほとんどの学生にクラスに友人が複数

いるので1の方がよい。

余白が足りなければ，答案用紙の裏に書いてもかまいません。
If you need more space, you may write on the back of the test paper.
If you need more space, you can write on the back of the test paper.
　《許可》を強調する場合は，may の方がよい。

ページが足りなければ知らせてください。
Please let me know if any pages are missing.

用紙が足りなくなったら，知らせてください。
If you run out of paper, please let me know.

余分な用紙を机の上に置いておきます。自由に使ってください。
1. I will put out some extra paper, so feel free to use it.
2. *I will leave some extra paper, so feel free to use it.

　2の leave は，試験を担当している教師が部屋を去っていなくなることを暗示させる。つまり，"Before I go, I'll leave some extra paper for you." という意味になる。もし教師がその場にいるのであれば，leave の代わりに put out という言葉を使わなくてはならない。通常は，試験を担当している教師が部屋を離れることはないので，1のように言わなくてはいけない。

質問があれば，黙って手を上げなさい。
1. If you have a question, raise your hand without saying anything.
2. If you have any questions, raise your hand without saying anything.

　2のように any questions という言い方も正しい。しかし，1のように a question と言った方が，後続の raise your hand という語句とマッチする。

質問があったら，そのつど知らせてください。
　Let me know if you have any questions.
　Let me know any time you have a question.
　Let me know at any time if you have questions.
　If you have questions, let me know anytime you want.

　　アメリカ英語では，「いつでも」を意味する any time は anytime のように1語でつづってもよい。ただ，接続詞的用法の場合には，any time のように2語でつづるのが普通である。イギリス英語では，at any time のように，前置詞の at を挿入するのが普通である。whenever も「いつでも」という意味の接続詞であるが，any time (anytime) よりも formal な響きがある。

問題ができた人は，30分過ぎたらいつ教室を出てもかまいません。
1. When you finish solving the problems, you may leave the room any time after the first thirty minutes have passed.
2. If you have finished solving the problems, you may leave the room any time after the first thirty minutes have passed.
3. If you are finished solving the problems, you may leave the room any time after the first thirty minutes have passed.
4. If you have finished solving the problems, you can leave the room any time after the first thirty minutes have passed.
5. If you are finished solving the problems, you can leave the room any time after the first thirty minutes have passed.

　　1が最も普通に使われる言い方である。

時間になるまで，退場してはいけません。
　You cannot leave the room until the time is up.

テストが終わるまで，退場してはいけません。
You cannot leave the room until the test is over.

答案用紙はいつ提出してもかまいません。
1. **You can turn in the test paper any time you wish.**
2. **You can turn in the test paper any time you want.**
    1と2はいずれでもよいが，wishを使った1の方がformalなニュアンスがある。

残り時間があと10分になったら，一度合図をします。
1. **I will let you know when there are ten minutes left.**
2. **I will let you know when there are just ten minutes left to finish.**
3. ***I will let you know when you have ten more minutes.**
    3のように you have ten more minutes と言うと，試験の制限時間を10分延長するという意味合いになってしまうから，もとの日本文と合わなくなってしまう。

あと10分で時間です。
1. **You have ten more minutes to go.**
2. **You have ten minutes more to go.**
    1と2では語順が異なるが，いずれでもよい。

はい。そこまで。
OK. Good.

時間です。やめてください。
Time is up. Please stop now.

時間になりました。書くのをやめてください。
Time is up. Please stop writing.

もう一度，名前を書いてあるかどうか確かめなさい。
　Check to see that you have written your name down.
　Make sure to see if you have written your name down.

答案用紙は，机の上に置いて退場しなさい。
　Go out of the room, leaving the test paper on the desk.
　Leave your test papers on the desk as you go out.

書くのをやめて，答案用紙を机の上に置いて退場してください。
　Stop writing now. Leave the answer sheet on your desk and leave the room.

答案用紙は裏返しにしてください。
　Turn the answer sheet over.

答案用紙は通路側に置いてください。
　Put the answer sheet on the aisle side.

答案用紙は通路側に裏返しに置いてください。
　Turn the answer sheet over and put it on the aisle side.

問題用紙も答案用紙も裏返しにしてください。
　Turn both the test paper and the answer sheet over.

問題用紙は持って帰ってもかまいません。
　You can take the test paper home.

時間が来たので，答案用紙を後ろから集めなさい。
　As time is up, collect the test papers starting with the back row.

時間になったので，答案用紙を後ろから前に送りなさい。
　As time is up, pass your test papers forward starting with

the back row.
　日本では最後尾の者が後ろから順番に答案用紙を回収したりするが，アメリカでは最後尾の者が1人で回収する代わりに，後ろから順ぐりに前に座っている者に渡していくのが普通である。

▶鉛筆を忘れました。
1. **I forgot to bring a pencil.**
2. **I forgot to bring pencils.**
　この場合には1のように a pencil の形の方が自然である。

▶筆記用具を忘れました。
I forgot to bring something to write with.

▶1枚紙が足りません。
We need one more sheet of paper.
Do you have one more sheet of paper?
We need another sheet of paper.

▶答案用紙が2枚足りません。
We need two more answer sheets.

▶もう1枚答案用紙をください。
May I get one more answer sheet?
Can I get one more answer sheet?
May I get another answer sheet?
Can I get another answer sheet?
One more answer sheet, please.

▶これはミスプリントではないでしょうか。
Isn't this a misprint?

▶これは白紙です。
This is a blank sheet of paper.

▶質問があります。
I have a question.

▶この問題の意味がわかりません。
I cannot understand this question.

▶消しゴムが落ちたので，拾ってもよいですか。
1. **Is it all right to pick up my eraser? It fell on the floor.**
2. **My eraser fell on the floor. May I pick it up?**
3. **May I pick up my eraser, as I dropped it?**
4. **May I pick up my eraser, since I dropped it?**

because は直接の原因を表す。as は付随的な理由を述べるときに使う。since は because と as の中間的な意味合いを持つ。落ちた消しゴムを拾うような状況では 3 の方が 4 よりも自然である。

3 と 4 で drop という語が使われているが，厳密には drop という語はふさわしくないというネイティブスピーカーがいる。人はふつう消しゴムを drop するのではなく，They get knocked off desks by mistake, and fall. というのがその理由である。

▶制限時間は何分ですか。
How many minutes do we have?

▶時間はあと何分ありますか。
1. **How many more minutes do we have?**
2. **How many minutes do we still have?**
3. **How many more minutes do we have left?**
4. **How many minutes do we have left?**
5. *****How many more minutes do we still have?**

1 と 2 とを合わせて 5 のように言うことはできない。つまり，How many more minutes ... still have ...? の形はふさわしくない。

1 授業開始　　*453*

▶もうできたので，提出してもいいですか。
1. May I hand this in? I've finished it.
2. I'm finished. May I hand this in?
3. May I turn this in, as I have finished it?
　　「理由」をつけて3のように1文にして言うよりも，1や2のように2つの文にして言う方が自然な言い方である。

C　試験終了後

試験はどうでしたか。
　How was the test?

試験は難しかったですか。
　Was the test difficult?

試験は思っていた以上に難しかったですか。
　Was the test more difficult than you had thought?
　Was the test harder than you had thought?

答案用紙はあさって返します。
　I will return your test papers the day after tomorrow.

答案用紙はこの次の時間に返します。
　I am going to return your test paper next time.

忘れ物がないようにもう一度チェックしてください。
　Please check once more so that you won't forget anything.
　Please check once more to see that you have not forgotten anything.

▶試験の結果を心配しています。
　I am worried about the results of the exams.

▶テスト問題を返してください。
Please give the test back to us.

▶テストの結果はいつわかりますか。
1. When will we know the results of the test?
2. When will we know how we did on the test?
  1 は standard，2 はやや informal な表現である。

▶鈴木先生，テストはいつ返してもらえるのですか。
Mr. Suzuki, when can we get our tests back?
Mr. Suzuki, when can we have our tests back?

▶鈴木先生，テストはどれくらいで返してもらえるのですか。
Mr. Suzuki, how soon can you give the test back to us?

▶鈴木先生，早くテストを返してください。
Mr. Suzuki, could you give our test paper back to us as soon as possible?
Mr. Suzuki, could you give our test paper back as soon as possible?

▶この問題の正解を教えてください。
Please tell us the answer to this question.

▶この試験は非常に難しかったです。
This test was very difficult.

▶次回はもっと易しいテストにしてください。
1. Please make a little easier test next time.
2. Please make the test a little easier next time.
3. Please make a test a little easier next time.
  1～3 はいずれでもよい。

▶試験時間が足りませんでした。
  1. **I didn't have enough time for the test.**
  2. **I ran out of time on the test.**
     1 は standard, 2 はやや informal な表現である。

▶予想していたところが試験に出ませんでした。
  1. **The test didn't cover areas I thought would appear.**
  2. **The test didn't cover what I had expected.**
  3. **The test didn't cover what I had studied.**
     1 ～ 3 はいずれも standard な表現である。

2　試験問題指示文

A　基本的な指示文

次の質問の答えを英語で書きなさい。
  Write the answers to the following questions in English.

次の質問に対するふさわしい答えを書きなさい。
  Write appropriate answers to the following questions.

次の文を読んで，問いに答えなさい。
  Read the following sentences and answer the questions.

今度はもっとゆっくり話します。用意はいいですか。
  I'll speak a little bit slower this time. Are you ready?

B 訳す

次の文を日本語に訳しなさい。
 1. Translate the following sentences into Japanese.
 2. Put the following sentences into Japanese.
 3. Put the following sentence in Japanese.
 4. Change the following sentences into Japanese.
　　1〜3の方が4よりも明確である。

次の文の下線を引いた部分を日本語に訳しなさい。
 Translate the underlined phrases in the following sentences into Japanese.

次の文を読み，下線部を日本語に訳しなさい。
 1. Read the following sentences and put the underlined area into Japanese.
 2. Read the following sentences and translate the underlined area into Japanese.
 3. Read the following sentences and change the underlined part into Japanese.
　　1と2の方が3よりも明確である。

次の文章を読んで日本語に訳しなさい。
 Read the following sentences and translate them into Japanese.

次の日本文を英文に訳しなさい。
 Change the following Japanese sentences into English.
 Put the following Japanese sentences into English.

C 正誤・異同を指摘する

次の文のうち，もし誤りがあれば訂正しなさい。
  Correct the errors, if any, in the following sentences.

次のそれぞれの文のうち，誤りがあれば指摘しなさい。
  Point out the errors, if any, in the following sentences.

次のそれぞれの文について，正しければ○，誤っていれば×を付けなさい。
  For each of the following sentences, write a ○ in front of each correct sentence and an × in front of each incorrect sentence.
  For each of the following sentences, write a ○ if the sentence is correct and an × if the sentence is wrong.
   　×の前にはaではなく，anを置くことになる。×は [éks] と発音するからである。○は circle と読む。

次の現在完了の用法が，正しければ○，誤っていれば×を付けなさい。
  For each of the following present perfect sentences, write a ○ if the use is correct, and write an × if it is incorrect.
  For each of the following present perfect sentences, write a ○ if the use is correct, and an × if it is incorrect.
  For each of the following present perfect sentences, write a ○ if the use is correct, and an × if it is wrong.
   　3では ... an × if it is wrong となっているが，バランスの上から incorrect という語を使った方がよい。correct と incorrect とは対応する関係にある。right に対応する言葉が wrong である。

接続詞の用法が正しければ○，誤っていれば×を書きなさい。
  Write a ○ if the use of the conjunction is correct and an ×

if it is not.

次の接続詞の用法のうち，正しければ○，誤っていれば×を文頭に付けなさい。
If the usage of the following conjunctions is correct, write a circle in front of the sentence ; if incorrect, write an ×.
If the usage of the following conjunctions is correct, draw a circle in front of the sentence ; if not, write an ×.

次の文章のうち，関係詞の用法が正しければ○，誤っていれば×を付けなさい。
In the following sentences if relatives are properly used, mark ○ , and if they are not, mark ×.

各組の文の意味が同じであれば○，違っていれば×を付けなさい。
For each of the pairs, if the meaning is the same, write a ○ and if the meaning differs, write an ×.

次の各組の下線部の発音が，すべて同じであれば○，1つでも異なるものがあれば×を付けなさい。
1. For each pair of the following words, mark ○ if all of the underlined parts have the same pronunciation, and mark × if they do not.
2. For each pair of the following words, mark ○ if all of the underlined parts have the same pronunciation, and mark × if they don't.

口語表現では don't, isn't, can't などのように省略して話すことの方が多いが，書き言葉，特に指示語などではむしろ省略しない形の方が普通である。1の方が2よりもよい。

D 書く

次の数字の読み方を英語で書きなさい。
Write out the following numbers in English.

次の数字をどのように読むか，英語で書きなさい。
Write in English how to read the following figures.

次のそれぞれの語句が答えとなる質問文を書きなさい。
Write question sentences so that the following words will be the answers.

次の文の下線を引いた部分が答えの中心になるよう，疑問文を作りなさい。
Make a question sentence so that the underlined word is the core of the answer.

What で始まる疑問文を2つ書きなさい。
Write two question sentences beginning with *What*.
　　"What" は英文の文尾にきているが，求められている文は "What ...?" のようになるので，上記の英文では "... with what." ではなく，"... with *What*?" を用いなくてはならない。

板書した語句を使って，文を2つ作りなさい。
Write two sentences using the hints on the board.

「将来の夢」について，500 語ほどのエッセイを書きなさい。
1. Write an essay of about 500 words on "My Dream of the Future."
2. Write an essay of about 500 words on "My Hopes of the Future."
3. Write an essay of about 500 words on "My Future."

4. *Write an essay of about 500 words on "My Future Dream."

　4 の My Future Dream はよさそうに見えるが，正式な用法ではない。1, 2, 3 のように言うべきである。

E　説明する

次の語句を簡単な英語で説明しなさい。
　Explain the following words in plain English.

次の熟語について，英語でその意味を説明しなさい。
　Explain the meaning in English of the following fixed expressions.

次の語句を例に示したように英語で説明しなさい。
　Explain the following words in English as shown in the example.

次の関係代名詞の用法を日本語で説明しなさい。
　Explain the use of the following relative pronouns in Japanese.

F　書き換える

次の文を，指示に従って書き換えなさい。
　Change the following sentences as indicated.

例文と同じように次の文を書き換えなさい。
　Change the following sentences in the same way as in the example.

次のＡからＧまでの文を，例に従って書き換えなさい。
1. Rewrite the following sentences A through G as shown in the example.
2. Rewrite the following sentences A through G after the example.
　　１の方が２よりもより自然な表現である。

次の文を疑問文に直しなさい。
Change the following sentences into the corresponding question sentences.
Change the following sentences into the corresponding interrogative sentences.

次のそれぞれの文を否定文に直しなさい。
Write the negative for each of the following sentences.
Change each one of the following sentences into the negative.
Negate each of the following sentences.

次のそれぞれの文を，過去時制で書きなさい。
Write each of the following sentences in the past tense.

次の名詞を動詞形に変えなさい。
1. Change the following nouns into their corresponding verbs.
2. Change the following nouns into the corresponding verbs.
　　１の方が２よりも自然な英文である。

次の名詞は形容詞に，形容詞は名詞に換えなさい。
Change the following nouns into adjectives, and adjectives into nouns.

462 Ⅵ テスト・試験

下線部の語を，ふさわしい形に換えなさい。
1. **Change the underlined word into an appropriate form.**
2. **Change the underlined word into the appropriate form.**

　1，2はいずれでもよいが，ニュアンスの違いがある。1は多くのふさわしい形がある場合，2は1つだけしかふさわしい形がない場合である。

次の各文を，主語を単数形にして書き換えなさい。
Rewrite each of the following sentences, changing the subject into the singular form.

次の各文を，主語を一人称にして書き換えなさい。
Rewrite each of the following sentences, changing the subject into the first person.

次の文の話法を換えなさい。
Change the narration of the following sentences.

次の各文を直接話法に書き換えなさい。
Put the following sentences in direct narration.
Put the following sentences into direct narrative.
Put the following sentences using direct narration.

直接話法は間接話法に，間接話法は直接話法に換えなさい。
Change direct narration into indirect narration and indirect narration into direct narration.

この文を受け身に換えなさい。
1. **Change this sentence to a passive sentence.**
2. **Change this sentence to a sentence in the passive.**
3. **Change this sentence to a sentence in the passive voice.**

　1の方が，2や3よりも自然である。
　「受け身」は the passive でも the passive voice のいずれでも

よい。

次の各文を受動態に書き換えなさい。
Rewrite the following sentences into the passive voice.

受動態は能動態に，能動態は受動態に換えなさい。
1. Convert each passive sentence to an active one, and each active sentence to a passive one.
2. Rewrite each sentence in the passive voice into one in the active voice, and each sentence in the active voice into one in the passive voice.
3. Rewrite the passive voice to the active voice, and the active voice to the passive voice.

　　1，2 はいずれでもよい。3 はやや不明瞭な表現である。1 は 2 よりも pedantic なニュアンスがある。
　　生徒が受動態と能動態に習熟していれば，Change the voice in each of the following sentences. と指示してもわかるであろう。

次の文の態を指示に従って書き換えなさい。
Change the voice of the following sentences according to the directions.

次の文を，直接目的語と間接目的語の語順を換えて，書き直しなさい。
Rewrite the following sentence, switching the direct object and the indirect object.

次の文を感嘆文に直し，さらに日本語に訳しなさい。
Change the following sentences into exclamatory sentences and translate them into Japanese.

次の文を，最上級を使った文に直しなさい。
Change the following sentences into the superlative form.

Change the following sentences into the superlative.

G つなぐ

２つの文を関係代名詞を使ってつなぎなさい。
Combine two sentences, using a relative pronoun.

関係代名詞を使って，２つの文を１つにしなさい。
Combine the two sentences, using a relative pronoun.
Join the two sentences into one, using a relative pronoun.

Ａ欄とＢ欄からそれぞれ１つずつ文を選んでつなぎ，複文にしなさい。
Choose one sentence each from Columns A and B, and combine them to make a complex sentence.

Ａ欄から主語を，Ｂ欄から述語を選んでつなぎなさい。
Choose a subject from Column A and an appropriate predicate from Column B, and combine them.

H 並べ換え・置き換え

形容詞を正しい順序に並べ換えなさい。
Rearrange the adjectives in the correct order.

（ ）内の語句を並べ換えて，正しい英文を作りなさい。
Unscramble the words in parentheses to make a correct English sentence.

（ ）内の語句を並べ換えて，意味の通る英語に直しなさい。
Arrange the words in parentheses and make correct Eng-

lish sentences.
Unscramble the words in parentheses to make a correct English sentence.
　　scramble は「ごちゃまぜにする」という意味である。unscramble はその反意語で、「乱れをもとに戻す」ということ。

過去形を現在形で置き換えなさい。
Substitute the past tense for the present.

次の各文で，you を he で置き換えなさい。必要であれば動詞も変えなさい。
In the following sentences, replace *you* with *he*. Change the verb, if necessary.

I　埋める・空所補充

次の空欄を埋めなさい。
Fill in the following blanks.

（　）の中に当てはまる言葉を記入しなさい。
Insert an appropriate word into the parentheses.

次の空欄に当てはまる語句を書き入れなさい。
Fill in the following blanks with suitable words.

次の空欄のそれぞれに適当な言葉を入れなさい。
Fill in each of the following blanks with the proper word.

必要であれば空欄に当てはまる語句を書き入れなさい。
Fill in the blank with an appropriate word, if needed.

466　VI　テスト・試験

次の各組の意味が同じになるように，（ ）に適当な言葉を入れなさい。
Insert a word into the parentheses so that each pair of the following sentences means the same.
　　pair は singular の扱いをする。
　　　This sock is dirty. These socks are dirty.
　　　This pair is dirty. Each pair is dirty.
　　　Each pair (of the following sentences) means the same.

（ ）の中に当てはまる前置詞を補いなさい。
Supply an appropriate preposition to the parentheses.
Supply an appropriate preposition for the parentheses.

空欄（A）〜（F）に当てはまる前置詞を書き入れなさい。
Fill in the blanks (A) through (F) with an appropriate preposition.

次のそれぞれの（ ）の中に当てはまる前置詞を書き入れなさい。
Write the appropriate preposition in each of the following parentheses.

抜けている接続詞を補いなさい。
Supply the missing conjunctions.

次の（ ）の中に，適当な接続詞を書き入れなさい。
Write a suitable conjunction in the following parentheses.

次の文の（ ）の中に必要な関係代名詞を入れなさい。
1. Fill in the parentheses with an appropriate relative pronoun.
2. Insert the necessary relative pronouns into the parentheses of the following sentences.
　　1の方が2よりもより自然な英語である。

2 試験問題指示文　*467*

次の各組の2つの文が同じ意味になるように，（　）の中に適当な言葉を書き入れなさい。
Insert an appropriate word into parentheses so that the two sentences of each pair mean the same.

次の日本文と同じ意味になるように，（　）の中に適当な言葉を補って文を完成させなさい。
1. **Supply words to the parentheses to make a sentence that means the same as the given Japanese sentence.**
2. **Supply words to the parentheses to make sentences that mean the same as the given Japanese sentences.**
3. **Supply words to the parentheses so as to make a sentence that means the same as the given Japanese sentence.**
4. **Supply words to the parentheses so as to make sentences that mean the same as the given Japanese sentences.**
　　1，2，3，4のいずれでもよいが，1，2の to make 〜 を 3，4 の so as to 〜 よりも好むネイティブスピーカーがいる。

空欄に，名詞の複数形を書きなさい。
Write the plural form of the noun in a blank.

J　完成させる

与えられた語句を使って文を完成させなさい。
Complete the sentences using the words provided.

次の各文を，適当な助動詞を補って完成させなさい。
Complete the following sentences with a suitable auxiliary.
　　助動詞は auxiliary でも auxiliary verb でもよい。

次の語群の言葉を1つ使って、各文を完成させなさい。
Use one of the following words to complete the sentences.

（　）の中に当てはまる助動詞を入れて、各文を完成しなさい。
Complete the sentences, using an appropriate form of can.

次のそれぞれの文の（　）の中に当てはまる語句を下の欄から選んで、文を完成させなさい。
Choose a suitable group of words from the lower column that fit into the parentheses to make a complete sentence.

K　選ぶ

次の英文を読み、本文の内容と一致するものを選びなさい。
Read the following English sentences and choose the items corresponding to the content.

本文の内容に一致したものを、3つ選びなさい。
Choose three statements that agree with the text.

次のうち、本文のタイトルとしてふさわしいものを選び番号で答えなさい。
Write the number of the statement that will make a good title for the text.

この段落の内容を最もよく表している文を選びなさい。
1. Choose the sentence that best describes what this paragraph is about.
2. Choose the sentence that describes the content of this paragraph best.
　　1の方がより自然な表現である。

2 試験問題指示文　469

4つの選択肢の中から，最もふさわしい答えを選びなさい。
  1. Choose the best answer from the four choices.
  2. Choose the best answer out of the four choices.
     1の方が2よりもよい。

例文と同じ種類の文を選び，記号で答えなさい。
  1. Choose the sentence of the same type as the example sentence and write the corresponding letter in the space provided.
  2. Choose the sentence similar to the example sentence and write the corresponding letter in the space provided.
  3. *Choose the same sentence as the example sentence and answer in alphabet.
     1，2はいずれもでもよいが，3は不自然である。もとの日本語には1が近い。

次の (1) ～ (6) と同じ文型の文を (A) ～ (F) から選びなさい。
  For each of the following sentences from (1) to (6), choose the corresponding sentence from (A) to (F) with the same sentence pattern.

それぞれの文に最も合う前置詞を選びなさい。
  Choose the preposition that best fits each sentence.

次の（　）の中の接続詞のうち，最もふさわしいものを選び番号で答えなさい。
  Write the number corresponding to the best conjunction in the following parentheses.
  Write the number of the best conjunction in the following parentheses.

次の（　）の関係詞のうち，最もふさわしいものを選びなさい。
  Choose the best relative from the following parentheses.

Choose the best of the relatives from the following parentheses.

下線部（A）と同じ意味を表す言葉を文中から探しなさい。
Find a word in the passage that has the same meaning as the underlined part (A).

次のそれぞれの（　）の中で，正しい方を選びなさい。
1. Choose the correct answer from the following pairs of words within parentheses.
2. *For each pair of the following parentheses, choose the correct answer.

　2はもとの日本文には近いが，意味が不明瞭である。1のように具体的に言うべきである。

　括弧の一方は parenthesis であるが，両方の括弧に言及する場合は parenthesis と言っても，parentheses と言ってもよい。

空欄に at, in, for のいずれかを入れなさい。
Fill in the blanks with an *at*, *in*, or *for*.

（　）の中に a か the を入れなさい。
Put either *a* or *the* in the parentheses.

それぞれの（　）の中から，can か may のいずれかを選びなさい。
Choose either *can* or *may* from the parentheses.

それぞれの文の（　）に当てはまる語句を右欄から選んで，記号で答えなさい。
Choose the corresponding word from the right column. Answer with the symbol representing the word.
Choose the corresponding word from the column on the right. Answer with the symbol representing the word.

次の副詞節の働きを a 原因・理由, b 時, c 条件, d 譲歩, e 目的・結果の中から選んで記号で答えなさい。
Indicate the role of the following adverbial clauses. Write a, if it is that of cause and effect ; b, time ; c, condition ; d, concession ; and e, purpose and result.

与えられた語句を用いて, 空欄を埋めなさい。
Fill in the blanks using the words given.

次の空欄に当てはまる語句を下の欄から選び, 番号で答えなさい。
Choose the appropriate word from the list below, that fits into the following blank, and write in the number.

次の文の（ ）に当てはまる言葉を下の欄から選びなさい。
For each set of parentheses in the following sentences, choose an appropriate word from the column below.

[æ] の音を持つ言葉を選んで, その番号で答えなさい。
Write the number corresponding to the word having an [æ] sound.

次の単語のうち, [æ] の音を含むものを選びなさい。
Choose the words that have an [æ] sound from the following words.
From the following words, choose the ones with an [æ] sound.

L ○で囲む

ふさわしい答えを○で囲みなさい。
Circle the appropriate answer.

( ) の中のふさわしい言葉を○で囲みなさい。
　Circle the suitable word within the parentheses.
　Put a ring around the suitable word within the parentheses.

正しい文を選び，その番号を○で囲みなさい。
　Choose the correct sentences and circle the corresponding numbers.

次のそれぞれの文で，目的語を○で囲みなさい。
　Circle the object for each sentence.

次のそれぞれの文の動詞を○で囲みなさい。
　1. For each of the following sentences, circle the verb.
　2. For each of the following sentences, put a ring around the verb.
　　　1の方が2よりも自然な表現である。

M　下線を引く

助動詞に下線を引きなさい。
　Underline the auxiliary verbs.
　Put a line under the auxiliary verbs.

すべての動詞に下線を引きなさい。
　Underline all the verbs.

それぞれの文の補語に下線を施しなさい。
　Underline the complement for each sentence.

次の各文の名詞に下線を引きなさい。
　For each of the following sentences underline the noun.

次のそれぞれの文のうち代名詞があれば下線を引きなさい。
　For each of the following sentences, underline the pronouns, if any.

それぞれの文に２つ誤りがある。誤りの箇所に下線を引きなさい。
　Each of the following sentences has two errors. Underline them.

N　×を付ける

該当する文の左に，×を付けなさい。
　Write an × to the left of the appropriate sentence.
　　日本語の中では×という記号は「間違い」を表すが，英語の中では「該当する」ことを表す。いくつかある選択肢の中から該当する答えを選ぶときには，□の中にこの×の記号を書き入れることが多い。
　　×は [krɔs] あるいは [eks] と読む。前者の読み方であれば a, 後者の読み方なら an となる。

正しい答えに×を付けなさい。
　Put an × by the right answer.
　Put an × in front of the right answer.

該当する（　）の中に×を書き入れなさい。
　Put an × in the appropriate parentheses.

O　要約する・まとめる

次のストーリーを簡単に要約しなさい。
　Summarize the following story briefly.

本文の内容を英語でおおまかにまとめなさい。
1. **Briefly translate (the content of) the book in English.**
2. **Give a brief translation of the book in English.**
3. **Translate the content of the book briefly in English.**
    1 は standard, 2 はやや formal, 3 はやや不自然な表現である。

次の文章を 300 語以内で要約しなさい。
Sum up the following passage within 300 English words.

Farewell to Arms を 300 語以内で要約しなさい。
1. **Summarize *Farewell to Arms* in 300 words or less.**
2. **Summarize *Farewell to Arms* in not more than 300 words.**
    1 の方が 2 よりもよい。

文法に注意して, リンカーンの伝記を 100 語以内の英語でまとめなさい。
1. **Bearing grammar in mind, summarize the biography of Lincoln in 100 English words (or less).**
2. **Paying attention to grammar, summarize Lincoln's biography in 100 English words (or less).**
    1 は standard, 2 はやや informal な表現である。

下線部 A はどんな意味か, 50 字以内の日本語でまとめなさい。
Sum up what the underlined passage A means within fifty Japanese characters.

次の段落を読んで, 大意を 50 字以内の日本語にまとめなさい。
Read the following paragraph and sum it up within 50 Japanese characters.

　　paragraph とは a distinct section or subdivision of a chapter, letter, etc., usually dealing with a particular point. ということであり, passage とは a noted sentence, paragraph, etc., of a written work or speech ということになる。

10 課の内容を日本語で 100 字以内でまとめなさい。
1. **Summarize the passage in Lesson 10 within 100 words in Japanese.**
2. **Sum up the passage in Lesson 10 within 100 words in Japanese.**
3. **Summarize Lesson 10 within 100 words in Japanese.**
4. **Sum up Lesson 10 within 100 words in Japanese.**

　　1〜4 はいずれでもよい。1〜3 は standard な表現であるが，4 はやや informal な表現である。passage という語を使うとより明確である。

P　句読点を打つ

次の各文に句読点を打ちなさい。
Punctuate the following sentences.

次の句読点の用法のうち，誤っていれば×を付けなさい。
1. **Write an × if the use of the following punctuation is incorrect.**
2. **Write an × if the use of the following punctuation is wrong.**

　　1 の方が 2 よりもよい。

次のそれぞれの文で，必要な箇所に句読点を打ちなさい。
Punctuate each of the following sentences in the right place.

Q　その他

次の文の種類を言いなさい。
　Indicate the sentence pattern of each of the following sentences.

次のそれぞれの文を主部と述部に分けなさい。
　Divide each of the following sentences into their subject and predicate.
　Divide each of the following sentences into the subject and the predicate.

次のそれぞれの文について，相当する箇所の下にS，V，O，Cを書きなさい。
　For each of the following sentences, write S, V, O, and C under the corresponding part.

3　採点・成績

A　返却前

隣の人と答案用紙を交換しなさい。
　Exchange your test paper with your neighbor.
　　neighbor のつづりはアメリカ英語。イギリス英語では neighbour となる。

まだ，採点をしていません。
　I haven't graded the papers yet.
　　アメリカでは，誤答に○を付け正解に何も印を付けなかったり，正解に ✓（チェックマーク）を付けたりする。通常の試験では平

均点で 50 点以上のものが求められるので，アメリカ式のように，正解には何もしるしを付けずに採点すると確かに時間的な節約にはなる。
　しかし，たまに，誤った答えにチェックマークを付けることもある。

最高点は 95 点でした。
　The highest score was 95.

平均点は 62 点です。
　The average score is 62.
　The average is 62.

60 点以下は追試験をします。
　I will give a make-up test for those who scored under 60.

▶テストの結果を知らせてください。
　Could you let us know the results of the exam?

▶平均点はいくらですか。
　What is the average score?

▶最高点はいくらですか。
　What is the highest score?

▶合格点は何点ですか。
　What is the passing score?
　　ふつう，合格するための最低点は 1 つしかない。したがって，the が必要である。

▶欠点は何点ですか。
　1. What is the passing score?
　2. What score is a D?

3. *What score is the D?

　　日本文を直訳すると3のような英文が考えられるが不自然な言い方である。1のように言わなくてはいけない。

▶この科目に合格するには何点必要ですか。
　How many points do I need to pass this class?

▶私たちの試験の成績は，ほかのクラスと比べてどうでしたか。
　How did the results of the exam of our class compare with those of other classes?

▶このクラスの平均点はほかのクラスと比べてどうですか。
　1. How does our class average on this test compare with those of other classes?
　2. How does the average score of this class compare with that of the other classes?
　3. How is the average score of this class, compared with those of the other classes?

　　1と2とでは意味が異なる。1はそれぞれのクラスの平均と比較する場合。2はほかのクラス全体の平均と比較する場合である。
　　3は話し言葉としては formal すぎる。1が最もふさわしい表現である。

B　返却後

テストは難しかったですか，簡単だったですか。
　1. Do you think the test was easy or difficult?
　2. Was the test easy or difficult?

　　1は，テストを受けた学生に対して，教師が客観的にテストの難易度を尋ねているケースである。
　　2は，テストをまだ受けていない学生が，すでにテストを受けた学生に対してその難易度を尋ねているようなケースである。

名前を呼ばれたら，答案用紙を取りにきなさい。
  1. **When you are called, please come here to get your paper.**
  2. **When you are called, please come up to get your paper.**
  3. **When you are called, please come here and get your paper.**
  4. **When you are called, please come up here and get your paper.**
     1，2の表現の方が3，4よりも自然である。

この問題は簡単じゃないか。
  1. **This exercise is easy, isn't it?**
  2. **This problem is easy, isn't it?**
     exercise は，しばしば a series or set of questions の意。

この問題は難しすぎたかな。
  I wonder if this question was a bit too difficult.
  I wonder if this question was a bit too tough.
  I wonder if this question was a bit too hard.
  I wonder if this question was a bit too complicated.

ここは，これ以上点をあげられません。
  1. **I can't give you any more points.**
  2. ***I can't give you more points than these.**
     日本語を直訳すると2のような文が考えられるが，2は不自然な言い方である。1の方がよい。

松本君，おめでとう。100点だよ。
  Matsumoto-kun, congratulations! You scored 100.
  Matsumoto-kun, congratulations! You got a hundred.
  Matsumoto-kun, congratulations! You got a perfect score.
  Matsumoto-kun, congratulations! It's a hundred percent correct.

松本君，今回の試験はあまりよくなかったけれども，この次の試験は頑張れよ。
1. Matsumoto-kun, you didn't do very well on the last test. Do better the next time.
2. Matsumoto-kun, you didn't do very well on the last test. Do a good job on the next one.
3. Matsumoto-kun, the last test was not good enough. Do a good job on the next one.
4. Matsumoto-kun, the last test was not so good. Do a good job on the next one.
5. *Matsumoto-kun, the last test was not so good, but do a good job in the next test.

  もとの日本語に引かれると，接続詞の but を使いたくなるが，5 のようにあえて but を使う必要はない。
  「この次の試験では」というとき，*in the next test は誤り。on the next test のように，前置詞は on を使うこと。

欠点を取った人は，今日の昼休みに私の部屋に来るように。
Those who failed the test, come to my office during lunchtime today.
Those who failed in the test, come to my office during lunchtime today.

  「(試験などに) 落ちる」場合，fail in the test, fail the test のいずれでもよいが，現在では in を省略することが多い。

採点ミスはありませんか。
Are there any marking mistakes?
Have I made any marking mistakes?
Have I made any mistakes in grading?

採点ミスがあったら持ってきてください。いま訂正します。
1. If there's a mistake in grading, please bring your paper to me. I'll correct it now.

2. If there's a grading mistake, please bring your paper to me. I'll correct it now.
3. If there are any grading mistakes, bring them up to me. I'll correct them now.
4. If there are any grading mistakes, bring them up to me. Let me correct them now.
5. *If there are any mistakes in grading, come to me. Let me correct them now.
    5の come to me という言い方はふさわしくない。

▶小川先生は，採点がからい。
Mr. Ogawa is a hard marker.
Mr. Ogawa is a hard grader.
Mr. Ogawa is hard in marking.
Mr. Ogawa is severe in marking.

▶試験は難しすぎました。
The exam was too difficult.

▶今度の試験は前回よりもずっと難しかったです。
This test was a lot more difficult than the previous one.

▶今度は易しい試験にしてください。
Next time, please make an easy test.
    少し demanding な表現であるが，親しい教師に対しては学生はこのように言うこともありうる。

▶私のテストはどうだったでしょうか。
How did I do on the test?

▶私はどれくらいのところでしょうか。
How did I rank on the test?

▶私の平常点を教えてください。
　Could you tell me how many points I have?

▶合格したでしょうか。
　Did I pass?
　Did I make it?

▶単位が取れそうでしょうか。
　Do you think I can get units for this class?
　Do you think I can receive credit for this class?
　Do you think I can pass this class?

▶ここは，採点されていません。
　This isn't graded yet.
　This hasn't been graded yet.

▶小川先生，部分点がありません。
　1. Mr. Ogawa, I didn't get any partial credit.
　2. Mr. Ogawa, I do not have any partial credit.
　3. Mr. Ogawa, I haven't got any partial credit.
　　　１のように過去形で表現してもよいし，２のように現在形で表現してもよい。
　　　３はあまり自然な表現ではない。

▶先生，合計点が合いません。
　These don't add up to the total score.

▶なぜそこはそのようになるのですか。
　1. Why should it be that way?
　2. Why should that be as it is?
　　　１の方が，２よりも自然な表現である。

▶この問題はどのようにして考えればいいのですか。
How should I tackle this problem?
How should I go about solving this problem?
　　go about は,「(仕事などに) 取りかかる」という意味の熟語。

▶これは採点ミスではないでしょうか。
Is this grading all right?
Is this graded correctly?

▶これは採点ミスだと思います。
1. I think there's a mistake in grading.
2. I think there's a grading mistake.
3. I am afraid you've made a mistake in grading.
4. I am afraid you've made a mistake in marking.
5. I am afraid you've made a grading mistake.
6. I am afraid you've made a marking mistake.
　　1や2の言い方の方が, 3〜6よりもよい。3〜6は you've 〜 のように, だれが採点ミスをしたかを強調した形になっているから, 相手の立場を考えるとあまり好ましい表現ではない。you という代名詞を使うかわりに, there's という無難な言い方にしたい。

▶合っているのに, ×をされています。
This is OK, but it is marked wrong.

▶これは辞書に載っていました。
This is what the dictionary says.

▶この問題は, これだけしか点がもらえませんか。
Is this all I get for this item?
Is this all I get for this question?
Is this all I get for this exercise?
Is this all I get for this problem?

▶英語の点は5教科の中で一番悪かった。
The English score was the worst among the five subjects.

C　成績

これは平常点に加えます。
I will count this toward your grade.

成績には授業中の発言も考慮します。
1. Your class participation will be counted toward your grade.
2. Your class activity will be counted toward your grade.
   1は自然であるが，2はあまり自然な言い方ではない。

レポートも成績に加えます。
1. Your report will be counted in your grade.
2. *Your report will be added toward your grade.
   日本語ではおかしくないが，2の表現ではreportがaddされることになり，ふさわしくない。pointsやscoresはaddすることができる。

試験を6割，平常点を4割として成績をつけます。
1. Sixty percent of your grade will be based on your test and the rest will be on your class participation.
2. *Your grade will be based on your test 60 percent, and the rest will be on your class activity.
   1は自然であるが，2は自然な言い方ではない。

今から今学期の成績表を配ります。
1. I am going to hand out your report cards now.
2. I am going to hand out your report cards from now on.
3. I am going to give you the report cards now.

4. I am going to give you the report cards from now on.
「今から」を直訳すると，from now であるが，1 や 3 のように，now とするか，2 や 4 のように from now on としなくてはいけない。

なお，just now（「たった今，今しがた」）は，現在完了と一緒には使えない。過去形とともに使わなくてはいけない。
　　*She has left Oita for Tokyo just now.
　　She left Oita for Tokyo just now.

どうすれば英語の成績が上がると思いますか。
　How do you think you can improve your English ability?

英語の成績と国語の成績とは，直接関係はありません。
　The English score has no direct connection with the Japanese language score.
　The English score has no direct correlation with the Japanese language score.

この成績では，希望の学校には入れませんよ。
　With these grades, you won't be able to enter the school you want.
　Having these grades, you will not be able to enter the school you want.
　I'm afraid you won't be able to get into the school you want with these grades.

成績表は直接保護者に送付します。
　I am going to send the report cards to your parents directly.

▶成績はどのようにつけるのですか。
　How will you grade us?

▶平常点は何割で計算するのですか。
How much weight will be given to daily classwork?
How many points will be put on daily classwork?
How many points will be credited to daily classwork?
　　　How much point というような表現はできない。points が普通名詞であるからである。
　　　classwork は class work のように2語ではなく，1語であることに注意。

▶成績はいつもらえるのでしょうか。
When can we get the report card?

▶今学期の成績が心配です。
1. I am worried about my semester grades.
2. I am worried about my grades for this semester.
　　　1の方が2よりも自然な表現である。
　　　アメリカの大学は，semester system か quarter system を採用している。前者は夏期期間も含めて1年を3つの期間に分け，後者は1年を4つの期間に分けている。

▶落第点を取ったらどうしたらよいですか。
What should I do if I get a D?
What shall I do if I fail the course?

▶英語の成績が伸び悩んでいます。
My English scores are not improving.

▶英語の点がだんだん下がっています。
1. My English scores are gradually getting worse.
2. My English scores are getting worse and worse.
　　　1の文で副詞の gradually が使われている。副詞の位置はほかの品詞に比べて比較的自由であると言われるものの，gradually の位置は，are という be 動詞の後が一番おさまりがよい。grad-

ually を文末に置いて,

  My English scores are getting worse gradually.
とすると, 抵抗を示すネイティブスピーカーがいる。

▶私の成績はクラスで何番目くらいでしょうか。
How do I rank in this class?

 「何番目」に相当する英語表現はない。上記のように別の言い回しをしなくてはいけない。

▶成績は親に知らせるのですか。
Are you going to send the report cards to our parents?

▶成績が下がると親がうるさいんですよ。
1. **My parents get upset with me when my grades get worse.**
2. **My parents scold me when my grades get worse.**
3. ***My parents get fussy when my grades get worse.**
4. ***My parents get fussy when my grades go down.**

 3と4の fussy には①気難しい, ②神経質な, ③〈衣服などが〉ごてごてした, などのようにいろいろな意味がある。しかし, ここではふさわしくない。

VII 授業の周辺

1 連絡・相談など

A 連絡・相談

わからないところがあれば，図書館に行って調べなさい。
1. If you have something you can't understand, go to the library and look it up.
2. If you have something you can't understand, go to the library to find out about it.
3. If you have something you can't understand, go to the library to check it out.
4. If you have something you can't understand, go to the library and check it.

　　4のように check it とすると，check には「妨害する」「照合する」「(所持品を一時的に) 預ける」などいろいろな意味があってわかりにくい。1, 2, 3のように言った方がいい。

この俗語に興味のある人は，図書館の俗語辞典で調べてごらんなさい。
If you are interested in this slang expression, why don't you look it up in a slang dictionary in the library?
If you are interested in this slang expression, why don't you check it in a slang dictionary in the library?

英語のいろいろな辞書については，図書館員に聞いてごらんなさい。
1. For information on various English dictionaries, please ask the librarian.
2. As for information on various English dictionaries, please ask the librarian.
3. If you need information on various English dictionaries, please ask the librarian.
4. *For information on various English dictionaries, please ask the librarians.

　辞書について聞く場合には，普通の図書館員であれば学生の質問に答えられるから，4 のように librarians と複数の形にしない方がよい。複数にすると，あたかも「1人では信用できないから」という意味合いを含むことになる。

まだ本を返していない人は，来週の金曜日までに必ず返してください。
1. Students who have not returned their books yet, be sure to turn them in by next Friday.
2. Students who have not returned their books yet, be sure to bring them back by next Friday.
3. If you haven't returned your books yet, be sure to bring them back by next Friday.
4. Students who have not returned the books yet, be sure to turn them in by next Friday.

　1, 2 では their books, 4 では the books となっている。their books という場合には，「(図書館から借り出して) しばらく使った本」というニュアンスがあるが，the books と言うとそういう意味合いはない。人称代名詞と定冠詞の使い方で意味の違いが生じる例文を挙げてみる。

　　① I returned my library book.
　　② I returned the book to the store.

　①の場合は，「(図書館からしばらく借りて使った) 本を図書館に返却した」というニュアンスがあるが，②の場合には，「(希望

していた本とは異なっていた）本を，本屋に返した」というようなニュアンスの違いがある。
　3 は casual な言い方である。

山本君，ちょっと相談したいことがあるんだ。
　Yamamoto-kun, I have something to talk to you about.

山本君，今日の放課後僕の研究室に来てくれないか。
　Yamamoto-kun, could you come to my office after school?
　Yamamoto-kun, can you come to my office after school?

山本君，お父さんにお会いしたいので，ご都合を聞いておいてくれないか。
　Yamamoto-kun, could you ask your father when he is available as I would like to see him?
　Yamamoto-kun, can you ask your father when he is available as I would like to see him?

山本君，近いうちにお母さんにお会いしたいのでそのように言っておいてくれないか。
　Yamamoto-kun, could you tell your mother that I want to see her one of these days?
　Yamamoto-kun, can you tell your mother that I want to see her one of these days?

▶西田先生，ちょっとご相談したいことがあるんですが。
　Mr. Nishida, I have something to talk to you about.

▶西田先生，英語のことでちょっとご相談したいことがあるんですが。
　Mr. Nishida, I have something to talk to you about English.

▶高橋先生，お願いがあるんですが。
  Mr. Takahashi, may I ask a favor of you?
  Mr. Takahashi, I have a favor to ask of you.

▶高橋先生，相談ごとにのっていただけませんか。
  Mr. Takahashi, could I come see you for advice?

▶先生，あることで困っているんです。
  I am in trouble.
  　「あることで」を無理に英訳して for something というような語句を付け加えると不自然な英語になる。

▶話を聞いてください。
  Could you listen to me?

▶鈴木先生，お暇なときはいつですか。
  Mr. Suzuki, when will you be free?

▶先生，今日の午後は研究室にいらっしゃいますか。
  Will you be available in your office this afternoon?
  Will you be available at your office this afternoon?
  Will you be in your office this afternoon?
  Will you be at your office this afternoon?
  　前置詞 in と at の使い分けは難しい。明確な使い分けのルールは定かではないが，in は話し手と聞き手が同一の建物か比較的近い建物にお互いがいるような場合，at はそれぞれが別の建物か遠くの建物にいるような場合に使われることが多い。
  　① I'll be in the business office for a few minutes.
  　② I'll be in my office from 3 : 00 to 5 : 00 today.
  　③ I'll be at the office until 9 tonight.
  　例えば，①は，ある高校の教師が別の教師に学校で言う状況である。the business office は the teachers' office を出て突き当たりのところにあるような場合である。

②は，教師が学生に対して言う表現であり，教師は学生が授業を受けている建物と同じ，あるいは隣接する建物にいることが想定される。
　③は，教師が学校から彼の妻に，用事があって学校に9時までいなくてはならないということを告げているような場合である。

▶今日の放課後，先生のお部屋にお邪魔してもいいですか。
May I come see you at your office this afternoon?

▶高橋先生，午後は空いていますか。ちょっとわからないところがあるんです。質問に行ってもいいですか。
Will you be available sometime this afternoon, Mr. Takahashi? I have something I don't understand. May I come to your office?
Will you be available sometime this afternoon, Mr. Takahashi? There's something I don't understand. When could I come and talk to you about it?
Will you be available sometime this afternoon, Mr. Takahashi? I have something I don't understand. Do you have time for me to come and talk to you about it?
Will you be available sometime this afternoon, Mr. Takahashi? There's something I don't understand. When do you have time for me to come and talk to you about it?

　Will you be available sometime? のように available のあとに修飾語句があれば問題ないが，Will you be available? のように何も修飾語句がないと sexual overtones がある。available を使うときには何か語句を添えたい。

▶英会話の教材を貸していただけませんか。
Could you lend me some English conversation materials?

▶英語の本を何か貸していただけませんか。
Could you lend me some English books?

▶高橋先生，お話とは何でしょうか。
1. Mr. Takahashi, what was it you wanted to talk to me about?
2. Mr. Takahashi, what was it you wanted to see me about?
3. Mr. Takahashi, what would you like to talk to me about?
4. *Mr. Takahashi, what would you like to talk to me?
　　１と２が最も普通の言い方である。
　　文尾の about は必要である。about がなければ非文法的。

第２回の英検は，８月１日から願書の受け付けが始まります。
1. Applications for the second English Step Test will be accepted starting August 1.
2. Applications for the second English Step Test will be taken starting August 1.
3. The application for the second English STEP Test is going to be received starting August 1.
　　１と２の方が３より自然な言い方である。

▶英検を受けたいのですが，どのような準備をしたらよいのでしょうか。
I'd like to take the STEP test, but how should I get ready for it?
I'd like to take the STEP test, but how should I study for it?
　　STEP は The Society for Testing English Proficiency, Inc.（財団法人日本英語検定協会）の省略形であるから大文字にする。

▶英検はいつあるのですか。
When is the STEP test going to be held?

▶英検は年に何回ありますか。
How many English STEP tests are there in a year?

▶先週教わったことが，英検に出ました。
What we learned last week appeared on the English STEP Test.

▶先週教わったことが，偶然英検に出ていました。
What we learned last week happened to be on the English STEP Test.
　　「テストに」というときには，前置詞に in ではなく on を使うことに注意すること。

B　生徒への気遣い

近ごろ風邪が流行っています。気をつけてください。
Bad colds are going around. Be careful not to catch one.
　　bad colds は a bad cold でもよいが，アメリカ人の中には文体的に a ＋普通名詞の単数形よりも普通名詞の複数形を主語に置くことを好む人もいる。ある種の風邪であれば a cold となる。

季節の変わり目なので，風邪に注意してください。
As the seasons are changing, be careful not to catch cold.

食中毒にかかりやすい季節です。食べ物には十分注意しましょう。
You are likely to get food poisoning at this time of year. Pay special attention to food.
You are likely to get food poisoning this time of year. Pay special attention to food.

寝冷えしないように注意しましょう。
Be careful not to catch cold in your sleep.
Be careful not to catch cold while you're asleep.

山本君，何か心配事があるの。
1. **Yamamoto-kun, are you worried about something?**
2. **Yamamoto-kun, is something worrying you?**
3. **Yamamoto-kun, is something bothering you?**
4. **Yamamoto-kun, do you have something to worry about?**

　　4 は，threatening あるいは humorous な響きのする言い回しである。1，2，3 の方がよい。

　　日本語としては「山本君，心配事があるんじゃないのか」は不自然ではないので，

　　*Yamamoto-kun, aren't you worried about something?
　　*Yamamoto-kun, don't you have something to worry about?

のように英訳すると奇異な文になる。「心配事があることを期待している」趣がある。

心配事があったら，いつでも私のところに来なさい。
　Whenever something bothers you, please come to me.
　Whenever something bothers you, please see me.

お父さんの様子はどうですか。
　How is your father?

▶日に日によくなっています。
　He's getting better day by day.

2　教師についての質問

A　教師の経歴

▶野中先生，どんなふうに英語を勉強されたのですか。
　Mr. Nonaka, how did you study English?

私は基本文を覚えて，できるだけ語いを増やすようにしました。
   I tried to memorize basic sentences and enrich my vocabulary.

私は英語の映画をできるだけ見るようにしました。
   I tried to see as many English movies as possible.

私はわからないところは英語の先生によく質問しました。
   I often asked my English teacher(s) about things I could not understand.
   I often asked my English teacher(s) the things I could not understand.

私は英語を母語とする人たちと，メールのやりとりをして英語を学びました。
   I learned English by exchanging e-mails with native speakers of English.
   I studied English by exchanging e-mails with native speakers of English.

私は英語の本をよく読みました。
   I often read English books I liked.

▶先生が英語教師になったいきさつを教えてください。
   Could you tell us how you became an English teacher?

英語が好きで，人と話すのも好きだったからです。
   I liked English and also liked to talk with people.
   I liked English and I also liked to talk to people.

▶山本先生は高校のとき，英語は得意だったのですか。
   Mr. Yamamoto, were you good at English when you were in high school?

英語は好きでしたが，成績はまあまあでした。
　I liked English, but my grades in English were only so-so.

英語はほかの学科に比べて，よい方でした。
　1. My grades in English were better compared with my other subjects.
　2. I was better at English than in my other subjects.
　3. English was better compared with other subjects.
　　　　1と2は自然であるが，3はあまり自然な言い方ではない。

英語だけはよかったですよ。
　1. I was good only in English.
　2. I was only good in English.
　3. Only English was good.
　　　　1と2は自然だが，3はあまり自然な表現ではない。

高校1年の頃は英語の成績はクラスで下の方でしたが，その後，頑張りました。
　My English grades were near the bottom of the class when I was a freshmen, but I tried harder afterwards.

▶山本先生はどのようにして英会話をマスターされましたか。
　How did you master English conversation, Mr. Yamamoto?

暇なときは，できるだけ英語のCDを聞くようにしました。
　When I had time, I tried to listen to CDs in English as often as possible.

英語のCDの後について声を出して会話練習をしました。
　1. I practiced conversations by repeating sentences aloud after the CDs.
　2. I practiced conversations letting out my voice after English CDs.

1は自然だが，2はあまり自然な言い方ではない。

毎日何らかの形で英語に触れるようにしました。
I tried to get as much exposure to English as possible every day.
I tried to expose myself to English in one way or another every day.

毎日努力はしていますが，私はまだ英語をマスターしてはいません。
I am making great effort every day, but I haven't mastered English.
I am making efforts every day, but I haven't mastered English yet.

▶どうしたら先生みたいに英語がうまくなれるんですか。
1. How can I become a good English speaker like you?
2. How can I become as good at English speaker as you are?
3. *How can I become a good English speaker as you are?
   3は誤り。as 〜 as は対応しなくてはいけない。

▶アメリカの大学について話をしてください。
1. Will you tell us something about American colleges?
2. Could you tell us something about American colleges?
3. May I ask you something about American colleges?
   3の質問は1や2と異なり，何かを具体的に知りたいというニュアンスがある。

それはよいですが，具体的にどんなことが知りたいですか。
That's OK, but what would you like to know about it more specifically?

それでは，アメリカの学生がどのように勉強しているかの話から始めましょう。
　Well, let me begin with how American college students are studying.

▶園田先生，海外旅行の話をしてください。
　Mrs. Sonoda, could you tell us about your overseas trip?
　Mrs. Sonoda, could you tell us about your trip overseas?
　　overseas は「海外の」という意味の形容詞としての用法もあるし，「海外に」という意味の副詞としての用法もある。なお，oversea という -s のない形もあるが，overseas のように -s を付けて使う方がより普通である。

それでは，海外旅行での失敗談について少し話をしてみましょう。
　Well, let me talk about my blunders on my trips abroad.
　Well, let me tell you about some blunders I made on my trips abroad.

B　教師の私的事柄についての質問

▶谷川先生，どんな国に行ったことがありますか。
　What countries have you been to, Mr. Tanigawa?

6つの大陸の国々に行ったことがあります。
　I've been to countries on six continents.
　I've been to countries in six continents.
　　前置詞は on でも in でもよい。

文化や宗教が全く異なる国々に行ったことがあります。
　I've been to countries which have totally different religions and cultures.

英語圏ではない多くの国々に行ったことがあります。
　I've been to many countries where English is not spoken.

▶中野先生，休みはどのように過ごされたのですか。
　1. Miss. Nakano, what did you do on your vacation?
　2. Miss. Nakano, what did you do on your holidays?
　3. Miss. Nakano, how did you spend your vacation?
　4. Miss. Nakano, how did you spend your holidays?
　　　1と2が最も自然な表現である。

故郷に帰って，英気を養いました。
　I returned to my hometown and came back refreshed.
　I returned to my hometown, and restored my energy.

大学時代の友人たちと，富士山に登りました。
　I climbed Mt. Fuji with my college friends.

映画を見たり，買い物をしてのんびりした週末を過ごしました。
　I spent a relaxed weekend by going to see the movies and going shopping.

▶先生の子供のころの思い出話を聞かせてください。
　1. Could you tell us about your childhood?
　2. Could you tell us about your childhood experiences?
　3. Could you tell us about your recollections of your childhood?
　4. Could you tell us about your recollections when you were a child?
　　　1, 2 は standard, 3, 4 は formal な表現である。

小学生のころ九州に住んでいましたので，九州のことを話します。
　I will tell you about Kyushu because I was living in Kyushu when I was an elementary school student.

▶中野先生，趣味は何ですか。
　Miss. Nakano, what are your hobbies?

趣味はいろいろありますが，とくにテニスが好きです。
　I have many hobbies, and I especially like tennis.

▶中野先生はどこのご出身ですか。
　Miss. Nakano, where are you from?

▶中野先生，どこのご出身かお聞きしてもよろしいですか。
　Miss. Nakano, may I ask where you are from?

▶お暇なときに，お邪魔してもいいですか。
  1. When you have time, could I come to see you?
  2. When you have time, could we get together to do something at your house?
  3. When you have time, could we get together at your house?
  4. Would it be all right if I came to your house some evening?
  5. When you have time, could I come to see you at your home?

　　もとの日本文は，文脈次第でいろいろな英訳が可能である。
　　1は，生徒が授業でわからないことがあり，教師に会いたいというときに使われる。
　　もし，「遊び」を意味するのであれば，2，3，4，5のように言うべきであろう。

C　教師の身なり

▶スーツがお似合いですね。
　You look good in your suit.

That suit looks good on you.

▶ネクタイがなかなか似合いますね。
You look very good with your necktie on.
You look very good wearing a necktie.
You look very good in your necktie.

▶ズボンに何かゴミがついています。
You have something on your pants.

▶片山先生，ズボンが汚れています。
Mr. Katayama, your pants are stained.
Mr. Katayama, your pants are dirty.

 日本語のパンツに相当する英語は，briefs, shorts, underpants などである。アメリカ英語の pants は日本語の「ズボン」に相当する。

▶森田先生，ボタンがはずれています。
Mr. Morita, your button is unfastened.

▶山口先生，ボタンが取れています。
Mr. Yamaguchi, a button has come off.

 この文を，
  Mr. Yamaguchi, your button has come off.
のように表現すると，「ボタンが1つしかない」ことを暗示させる。

▶山口先生，ボタンがコートから取れています。
Mr. Yamaguchi, a button has come off your coat.

▶中山先生，髪に何かついています。
Mr. Nakayama, there's something in your hair.

VIII 終業

1 終業間近

あと10分したら会議があるから，今日は授業を早めに終わります。
Let me dismiss this class a little early. I have to attend a meeting.

　「授業を早めに終わる」を *quit this class a little early のようには表現できない。quit this class は「授業に出席するのを止める」という意味になってしまうからである。

あと7分ある。
1. **We have seven extra minutes.**
2. **We have seven minutes extra.**
3. **We have an extra seven minutes.**
4. **We still have seven more minutes.**
5. **We still have seven minutes more.**
6. **We still have seven more minutes left.**
7. **We still have seven minutes left.**

　「あと7分」と言うとき，不定冠詞の an は1や2のように付けなくてもよいし，3のように付けてもよい。
　left も4や5のように付けなくてもよいし，6や7のように付けてもよい。

もう数分ありそうだ。
　It looks like we have a few minutes left.

It looks like there are a few minutes left.
We seem to have a few minutes left.
There seem to be a few minutes to go.

もう時間か。
It's time to stop now.
It's time to finish now.

「授業を終える」というとき，stop, finish のいずれでもよい。finish はイギリスで好んで使われる。

もうこんな時間か。
Is it this late already?

疑問文で already を使うと，《驚き》を表す。
already は，ふつう be 動詞や助動詞 have の後に置くが，省略文の場合にはその前に置く。

I have already done it.
I already have.

もっと時間があればなあ。
1. **I wish I had more time.**
2. **I wish I had more time left.**
3. **I wish there were more time left.**

1，2，3 はいずれも仮定法（subjunctive）の用法である。
3 の were は，現在 was の形で使われることも多い。

もう 10 時半か。やめなくては。
It's already 10 : 30. We must stop now.

終わりにしましょう。
We'd better stop now.
We'd better finish now.
We'll have to stop now.

1 終業間近

これは今日は終わりそうにありません。
1. I don't think we have enough time to finish this today.
2. I don't think we've got enough time to finish this today.

  1は標準的な表現。2のようにgotを入れるのは口語的な表現である。

次の時間，これを続けて説明します。
  I'll continue explaining this next time.
  I'll continue to explain this next time.
  I'll continue with the explanation of this next time.
  I'll go on explaining this next time.

時間がなくなってしまいましたが，来週この問題を続けます。
  We've run out of time, but let me go on with this exercise next week.
  We've run out of time, but I'll go on with this exercise next week.

次の時間にはこの問題は終わると思います。
  I think I'll be able to finish this exercise next time.

もうひとこと言うのを忘れていました。
  I forgot to say one more thing.

今日の授業でやったことについて，質問はありますか。
  Do you have any questions on what we did today?

今日の授業でやったことについて，質問はありませんか。
1. Don't you have any questions on what we did today?
2. As far as what we went today, don't you have any questions?

  1の方が2よりも自然な響きがある。

教室の時計は進んでいます。
The clock in this room is fast.

教室の時計は遅れています。
The clock in this room is slow.

ちょっと待ちなさい。
1. **Hang on a minute.**
2. **Just a minute.**
3. **Just a second.**
4. **Hold on a minute.**
5. ***Wait for a moment.**

　2はネイティブスピーカーを angry, あるいは upset な気持にさせることがある。4も upset な気持にさせることがある。しかし, 4は電話で相手と話をしていて, 何かを取ってくるようなときにも使える。

　日本語の「待つ」ことに関する言い方は, 正しく英語に訳されていない場合がある。外国人が最初に覚える日本語表現の1つに「ちょっと待って！」があるが, 日本人はしばしば「待て」という言葉を使うから, 「待て」に相当する英語の wait を多用しすぎる。ネイティブスピーカーは wait という語を使わずに, 別の表現で相手に待ってほしい気持ちを表すことが多い。例えば,

　　I'll go get it and be right back.
　　Please excuse me.
　　I'll answer the phone and be back as soon as possible.
　　I'll answer the phone and come back as soon as I can.
　　I won't be long.
　　I'll be back with you in a moment.
　　I'll get back to you in a moment.

などのような言い方をする。こうした婉曲的な表現に慣れているネイティブスピーカーに対して日本人が wait という語を多用すると, "Well, I wasn't going to run away, after all!" という気持ちをつい抱かせてしまう。

席に戻ってください。
1. **Please go back to your seats.**
2. **Back to your places.**

　　2 はあまりにも abrupt で curt な感じがする。1 の方がよい。

▶小山先生，もう時間です。
Time is up, Mr. Oyama.

　　「もう時間です」という日本語を英語に訳すと Time has come. のような英文が考えられるが，has come を使えば，「何かを始める時間がとうとう来た」ということになる。
　　「もう残りの時間がなくなった」という意味では Time is up. と言う。

▶鈴木先生，時間になりました。
1. **Mr. Suzuki, the time is up.**
2. **Mr. Suzuki, time is up.**
3. **Mr. Suzuki, the time has come for us to stop.**

　　日本語を直訳すると，*Mr. Suzuki, the time has come. でもよさそうであるが，このように言うと，Mr. Suzuki, the time has come to do what? のように取られてしまう。
　　3 は文語的な響きのする文である。

▶森山先生，時間が過ぎています。
Mr. Moriyama, there's no more time left.

　　上記のほかに，The period is over. などのようにも言える。

2　連絡・指示など

この次の時間は，CALL 教室に行ってください。
　Please go to the CALL for the next class.
　The next class will be in the CALL.

今度の英語の時間には，必ずワークブックを持ってきてください。
1. **Be sure to bring your workbook to the next English class.**
2. **Be sure to bring the workbook for the next English class.**

　　1の方が2よりも自然な表現である。2のように ... bring the workbook for 〜と言うと，「次の英語の授業のためのワークブック」というニュアンスが強くなるからである。

来週の月曜日は祝日ですから，授業はありません。
1. **Next Monday is a national holiday, so we won't have a class.**
2. **Next Monday is a national holiday, so we won't have class.**
3. **Next Monday is a national holiday, so we have no class.**

　　1や2の方が3よりもよい。
　　「祝日」のことを，red-letter days とも言う。black-letter days と言えば「不幸な日」や「厄日」(unlucky days) のことを言う。

来週の月曜日は休みだということを言い忘れるところだった。
I almost forgot to say that next Monday is a holiday.

　　英語では forgot のように過去形で表現する。

委員長は，昼休みの時間に職員室に来るように。
I would like the class leader to come to the teacher's room during the lunch break.
I would like the class leader to come to the teacher's room during lunch break.
I would like the class leader to come to the teacher's room during the lunch hour.
I would like the class leader to come to the teacher's room during lunch hour.

　　the lunch break，the lunch hour の the は省略してもよい。

田中君，職員室にすぐ来なさい。
Tanaka-kun, come to the teachers' room immediately.

3 終業時の表現

これで終わります。
　1. That's it.
　2. That's it for now.
　3. We'll stop for now.
　4. We'll finish up with this.
　5. I'll stop here.
　6. Let me stop here.
　7. Let me end class here.
　　　1～6の方が7よりもよい。
　　　1のThat's it. は単独に使うといろいろな意味がある。例えば，①その通りだ，②それが問題だ，③もう駄目だ，④やれやれ，など。

今日はここまでにします。
　That's it for today.
　So much for today.
　That's all for today.
　That will do for today.

時間がきた。ここでやめましょう。
　1. Time is almost up. I'll stop here.
　2. Time is almost up. Let's stop here.
　3. Time is almost up. Let me stop here.
　　　3のLet me stop here. は正しい英語表現であるが，この場合，1や2の方がふさわしい。Let me ... は学生に許可を求めているニュアンスが強いからである。

VIII 終業

ベルが鳴りました。これで終わります。
  That's the bell. It's time to stop.

少し早いが終わります。
  It's a bit early, but let's call it a day.
  It's a bit early, but let me end class.
  We have some time left, but this is it for today.
  Let me dismiss class even though the period is not over yet.

数分早く終わったようだ。
  I seem to have finished a few minutes earlier than usual.
  I seem to have finished a few minutes early.

切りがいいので今日はここまでにしましょう。
  This is a good place to stop. So much for today.

ベルがもう鳴ってしまった。
  The bell has already rung.

5分過ぎてしまいました。終わります。
  I'm five minutes over. I must stop here.
  We're five minutes over. We must stop here.
  We've gone five minutes over. We must stop here.

時間のたつのは早いですね。
  Time goes by very fast, doesn't it?
  Time flies.

ドアはきちんと閉めてください。
  Shut the door tightly.
  Shut the door completely.
  Shut the door all the way.

いすを入れて帰ってください。
1. **Push your chair in and leave.**
2. **Put your chair in and leave.**
   2の put ～ in は「何かの中に」という意味合いが強いので，1のように push ～ in の方がよい。

ベルが鳴るまで静かに座っていなさい。
Please sit quietly until the bell rings.

ベルが鳴ったから，片付けて出てもいいですよ。
There's the bell. You can put things away and go.
There's the bell. You can put your things away and go.
That's the bell. You can put your things away and go.

ベルが鳴ったから，帰る準備をしてもいいですよ。
There's the bell. You can get ready to go.

今日はいつでも会えますよ。
You can see me any time today.

あさってまた会いましょう。
See you the day after tomorrow.

来週の木曜日にまた会いましょう。
I'll see you again next Thursday.
   I'll は省略して，See you again next Thursday. のように表現してもよい。

来週はいません。
I will not be here next week.
I won't be available next week.

いい週末を過ごしてください。
Have a nice weekend.

いいクリスマスを過ごしてください。
Have a merry Christmas.

　　Have a ～ という表現は，いろいろな状況で使える。例えば，友人がアメリカ旅行をするとき，Have a nice trip to America. などのように言える。日本に初めてやってきた外国人の旅行者に対して Have a nice stay in Japan. と言えば，相手は相好を崩して，Thank you. というような答えが返ってくるであろう。

夏休みは，くれぐれも事故を起こさぬように注意してください。
Try not to have an accident during the summer vacation.
Be careful not to have an accident during the summer vacation.

夏休みのあとまた会いましょう。
See you after summer vacation.

　　アメリカの大学では，夏休みが大変長い。正味3か月はある。中間テストもすべて夏休みまでには終えてしまうので，学生は3か月の休みを勉強を離れて有意義に過ごすことができる。アルバイトにいそしんだり，旅行をしたり，あるいは大学の夏季講座を受講したりと各人各様の過ごし方が可能である。

IX ネイティブスピーカーの英語表現実例

　クラスでどのような英語表現を使うかはクラスの内容によるが，そのクラスを担当する英語教師によるところも大きい。以下は，6人のネイティブスピーカーの授業を参観し，授業のなかで使われた表現を簡単にまとめたものである。教室英語表現の参考例として挙げてみる。重複して使われた表現は一度しか記載していない。

1　ネイティブスピーカーの教師1

A　授業進行

生徒を座らせるとき
　Sit down.

生徒全員に授業を進めてよいか様子をうかがうとき
　May I go ahead?

少し急いで授業を進めたいとき
　We are in a little bit of a hurry.

新しいことを始めるとき
　Shall we start?

言葉遊びをするとき
  Let's start the word puzzle.

英語で説明して，生徒にそれがどんな言葉であるか当ててほしいとき
  What is the word?

生徒にこんな方法があるというヒントをあげるとき
  You can go this way.

ヒントなしでゲームに挑戦させるとき
  Maybe no hints this time.

問題が簡単そうなのでヒントを与えないと言うとき
  No hints this time.

挙手をうながすとき
  Raise your hands, please.

できるだけクラスの全員に当てたいとき
  I don't want to ask the same people.

ある生徒に始めてほしいとき
  Can you start this sentence?

答えのわかる生徒がいないとき
  Nobody?

答えのわかる生徒がだれかいてほしいと願うとき
  No response?

簡単な答えであるのに，だれも答えようとしないとき
  Come on, it's easy.

まだ応答していない生徒を強制的に立たせるとき
  People who have not answered, stand up! Right now!

1人の生徒が勇気を出して言った答えが正解だったとき
  Yes!

生徒が聞き間違えたとき
  No, listen more carefully.

生徒の解答にあいづちを打つとき
  That's right.

部分的に解答した生徒に全部を言わせるとき
  Say the whole thing.

ある生徒が答えたので，他の生徒に意見を尋ねるとき
  Anybody else?

ある生徒が言った答えがその前に答えた生徒の答えと同じであるとき
  That's what he said.

次の問題に移るとき
  Next one.

12番の問題をするにあたって
  OK number twelve. Here we are.

テープを聞かせたり，自分の朗読を聞かせたりして解答させるとき
  Please listen and try to answer.

生徒に1つの単語の発音のしかたを尋ねるとき
  How do you pronounce it?

すべての単語を皆で発音練習したいとき
   Let's pronounce all the words, OK?

「まだ～をしていないのですか」と言うとき
   Not yet?

生徒の注意をうながすとき
   Listen carefully, OK?

生徒全員の注意を引いて，聞き取り練習をさせるとき
   Everybody, ready?

生徒全員の注意をうながすとき
   Everybody, OK?

生徒全員に同時に答えさせようとするとき
   All of you try to answer together, OK?

本来の質問ではなく，横道にそれた質問をするとき
   What is ..., by the way?

「もっともっと～している」の～とは何かを尋ねるとき
   Getting more and more what?

ある事柄の後で，質問が２つあると言うとき
   I have two questions afterward(s).

最後の質問をするとき
   The last question is ...

可能性の有無を確認するとき
   That's possible, right?

一方的に説明するのではなく，相手の注意を引きたいとき
　　You know ...

英語で状況を説明してほしいとき
　　Please explain the situation in English.

「だれも説明できる者がいないのか」と言うとき
　　Nobody can explain this?

ある生徒が何かを一生懸命に説明しようとしているとき
　　Yes? ... Yes? ... Yes?

ＤＶＤを使った授業に切りかえるとき
　　Well, let's go on to the DVD.

テレビをつけるとき
　　I'm gonna turn the TV on.

残り時間があまりないとき
　　Time is running short.

「また来週会いましょう」というとき
　　See you next week. See you ...

B　生徒とのやりとり

「君たち」と言うときの親しい表現
　　You guys ...

教室がザワザワして授業が始めにくいとき
　　Please settle down so we can start.

教室がザワザワしているので，静めたいとき
　　Shh ...

生徒が授業中私語をしたので，軽くたしなめるとき
　　During the break, it's OK.

自分の言ったことが生徒に理解できたかどうか確かめるとき
　　OK?

生徒が何か言おうとしたが聞き取れなかったので
　　What?

生徒の言うことが理解できなかったので
　　Huh? / Eh?

早く応答するようにうながすとき
　　Quick, quick, quick.

「自分の出した問題が簡単すぎて面白くない」というようなとき
　　This is very simple, so it's not so interesting.

簡単な問題だけでなく，時にはいたずらな問題をも出すことの前触れ
　　I'm a little tricky sometimes.

今まで言ってきた事柄から話題を転じるとき
　　So, anyway.

生徒にあることについて詳しく尋ねたいとき
　　What is this about?

生徒に自分の教えている方法がふさわしいかどうか聞くとき
　　Do you like the way I am teaching?

使い方を尋ねるとき
　How do they use these ...?

生徒の応答が好ましいとき
　That's right.

知りたかっただけだというようなとき
　I just wanted to know.

熱心に勉強している生徒を激励するとき
　You've been doing pretty well, so far.

あまり勉強する気のない学生がいるので，それを少し皮肉を込めて言うとき
　Some students are not really trying, huh?

英検の2級に全員パスするように激励するとき
　This year, everybody should pass STEP Two, huh?

全員で一緒に行動してもらいたいとき
　Everybody together this time.

C　トラブル・間違い

教師が黒板に書いた単語のつづりの誤りを生徒に指摘されて
　Oh, sorry. Thank you very much. If I make a mistake like this, please point it out immediately. Don't wait. OK?

（自分でばかばかしいような）間違いをしでかしたようなとき
　I goofed it up, now.

ビデオの操作がうまくいかず，テレビが邪魔をするとき
  The TV is going to annoy us every time I stop it.

教科書をどの位置から始めてよいかわからなかったが，やっとわかったようなときに
  Here we are.

説明などをしていて間違いに気づき，最初からもう一度始めたいときなど
  I'll start again. I'm sorry.

2　ネイティブスピーカーの教師2

A　授業進行

あることの説明を成し遂げて
  Now I've finished that.

テキストをどれくらい終えたかを生徒に聞くとき
  How far have we gone in this book?

前回の授業でどこまでやったかを確認するとき
  What page were we on?

前回は31ページをやったという表現
  We were on page 31.

説明の途中で，あることについて生徒に質問するとき
  What is this, by the way?

早口言葉などを練習させるとき
　Can you say all the words in one minute?

生徒にあることをするようにうながすとき
　You go ahead and do your work. I'll take care of this.

ジャンケンポンの英語
　Stone, scissors, paper.

次がだれかと言うとき
　Who's next?

B　生徒とのやりとり

教師が生徒にあいづちを打つとき
　You did it too.

自分が忘れっぽいことについて
　I keep forgetting.

生徒が具合が悪くて早引きしたいと言うとき
　OK, take care now.

3　ネイティブスピーカーの教師3

A　授業進行

たとえて言うとき
　It's like a camping car.

〜について聞いたことがあるかと尋ねるとき
   Have you ever heard of Tijuana?

後でその話をすると言うとき
   I'll tell it to you later.

話を遮って何か言うとき
   I should interrupt you and say ....

相手の意見を確かめるとき
   You agree with me?

生徒から難しい質問を受けてちょっと考えるとき
   Mmmm.

B 生徒とのやりとり

差し支えなければ話してほしいと言うとき
   Maybe you can tell us about it.

生徒が見た映画について説明をしてほしいとき
   What is the movie about?

映画の種類を知りたいとき
   What kind of movie was it?

生徒に助け舟を出して話をうながすとき
   It's about New York?

4　ネイティブスピーカーの教師4

A　授業進行

「テキストを忘れたのか」と言うとき
　　Did you forget your textbook?

「言いたいことはほかにないのか」とうながすとき
　　Is that all?

どの問題をするか説明するとき
　　We'll do number 1.

生徒の意見に同意しないとき
　　I don't think so.

つづりを聞くとき
　　How do you spell it?

生徒にポイントを与えるとき
　　Two points for you.

自分の希望することを相手が言ったとき
　　That's what I want.

違いがわかるかどうか聞くとき
　　You know the difference?

自分の言うことをよく聞くようにと言うとき
　　Listen to me very carefully.

5　ネイティブスピーカーの教師5

A　授業進行

「だれかが同じことを言った」と言うとき
　　Somebody told me the same thing.

ビデオを見せるとき
　　Tonight, I'm going to show you the video.

一緒にビデオを見るとき
　　Shall we enjoy this video?

ビデオを始動するとき
　　Let's start.

見る予定のないところをつい見てしまったとき
　　Not this part.

これは〜と関係があると言うとき
　　This is connected with ....

「今でもこれは続いている」と言うとき
　　Even now this continues.

覚えているかどうか尋ねるとき
　　Do you remember ...?

もう一度CDを聞かせるとき
　　I'll play the CD again.

「その通り」と言うとき
   That's it!

「〜を強調したいときは」と言うとき
   When we want to emphasize ....

ヒントを与えるとき
   I'll give you a hint.
   I'll give you hints.
   I'll give you some hints.

どちらでもよいと言うとき
   It doesn't make any difference.

B　生徒とのやりとり

休みについて聞くとき
   Did you have a nice holiday last week?

休暇はどうだったか尋ねるとき
   How was your vacation?

「体の調子がすぐれなかった」と言うとき
   I was in bad condition.
   I was in bad shape.

「調子がよくなっている」と言うとき
   I am getting in better shape.

「からかったんだ」と言うとき
   I'm teasing you.
   I'm kidding you.

「平均点はどれくらいか」と言うとき
　What's the average?

「信じられない」と言うとき
　It's incredible.

あいさつを簡単に言ってもらいたいとき
　Would you like to say a few words?

どうしたのかと言うとき
　Anything happened to you?

6　ネイティブスピーカーの教師6

A　授業進行

前回の授業内容の説明をするとき
　Last Friday, we did a lesson. We were talking about ....

付け加えて言うとき
　Also, ...

質問の有無を確かめるとき
　Do you have any questions about this part?
　Do you have any question about this part?

質問がないので次に進むとき
　No questions? OK, then ....
　No question? OK, then ....

別の例を示すとき
   Another example.

次の練習問題に移るとき
   Let's go on to Part 3.

練習問題の指示
   Please take one minute and read Part 2 again to yourself.
   You may look at the picture, but you try to remember the story.
   I am going to say wrong sentences about the story. I want you to correct my sentences.
   Please look at the picture only and listen.

B　生徒とのやりとり

自分の話をしながら，結論を述べたいとき
   ... so anyway, ...

口ごもったとき
   Ahhh.

流ちょうに説明できず，自分なりの結論を述べたとき
   OK, so ....

ちょっと考えてから生徒の意見に同調するとき
   Mmmm. OK.

生徒を非常にほめるとき
   OK, very good.
   Oh, that's nice.

関連語い集

1 学問・学科名

　　**は小・中学校，*は高等学校の科目名。

【あ行】
医学 medical science; medicine
　アレルギー学 allergology
　胃腸病学 gastroenterology
　ウイルス学 virology
　衛生学 hygiene
　衛生統計学 health statistics
　眼科学 ophthalmology
　肝臓学 hepatology
　寄生虫学 paleontology
　救急医学 emergency medicine
　胸部外科学 thoracic surgery
　形成外科学 plastic and reconstructive surgery
　外科臨床医学 surgery
　血液学 hematology
　肛門学 proctology
　呼吸器学 pulmonology
　産科学 obstetrics
　疾病学 diseases
　耳鼻咽喉科学 otorhinolaryngology
　腫瘍学 oncology
　循環器学 cardiology
　消化器学 gastroenterology
　小児医学 pediatrics
　食事療法学 dietetics
　神経科学 neuroscience
　診断学 diagnostics
　スポーツ医学 sports medicine
　整形外科学 orthopedics
　精神医学 psychiatry
　精神身体学 psychosomatic medicine
　精神病理学 psychopathology
　精神分析学 psychoanalysis
　男性病学 andrology
　内科学 internal medicine
　内分泌学 endocrinology
　脳科学 neuroscience
　脳神経外科学 neurosurgery
　泌尿器学 urology
　皮膚科学 dermatology
　病理学 pathology
　婦人科学 gynecology
　法医学 forensics
　放射線医学 radiology
　麻酔学 anesthesiology
　免疫学 immunology
　予防医学 preventive medicine
　リューマチ学 rheumatology
　臨床神経学 clinical neurology
　老人医学 geriatrics
遺伝学 genetics
英語 English ; the English language**
　　「英語」は English でも the English language でもよい。
　近代英語 Modern English
　　初期近代英語 Early Modern English
　　後期近代英語 Late Modern English

古代英語 Old English
　　略してOEと言ったりする。700〜1100年代の英語。
実用英語　practical English ; living English
商業英語　commercial English ; business English
中期英語　Middle English
　　以前は「中世英語」と呼んだりしたが, Middle Ages（中世時代）とは年代が一致しないために，この名称は使われなくなった。1100〜1500年ころの英語を言い，MEと略すこともある。
英語学　English philology ; English linguistics
　　English philology は史的あるいは比較的な研究をする言語学をいい，共時的に研究する場合は English linguistics という。
英作文　English composition
英文法　English grammar
栄養学 dietetics
園芸学 horticulture
音楽 music**

【か行】
会計学 accounting
　簿記　bookkeeping
外国語（英語）* foreign language (English)
　英語 I, II* English I, II
　オーラル・コミュニケーション I, II* oral communication I, II
　ライティング* writing
　リーディング* reading
　コミュニケーション英語基礎* basic English communication
　コミュニケーション英語 I, II, III* communicaiton English I, II, III
　英語表現 I, II* English expression I, II
　英語会話* English conversation
　イタリア語 Italian
　韓国語 Korean
　スペイン語 Spanish
　中国語 Chinese
　ドイツ語 German
　フランス語 French
　ポルトガル語 Portuguese
　ラテン語 Latin
　ロシア語 Russian
解剖学 anatomy
海洋学 oceanography
　海洋動物学 marine zoology
　海洋物理学 oceanophysics ; physical oceanography
科学 science
　医学情報科学 medical informatics
　宇宙科学 space science
　応用科学 applied science
　核科学 nuclear science
　画像科学 imaging science
　環境科学 environmental science
　計算機科学 computer science
　行動科学 behavioral science
　材料科学 materials science
　自然科学 natural science
　社会科学 social sciences
　純正科学　pure [abstract] science

食品科学 food science and technology
神経科学 neuroscience
性科学 sexual science; sexology
政策科学 policy science
精神科学 mental science
地球科学 geoscience
地球惑星科学 earth planetary science
認知科学 cognitive science
文化科学 cultural science
輸送科学 transportation science

化学 chemistry
医化学 medical chemistry
応用化学 applied chemistry
海洋化学 chemical oceanography
化学機械工業 chemical engineering
化学力学 chemical dynamics
化学量論 stoichiometry
金相学 metallography
顕微化学 microchemistry
光化学 photochemistry
工業化学 industrial chemistry
極微量化学 ultramicro chemistry
実験化学 experimental chemistry
実用化学 practical chemistry
純正化学 pure chemistry
生化学 biochemistry
精密化学 fine chemistry
石油化学 petrochemistry
総合化学 synthetic chemistry
地球化学 geochemistry
電気化学 electrochemistry
熱化学 thermal chemistry
農芸化学 agricultural chemistry
農産化学 chemurgy
物理化学 physical chemistry
分析化学 analytical chemistry
放射化学 radiochemistry
無機化学 inorganic chemistry
冶金化学 metallurgic chemistry ; metallurgy
有機化学 organic chemistry
理論化学 theoretical chemistry

家庭* home economics
家庭基礎* basic home economics
家庭総合* integrated home economics
生活技術* life style technique

家庭科** home economics
環境学 environmental studies
観光学 tourism
看護学 nursing science
岩石学 petrology
記載岩石学 petrography
火山学 volcanology
技術** technical course
気象学 meteorology ; climatology
物理気象学 physical meteorology
教育学 pedagogy
行政学 science of public administration
経営学 business administration
病院管理学 hospital administration
軍事学 military science
経済学 economics
音響効果農業経済学 acoustics

agricultural economics
近代経済学 modern economics
農業経済学 agronomy
マクロ経済学 macroeconomics
マルクス経済学 Marxian economics
ミクロ経済学 microeconomics
芸術* arts
音楽Ⅰ, Ⅱ, Ⅲ* music I, II, III
工芸Ⅰ, Ⅱ, Ⅲ* crafts production I, II, III
書道Ⅰ, Ⅱ, Ⅲ* calligraphy I, II, III
美術Ⅰ, Ⅱ, Ⅲ* fine arts I, II, III
絵画 painting
彫刻 sculpture
結晶学 crystallography
言語学 linguistics
意味論 semantics
応用言語学 applied linguistics
音声学 phonetics
音素論 phonemics
言語学概論 an introduction to linguistics
「～概論」は, an introduction to ～を学問名に付加すればよい。
記述言語学 descriptive linguistics
構造言語学 structural linguistics
語用論 pragmatics
社会言語学 sociolinguistics
神経言語学 neurolinguistics
心理言語学 psycholinguistics
対照言語学 contrastive linguistics
統語論 syntactics
認知言語学 cognitive linguistics
比較言語学 comparative linguistics
歴史言語学 historical linguistics
建築学 architecture
設計法 design
都市計画 city planning
工学 engineering
遺伝子工学 gene engineering
化学工学 chemical engineering
機械工学 mechanical engineering
金融工学 financial engineering
経営工学 industrial engineering
原子力工学 nuclear power engineering
材料工学 materials engineering
情報工学 information engineering; computer science
信頼性工学 reliability engineering
生物工学 bionics; biotechnology
電気工学 electrical engineering
電子工学 electronics
土木工学 civil engineering
人間工学 human engineering ; ergonomics
微小工学 nanotechnology
ロボット工学 robot engineering

考古学 archeology
鉱物学 mineralogy
　鉱物化学 mineral chemistry
公民* civics
　現代社会* contemporary society
　政治・経済* politics and economics
　倫理* ethics
国学 study of Japanese classical literature
国語* Japanese
　現代文* comprehensive Japanese
　国語Ⅰ, Ⅱ* Japanese language I, II
　国語表現* Japanese expression
　古典* classics
　古典講読* appreciation of classics
国語** Japanese ; the Japanese language
湖沼学 limnology
古書本学 paleography

【さ行】
細菌学 microbiology
　応用細菌学 applied microbiology
歯学 dentistry
　口腔外科 oral surgery
　歯科衛生学 dental hygiene
　歯列矯正学 orthodontics
辞書学 lexicography
社会** social studies
社会学 sociology
　社会福祉学 the study of social welfare
宗教学 science of religion

修辞学 rhetoric
獣医学 veterinary science
習字** calligraphy
商業* commerce
情報* computer science
　情報Ａ, Ｂ, Ｃ* computer science [information science] A, B, C
食品学 food science
植物学 botany ; phytology
　古植物学 paleobotany
　植物解剖学 phytotomy ; plant anatomy
　植物化学 plant chemistry ; phytochemistry
　植物記載学 descriptive botany
　植物形態学 plant morphology ; morphological botany
　植物社会学 phytosociology ; plant sociology
　植物生態学 plant ecology
　植物生理学 plant physiology ; physiological botany
　植物地理学 geographic botany ; plant geography
　植物病理学 plant pathology ; phytopathology
　植物分類学 systematic botany ; plant taxonomy
女性学 women's studies
神学 theology
心理学 psychology
　計量心理学 psychometrics
　健康心理学 health psychology
　社会心理学 social psychology
　スポーツ心理学 sports psychology
　犯罪心理学 criminal psychology

臨床心理学 clinical psychology
人類学 anthropology
　自然人類学 physical anthropology
　象徴人類学 symbolic anthropology
　文化人類学 cultural anthropology
　霊長類学 primatology
神話学 mythology
水文学 hydrology
数学 mathematics**（小学校は **arithmetic**）
　応用数学 applied mathematics
　解析 analysis
　確率 probability
　幾何 geometry
　　位相幾何学 topology
　　立体幾何学 solid geometry
　高等数学 higher mathematics
　三角関数 trigonometric function
　算術 arithmetic
　集合 set
　数学Ⅰ, Ⅱ, Ⅲ* mathematics I, II, III
　数学 A, B, C* mathematics A, B, C
　数学基礎* Basic Mathematics
　積分 integral calculus ; integration
　代数 algebra
　等式 equality
　微分 differential calculus : differentiation
図画工作 drawing and crafts**
政治学 politics
　環境政治学 ecological politics
　国際政治学 international politics
　地政学 geopolitics
　比較政治学 comparative politics
生態学 ecology
生物学 biology
　海洋生物学 marine biology
　計算生物学 computational biology
　形態学 morphology
　古生物学 paleontology
　細胞生物学 cell biology
　進化生物学 evolutionary biology
　生殖生物学 reproductive biology
　生物気候学 bioclimatology ; bioclimatics
　淡水生物学 freshwater biology
　内細胞生物学 endocytobiology
　農業生物学 agrobiology
　発生生物学 developmental biology
　微生物学 microbiology
　分子生物学 molecular biology
生理学 physiology
総合的な学習の時間* period for integrated study
組織学 histology

【た行】
体育 physical education (P.E.)**
地域研究 area study
地質学 geology
　海洋地質学 marine geology
　地史学 historical geology
　地質工学 geotechnology
地震学 seismology

1 学問・学科名

地理 geography
地理学 geography
　地形学 topography
地理歴史* geography and history
　世界史Ａ，Ｂ* world history A, B
　日本史Ａ，Ｂ* Japanese history A, B
　地理Ａ，Ｂ* geography A, B
哲学 philosophy
　インド哲学 Indian philosophy
　形而上学 metaphysical philosophy
　宗教哲学 philosophy of religion
　西洋哲学 Western philosophy
　東洋哲学 Eastern philosophy
天文学 astronomy
　位置天文学 positional astronomy
　エックス線天文学 X-ray astronomy
　ガンマ線天文学 gamma ray astronomy
　記述天文学 descriptive astronomy
　銀河天文学 galactic astronomy
　航海天文学 nautical astronomy
　恒星天文学 stellar astronomy
　紫外線天文学 ultra-violet astronomy
　実地天文学 practical astronomy
　重力波天文学 gravitational astronomy
　赤外線天文学 infrared astronomy
　電波天文学 radio astronomy
　統計天文学 statistical astronomy
　ニュートリノ天文学 neutrino astronomy
　理論天文学 theoretical astronomy
統計学 statistics
道徳 moral education
動物学 zoology
　貝類学 conchology
　魚類学 ichthyology
　昆虫学 entomology
　鳥類学 ornithology
　動物解剖学 zootomy ; animal anatomy
　動物構造学 zoophysics
　動物心理学 animal psychology ; zoo-psychology
　動物生態学 zoo-ecology
　動物生理学 animal physiology
　動物測定学 zoometry
　動物分類学 zootaxy ; zoological taxonomy
　動物力学 zoodynamics
毒物学 toxicology
特別活動 special activities
図書館学 library science

【な行】
日本学 Japanology
農学 agricultural science

【は行】
博物学 natural history
犯罪学 criminology
美学 aesthetics
　デザイン学 science of design

美術史 art history
美術** art
物理学 physics
　宇宙物理学 astrophysics
　応用物理学 applied physics
　海洋物理学 physical oceanography
　化学物理学 chemical physics
　原子物理学 atomic physics
　実験物理学 experimental physics
　精神物理学 psycophysics
　生物物理学 biophysics
　地球物理学 geophysics
　天体物理学 astrophysics
　物理光学 physical optics
　物理的音声学 physical phonetics
　理論物理学 theoretical physics
文学 literature
　江戸文学 the literature of the Edo period
　記録文学 documentary literature
　近代文学 modern literature
　国民文学 national literature
　古典文学 classical literature
　児童文学 juvenile literature
　通俗文学 popular literature
　田園文学 pastoral literature
　動物文学 animal literature
　都会文学 urban literature
　比較文学 comparative literature
　遊蕩文学 degenerate literature
文献学 philology
法学 jurisprudence
　刑法学 criminal law
　憲法学 constitutional law
　民法学 civic law
保健体育** physical and health education
保健体育* health and physical education
　体育* physical exercise
　保健* health

【ま行】
民俗学 folklore, folkloristics
民族学 ethnology, ethnic studies

【や行】
薬学 pharmacology
冶金学 metallurgy
優生学 eugenics

【ら行】
理科** science
　化学 I, II* chemistry I, II
　生物 I, II* biology I, II
　地学 I, II* earth science I, II
　理科基礎* basic science
　理科総合* comprehensive science
　物理 I, II, III* physics I, II, III
力学 dynamics
　大気力学 atmosphere dynamics
　記号力学 symbolic dynamics
　個体力学 solic dynamics
　天体力学 gravitational astronomy
　統計力学 statistical mechanics
　熱力学 thermodynamics
　流体力学 fluid dynamics
　量子力学 quantum mechanics
林学 forestry
倫理学 ethics

歴史 history
歴史学 history
  古代史 ancient history
  西洋史 Occidental history
  世界史 world history
  東洋史 Oriental history
  日本史 Japanese history
  歴史地理 historical geography
  歴史哲学 historical philosophy
老人学 gerontology

2 文法関連語い

語源 etymology
文法 grammar
  文法的な grammatical
  文法的に grammatically
品詞 parts of speech
  名詞 noun
    可算名詞 countable noun
    固有名詞 proper noun
    集合名詞 collective noun
    抽象名詞 abstract noun
    不可算名詞 uncountable noun
    普通名詞 common noun
    物質名詞 material noun
  代名詞 pronoun
    関係代名詞 relative pronoun
    疑問代名詞 interrogative pronoun
    再帰代名詞 reflexive pronoun
    指示代名詞 demonstrative pronoun
    所有代名詞 possessive pronoun
    不定代名詞 indefinite pronoun
    人称代名詞 personal pronoun
  動詞 verb
    完結動詞 conclusive verb
    規則動詞 regular verb
    群動詞 group verb
    再帰動詞 reflexive verb
    自動詞 intransitive verb
    述語動詞 predicative verb
    準動詞形 verbal
    状態動詞 stative verb
    他動詞 transitive verb
    不規則動詞 irregular verb
    本動詞 main verb
  助動詞 auxiliary verb
  不定詞 infinitive
    原形不定詞 bare infinitive
    受動態の不定詞 passive infinitive
  動名詞 gerund
    受動態の動名詞 passive gerund
    名詞的動名詞 nominal gerund
  分詞 participle
    過去分詞 past participle
    現在分詞 present participle
    進行形 progressive form
  形容詞 adjective
    数量形容詞 adjective of quantity
    性質形容詞 adjective of quality
    代名形容詞 pronominal adjective
  副詞 adverb
    関係副詞 relative adverb
    疑問副詞 interrogative adverb

様態の副詞 adverbs of manner
前置詞 preposition
　群前置詞 group preposition ; phrasal preposition
接続詞 conjunction
　群接続詞 group conjunction
　従属接続詞 subordinate conjunction
　相関接続詞 correlative conjunction
　等位接続詞 coordinate conjunction
間投詞 interjection
冠詞 article
　冠詞の衝突 conflict between articles
　定冠詞 definite article
　不定冠詞 indefinite article
限定詞 determiner
　定限定詞 definite determiner
　不定限定詞 indefinite determiner
連結詞 copula
数詞 numeral
助数詞 numerative

数 number
外来複数 foreign plural
単数 singular number
複数 plural number
不変化複数 unchanged plural

人称 person
一人称 first person
二人称 second person
三人称 third person
総称数 generic number
総称人称 generic person

性 gender
女性 feminine gender
男性 masculine gender
中性 neuter gender

格 case
格文法 case grammar
主格 nominative case
所有格 possessive case
対格 accusative case
二重所有格 double possessive
二重属格 double genitive
副詞的対格 adverbial accusative
目的格 objective case
与格 dative case

時制 tense
過去 past
過去完了 past perfect tense
現在 present
現在完了 present perfect tense
時制の一致 sequence of tenses
時と場所 time and place
話し手の現在 speaker's present
未来 future
未来完了 future perfect tense
歴史的現在 historic(al) present

活用 conjugation
活用させる to conjugate
規則活用 regular conjugation
不規則活用 irregular conjugation

態 voice
受動態 passive voice
動作受動態 actional passive
能動態 active voice
能動受動態 activo-passive

法 mood
仮定法 subjunctive mood
直接法 indicative mood
命令法 imperative mood

比較 comparison
  原級 positive degree
  最上級 superlative degree
  絶対最上級 absolute superlative
  比較級 comparative degree
  比較の comparative
  劣等比較 comparison of inferiority
話法 narration
  間接話法 indirect narration
  直接話法 direct narration
  描出話法 represented speech
文 sentence
  文の種類 kinds of sentences
    肯定文 affirmative sentence ; assertive sentence
    重文 compound sentence
    単文 simple sentence
    複文 complex sentence
    平叙文 declarative sentence
    否定文 negative sentence
      全否定 total negation
      部分否定 partial negation
    命令文 imperative sentence
    疑問文 interrogative sentence
      一般疑問 general question
      間接疑問 independent question
      修辞疑問 rhetorical question
      熟考疑問 deliberative question
      選択疑問 alternative question
      特殊疑問 special question
      Yes-No疑問 Yes-No question

  感嘆文 exclamatory sentence
構文 construction
  意味構文 construction according to sense
  独立分詞構文 absolute participial construction
  分詞構文 participial construction
文の要素 elements of a sentence ; sentence element
  主語 subject word
    形式主語 it formal it
    文主語 sentential subject
  節 clause
    継続節 continuative clause
    形容詞節 adjective clause
    従節 dependent clause
    主節 main clause ; principal clause
    等位節 co-ordinate clause
    副詞節 adverb clause
  目的語 object
    間接目的語 indirect object
    結果の目的語 object of result
    再帰目的語 reflexive object
    直接目的語 direct object
    同族目的語 cognate object
    二重直接目的語 two direct objects
  補語 complement
    主格補語 subjective complement
    目的格補語 objective complement
  句 phrase
    句接続 phrasal connection

形容詞句 adjective phrase
動詞句 verb phrase
特定的名詞句 specific noun phrase
副詞句 adverb phrase
名詞句 noun phrase

その他
一致 agreement
仮定法相当語句 subjunctive equivalent
関係詞節縮約変形 relative clause reduction
疑問符 question mark
却下条件 rejected condition
強調 emphasis
結果 result
原因 cause
後方照応 cataphoric
削除 deletion
三主要形 three principal parts
支柱語の one prop-word one
修飾 modification
修飾する to modify
条件 condition
状態 state
状態語 stative word
譲歩 concession
省略 ellipsis
前提 presupposition
前方照応 anaphoric
程度 degree
動作 action
二重制限 double restriction
派生接辞 derivational affix
非定形 finite form
付帯状況 attendant circumstances
文接続 sentential conjunction
分裂文 cleft sentence

母型文 matrix sentence
無標形 unmarked form
目的 purpose
理由 reason

3 発音関連語い

a 発音器官
口 mouth
口蓋 palate
口蓋音 palatal sound
口蓋垂 uvula
口腔 oral cavity
硬口蓋 hard palate
軟口蓋 soft palate
咽頭 pharynx
喉頭 larynx
鼻腔 nasal cavity
唇 lips
上唇 upper lip
下唇 lower lip
舌 tongue
後舌面 back of the tongue
舌先 tip of the tongue
歯 (単数) **tooth**
(複数) **teeth**
上歯 upper teeth
下歯 lower teeth
前歯 front teeth
歯茎 gum ridge
上歯茎 upper gum ridge
下歯茎 lower gum ridge
気管 windpipe
声帯 vocal cords
声門 glottis
肺 lungs

b 発音関連語い
発音 pronunciation

3 発音関連語い

言語音 speech sound
発音する to pronounce
発音記号 phonetic symbols
無声音 voiceless sound
有声音 voiced sound

母音 vowel
 あいまい母音 obscure vowel ; schwa
 基本母音 cardinal vowel
 口母音 oral vowel
 後母音 back vowel
 混成母音 mixed vowel
 三重母音 triphthong
 自然母音 natural vowel
 自由母音 free vowel
 静母音 static vowel
 前母音 front vowel
 単母音 monothong ; simple vowel
 短母音 short vowel
 中央母音 central vowel
 長母音 long vowel
 動母音 kinetic vowel
 二重母音 diphthong
 半母音 semi-vowel
 複母音 compound vowel
 閉母音 close vowel
 母音接続 hiatus
 母音類 vocoid
 無声母音 voiceless vowel
 有声母音 voiced vowel
 抑止母音 checked vowel
 わたり母音 glide vowel

子音 consonant
 明るい l clear l
 暗い l dark l
 単子音 single consonant
 二重子音 double consonant
 複子音 compound consonant
 無声子音 voiceless consonant
 有声子音 voiced consonant

子音的母音 consonantal vowel

c 調音法による子音の分類
 円唇音 round
 側音 lateral
 単せん動音；流動音 trill
 破擦音 affricate
 破裂音 plosive
 反転音 retroflexion
 鼻音 nasal
 閉止音 stop
 摩擦音 fricative
 流音 liquid
 わたり音 glide

d 調音点による子音の分類
 喉音 gutteral
 口蓋音 palatal
 硬口蓋音 hard-palatal
 歯音 dental
 歯間音 interdental
 歯茎音 alveolar
 歯茎・口蓋音 alveo-palatal
 歯擦音 sibilant
 唇音 labial
 唇歯音 labio-dental
 声門音 glottal
 声門破裂音 glottal stop ; glottal plosive
 軟口蓋音 soft-palatal
 両唇音 bilabial

e 強勢・音調
息 breath
 息の段落 breath group
強勢 stress ; stress accent
 移動アクセント mutable ac-

cent
高低アクセント pitch accent ; musical accent
強勢二重語 stress doublets
強勢の移動 stress shift
強勢法 accentuation
強勢をおく to stress
語強勢 word accent
弱勢化 unstressing
第１アクセント primary accent
第２アクセント secondary accent
強さアクセント dynamic accent
二重強勢 double stress
文強勢 sentence accent ; sentence stress
リズムの強勢 rhythm stress

イントネーション intonation
イントネーション型 intonation pattern
イントネーション曲線 intonation contour
イントネーションを上げる to raise intonation
イントネーションを下げる to lower intonation
音調言語 tone language
音調符号 intonation mark
下降調 falling intonation
好音調 euphony
降昇調 falling-rising intonation
昇降調 rising-falling intonation
上昇調 rising intonation
水平調 level intonation

鼻音化 nasalization
鼻音化する to nasalize

転写 transcription
転写する to transcribe

つづり spelling

f 音
異音 allophone
音の高低 pitch
音の長さ duration
音質 quality
音声 phone
音声の発声 phonation
音量 quantity
楽音 musical sound
きこえ sonority
気息音 aspirate
逆音 inverse sound
緊張音 tense
継続音 continuant
硬音 fortis
字音 alphabet
弛緩音 lax
自然音 natural sound
舌もつれ発音 lisp
すー音 hissing sound
成形音 formant
南部の引き延ばし発音 Southern drawl
閉鎖音 stop
連音 sandhi

g 音声変化
異化 dissimilation
逆行同化 regressive assimilation
偶発同化 accidental assimilation
語中音添加 epenthesis
語中音消失 syncope

語頭音添加 prothesis
語頭音消失 aphaersis
語頭母音消失 ahpesis
語尾音添加 paragoge
語尾音消失 apocope
重音脱落 haplology
省略 elision
同化 assimilation
 前進同化 progressive assimilation
 相互同化 reciprocal assimilation
無声化 devocalization
 無声化する to devocalize
無声の non-voiced
有声化 vocalization

h 発音
快活な調子 lilt
気息発声 aspiration
休止 pause
強形 strong form
国際音声学協会 IPA (International Phonetic Association)
弱形 weak form
縮約 contraction
調音 articulation
調音器官 articulation organ
調子 tone
つづり字発音 spelling pronunciation
東部型発音 Eastern type
東部方言 New England dialect
南部型発音 Southern type
直しすぎ hypercorrection ; over correction
音色 timbre
発音記号 phonetic symbols
鼻声 nasal twang
反転 retroflexion ; inversion
標準発音 standard pronunciation
容認発音 received pronunciation
流動音；巻舌音 rolled

i その他
意味の段落 sense-group
音位転換 metathesis
音声表象 sound symbolism
音節 syllable
音素 phoneme
音標表記 phonetic transcription
音標文字 phonetic alphabet
開音節 open syllable
擬声 onomatopoeia
脚韻；押韻 rhyme
強弱格 trochee
強調 emphasis
共鳴 resonance
均勢 level stress
緊張度 tension
句読法 punctuation
形式語 form word
声 voice
ささやき whisper
詩の中間休止 caesura
終止符 period ; full stop
純正英語 king's English
省略記号 apostrophe
対照 contrast
短縮形 contract form
つづり spelling
つづり字の二重式 dual system
同音異義語 homonym
添加 addition

同形異義語　homograph
同字異音語　heterograph
同綴異音異義語　heteronym
早口言葉　tongue-twister
不協和音　cacophony
複合語　compound word
分節　syllabic division
分節部　syllabic element
分節法　syllabification
閉音節　close syllable
閉音節語　close-syllabics
方言　dialect
黙字　mute ; silent letter
連字；合字　ligature
連字符　hyphen
連声　liason

4　英作文関連語い・表現

英作文　English composition
　高等英作文　advanced English composition
　自由英作文　free English composition
作文　composition
　作文する　to compose
　作文がうまい　be good at composition
　作文の題　the title of a composition
　作文の題材　a subject for a composition ; a theme for a composition
　作文問題　composition exercises
　作文を添削する　to correct a composition
　作文を〜に添削してもらう　to have one's composition corrected by 〜
添削　correction
書く　to write
　いいかげんな書き方　sloppy writing
　英語を書くのがうまい人　a good writer of English
　英語を書くのが下手な人　a bad writer of English; a poor writer of English
　1行おきに書く　to write on every other line
　インクで書く　to write in ink
　美しく書く　to write beautifully
　英語で書く　to write in English
　鉛筆で書く　to write in pencil; to write with a pencil
　　「鉛筆で書く」というとき，前置詞は in でもよいし with でもよい。ただし in を使う場合には不定冠詞の a を付けないことに注意。
　大きく書く　to write large
　遅く書く　to write slowly ; to write slower
　小さく書く　to write small
　書き方　writing
　書き尽くす　to write and write ; to write oneself out
　書き直す　to write over
　書き間違い　a writing mistake
　書くこと　writing
　書く人　writer
　書くペンがない　do not have a pen to write with; have no pen to write with
　　have no pen to write with は，イギリス英語ではよく使われる。

紙に書く to write on paper
辛うじて書く to write with difficulty
簡潔に書く to write briefly ; to write concisely
口で言って〜を書かせる to dictate 〜
字を上手に書く to have good handwriting
字を下手に書く to have bad handwriting
自由に英語が書ける to write English with ease
上手に書く to write well
すらすらと書く to write with ease
草書体で書く to write cursive
即座に書く to write off
2ページ書く to write two pages
はっきりと書く to write plainly ; to write clearly
速く書く to write faster
ペンで書く to write with a pen
ボールペンで書く to write with a ballpoint pen
〜を書いてもらう to have a person write 〜
〜を書かせる to get a person to write 〜 ; to tell a person to write 〜

つづり spelling
誤ったつづり wrong spelling ; misspelling
異なったつづり字法 a variant spelling
正字法 orthography
正しいつづり correct spelling

つづり字改良運動 spelling reform
　発音されていない黙字などを省略して，できるだけ実際の発音に近いつづり字を案出することをいう。例えば, through を thru と書いたり, light を lite と書いたりすることなどがそうである。英語の漫画にはこの手法を用いるものが多い。
つづり字競争 a spelling match ; a spelling bee ; a spelldown ; a spelling contest
　一定数のつづりの違いがあると失格として座らせるつづり字競技のことをいう。
つづり字発音 spelling pronunciation
　実際のつづりとは違った発音をする言葉に対して，つづり字の通りに発音することをいう。例えば, often [ɔ(:)fən] を [ɔ(:)ftən] のように発音したりすること。
つづりの間違い a spelling mistake; an orthographic mistake ; incorrect spelling
　a spelling mistake は普通よく使う表現であるが，an orthographic mistake は専門的な感じのする表現である。
つづりの練習 spelling exercises ; orthographic exercises
つづる to spell
表音的つづり法 a phonetic spelling

間違い mistake
　英語学では間違いを2種類に分けることがある。mistake と

は，正しい答えを知りながらうっかりしていて間違うことをいい，error とは，知らないで間違うことをいう。
誤った文章 erroneous sentences
誤りではない be not a mistake
誤りなし no mistake
誤植 printer's error
文法的な誤り a grammatical mistake ; mistakes in grammar
間違いの mistaken ; erroneous ; wrong ; false ; incorrect
間違う to make a mistake
間違っていない be right ; be correct
まるで間違っている be completely mistaken ; be absurdly mistaken ; be quite wrong ; be dead wrong
容認できる be acceptable
AとBを取り違える to take A for B

句読点 punctuation marks
句読点なしで書く to write without punctuation
句読点を付ける to punctuate ; to put in punctuation marks ; to put punctuation marks ; to use punctuation marks
簡略句読 open punctuation
精密句読 close punctuation

文体 style
簡潔な concise
口語法 colloquialism
口語体の colloquial
上品な elegant
平易な easy ; plain

文語体の literary

文法 grammar
文法的な grammatical
文法的に正しい be grammatically correct
文法的な正しさ grammatical correctness
文法的に間違っている be grammatically incorrect

慣用句 idiom
　日本語でイディオムのことを熟語・成句と訳したりすることがあるが，厳密には idiom には２種類ある。語い的・意味的なものと，語法的なものとである。例えば，前者には be interested in や make use of などがある。後者の例としては It's me. などがあげられる。日本語でイディオム，熟語，成句などという場合には，前者を指すことが多い。
慣用的に idiomatically
慣用的な表現 idiomatic expressions

5 "読み" 関連語い

読み・朗読 reading
音読 reading aloud
音読する to read aloud
斉読 reading in chorus ; choral reading
斉読する to read in chorus
精読 intensive reading
熟読 careful reading
熟読する to read thoroughly; to read carefully; to read with care

速読 rapid reading ; fast reading
速読術 speed reading
速読する to read fast
棒読み reading in a singsong manner
黙読 silent reading
黙読する to read silently
読む to read
乱読 unsystematic reading
乱読する to read at random
流ちょうに読む to read fluently

休止 pause
意義段落 sense group
休止を置く 1. to pause ; 2. to put a pause ; 3. to place a pause
　1，2，3のいずれも可能であるが，1が一番自然な感じである。2と3はほぼ同一。
休息単位 breath group

リズム rhythm
リズム法 rhythmics

6 意味・読解関連語い

意味 meaning
ある意味では in a sense
意味する to mean
意味を失う to lose its meaning
真の意味において in the true sense of the word
意味を誤解する to misunderstand the meaning
意味をつかむ to grasp the meaning
意味をなさない to make no sense ; do not make sense ; does not stand to reason
　make sense は，It doesn't make sense. という言い方も，They don't make sense. という言い方も可能である。（後者の場合には they が several words あるいは sentences などを指す）。しかし，stand to reason は It doesn't stand to reason. という言い方はできるが，*They don't stand to reason. という言い方はできない。ちょうど，It's raining. という言い方は可能でも，*They're raining. という言い方が不可能である関係に似ている。こうした理由から，does not stand to reason という形でここでは掲載されている。
意味を理解する to understand the meaning ; to comprehend the meaning
一般的な意味で in a general sense
おおよその意味 general meaning
厳格な意味において in a strict sense
異なった意味 different meaning
正確な意味 precise meaning
漠然たる意味で in a vague sense
比ゆ的な意味 figurative meaning
広い意味で in a broad sense
本来の意味 original meaning
文字どおりの意味 literal

meaning
反対の意味 opposite meaning
   反対の opposite
   反意語 antonym
派生語 derivative
同じ意味 the same meaning
   同じような意味 about the same meaning
   同義語 synonym
   同義語的な synonymous
語源 etymology
   語源学者 etymologist
   語源的な意味 etymological meaning
   語源的に etymologically
直訳 literal translation
   直訳する to translate literally
   直訳的に literally
意訳 free translation
翻訳 translation
   翻訳する to translate
   英語を日本語に翻訳する to translate English into Japanese
俗語 slang
   俗語的表現 slang expression
   俗語的な slangy
文脈 context
   文脈上の contextual
音訳 transliteration
   音訳する to transliterate
状況 situation
   状況の situational

索 引

＊太字は本文で節・項として扱っている箇所を示す（頻出語はそれ以外の場合を省略）。

【あ行】
あいさつ **6**, 528
合図 444, 449
あいづち 517, 523
空いている 493
空いている席 4, 31, 42
相手を探す 141
明るいエル 265
アクセント **282**
あけましておめでとう 9
与えられた語句 467, 471
頭が痛い 61
暑い 24
集める 234, 450
当てはまる語句／言葉 465, 470, 471
当てる 516
あとについて読む 70, 71, 81, 106
アポストロフィー 309
余る 203, 206
雨 25
アメリカ英語 263, 298, 300, 377, 394, 432, 433
誤り 155, 457, 473, 521
暗記 132, 345
アンダーライン（→下線）213
言い換える 413
いい質問 160
言いたいこと 246, 251, 342
言い忘れる 249
委員長 152, 510
言うことをまとめる 246
家で 87, 107
家に帰る 61
家に連絡する 62
息継ぎ 399
イギリス英語 263, 298, 300, 394, 432, 433
意見を言わせる **122**
意見を尋ねる 517
医者に寄る 19
いす 41, 513
いすを後ろに傾ける 50
いすをガタガタさせる 50
急ぐ 515
いたずらな問題 520
１行飛ばし 81
一語一語訳す 98
一人称 462
一致 349, 468
一般疑問文 404
いつまでに 89, 229
異同を指摘する **457**
…以内 318, 474, 475
居眠り 49
意味の違い 324, 328, 331
医務室 61
意訳 97, 98, 103
（…と）言われている 236
韻 260
飲食物 32
インターネット 428
イントネーション 286, **287**,

409
引用句　328
引用符　412
受け身　462
後ろから　450
後ろに置く　381
後ろの人　185，445
歌　184
移る　139，517
埋める　**465**，471
裏　107，321，447
裏返し　450
上着を着る／脱ぐ　25
映画　**196**，497，501，524
英会話　423，429，493，498
英検　494，495，521
英語が好き　184，194
英語の本　426，493，497
英語や英語文化に関する知識　**430**
英語を学ぶ意義　**426**
英作文　**311**，353
英訳　100，**322**
エッセイ　459
選ぶ　**468**
絵を換える　190
円唇母音　269
鉛筆　54，442，443，451
鉛筆で　87，89
遠慮なく　70，158，170
大雨　20
大きさを比較する　240
大きな声で　26，38，70，77-79，258
大きな声を出す　117，177
大きな字を書く　93
大雑把に言う　251
おおまかに説明する　335，474
大文字　84，85，301，348，354，356，360，363，366
おおよその訳　96
おおよその意味　335
置き換え　**464**
補う　466，467
起こす　50
遅すぎる　168
落ち着く　176
音が小さい　27，43
おなかが痛い　57，61
同じ　458
同じ意味　327，328，467，470
同じ種類の文　469
お願い　492
おはよう　7
覚える　422，423
思い出す　249，250
思い出話　501
面白かった　194，195
面白くない　520
終わります　195，511，512
音節　**277**，284，285
音読　**290**

【か行】
カーテン　23，195
海外旅行　500
外国語　299，429
外国人　420，424
解答　162，517
回答器　188
該当する　473
解答用紙　443
会話　80，81
会話練習　**140**，209，498
返す　453，454
顔色　56，58
顔が赤い　57
書かせる　**84**

鏡　274
かかる　337, 386, 399, 401
(…と)書かれている　236
書き換える　**460**
書き方　**297**
書き取らせる　**114**
書き直す　350, 351, 410, 463
書く　**297**, **459**
学習活動の指示　**67**
学習への姿勢　**177**
学習方法　**417**
確信して言う　243
書く力　313, 315, 316
書くもの　89
過去完了　411
過去形　375, 379, 411
過去時制　411, 461
過去分詞(形)　374, 375, 377, 411
加算名詞　365
貸す　442
風邪　12, 15, 28, 51, 56, 495
下線　76, 117, 219, 395, 456, 459
下線部　415, 456, 458, 462, 470, 474
下線を引かせる　**125**
下線を引く　**472**
課題をさせる　**106**
カタカナ語　432
活用　375, 377, 386
家庭学習　**225**
仮定して言う　244
必ずしてほしい　246
可能性の有無　518
からかう　527
体の調子　527
仮主語　352
借りる　217, 446
勘　291

考えを言う　245
環境　**21**
関係代名詞　371, **372**, 399, 464
関係副詞　384
換言する　242
冠詞　**392**
完成させる　**467**
間接目的語　357, 358, 463
間接話法　(→話法)　412, 413, 462
感想(文)　89, **183**, 200
感想を述べる　246
簡単な英語で　326, 328
間投詞　**401**
カンニング　442
聞かせる　**110**
聞き取り　111, **184**, 518
聞き取れない　520
聞き取れるか　**26**
機器の操作　**32**
機器のトラブル　**42**
聞き間違える　517
聞く　**253**
期限　230, 234, 235
記号で　469-471
聞こえる　26, 27, 36, 445
聞こえない　28, 29, 43, 78
既習部分の確認　**65**
季節の変わり目　495
規則動詞　375
気遣い　**495**
機能語　255, 260, 287, 350, 388, 389, 414
気分が悪い / よくない　60, 61
希望　**183**
基本的指示　**67**
期末試験 / テスト　183, 439
疑問詞　287
疑問代名詞　371

疑問副詞　385
疑問文　287, 289, 290, 354, 403, 404, **406**, 459, 461,
休暇　9, 527
休止　295
教科書　50, 54, **207**, 522
教科書を使う　**104**
行間を空ける　86, 93
強形　395
教材　493
教室で使うもの　**202**
教室を出る　448
教師についての質問　**496**
教生　11
強勢　270, 271, 279, 350, 389
強調　350, 351, 403
きりがない　241
起立　6
規律　**46**
切る　294-296
きれいに書く　85, 93
緊張　269, 271
クイズ　346
空気の流れ　264, 269
空気を入れ替える　25
空所補充　**465**
空白部分　86
空欄　67, 391, 465, 467, 470, 471
区切り　**294**
口ごもる　529
口の開き方　**272**
唇について　**275**
唇を軽くかむ　264
唇をすぼめる　272, 276
唇を丸める　276
口を大きく開ける　77, 271, 275
句読点　88, 296, **307**
句読点を打つ　**475**

組む　84
暗い　22
暗いエル　265
繰り返して言う　241
グループを作る　141
苦しい　58
詳しく述べる　240
群接続詞　398
蛍光灯　22
形容詞　**380**
形容詞形　382-384
経歴　344, **496**
ゲーム　516
激励する　521
消しゴム　55, 443, 452
欠席　12, **14**
欠点　477
元気がよい　177
元気です(か)　8, 9
研究室　491, 492
原形　378
現在完了　411
現在形　411
現在分詞　374
現代英語　431
語い　**345**, 418, 422, 497
合格　478, 482
合格点　477
交換する　206, 476
合計点　482
口語(的)　377, 397, 416
後舌面　269
肯定文　289, 349, 406
口頭で　224
構文　416
公用語　430
古英語　431
声が小さい　28
コールボタン　35, 39

語学　344
語句　459, 460
語句の理解　**323**
黒板　**218**
黒板に行く　67
黒板に書く　67, 68, 89-92
黒板の字が見えるか　**30**
語群　468
語形変化　379
語順　**402**
答えのチェック　108
答えの中心　459
語頭　265
異なる意見を述べる　242
言葉遊び　516
語尾　265, 288, 374
困っている　492
ゴミ　21, 503
コメント　123
小文字　84, 302
固有名詞　366, 396
コロン　308
こんにちは　7
コンマ　308, 311

【さ行】
再帰代名詞　371
最高点　477
最後に　252
再試験　437
最上級　463, 381-383, 385, 416
採点　51, **476**, 481, 482
採点ミス　480, 483
作者　251, 252, 339-343
作品　343, 344
作文　**311**
雑音　45
寒い　24
ザワザワ　520, 521

賛成する　123
三人称単数現在　374, 379
シー！　47
子音　**264**
ジェスチャー　200
視覚教材を使う　**135**
字が小さい　81, 93
しかる　**48**
時間がきた　511
時間がない　506
時間です　449, 509
時間内に　317
始業のあいさつ　**6**
試験　**435**
試験結果　437
試験に落ちる　441
試験に出そう　436
試験の結果　441, 453, 454
試験(の)範囲　436, 437
試験問題　443, **455**
私語　47, 48, 446, 520
事故　514
指示　**509**
指示代名詞　371
事実に基づく　343
指示に従って　460, 463
指示文　**455**
自習　59, **151**, 205
辞書　**211**
字数　318
静かにさせる　**46**
時制　101, **411**
時制の一致　411
自然な英語　322
自然な日本語　98
したがって　236
下唇を軽くかむ　275, 276
舌先　265-268
下の欄から　468, 471

舌をかむ 269
舌を丸める 265
失敗談 500
質問の有無 **157**
質問文 459
実力考査 210
私的事柄 **500**
自動詞 356, 358, 373, 378
自分で 139
字幕 198, 199
指名されて **153**
締め切り 207, 321
謝罪 **51**
邪魔をする 69
ジャンケンポン 523
ジャンル 340
習慣 433
終業時の表現 **511**
集合名詞 365
修飾 294, 380-384, 387, 405
修飾関係 103
従属節 350, 411
集中する 417
自由に使う 447
重文 398
週末 514
重要なこと/点 252
主格補語 360, 361, 363
授業開始 **63**
授業後の課題 **225**
授業参観日 22
授業の進め方 **167**
授業の予定 235
熟語 323, 348, 422, 460
宿題 55, 149, **225**, **229**, **231**
主語 **348**, 354, 355, 364, 403, 409, 410, 462, 464
主人公 343
主節 411

出欠 **11**
述語 **354**, 464
出身 502
出席 **11**
出席番号 6, 99, 444
出席を取る 11
述部 354, 355, 360, 411, 476
述部形容詞 382
受動態 (→態) 350, 351, 357, 402, 405, 409, 410, 463
主部 476
趣味 502
シュワ 270
順序 380, 383, 464
順序だって話す 236
順に送る 232
順番に 73, 121
準備ができた 64
状況を説明する 519
小説 339, 340
冗談 248
小テスト 226
証明する 242
省略 349, 352, 353, 361, 371, 372, 376, 377, 399, 410, 414, 416
ジョーク 433
職員室 59, 159, 223, 510, 511
叙述名詞 369
助動詞 **378**
所有代名詞 371
印をつける 131
新出語い 346
新出単語 70, 76, 88, 117, 128, 145, 164, 207, 219, 226, 228, 261, 262, 292, 335
身体状況 **56**
新任教師のあいさつ **10**
心配事 496

図　106, 136, 193
スイッチ　33, 36, 41, 44
随筆　340
進む　138
ストレス　282, 283, 285, 286, 395
ストレスアクセント　282, 286
スピード　112
スピードリーディング　294
スペリング　129, 181, 305, 306, 368
スライド　**190**, **194**
すらすら書ける　311
すらすら読む　292, 293
〜するために　237
座らせる　515
座る　3-5, 67
正解　322, 323, 454, 517
制限　318, 320
制限時間　452
正誤を指摘する　**457**
成績　417, 418, 441, **476**, 498
成績表　484, 485
声帯を振動させる　264
生徒とのやりとり　**157**, **519**, **523**, **524**, **527**, **529**
生徒の返答に対して　**171**
制服　58
整理　205
席がえ　70
席につく　3
席に戻る　48, 509
席を代わる　4, 6, 45
接辞　370, 383
接続詞　384, **397**
設備　**32**
接尾語　375
接尾辞　368
説明する　**460**

セミコロン　308, 397
先行詞　372
選択疑問文　290
選択肢　469
前置詞　357, 358, **388**, 398
相関接続詞　397
掃除当番　21, 22
総称　394
相談　**489**
相当する箇所　476
俗語　215, 489
そこまで　76, 77, 100, 449
その通り　172, 527

【た行】
態　**409**
…対…　241
題　317
ダイアローグ　210
大意　122, 474, 475
大学入試　210, 388
退室　**41**, **59**
退場　448-450
タイトル　468
代名詞　350, **370**
確かめる　203, 520
たしなめる　520
助け舟　524
正しい答え　473
正しい方　470
立たせる　517
立ち歩く　140, 141, 151
立ちなさい　67
脱線　247
他動詞　357, 373, 378
たとえる　523
ダビング　40
だらだら　417
足りない　203, 206, 320, 321,

447, 451, 455
足りる 203
単位 230, 482
単語 **345**, 422, 423
単語力 413
男女別 5
単数(形) 351, 367, 370, 462
端的に言う 250
担任 11
暖房 24
違い 324, 325, 328, 329, 331, 332
違う 458
遅刻 **16**
着席 **3**, 6
注 335
注意事項 **441**
注意をうながす 518
注意を引く 518, 519
中間テスト 183, 227, 435, 437, 438
中期英語 431
抽象名詞 366, 369, 397
中立 270
調音器官 269, 271
聴解力 256
調子 80, 188, 287
チョーク 54, 90, **218**
直接目的語 357, 358, 463
直接話法 (→話法) 412, 413, 462
直訳 97, 98, 103
著者 339, 344
チンプンカンプン 332
追試(験) 165, 438, 441, 477
ついていく 418
ついていけない 171
通じる 125
次に移る 136

次の課・章などに移る **139**
次の人 77
次のページに進む **138**
付け加える 242, 528
都合 491
続き 195, 201, 202
つづり 181, 211, 215, 224, **298**, 346, 362, 521, 525
つづりと発音 260, 298
つなぐ 400, **464**
つめて書く 94
強く発音する/しない 368, 371, 377, 380
強く読む 373, 387
定冠詞 383, 392
提出 449, 453
訂正 179, 180, 302, 457, 480
丁寧語 379
丁寧さ 289
手書き 320
手紙 316
適当な言葉 466, 467
テストに出る/出す 132, 133, 228
手伝う 202
テレビ 519, 522
手を上げさせる **119**
手を上げる 158, 165, 212, 231, 292, 447
天気 371
電気をつける 22, 195
添削 322
電子辞書 216
電車に乗り遅れる 17
ドア 512
問いに答える 455
トイレ 60
答案用紙 54, 443, 445, 447, 449-451, 453, 476, 479, 480

同意する 244
等位接続詞 397, 398
同義語 347
動詞 **373**
動詞形 368, 375, 461
登場人物 199
動詞用法 377
動詞を重ねる 377
同調する 529
時 371
得意 497
特徴について述べる 240
時計 508
どこから 210
どこからどこまで 83, 95, 130, 147, 351, 355
どこまで 83, 102, 201, 522
どこを 83, 101, 153
年明けのあいさつ **9**
図書館 152, 489, 490
途中での退室 **59**
読解 **323**
読解力 256
隣の教室 29
隣の人 69, 81, 106, 140, 208, 209, 476
飛ばす 139, 190
止める 112
友だち 446
トラブル **42**, **521**
取り換える 204, 207
努力 178, 182, 417

【な行】
内容語 260, 368, 373, 385, 414
内容を問う問題 167
直す 263, 461, 463
長さ 318, 320
慰める **182**

夏休み 514
名前 444, 450
名前を書く 233
名前を呼ぶ 91, 479
並べ換え **464**
軟口蓋 269
何番目 487
似合う 502, 503
苦手 421, 423, 424
〜については 239
〜について話す 238
日記 312
日本語 432
日本語で 113, 166, 177, 189, 338, 339, 460, 474
〜にもかかわらず 238
入室 **32**
〜によると 237
人称 349
人称代名詞 371
抜けている 307
ネイティブ 425
寝過ごす 16, 18
熱がある 9, 57, 61
熱っぽい 56
寝冷え 495
眠る 50, 52
能動態 (→態) 350, 405, 409, 410, 463
ノートに写させる **127**
ノートに写す 114, 116
ノートに書く 67, 86-89, 128
ノートを集める 152
ノートを出す 69
ノートを提出する 152
ノートを取る 129
残り時間 449, 519
載っている / いない 148, 212, 215-217

【は行】

パーセント　194, 200, 201, 241
…倍　240, 241
配布　443
配布物　**202**
ハイフン　301
歯茎　265
白紙　206, 451
励ます　**182**
「始め」　444
始めます　63, 64
恥ずかしがらずに　120
パスワード　33
パソコン　34, 42
×　181, 457, 473, 475, 483
発音　**257**, 374, 395, 484
発音器官　264
発音記号　214, **280**
発音させる　**117**
発音しない文字　299
発音のしかた　517
発音練習　518
はっきり話す　28
発言させる　**119**
発表させる　**122**
発表する　183
×をつける　**473**
話を切り出す　235
話を遮る　524
話を元に戻す　247
話す力　316
歯の裏　266
省く　410
早口言葉　523
速く読む　186, 426
速すぎる　83, 110, 168, 169
早寝早起き　19
早引き　523
早めに終わる　505

破裂音　266
パワーポイント　**190**
範囲　346, 436, 437
反意語　346, 347
パンク　16, 17
番号　444
番号で　471
番号の順番に座る　3
班ごとに座る　3
板書　88, 91, 219
反対意見　123, 124, 245
(〜から)判断する　238
半分　241
ヒアリング(力)　256, 425
比較級　381, 383, 385, 386, 416
悲劇　340
筆記体　85
筆記用具　55, 443, 451
日付　205, 445
ピッチアクセント　282, 286
ピッチを上げる　407
否定文　461
ビデオ　135, 522, 526
一人で　72
皮肉　521
非人称の it　349
暇　492, 498, 502
比喩的　328
病気　**56**
ピリオド　308
昼休み　510
品詞　352, 356, 358, 363, 401, 414
ヒント　343, 440, 516, 527
ブース　32
付加疑問文　**407**
不加算名詞　365, 366, 394
不規則動詞　375
副詞　**384**

副詞形　385
復習　131, 137, 144, 148-**150**, 210, 228, 420, 436
複数(形)　351, 353, 367, 369, 370
複文　350, 464
ふさわしい形/答え/言葉　461, 469, 471, 472
伏せる　106, 444
普通の速さで　115
普通名詞　365, 394, 396
物質名詞　366, 367
不定冠詞　383, 392, 395
不定代名詞　371
不定詞　374, 376, 379
部分点　482
冬休み　9
ブラインド　23, 190, 195
振り返る　249
プリント　**202**
プロジェクター　43, 195
ブロック体　84, 85
文化　500
文学作品　**339**
文型　128, **364**, 469
文章語　397
文章の理解　**331**
文頭　355, 387, 400, 403-406, 458
…分の1　241
文の理解　**331**
文尾　289, 387, 406, 407
文尾を上げる/下げる　408, 407
文法　314, 322, **348**, 474
文法事項　416
文法的に説明する　223
文法力　418
文末(→文尾)　290
文脈　287, 323, 327, 345, 354, 389

ペアを組む　140
平均点　477, 478, 528
平常点　122, 159, 482, 484, 485
平叙文　289
ヘッドセット　35, 36, 38, 41
別の例　529
部屋の状態　**21**
ベル　512, 513
返却　**476**, **478**
変種　430
ペンで　87, 89
ペンパル　314
母音　**269**, 273, 393
ポイントの指示　**130**
放課後　159, 491, 493
方言　430, 433
ポーズ　294-296
ボケている　191
保健室　60, 61
補語　**359**, 364
母語　429
補講　438
保護者　485
ボタン　503
ホッチキス　203
ほめる　529
ボリューム　28, 39, 44
本題に入る/戻る　247, 248
本動詞　374, 378, 379
本を返す　490
本を読む　345

【ま行】
マイク　29, 36, 38, 186, 187
マウス　34
前に送る　450
前のページに戻る　**137**
前の方に座る　6

前の方につめる　27
まじめに言うと　249
間違い　14, 175, 176, **179**, 259, 302, 303, 426, **521**, 522
間違いを指摘・訂正させる　**154**
間違う/間違える　121, 133, 165, 224, 302, 306
待ちなさい　508
まっすぐ書く　93
待って　166
まとめ　138
まとめる　336, **473**
窓を開ける/閉める　24, 25
真似をする　110
まぶしい　31
○　457
○で囲む　**471**
見えにくい　204
短くする　415
ミスプリント　179, 204, 207, 443, 451
身なり　**502**
みんなで　73, 81
向かい合う　141
難しい質問　160, 524
名詞　**365**
名詞形　368
命令文　349, 352, 408
メール　497
目が悪い　6
黙字　300
目的格　372
目的格補語　360, 361, 363
目的語　350, **356**, 364, 409
黙読　82, 128
持ち込む　437
最も合う　469
最もふさわしいもの　469
戻す　190

戻る　111, 137
モニタースピーカー　38
問題集　162
問題の指示　**188**
問題用紙　444, 450

【や行】
やあ　9
訳させる　**95**
訳す　**456**
役割を決める　81, 106
役割を交替する　141
易しい英語で　113, 332
休み　501, 510, 527
休み明け　**9**
破れている　207
やめてください　449
やめなさい　76
友人　501
有声音　265
ゆっくり説明する　168
ゆっくり話す　28, 112, 115, 168, 184, 455
ゆっくり読む　84, 115
由来する　432
用紙　447
用事を思い出す　59
様子が変　58
様子をうかがう　515
用法　352, 388, 395, 457, 460
要約する　250, **473**
よく使う表現　**235**
よくできました　171, 172
抑揚　80, 288, 289, 295, 408
予告　**435**
横に動く　225
横道　518
汚れ(てい)る　58, 207, 503
予習　50, **142**, 150, 151, 154,

159, 209, 419
予想 455
よそ見 49
余白 447
予備 39, 40
夜ふかし 16
余分な時間 318
余分な用紙 447
読ませる **70**
読み **184**, **290**
読み方 84, 459
読む **290**
弱く発音される 394

【ら行】
ライト 190
落書き **55**
落第点 486
ラッシュ 51
ラテン語 431
理解の確認 **162**
リズム 260, 288
リモコン 43
略語 378
類義語 347
類似 333
礼 6
例外的状況 **56**
例に従って 460
例文 460
例をあげる 166, 240, 348
列 99, 121, 202, 232
レポート 181, **234**, 484
連語 95
練習問題 226, 227, 436, 529
連絡 **489**, **509**
ロールプレイ 140
ログアウト 42

ログイン 34
録音 35, 36, 45, 185, **187**
ロッカー 62

【わ行】
ワークブック 510
忘れ物 **54**, 453
話題を転じる 520
和文英訳 **322**
話法 **412**, 462
和訳 **338**
割合 241

【英語・アルファベット】
a 392, 396, 397,
BBC 英語 431
be 動詞 354, 360, 374, 377, 403, 404, 406
CALL 教室 **184**, 438, 509
CD 35, 37, 39-41, 45, 111, 498, 526
CD のあとについて読む 71, 185
CD プレーヤー 54
do 374, 352
DVD 40, 519
ID 33
IPA 280
it 371
Let's 408
LSA 280
never 403
so 405
that 397, 399, 400, 412
that 節 399, 401
the 383, 385, 392, 394-397
WH 言葉 407
what 372

参考文献

安藤賢一（1985）『演習英語音声学』成美堂.
一色マサ子, 松居千枝（1980）『英語音声学』朝日出版社.
小栗敬三（1983）『英語音声学』篠崎書林.
小稲義男（編）（1989）『新英和大辞典　第5版』研究社.
小西友七（編）（1988）『ジーニアス英和辞典』大修館書店.
小林兼之（1983）『英文法　基礎編』開隆堂.
小学館（1988）『英語図詳大辞典』.
染矢正一（1989）『英語ここがわからない』明日香出版社.
染矢正一（1991）『英語発音の基本演習』Macmillan LanguageHouse.
染矢正一（2010）*Basic English Pronunciation for Japanese*. 三修社.
Someya, Masakazu and Fred Ferrasci. (1990) *Fresh Preps*. Macmillan LanguageHouse.
染矢正一, Fred Ferrasci. (2003) *Reading Shukan ST*. Eihosha.
染矢正一, Fred Ferrasci. (2007)『ホームステイ英会話ナビ』南雲堂.
Someya, Masakazu and Fred Ferrasci. (2010) *World Heritage on DVD*. Nan'undo
Someya, Masakazu et. al. (2011) *Asian Crossways*. Kinseido.
Someya, Masakazu et. al. (2013) *Aiming for the Top*. Sanshusha.
高梨健吉（編）（1985）『アイテム76　新総合英語』美誠社.
竹田明彦（1990）『学校用語英語小事典』大修館書店.
田中長敬（1970）『教室英語の運用』開隆堂.
田中好夫（1985）『アイ・シー・オール』学習研究社.
増田剛（1974）『新英和大辞典　第4版』研究社.
安井稔（1984）『英文法総覧』開拓社.
Ferrasci and Masakazu Someya. (1987) *A Unified Approach to American English*. 成美堂.
Holman, C. Hugh. (1972) *A handbook to Literature*. The Odyssey Press.
Hughs, Glyn S. (1987) *A Handbook of Classroom English*. Oxford Uni-

versity Press.
Warriner, John E. et al. (1965) *English Grammar and Composition*. Harcourt, Brace and World.

[ウェブサイト]
オンライン英英辞典 & 各種辞書
　http://english.chakin.com/eul-dictionary.html#b2
中学校学習指導要領解説　外国語編
http://www.mext.go.jp/component/a_menu/education/micro_detail/__icsFiles/afieldfile/2011/01/05/1234912_010_1.pdf
高等学校学習指導要領解説　外国語編　英語
http://www.mext.go.jp/component/a_menu/education/micro_detail/__icsFiles/afieldfile/2010/01/29/1282000_9.pdf

[著者紹介]

染矢正一（そめや まさかず）
カリフォルニア州立大学大学院　文学修士。
元大分県立芸術文化短期大学教授。
著書:『英単語使い分けの弱点』（ジャパンタイムズ）
　　　Basic English Pronunciation for Japanese　（三修社）
　　　World Heritage on DVD　（共著　南雲堂）
　　　Aiming for the Top　（共著　三修社）
　　　ほか多数。
趣味:旅行，農業，ソフトボール，テニスなど

新版 教室英語表現事典
© SOMEYA Masakazu, 2013　　　　　　　　NDC837／x, 565p／19cm

初版第 1 刷──2013年8月10日

著者──────染矢正一
発行者─────鈴木一行
発行所─────株式会社 大修館書店
　　　　　　　〒113-8541　東京都文京区湯島 2-1-1
　　　　　　　電話 03-3868-2651（販売部）　03-3868-2294（編集部）
　　　　　　　振替 00190-7-40504
　　　　　　　[出版情報] http://www.taishukan.co.jp

装丁者─────岡崎健二
印刷所─────横山印刷
製本所─────牧製本

ISBN978-4-469-04178-1　Printed in Japan

Ⓡ本書のコピー，スキャン，デジタル化等の無断複製は著作権法上での例外を除き禁じられています。本書を代行業者等の第三者に依頼してスキャンやデジタル化することは，たとえ個人や家庭内での利用であっても著作権法上認められておりません。